THE
FRENCH
ROTHSCHILDS

Books by Herbert R. Lottman

Albert Camus: A Biography

*The Left Bank: Writers, Artists, and Politics from the
Popular Front to the Cold War*

Pétain, Hero or Traitor

The Purge

Flaubert: A Biography

Colette: A Life

The Fall of Paris: June 1940

THE FRENCH ROTHSCHILDS

THE GREAT BANKING DYNASTY THROUGH
TWO TURBULENT CENTURIES

Herbert R. Lottman

CROWN PUBLISHERS, INC.

NEW YORK

Published by Crown Publishers, Inc., 201 East 50th Street, New York,
New York 10022. Member of the Crown Publishing Group.

Random House, Inc. New York, Toronto, London, Sydney, Auckland

CROWN is a trademark of Crown Publishers, Inc.

Manufactured in the United States of America

Design by Lenny Henderson

Library of Congress Cataloging-in-Publication Data

Lottman, Herbert R.
    The French Rothschilds : the great banking dynasty through two
turbulent centuries / by Herbert R. Lottman. — 1st ed.
        p.   cm.
    1. Rothschild family.   2. Bankers—France—Biography.   3. Banks
and banking—France—History.   I. Title.
HG1552.A1L68   1995
332.1'092'244—dc20
94-41337
CIP

ISBN 0-517-59229-0

10 9 8 7 6 5 4 3 2 1

First Edition

CONTENTS

1 *An End and a Beginning*   *1*

2 *Fighting Napoleon*   *6*

3 *King of the Jews*   *14*

4 *The Great Baron*   *24*

5 *Hard Times*   *33*

6 *Another Emperor*   *42*

7 *The Next Generation*   *51*

8 *French Barons*   *64*

9 *The Brothers Rothschild*   *74*

10 *"Jewish France"*   *84*

11 *Russia and Palestine*   *94*

12 *Dreyfus?*   *109*

13 *Fin de Siècle*   *118*

14 *Edouard*   *126*

15 Tightening Circles — 138

16 The Extended Family — 146

17 War and Peace — 154

18 Saving the Franc — 165

19 Before the Depression — 178

20 Guy's Apprenticeship — 188

21 The Two Hundred Families — 200

22 Rothschilds at War — 208

23 Vichy — 219

24 Goering — 228

25 France Without Rothschilds — 239

26 Liquidating the Liquidators — 250

27 Revival — 261

28 The Banks Rothschild — 273

29 The Big Change — 283

30 Mitterrand's Folly — 294

31 Edmond and the Others — 304

32 Modern Times — 315

33 Rothschild Legends — 325

34 King David — 334

Acknowledgments — 343

Notes — 345

Index — 393

THE
FRENCH
ROTHSCHILDS

AN END AND A BEGINNING

ebate in the French Parliament, despite the sensitivity of the issue—questioning the sanctity of private property—concluded with the resounding impact of a hammer's blow: swift, irrevocable. With the coming to power of François Mitterrand, France's first Socialist president, in May 1981, followed soon after by legislative elections that gave his party a parliamentary majority, the French left seemed mesmerized by quasi-religious fervor, and in that atmosphere economic common sense easily gave way to righteous wrath. To many well-intentioned politicians it seemed pure justice to nationalize wealth, and why stop short of the Rothschilds? No matter that the parliamentary majority would be obliterating a century and a half of French history; the important thing was to track down and stamp out the very image of "rich as a Rothschild" (a phrase and a notion that went back to Stendhal).[1] "Do you take me for Rothschild?" was the instinctive rebuke of every exasperated parent to every demanding child.[2]

The determination of the left side of the assembly (Communists allied to Socialists) stunned a banking family that had experienced ignominy in many forms—spoliation during the Nazi occupation of France, humiliation by Philippe Pétain's Vichy regime, not to speak of recurrent outbursts of anticapitalist, anti-Semitic vituperation and violence from both left and right going back a century and more. They were being told that they could no longer do what they had always done, reflected Baron Guy de Rothschild, head of the family bank (after his father, Edouard, and Edouard's father, Alphonse, and Alphonse's father, Jacob or James, founder of the French dynasty). But it was worse than that. It was as if they were being told to move out of their own home—so much was the Banque Rothschild, domiciled for over a century and a half on Rue Laffitte, part of their lives.[3]

His initial reaction was anger; better that, he reflected, than to give way to depression. After a debate spread over thirteen days and thirty-three sessions, Parliament voted for nationalization of the Rothschilds and over three dozen other banks and financial groups, together with five industrial groups, on October 26, 1981.[4]

Within days, Guy was ready with a scorching farewell; it made the front page of the most influential newspaper in Paris. "A family whose name is associated with an eminently capitalistic banking institution was bound to see the shrinking of its activities as French society became increasingly socialized since the beginning of this century." He cited some of the depredations to which the Rothschilds had been subjected in his time: the seizure of the railroads (a traditional Rothschild fief) by the Popular Front government of the mid-1930s, the extension of state authority over the Banque de France (of which Guy's father had been an influential director).

Rothschild knew that over the years his family had become "the proverbial symbol of wealth," and it had lived up to that image. But had they been the only capitalists in France? Elsewhere, he pointed out, notably in the United States and Britain, prosperity and experience were encouraged. Even in France the service rendered by his family to fellow citizens—the Rothschild hospitals and schools and low-cost housing, the masterpieces donated to state museums, the subsidies to the arts and sciences—had not gone unnoticed. Yet he knew that the Rothschilds necessarily aroused instincts of jealousy. He himself had found his name a handicap, as when, after serving the Gaullists in the Second World War, he had failed to receive an appointment that would have allowed him to continue in his country's service. Earlier it was the Vichy regime that had stripped his father and his uncles of French nationality, and of course had appropriated their bank. "A Jew to the Pétain regime, a pariah under Mitterrand, that's enough for me," he concluded. "To rebuild on ruins twice in a lifetime is once too much." Speaking to a reporter for the German news weekly *Der Spiegel,* he declared with more heat: "The Rothschilds are tired of working in France, where governments demolish their property every forty years."

Yet Baron Guy was gratified to see that press and broadcast media in Europe—and as far away as the United States—picked up and magnified the impact of his declaration. It signified that the Rothschild name still counted. This bank employing 2,000 persons, serving 70,000 clients, an industrial and trade group that, with its subsidiaries around the world, provided an additional 30,000 jobs, could not be gobbled up by Big Government without leaving blood on the ground.[5]

There might have been a way to do what the government felt it had to do (so he told an interviewer) without virtually banning the Rothschilds. But it was clear that this would not have satisfied those calling for a radical solution. Guy let it be known that he himself had voted Socialist after the Second World War—a natural reaction to the Vichy years. But banks belonged in the private sector, thrived in an atmosphere of competition; when they were no longer allowed to operate freely, it was the economy's loss. Against that he also knew what he was up against in France. "To politicians on the extreme left we are the quintessence of evil."[6]

A cousin of Guy, the filmmaker Nicole Stéphane, felt that a visit to the bank on Rue Laffitte was the least she could do; she found Guy packing up. Although he made no effort to conceal his feelings, she noted that he held his head high. "Obviously afflicted," she thought. "But also the stiff upper lip."[7] Receiving a correspondent of Britain's daily *Guardian,* Baron Guy showed an office emptied of personal effects. "This has been my home," he explained, "perhaps even more than where I live because I've changed places where I live. This has been my constant home in every respect for the last 50 years." He characterized the government's acts as precipitous, "as if they [were] being pursued by an enemy and they wanted to burn everything before the enemy caught up with them, which is totally absurd." Would the family pursue its activity? "If something which would be respectable and valuable enough to be called 'The House of Rothschild' in France will survive or revive I can't tell," was his reply.[8]

Soon after that, at the traditional year-end reception for employees of the bank, Baron Guy became aware of the disarray of long-time associates, some of them fighting back tears. For them, as for himself, it was the end of a world.[9]

Guy's son David was to celebrate his thirty-ninth birthday during the weeks of moving out of Rue Laffitte; for David too, what hurt most was being evicted from what was truly home. He had all but grown up on that street—first in the historic house of James, founder of the French Rothschild dynasty—a neoclassical three-story mansion that had been the home of Napoleon's feared police minister, Joseph Fouché, then in the functional building that replaced it in the 1960s. His friends were there; he was being separated forcibly from these friends. In retrospect, he'd come to understand that nationalization had been more of a psychological shock than a financial disaster, for the Rothschilds were being stripped of their investments at a time when the business climate was anything but promising (but that was no longer a Rothschild worry!).

Later still, the wrenching experience could even seem positive. For it had removed layers of activity into which the Rothschilds had ventured over the years, and that often proved more trouble than they were worth. Indeed, thanks to the Socialist-Communist takeover of France's economic giants, it seemed possible that the Rothschilds could return to their historic calling, merchant banking, in the spirit of their forebear James, known as the Great Baron.[10] Perhaps his nineteenth-century dedication was what the late twentieth century needed most.

They had something to build on. In New York, for example, the French family shared a financial partnership with their British cousins that had escaped nationalization; Guy would move there to see what he could do about developing its potential.[11] In France they still owned a small investment house for portfolio management, called Paris-Orléans, until then one of the vehicles by which the family had exercised control of the Paris bank. As the threat of nationalization grew, David de Rothschild, working as part of a three-member directorate with his cousin Nathaniel and a longtime bank manager, Jacques Getten, began to transform Paris-Orléans into a financial institution that was not quite a bank but could exercise some of the functions of an investment bank all the same, mobilizing the resources of its partners and clients for profitable ventures in industry and finance.

They had six months ahead of them—or so they assumed, at the time of Mitterrand's election. While other groups targeted by the government took more decisive steps to move assets out of reach of the nationalizers, or worked behind the scenes to shield themselves from takeover, the Rothschilds resolved to let government do what governments do, and then simply to start over again.

The Rothschild name disappeared from the sign over the door of the building on Rue Laffitte; it would appear again on another sign over another door.

Fighting Napoleon

To make sense of the beginnings of the fabulous Rothschild family, it helps to remember the paramount importance of being in the right place at the right time—Mayer Amschel Rothschild was there—and then to appreciate the function of an individual at once elevated and humiliated to the condescending condition of court Jew, despised for what he was, admired and solicited for what he could provide. Not being allowed to own or to use land, Jews in pre-Revolutionary Europe could handle *money*, could change it or lend it, and trade in precious metals; when recognized as useful to a prince, they became suppliers to the court, managing their lord's business (and sometimes his property). Few reigning families in postfeudal Europe lacked a Jewish moneylender in their entourage; no wonder that Jews were ready for the age of banking when it came (along with another oft-despised minority, the Protestants).

There is no environment we can imagine more depressing than the European ghetto; there were limits to what a man of ambition, even with success, could do to alleviate its distress, and nothing he could do to escape it. The free city of Frankfurt am Main, in postmedieval Europe, was anything but free for Jews, obliged as they were to reside in overcrowded houses along a sunless lane, in the disorder of this sewerless prison yard circumscribed by old

town walls on one side and a moat on the other, locked in at night
and on Sunday, subject to the wearing of distinctive dress, to
discriminatory taxes and tolls; they were the constant prey of gratuitous insult, and not infrequently targets of violence. Unable to
practice crafts or to sell certain kinds of produce and denied
ownership of property, Jews were also nameless; one might make
a family name of an otherwise meaningless signboard over his shop
(*Rothschild* is from the German for "red shield"). Born in the
ghetto on February 23, 1744, Mayer Amschel grew up in his
parents' place of business, deprived of playing fields and gardens,
his father a dealer in general goods including hardware, supple-
menting his income with money-changing.

History and legend show the son to have been exceptionally apt
at handling coins new and rare, but we don't have to be told that
Mayer Amschel was exceptional; how else explain the wealth and
influence he acquired in his lifetime, and the setting up in business of five sons who were to change the economic history of their
continent?[1]

All his life, Mayer Amschel would dwell above his workplace in
the dank Judengasse, as if subhuman and prisoner, his situation
and that of his family remaining in Frankfurt improving by tiny
increments over the years that his sons in other European capitals
came to be treated as equals (at least) by their financial peers.
Mayer's story has been told and thrice told: assistant and money
changer to his father at ten, orphan at twelve, obliged to be a
parent to still-younger siblings. Learning enough about old coins to
be counselor as well as procurer to titled collectors. And although
a Rothschild archivist reminds us that we don't really know for
sure how the young man's expertise won the confidence of the court
of Hesse, somehow at the age of twenty-five he was appointed
official supplier to that court; he was also a purveyor of rare coins
and precious art objects to any and all who could afford them.[2]

The princes of Hesse were redoubtable purveyors themselves—
purveyors of their able-bodied subjects, who were trained as soldiers, rented abroad as mercenaries. A wicked story is told of Prince
Frederick II, father of Wilhelm IX: By agreement the prince re-

ceived a premium when members of his mercenary force died in the service of a foreign employer; the greater the death toll, the richer he became. "Your men don't die easily," Frederick complained to one of his generals. "Don't forget that my coffers are empty."[3]

True or not, the story is indicative of a climate in which the rulers of this province became rich by selling bodies for cash. When Wilhelm IX inherited his father's charge at Cassel, he was an extraordinarily prosperous businessman, wealthier than princes who ruled far larger domains. These entrepreneurial princes made use of equally entrepreneurial men of finance such as Carl Frederick Buderus, who enters history only because he recognized the talents and the utility of the ghetto dealer in old coins, Mayer Amschel. In those times, when money signified bulky bullion or clanking coins whose movement was awkward at the least, and usually dangerous, the incipient merchants and money changers, whose word and signature could replace physical transfers, were worth the commissions they commanded. It was particularly useful to have a Rothschild, far removed from the banking community, for discreet transfers of cash, for rapid conversions of foreign currency. Mayer Amschel's fortune was under way.[4]

So was his family. In August 1770, at the age of twenty-six, Mayer Amschel married seventeen-year-old Gutele Schnapper, daughter of a ghetto merchant; their first child to survive was a girl, followed in 1773, 1774, and 1777 by sons Amschel—the first of the family to bear Rothschild as a family name[5]—Salomon, Nathan; then and until much later only sons were to count (and be counted). Two more daughters were born to the couple, then Carl (1788), again two daughters, then, on the fifteenth of May, 1792, the last of the children of Mayer Amschel and Gutele, Jacob Mayer, who would become known internationally as James, founder of the French branch of the Rothschilds, hero of our story.

By then the family was living in more ample quarters (this house happened to have a green shield over the door). But the address—Judengasse—hadn't changed, nor had the subjections. In their time the disposable revenue of the household could be compared to that of another Frankfurt family, the Goethes, but *their* home was a mansion.

We don't have a single portrait of Mayer Amschel, founder of the

Rothschild clan, either as young entrepreneur or as sage and elder, although he was surely among the richest and in any case the most famous product of the Frankfurt ghetto (portraits come in with the next generation). But an early-twentieth-century witness, Count Corti, was able to visit and to describe the house with the green sign above the door some time before the Second World War. We cannot do the same because Allied bombs flattened old Frankfurt, and the ghetto with it.[6]

By January 1800, when Mayer Amschel's sons were grown men and full partners—father and sons now held official charges under their prince—the Rothschilds took another giant step, becoming agents of the court of the Austrian emperor in Vienna. Their most remunerative activity continued to be moving money, whenever possible via letters of exchange rather than sacks of coins, between Britain and the continent. They also took on an increasing proportion of their prince's investments, often in the form of loans to other states. At times the Rothschilds were expected to conceal the role of the prince in the transaction, placing themselves in the middle. Their reputation, as well as their commissions, grew.[7]

At this point, the dawn of their international careers, the commencement of their travels abroad, to be followed by the establishment of branches abroad, discerning contemporaries could observe signs of what would later be recognized as the Rothschild style: absolute loyalty among family members, discretion in handling the business of others, a speed and efficiency in moving messages and money extraordinary for their times. Above all—and notwithstanding their uncanny success in getting goods and currency across frontiers and between warring nations—a keen sense of honor, a refusal to take shortcuts or to shortchange their clients (qualities that would astonish and conquer these clients, kings among them).

Revolutionary France declared war on Austria in 1792. Wilhelm of Hesse was on Austria's side, and Napoleon would not forget that. But Wilhelm did not wage war, he lent money, and rented more soldiers to England; the Rothschilds, as discreet agents, did not suffer thereby. In 1795 Mayer Amschel attained Frankfurt's highest tax bracket, based on declared or estimated earnings. By the end of the century, that city had become a relay between England

and the rest of the continent, both as banking hub and transit point for merchandise from England destined to all the German states, to the point that it made sense to export a Rothschild, twenty-one-year-old Nathan, to represent the family in London. The British firm was born.[8]

Nathan took part of the family fortune with him. Henceforth, during the Napoleonic wars, he was a vital link in the transfer of funds and goods, much of which had to be run through blockades. Throughout these years, and despite his professed neutrality, Wilhelm of Hesse was a significant trader with Britain, lender to the British (including their Hanoverian royalty).

Napoleon was defeated on the financial battlefield, a Marxist historian would say. Neither his war machine, however fearful, nor his virtual colonization of conquered nations succeeded in destroying the economic links between the United Kingdom and the continent.[9] Young Jacob, soon to prefer the name James, received his baptism of fire on this battlefield.

He had begun to deal with customers at age thirteen, the time of his bar mitzvah in this family ever respectful of religion. He accompanied his father on business trips, especially to call on persons who had borrowed money from the prince of Hesse (and even so, these sorties from the ghetto required special permission). We can document the existence of James so early thanks to letters sent to Nathan in London by his father, letters carefully preserved in the archives of the London bank, intelligently read by James's biographer.[10] Then and later so many tall tales were told of the rise of the Rothschilds during Napoleon's reign that we must be grateful for the documentation that has been uncovered and preserved: contemporary correspondence, diplomatic dispatches, even police reports.

Count Corti paints the portrait of an opportunistic Prince Wilhelm of Hesse, hesitating to take sides in war (say, with Prussia against France in 1806), waiting to see from which party he could make more profit. Little good it did Wilhelm; Napoleon decided for him, occupying the prince elector's territories, threatening his wealth. The head of the house of Rothschild found ways to serve the exiled Wilhelm while maintaining good relations with the new ruler of Frankfurt, Napoleon's appointee Carl von Dalberg, a broad-minded archbishop who seemed to be offering a more promising future to the population of the ghetto.[11] In 1808 Mayer Amschel, as spokesman for the Jewish community, was able to negotiate, for a lump sum representing twenty years of taxes—the discriminatory taxes levied on affluent Jews—equal rights for ghetto residents.

Times were indeed changing. The Rothschild sons were different from their father, less ritually Jewish in dress, in respect for dietary laws and the interdictions of the Sabbath (they'd even write letters on the obligatory day of rest—making sure they were out of his sight).[12]

Protected though they might be by Napoleon's German viceroy in Frankfurt, Prince-Archbishop von Dalberg—who was both a secret sympathizer with Prince Wilhelm and a friend (or at least not an enemy) of Jews—the Rothschilds had some narrow escapes, as in May 1809, when the police moved in to search their premises for evidence of collusion with the absent Wilhelm; both James and his brother Salomon were detained in their shop while the search went on. Little was found; members of the family, noted the police report, had been "extremely clever."[13] By then the association of Mayer Amschel and his sons still living at home—but not Nathan—had become formalized in a company registered as M. A. Rothschild and Sons. Its capital was divided among father M. A. (twenty-four shares) and sons Amschel and Salomon (twelve shares each) and Carl and James (*one* share each). Indeed, it was stressed that James got a share despite his tender age—he was eighteen—because of the "scrupulous manner in which he had handled the business to which he was assigned." A scholar who examined the document observed that it did not refer to the Rothschilds as merchants, speaking rather of their lending, letters of exchange, mortgages, and other financial transactions. It has also been said that the division of capital into fifty shares was designed to make it easier to divide by five when the time came to apportion the shares equally among the sons—Nathan of London being included this time.

There were no shares for daughters, spouses, or descendents—then or later; nor could any of the brothers withdraw from the firm with his capital. The cement that was to build the firm and then to preserve it had been put into place.[14]

*   *   *

The Rothschilds didn't make it easy for enemies—or friends—to pin them down. We can only presume that the son whose presence was reported by the French police at Gravelines, near Dunkirk on France's Channel coast, was James; logically it was, for it was he who would go on to settle in Paris. The founder of the French Rothschild dynasty hadn't yet attained his eighteenth birthday. He arrived in France with a properly executed passport from Frankfurt's Grand Duke Dalberg, found lodgings on a street aptly named Rue Napoleon, declared himself formally to the authorities, and then set about strengthening the chain that made possible the three-way traffic of British gold and continental bills of exchange between England, France, and the rest of Europe, for the benefit of Prince Wilhelm, his agents and allies, and other Rothschild clients. This was to the immense profit of the risk-taking Rothschilds, who were slipping through Napoleon's continental blockade in carriages with secret compartments for gold and bank papers, while James (alone or with the help of his older brothers) had somehow convinced Napoleon's treasury minister Nicolas Mollien that the outflow of gold from London would weaken France's historic enemy. . . .[15]

Nathan and James were henceforth the luckiest of the Rothschilds: they breathed freer air. Britain's political liberty opened most doors (except that of Parliament) to a Jewish subject of His or Her Majesty—Nathan was naturalized a British subject as early as 1809. In France, Jewish institutions were rigidly centralized under Napoleon, who did much to slow the original impetus given by the Revolution to Jewish emancipation in 1791. Nevertheless, despite a return to certain pre-Revolutionary constraints in the final years of Napoleon's empire, French Jews enjoyed extraordinary liberty for their times, released from most of the interdicts suffered by their cousins in Frankfurt or Vienna.[16]

James was in France—in Gravelines, Dunkirk, or Paris—when his father died on September 12, 1812. (Only sons Amschel and Carl were present in Frankfurt, allowing Count Corti to puncture the legend that on his deathbed Mayer Amschel divided the world among his descendents.)[17] From that moment on, Nathan, a modern banker firmly established in the shadow of the Bank of England, was all but formal head of the clan; now the roles of the

Rothschilds as bankers of kings, as masters of Europe's most efficient transport network for delivery of money and documents, could be exploited to the full. Not without occasional setbacks, however: to a France ever at war, the ubiquity of the Rothschilds had to be worrying.[18]

It was only then that Jacob really became James, as he assumed Parisian dress and manner—without ever losing that heavy German accent mimicked all his days by admirers as well as enemies. He'd learn to dance, to ride; he'd go to fancy dress balls—assuring his brother and senior partner in London that he was doing so only to meet people who could be useful. Soon he'd have a respectable house on Rue Le Peletier, in Paris's new business and banking district, with doorkeeper and domestic servants, a coachman—at a cost as upsetting to him as he knew it would be to his brothers.[19]

Napoleon's defeat—the first of them—facilitated Rothschild business in France. In 1814 James was able to register his bank at the Paris Tribunal de Commerce. This same year he was on the receiving end of British funds to be handed over to the restored king, Louis XVIII, on his return from exile in England—James's first direct contact with a crowned head. At the age of twenty-one James was responsible for the movement of millions of francs yearly; in an eight-month period in 1815 (when he was all of twenty-three) his reported profit exceeded a million—that would be some 22 million present-day francs.[20] Still, the brothers shared in each other's prosperity, James holding a one-eighth share of his brother's London bank, three-sixteenths of Frankfurt, and as much of Paris.[21]

Not even Napoleon's return to France from forced exile in Elba in March 1815 could disrupt the growth of their banks, although it could contribute one more legend to the Rothschild story, which has it that Nathan watched the Battle of Waterloo from a hill (or was informed of Napoleon's final defeat by carrier pigeon), enabling him to make a killing on the London stock market. In truth, the always expeditious Rothschild messenger service did get the news to Nathan early, but being a good Englishman he informed the British government at once. The Rothschilds became still richer—but they were not the exclusive beneficiaries of the victory.[22]

KING OF THE JEWS

*M*odern banking, with its inordinate movements of capital, its dizzying risk-taking, came into existence even before the industries in whose development it was to play so great a role. The first significant customers of the new banks were nations, not individual businessmen—heads of state, treasury ministers in need of funds for war (or to pay for lost wars), and for public works in peacetime. A French economic historian reminds us that these archetypal institutions—the merchant banks—derived from trading companies, dealers in merchandise as well as currencies, who speculated as readily in cotton and iron, say, as in commercial paper.

A nation, France for example, could replenish its treasury with long-term bonds offering attractive interest payments. A Rothschild family, with its own considerable resources, could take, if not a whole government loan, at least a large part of it, on its shoulders. This signified that kings and their ministers could get all the cash they needed on demand, letting the Rothschilds and their banking peers handle the details as to where it would come from, how it would be repaid. Merchant banking, with its emphasis on the financing of industrial development, came into its own in the wake of the French Revolution, on the heels of the Bonapartes, concomitant with the coming to power of the businessmen monarchs of the nineteenth century and the new untitled upper class that populated their courts.[1]

Follow the ascension of James, the lad behind the counter of the Frankfurt ghetto shop, as he emerges almost overnight as a leading actor in the economy of his adopted country. In 1815 he was still a junior partner in the spreading Rothschild enterprises, judging from the distribution of capital among the male descendents. Three years later, by which time their assets had grown by a multiple of nearly thirteen (to 42,528,000 francs, some 935 million of today's francs), James was virtually on a par with all the brothers save Nathan. By then he held a three-sixteenths share of his Paris bank. So did all his brothers save Nathan, who had a four-sixteenths share, as well as half the capital of the London bank, and a slightly higher share (again four-sixteenths) than his brothers of the assets of their original Frankfurt company.

Seven years later the brothers' capital had more than doubled, by which time Paris had become the biggest Rothschild bank of the lot, although Nathan, as senior partner—not because of age but for having been the first to go out into the world and to prove himself in foreign banking—continued to hold a higher equity than his siblings.[2]

Thanks to the indefatigable research of the economic historian Bertrand Gille, who was put to work on the bank archives by mid-twentieth-century Rothschilds, we can follow the impressive achievement of young James, who in the first years of the post-Napoleonic Bourbon reign entered the small club of merchant bankers handling French government loans. By 1817, a few days before his twenty-fifth birthday, his bank formed part of a syndicate handling a government issue designed to liquidate war reparation debts; earlier he had been involved in the physical transfer of money owed by France to Austria.[3]

As for Austria . . . It would indeed be difficult to exaggerate the significance of the brothers to that empire. It is relatively *easy* to demonstrate how precious they were to Austria's all-powerful chancellor, that Prince Clemens von Metternich who virtually ruled the continent after the Congress of Vienna reorganized post-Napoleonic Europe. At a time and in a place that scorned Jews, the Rothschilds were now to be ennobled; true, it was not a spontaneous gesture by

Metternich, but rather the product of skillful handling of the prince and his advisers by Salomon, the Rothschild brother who spent most of his time in Vienna to serve that court. But only Metternich could push through a proposal to make barons of tradesmen, and Jewish tradesmen at that. Their titles were confirmed before the end of 1816; Baron James in Paris was twenty-four.

James as well as Salomon became an *Austrian* baron, but the title suited nineteenth-century Paris very well. Salomon had proposed five arrows for their coat of arms to signify the ramifications of the bank in Frankfurt, London, Paris, Vienna, and Naples (where the Rothschilds were represented by Mayer Amschel's next-to-last son, Carl, who had been dispatched to the Kingdom of the Two Sicilies in 1821); they got only four, and four titles (as a British subject, Nathan had been omitted from the honors, an omission he found suited him well).[4]

James, in any case, was on his way. He knew where power resided under the Restoration monarchy, and laid siege to the ministers who counted. Whatever this child of the Judengasse may have looked like in those first years, however strange his dress and manners and speech, he forged ahead, as letters to his brothers show so graphically. In a letter to Nathan, for example, he refers to a formal reception given by one of the great bankers of the day, Jacques Laffitte, to which he hadn't been asked. "It's jealousy," he wrote (in Yiddish, using the Hebrew alphabet—the brothers' best code). "They don't want us to become even more important . . . I don't have a house in which to receive guests. A household without a wife is a ship without a captain."

He rendered service to the Duke of Orléans—who would remember it when he became Louis-Philippe, "Citizen" King of the French. He became an intimate of Elie, Duke Decazes, before *he* became first minister to King Louis XVIII. One of the first acts of James after winning his barony and celebrating his twenty-fifth birthday was to invite the Duke of Wellington to dinner—and the duke knew better than to refuse. The new baron could even invite a Metternich—something his brother Amschel wasn't able to do in Germany, or his brother Salomon in Metternich's own capital.

One didn't necessarily love the new Jewish bankers, but one respected them—at the very least, one maintained courteous relations with them. Anka Muhlstein notes that at the time of an outbreak of violent anti-Semitism in the German provinces in 1818, James in Paris had Prussian and Austrian diplomats at his table.[5]

That year, 1818, marks the preeminence of the brothers over all other European bankers, and this is saying much, saying it about Prussia, Russia, Austria, Spain, the Bourbon Kingdom of Two Sicilies in Naples, as well as about France and the United Kingdom. (By then James in Paris and Nathan in London were Austrian consuls, appointed by the Emperor.) What their activities had in common was an "interiorization" of foreign loans. Before the Rothschilds, an investor in the bonds of another nation would have to collect interest in the country of origin, with all the risk that might involve, and at whatever rate of exchange happened to prevail. The brothers reduced the risk to borrowers by taking full responsibility for the loans they underwrote, so that a Frenchman could buy Russian bonds in Paris, in French currency, and collect on them in Paris, also in francs (via the Rothschild bank).[6]

One unforgettable event took place in 1818, with James's purchase of the town house of Joseph Fouché, minister of police under Napoleon, then exiled to Prague. It was located in the heart of Paris's financial district, close to the headquarters of the then-dominant banker Jacques Laffitte (on a street later to be renamed Laffitte). And a grand house it was, with an ample courtyard behind the gate, a garden at the rear; it was more than adequate to receive nobility—or the wealthiest investors of the day. The main building, faced like all of Paris's noble residences in sober gray limestone, was to be Baron James's living quarters; it had a columned porch, steps leading up to it through three archways. The bank offices would be lodged in two wings constructed of the same noble materials, with similar paneled windows and doors. Few Parisians could boast of better quarters, and it remained a suitable place for a Rothschild bank until the sixth decade of our own century.[7]

Henceforth Baron James de Rothschild was to be at the center of his adopted country's political and economic life. The absence of war made it possible to focus on business, a lesson the Rothschilds were never to forget: they would always represent the peace party, except when their commitment to the nation to which they owed allegiance required that they fuel its war (it would happen in 1823, when James funded the campaign of the king's nephew, the Duc d'Angoulême, to put a king back on his throne in Spain).[8]

As a consular representative of the Austrian emperor, James could go everywhere, but it is clear that his best asset was neither his title nor his rank, rather the services he could provide. One of these services was the already legendary courier network, which even French prime minister Count Joseph de Villèle preferred to his own diplomatic pouch.[9] Austria's envoys in London, Frankfurt, and Paris also discovered that the Rothschild network could be more reliable than their own.

Sometimes the sudden arrival of a Rothschild courier would provoke a run on a local stock market; was he carrying bad news, or simply an order to sell—or to buy? In periods of tension— notably in Naples—Rothschild couriers would change clothing and carriages before entering the city so as not to be recognized. Of course, the family would be accused of manipulating information to their advantage, to make stocks rise (or fall).[10]

Another Rothschild strategy that paid off in the early years was the focus on transactions, leaving it to others to invest in specific industries—with all the risks this entailed for the nonexpert. In 1823, by skillful bidding, James won the management of a major French government loan against long-established rivals.[11] Henceforth he was a partner in every significant financial operation undertaken by France. Having paid a friendly call on James one morning, Metternich's son Victor described the scene to his father: "At that hour his office resembled a veritable magic lantern, with people of every sort of dress and expression coming and going. . . . While we spoke we were often interrupted by brokers announcing stock quotations to the grand master."[12]

In choosing a bride, James was as circumspect as he was in meditating a stock purchase. His best choice was brother Salomon's daughter Bettina; James was now thirty-two, she thirteen years his junior. Marrying a niece was the best thing a Rothschild could do, keeping both money and secrets in the family. And the family was at full strength for this marriage, celebrated on July 11, 1824, at the site of its founding, the Frankfurt ghetto house still occupied by Mayer Amschel's first son, Amschel, and his widow, Gutele. (Nathan would soon marry off his own daughter to Salomon's son. Of eighteen marriages contracted among Mayer Amschel's grand-children, sixteen would unite first cousins. The banking Roth-schilds showed by their behavior that they didn't require alliances with other banking families to prosper.)[13]

The groom was no beauty; even his friends would say so. Jules Michelet mentions his "profile of an intelligent monkey"; Heinrich Heine saw him as "distinguished and negligent."[14] Betty *was* a beauty; well tutored and well traveled, she adapted comfortably to Paris, and Paris adopted her, socially speaking, even more than it had James; she seems at home in the portrait Ingres painted for the house on Rue Laffitte, and represents its elegance. "On Saturday we dined at a sumptuous feast at Rothschilds," Lady Granville (wife of British ambassador Lord Granville Leveson-Gower) in-formed her sister Lady Carlisle. "He has married his niece, a pretty little Jewess, née coiffée, a very good thing at Paris, for just out of her nursery she does the honours of her house as if she had never done anything else."[15] The young baron was already distin-guishing himself as a man about town, patron of the arts. He'd be seen at the right restaurant, the right theater; none of the brothers adjusted as well to the social climates of their adopted countries (not even Nathan in London).[16]

Part of the reason, his biographer dares say, was the absence of a tightly structured Jewish community enforcing compliance with ritual; Baron James could remain a Jew without observing all the laws of traditional Jewry.[17] When he took up Jewish causes, they might concern unfortunate brethren in Germany and as far away as Russia or Damascus; Paris would not be part of the problem in his lifetime.

It seemed so easy, in Metternich's Europe, to make money with money. But crisis would come, the first signs of it in 1825–26. The decline in business activity extended across the European conti-nent, yet the brothers—with their multifaceted banking facilities augmenting the possibilities of mutual aid—seemed to weather it better than most. (No surprise; archivist Gille shows that the combined capital of the Rothschilds in the last years of the 1820s exceeded that of any other banking group, largely surpassing that of the Banque de France.)[18] Still, the French situation could not have been worse, with Charles X (who had come to the throne in 1824) unwilling to compromise in an increasingly tense social and political climate, not even with his bourgeoisie.

Despite the ominous signs, James de Rothschild seems to have accepted the assurances of the Bourbon king and his ministers that all would go well. Contemporary accounts stress James's lack of preparation for the debacle when it occurred: a series of decrees in late July 1830 dissolved the troublesome Chamber of Deputies, called for new elections under rules that stifled dissent, restricted press freedom.

This time the Bourbons were not to survive. Barricades went up, manned by insurgents drawn from the working class and students, joined by a disbanded national guard whose members had kept their arms, soon to be commanded by General La Fayette. Successively the city hall, Notre-Dame Cathedral, and the Louvre and Tuileries palaces were seized by the mob. With the abdication of Charles X, last of the Bourbons, the popular Duke d'Orléans moved in to rule as Louis-Philippe. All this, as Salomon de Rothschild explained in a report to Prince Metternich, without damage to public or private property.[19]

Yet the crisis had sent government bonds crashing, threatening the foundations of more than one monarchy. And the Rothschilds had been caught napping. To compensate, they could profit from the coming to power of a friend. "You know me well enough," the new king reminded James at a reception shortly after coming to power. "France was clearly leaning toward a republican form of government. . . . The monarchal principle won out over anarchy. . . . Nothing is dearer to me than peace in Europe."

Balm to the baron. To Metternich also—and James made sure he heard those words.[20] Henceforth the Rothschilds served both Louis-Philippe and Metternich—and peace between their nations—at a time when small crises (such as a dangerous dynastic change in Belgium) threatened to trouble the status quo among the major powers. "The entire world is arming and this frightens me,"

James wrote to Salomon—in a letter he knew his brother would show to "uncle," their code name for Metternich. "If uncle wishes peace and convinces our [French] government that he does, peace will be maintained." With peace, making money became possible again.[21]

Nothing could stop Baron James's ascension now. He'd dine at the king's table, or the king's sons might show up to dine at his. These years have been called "the reign of stock-jobbing and speculation"; one of the Rothschild historians suggests that James had an honored place in it.[22] Closer scrutiny shows that the rise of the Rothschilds was slower and surer. They took all useful precautions, refused all risks. It happened that the financial capital of Europe—thanks to its legion of bondholders prepared to invest not only in French loans but in foreign issues as well—was Paris.[23] And in France James had become—in the phrase of one of his clients, Honoré de Balzac—"the prince of money."[24]

Seemingly without humor, the social philosopher Charles Fourier envisioned the head of the French Rothschilds as King of Judea. He expected that the family would be able to rebuild an Israelite kingdom in Jerusalem, allowing them to emancipate Christians as well as Jews, since Jerusalem was then under the thumb of the Ottoman Turks.[25]

Whatever their image in popular fantasy, the brothers were hardly interchangeable. Salomon, in Vienna, had begun to involve himself in heavy industry, and would soon become master of the mighty ironworks of Vitkovice (Witkowitz) in Austria's Czech province. He was also the first brother to invest in building railroads, long before James was ready to do so.[26] In the 1830s the Rothschilds momentarily found themselves on opposite sides in an apparent *casus belli*, the succession to the Spanish throne, when France and Britain declared for the king's daughter, Austria for his absolutist brother.[27] But most of the time the brothers acted *en bloc*, and when they did they could make an emperor anxious.

Henceforth there was a recognizable Rothschild style that would see one or more of the brothers underwrite a sizable government bond issue, serving—thanks to their good name—as the moral guarantor vis-à-vis investors, even when they were not the sole managers of the loan but headed a syndicate of bankers. Their stock in trade was unerring knowledge of how money behaves, how to play rates of exchange, terms of interest. The bigger the loan the better, although they made sure not to risk their own money; it was enough that they offered the backing of their name. Their best asset was the Rothschild network of banks, making it possible for bonds of one country to be issued in all significant currencies, the bondholders assured that they'd be paid in their own.[28]

Soon enough the brothers were being talked about in another growth market, the United States; it made sense to lend money to America's nascent industry. They found just the right man to represent them in August Belmont, a Hessian Jew who had begun as an apprentice at the Rothschild bank in Frankfurt. At the age of twenty-three, Belmont was in New York, en route to a Rothschild assignment in Havana, when a financial crisis and the failure of the regular Rothschild broker on Wall Street convinced him that he should go no further. Thus began an American saga, for banker Belmont would not only serve the Rothschilds but his own ambitions, ending up as chairman of the Democratic party, a welcomed visitor and adviser at the White House.

Had they seen fit to stake out a major position in the United States, Belmont might have done even more than he did do for the Rothschilds; they could have had a bank in New York, managed, say, by a younger member of the family. There were frequent rumors in both the European and American press that they'd do just that. But the Rothschilds preferred to leave it to Belmont, who served long years as their agent, and to everybody's satisfaction.[29]

There was another fateful decision to make, but this time circumstances forced James's hand. He thought he knew one thing and only that thing: money, and how to make it grow. When an entrepreneur wished to buy or to found an industrial venture, he might borrow from Rothschild to do so; Rothschild involvement ended there.

But times were changing. Governments weren't borrowing through banks as much as they used to (tax collection was improving), while new developments in manufacturing, transportation, and communications called for investment on a scale the Rothschilds understood. His biographer, Anka Muhlstein, shows how James was infected by the enthusiasm of one of his young employees, a Sephardic Jew from Bordeaux, Emile Péreire, himself inspired by the doctrines of the economic idealist Saint-Simon, whose followers prescribed the building of railroads as the first step in an industrial revolution. James did take the first step, and the expansion of industry did indeed follow.[30]

In 1835—the year Fourier saw James as king of the Jews— France was considerably behind Britain in the development of rail transportation; what lines existed served to move coal. But then the dreamers began to dream. The best guess is that the Pereire brothers—broker Emile and Saint-Simonian publicist Isaac—were behind the first concrete plan for a passenger line. It happened to be a line that would have considerable visibility, since it was to connect the French capital to nearby Saint-Germain-en-Laye. Surely encouraged by his brothers Nathan and Salomon, both already committed to railways in their respective territories, James became an investor in the projected line, with Emile Pereire as project manager.

The service was inaugurated in August 1836, and it was an immediate success. A year later the French Rothschilds won the bidding for a second railroad route to Versailles along the right bank of the Seine, and this time led the list of investors.

James had been bitten. France's northeast represented the country's industrial base, the source of its fuel; and yet there were investors who hesitated to build a rail link to it because of the unprecedented cost of such a project, the concern that rival lines might place the investment in jeopardy. Railroads seemed to call for an act of faith. And then France had begun to feel the effects of another recession at the end of the 1830s; it was a time to reassess visionary projects, to scrutinize the plans of the engineers with greater care. "At this moment," James confided to his associates, "I am not enthusiastic about railroads."[31]

THE GREAT BARON

*H*e never lost his accent, a comical one to the French. Nor would Baron James de Rothschild bother to acquire French nationality. But he did acquire a court composer in the person of Gioacchino Rossini, who, after writing three dozen operas in his native Italy (including *The Barber of Seville*), settled in Paris in 1824 at the age of thirty-two (James's age); there he created his last opera, *William Tell*, and a great deal of occasional music—some of it on command for the Rothschilds. Rossini accompanied James in 1836 to the wedding of Nathan's son Lionel and Carl's daughter Charlotte; although Lionel lived in London and Carl in Naples, the ceremony was once again held in the town where it all began—Frankfurt.[1]

Perhaps the great Ingres should be called court painter, for his oil painting of James's wife is virtually the official portrait. An equally confirmed talent, the chef Marie-Antoine Carême, who had cooked for the Prince de Talleyrand, now presided over the kitchens of Baron James.[2]

There was even an unofficial poet laureate in Heinrich Heine, that very Parisian German who reported regularly on James's private and public faces for readers of the German gazettes, and who composed an ode (at least one) to James's Bettina, one of the "angels without wings" who protect men from misfortune.

Bettina, or Betty as she'd be called, did appear an easy mark for seekers of alms.[3] Her great-niece Constance Battersea saw her as invaluable to James "for the social support she gave him in the influential position that he owed to his financial genius." She was given credit for the family's contribution to the development of Jewish schools, hospitals, social services; she could write Hebrew and Yiddish, and respected religious tradition more than her husband did. *He* might say, when going to work on a Saturday, the obligatory Sabbath day of rest, "My good lady would not go out today, but I must do such-and-such things."[4] Yet in 1839, when Nathan's daughter Hannah married outside the faith (married the brother of the Earl of Southampton, Henry Fitzroy), the baron was beside himself with rage. "This marriage makes me absolutely ill," he wrote to Hannah's brother Nathaniel. He wished to see her disinherited. "For my part, I have made up my mind that neither my wife nor my children will ever see Hannah again."[5]

By then James had acquired, as his in-town residence, an imposing eighteenth-century mansion on Rue Saint-Florentin, at the corner of the monumental Place de la Concorde. It had been the last home of Talleyrand; henceforth it was to be the address of the reigning Rothschild—until the Second World War brought the Nazis to Paris. Its sober façade—built according to the plans of Jacques-Ange Gabriel, architect of Louis XV in general and of his Place de la Concorde in particular—betrays little of the elegance found just inside its massive gate: the courtyard, with its statues perched in niches, has since been classified a historical monument. The true graces—a succession of drawing rooms that became as many art galleries—were reserved for the guests who were to crowd in for the legendary balls given in James's time, then in the time of his son Alphonse, and then by Alphonse's son Edouard.

What he did, he did grandly; the club he joined would have to be the best. (Being Austrian consul made that possible.) Even his charities had to be on the grand scale, and three clerks were employed to do nothing but process applications for succor. Of course James would also have to be a connoisseur of food and wine, loving every sip of that velvety Château Lafite whose vineyards in Bordeaux he'd purchase only in his final year.[6]

He began to amass one of Europe's great collections of art (a letter read by his biographer has him *selling* a Rembrandt as early as 1840).[7] "Yesterday," Balzac wrote the far-off Anna Hanska, the woman he was courting for her money but also for the near impossibility of the relationship, "I ran into Rostchild [*sic*], meaning all the wit and all the money of the Jews."[8] Notoriously naive about financial matters, the novelist assumed that just knowing a Rothschild might make his fortune. "For three weeks," he confesses to Anna, "I've been hoping that Rostchild [*sic*] would help me sort out my affairs as I requested that he do, but enough of that; if I have to ask him twice I prefer poverty and work."[9]

The times were friendly to personal initiative. France had entered the era when everything had to be built, or made new. James was to become the most important Rothschild of them all on the death of Nathan in 1836.[10] "Do you know who is viceroy and even king in France? It's Rothschild." So Countess von Nesselrode wrote to her husband, Karl, foreign minister of Czar Nicholas I, after dining at James's table. She has listened to Baron James say of France's cabinet ministers, "I know them all; I see them every day, and when I find that what they're doing is contrary to the government's interest I call on the King—I see him whenever I wish—and tell him what I think. Since he knows that I have a lot to lose and that I desire nothing more than tranquillity, he trusts me completely." The countess informs her husband that everybody who matters shows up at the Rothschild house, with the baron behaving "as a Richelieu, receiving or not according to his mood."[11]

How James was seen in 1844 (or wished to be seen, for he may well have subsidized the writer) bursts from the pages of a flimsy tract lauding "a royalty more solid than a constitutional monarchy"; had the Rothschilds existed during the reign of the Sun King, says this hagiographer, their fortune might well have irritated Louis XIV. Lest this be considered damning, the author gives credit to the Rothschilds for recent industrial progress; they are the Medicis of their time.[12]

Such uncritical tribute could make even a Metternich wince, despite his enduring connections to the family. So he indicates in a note to his ambassador Rudolf Apponyi in 1845: "In France the

house of Rothschild plays a more significant role than any government, for obvious reasons which I don't necessarily consider
good nor particularly moral. . . . These are people who pretend to
be philanthropists and who bury criticism under a pile of money."[13]

Fawning over and profiting from Rothschilds while finding it
uncomfortable to embrace them was something Rothschilds were
used to. And what James was experiencing in France, his procon-
sul August Belmont would find on the still-fragile American continent, where James hadn't hesitated to extend credit to the cotton
industry, as well as to state and federal treasuries, when other
French bankers (and the Bank of England) abstained, thus helping
to stem a monetary crisis in that nation suffering from growing
pains.[14] But Belmont's role as a Democratic party kingmaker in
pre–Civil War days expectedly led to charges that "Jew gold" was
being used to win the presidency. On balance, association with
Rothschild would end up becoming a plus for Belmont, for wealthy
Jews were admired as much as they were feared.[15]

But America was still a secondary power in the age of Metternich. What counted was Belgium, tiny but pivotal, and desperately
in need of support at a time when its independence within guaranteed frontiers was only then being recognized—and only because France and Britain made sure that the Netherlands respected
it. "My opinion," James wrote to his associates in March 1839, "is
that settlement of the Belgian question will be followed by a need
of money and that we should take advantage of that moment to
become total masters of that country's finances."[16]

One could involve oneself in a nation's affairs for profit; that much
was accepted by the new international bankers. But could one do the
same for moral or even personal reasons? The context, in 1840, was
a Middle Eastern crisis that saw France supporting the Egyptian
viceroy Muhammad ᶜAli in his revolt against the Ottoman Empire.
In February of that year the father superior of a French Capuchin
order disappeared in Damascus; somehow France's consuls there
went along with the age-old calumny that Jews committed ritual
murder to obtain Christian blood for the feast of Passover. It took no
more than their endorsement for leaders of the local Jewish community to be rounded up and tortured (some died, some made false
confessions). Two of the victims happened to be Austrian nationals;

that brought Metternich into the picture, tying the Damascus affair into the complicated quilt of European conflict. Austria's allies Prussia, Russia, and Britain stood with Metternich against France, in a crisis that seemed to hang on what the Talmud prescribed.

James intervened, taking up the matter with unsympathetic Adolphe Thiers, the French prime minister. He also made use of the press, but Parisians were more likely to find support for the anti-Jewish "blood libel" in their daily papers than its contrary. Before the crisis was resolved, Heinrich Heine was reporting on French Jewish reaction—or lack of reaction—to the Damascus affair, and publicly congratulating Rothschild for his intervention.[17]

The debate reached the floor of Parliament, Thiers defending his misguided diplomats in the name of patriotism. The plight of their Oriental brethren led to the first significant collaboration of European Jews across national boundaries, with leading community figures such as Sir Moses Montefiore in London and Adolphe Crémieux in France sailing to the Orient to meet both the Ottoman sultan and dissident Muhammad ʿAli. The intervention of James de Rothschild was more discreet, but he had the ear of Louis-Philippe. Eventually Muhammad ʿAli would submit to his sultan, and the Jews of Damascus receive justice.[18]

Clearly peace was their business, and when it seemed threatened, one was sure to find a Rothschild riding to the rescue. During the Middle Eastern crisis, James made it a point to inform Metternich that France wasn't pushing for war (he had it from the lips of Louis-Philippe himself). "By what right and under what pretext does this king of finance concern himself with our affairs?" demanded Le Constitutionnel, a newspaper known to be the mouthpiece of Premier Thiers. "If France is not my country," James replied (in a letter published by the same newspaper), "it's at least the country of my children. I have been living here thirty years, my family is here, and so are my friends and all my activities."

In the end peace was saved, and the king found that he could do very well without Adolphe Thiers.[19] Soon after that, writing for German readers, the amiable Heinrich Heine noted how well Baron

James was looking these days. "The prophets of the stock exchange, who know exactly how to decode the facial expressions of the great baron, assure us that the swallows of peace are nesting in his smile. . . . Even the baron's sneezes, they add, speak of peace."[20]

Still earlier, it had seemed vital to Prince Metternich to have Rothschild on his side during the protracted rivalry for the Spanish throne, a rivalry that exploded in armed conflict pitting the powers supporting the infant daughter of the deceased Ferdinand VII against those lined up with the dead king's brother Don Carlos (and both sides expected Rothschild support). It was France and Britain, favoring Isabelle II, against Metternich's Austria, and Metternich was not the last to learn that his protégé James had won a fabulous mercury mine concession from the regent Marie-Christine (ruling for her six-year-old daughter). Don Carlos lost, and with him his Austrian backers; the Rothschilds kept their mercury mines, which, with their Austrian holdings, added up to an international monopoly.[21]

Hence those rails that were to link the French capital to the heartlands of mining and industry, to the Channel coast, to the Mediterranean: this was the great work of the 1840s. It called for cooperation of the kind the Saint-Simonians had imagined, as well as government assistance in infrastructure and for necessary expropriations of land. But it was up to the new entrepreneurs to put down the rails, to place iron horses atop them. And that called for an injection of capital of a magnitude unknown until then, with a magician's gift for raising funds; James had that gift. "At this moment," Heinrich Heine reported, "the whole population of Paris forms a single chain transmitting an electrical charge." The poet felt himself in the grip of a "sinister tremor, of the kind we feel when something prodigious and unheard of occurs whose consequences are immense and incalculable." He could have been talking about the Apollo moonwalk. "We feel only that our existence is being drawn or rather launched into new orbits, that we are entering a new life, with new joys and new sufferings. . . ." In this remarkable account of the industrial revolution as observed by an eyewitness, Heine compared the advent of railroads to the discovery of America or the invention of gunpowder or of the printing press; as if reporting the event on a news broadcast, he painted a picture of all the world's mountains and forests marching on Paris.

The chronicler also described the mechanisms by which France was getting these magic machines: the great corporations being founded, the beguiling prospectuses inviting the public to subscribe for shares. Stock offerings listed the sponsors of the new enterprises, who included princes and dukes as well as bankers and industrialists. "One almost hears the trumpet calls and the big drums as Pagliaccio invites the honorable public to take seats from the stage of his carnival shack."

And so to the house of Rothschild, where "each share of a company that this firm accords is a favor or rather . . . a gift of money which Mr. de Rothschild makes to his friends." Indeed, since Rothschild railway shares were already worth more than their face value, anyone asking the Baron James for newly issued stock was literally begging. And everybody begged; Mr. de Rothschild was the hero of the day.

It wasn't easy to be James de Rothschild, Heine wanted it known, for "the poor baron is adulated, harassed, and tortured without a moment's respite" by his admirers. In turn, Baron James admired the great writers of the past—Homer, Dante, Shakespeare. . . . At least *they* weren't after him for shares in the Northern Railway.[22]

Honoré de Balzac was also a writer, but a living one—and he *was* asking for shares. This prolific storyteller, who was usually just one manuscript ahead of bankruptcy, was irresistibly attracted to the banker; he couldn't afford not to be. He had indeed called on Rothschild, who promised him a few shares (so he confided to Madame Hanska). In fact he was quite prepared to invest everything he had in railroads, but when he said as much to James, he "leaped from his chair" to tell the improvident Balzac, "I'd never advise a friend to invest everything he possesses."[23]

Skillful maneuvering had placed the baron in the driver's seat. In 1845 his Compagnie du Chemin de Fer du Nord was granted the potentially lucrative route from Paris northeast through France's mining and industrial heartland to the Belgian frontier. Soon enough there would be a place for a Rothschild investment in the eastern route to Strasbourg and the southern route to Lyon, with more to come.[24]

But now a groundswell of opposition to the pretentions of this Frankfurt Jew began to manifest itself, a reaction (given the Great Baron's notoriety, his visibility, and the character of Catholic, agricultural France) that should not surprise. What surprises is the extent to which expressions of anti-Jewish hostility came from the left, from incipient Socialists, beginning with Pierre Proudhon (for whom, in any case, property was theft). For Proudhon the Jew was "anti-productive," an "intermediary, always fraudulent and parasitical." That other early Socialist, Charles Fourier, sought to discredit the rival Saint-Simonian movement because Jews were active in it. (Both Proudhon and Fourier entered the history books with a somewhat more positive image.) Such positions allowed historian Robert Byrnes to conclude that in the decades before 1880 *most* anti-Semitism came from the left and not the right.[25]

Take Proudhon's disciple Alphonse Toussenel, whose two-volume exposé, *Jews: Kings of Our Time,* published by a socio-anarchist group in 1845, was the century's first manifestation of nonreligious anti-Semitism born of the industrial revolution. For Toussenel, "Jew" signified exploiter; one didn't even have to have been born Jewish to be a "Jew" in his terms. He said he employed the word *Jew* as he would *banker* or *money changer*; he recognized the Jewish contribution to humanity, just as he was aware that Protestants were as prominent as Jews in the ranks of high finance. Alas, he said, all "Bible readers"—Jews or Geneva or Dutch or Anglo-American Protestants—seemed convinced "that God granted his servitors the monopoly of exploitation of the globe, for all these mercantile peoples bring to bear, in the art of ransoming humanity, the same religious fanaticism."[26]

Quite expectedly, Toussenel attacked the government's railroad concessions to the Rothschilds. "Thus does high finance dominate everything; Jewish interests are visible all about us."[27] It is easy to see how Toussenel's treatise became a Bible for anti-Semites, in his time and later.

In May 1846, when a spectacular accident occurred on the Northern Railway near Arras—a derailment on a dike, causing a considerable number of deaths and injuries[28]—the pamphleteers were ready. One of them, identifying himself as "Satan," in a thirty-six-page *Histoire édifiante et curieuse de Rothschild Ier, Roi des Juifs* blamed "this Jew's gold" for Napoleon's defeats as well as for the deaths of the railroad passengers. For this polemicist, the Rothschilds had corrupted Parliament to obtain a rail monopoly, and James was "a capitalist who grows wealthy while working fathers are stripped of their last piece of bread."[29] A reply to "Satan" attributed to Baron James—but which he certainly hadn't touched or paid for—points out that the official report on the accident exonerated James's railroad. "Go to all the banks and exchanges of Europe, I defy you to discover a single operation of the house of Rothschild that lacks honesty and integrity."[30]

In a reply to that reply, "Satan" says his only purpose is to combat "the new financial feudality," to denounce Rothschild as "king of the Jews, which is to say leader of the speculators . . . , flagbearer of a party . . . that seeks to pervert France. . . ."[31]

And that was only the beginning.

HARD TIMES

King of the railroads, king of the Jews: the great baron at his zenith. Once again let Heine, a frequent caller at the bank, describe how "men of all classes and faiths, Gentiles as well as Jews, bow low and grovel before him"—this written for all the world to see—at least the world in and around Augsburg, Germany, where Heine's occasional letters from France were published. For Heinrich Heine, better known to us as poet and essayist, a lay Jew and a revolutionary in vision, lived during his self-exile in Paris in part by political journalism. Rothschild, who was most things Heine stood against, could only fascinate him.

"I have seen people who on approaching the great baron shudder as if they had touched an electric current," Heine went on. They approached him as Moses coming into the presence of his deity. "For money is the God of our times, and Rothschild His prophet."

One day, as a servant walked through the bank carrying the baron's chamber pot, the German writer looked on as a stockbroker raised his hat to this object deemed sacred. Heine was convinced that this man unknown to him would one day be a millionaire.[1]

* * *

Life at home was more serene, James and Bettina presiding over a model family. Their firstborn was a daughter, Charlotte. Two years later, on the first of February, 1827, came Alphonse (one of the chief protagonists of this story), followed in two more years by Gustave, six years after that by Salomon James. By the time Edmond was born, on August 19, 1845, monkey-faced James was fifty-three years old and Betty still beautiful; that set tongues to wagging. "Madame James gave birth to a fat little boy whose confection doesn't seem to have cost James much effort," Balzac told his Anna, adding with equal malice: "Jews have to make something on everything they do and even on what they don't do." (Of course Balzac hadn't stopped counting on James for financial advice.)[2]

While waiting for Alphonse and his brothers to grow up, James borrowed a son from Nathan in London—Nathaniel—and promptly married him to daughter Charlotte. They'd get an apartment on the rear garden at Rue Laffitte, later a house of their own at 33 Rue du Faubourg Saint-Honoré, until then the embassy of Czarist Russia. Nathaniel would never give up his British nationality, although he'd stay in Paris as long as he lived. He and Charlotte became the founders of the "English" line of the French Rothschilds, which has survived and sometimes thrived to our day. These Rothschilds seldom bothered about banking, but at least one of them became a celebrity in his own right: Henri de Rothschild, physician and scientist, playwright and sportsman, and a Parisian bon vivant who made the papers more often than his banking cousins were doing. And then there was Henri's son Philippe, who employed his talents as a publicist to build up the Bordeaux vineyards of his branch of the family into a famous label, Mouton-Rothschild.[3]

As first son and crown prince of the French Rothschild empire, Alphonse was going to get the best that money (and ingenuity) could provide. Archivist Bertrand Gille, who went over the accounts, found that the household consumed considerable sums of cash for that time, and none was spared on the education of Alphonse and his brothers. They were taught German and English as well as the language of the country, studied Hebrew and the Bible. (James's biographer, Anka Muhlstein, who read his letters, reminds us that while Alphonse and his brothers considered French their first language, and even their mother spoke and wrote that language fluently, the Great Baron almost never wrote in French or even in German—preferring his ghetto Yiddish).[4]

Young Alphonse learned to ride, to draw, and to dance in society. He appeared in public for the first time in 1845 (the year of Edmond's birth); the cost of his formal costume is also known. Unlike his father, Alphonse was to become a French citizen through naturalization (it happened in the tumultuous year 1848, which was also the year he graduated from law school).[5]

There were summers on the fashionable Channel coast (chiefly at Dieppe). Edmond remembered growing up not on the Place de la Concorde but in a Louis-Philippe castle in the middle of a 250-acre park on the Seine River, just outside Paris in Boulogne; from his window he'd watch the fashioning of the Bois de Boulogne, the digging of its artificial lakes.[6] A contemporary witness marvels at how the happy household spilled over to the bank on Rue Laffitte, as chubby little Edmond played at riding horseback on his father's cane, blowing a trumpet during the otherwise austere working day.[7] At home there were celebrated soirées, with recitals by the likes of Chopin, Liszt, Berlioz. Mocking, curious, or respectful, the aristocracy couldn't afford not to be there.[8]

Evil gossip didn't seem to leave marks. Just as James was rumored not to have sired Edmond, so James was said to be the adulterous father of a successful lawyer who would become one of the models for Proust's Charles Swann.[9] Balzac found James crude, enjoying rough humor. "It makes Madame James weep," Balzac told Anna. (The baroness is now Balzac's angel, having conceived Edmond with a lover.)

One day Balzac called on James on behalf of a poor woman who was seeking a license to open a small shop. Is she pretty? asked James. Had Balzac slept with her? "One hundred twenty-one times!" Balzac replied jokingly. "And if you want her I'll give her to you." James wished to know if the woman had children; when told that she had none, he said that he only assisted mothers. (Balzac comments to Anna that this is an excuse; had James been told that the poor woman did have children, he'd have replied that he couldn't abide immorality.)

Balzac decided that James had aged—aged ten years in the last twelve months. "Business is killing me," he told Balzac in February 1846. But the novelist is without pity for this Jew a hundred times millionaire. The scene switches to the Rothschild mansion. "Madame James is of a ravishing graciousness," Balzac croons to Anna. *She* will help the poor woman obtain the needed license."[10]

These were bad years; James might well seem prematurely old. He played a crucial role in alleviating famine after the failure of the wheat harvest in 1846, importing supplies from better-endowed regions of the Mediterranean basin; more, he made it easy for the French to buy the wheat, keeping prices down. Later his public-spirited efforts would be seen as a way to buy off the people's resentment of the leisure and merchant classes.[11] A historian noted that even after James sold wheat at a loss and subsidized the price of bread, he wasn't trusted; there were allegations in the popular press that the bread wasn't bread at all but plaster mixed with arsenic, or that the baron was only seeking to get rid of damaged flour. There was another rumor that he concealed the poor quality by mixing bad flour with sweet almonds (as if sweet almonds weren't a lot more costly than flour).[12]

By then France had entered into a full-dress crisis, seemingly a consequence of the sopping up of available capital for industrial expansion. Credit tightened, threatening new industries—not least the new class of railroad entrepreneurs. Share prices slipped, then plunged. Imprudently, clearly because he misjudged the extent of the recession, James agreed to underwrite a major French state loan in November 1847. The unimaginable: in the face of company failures, even a Rothschild couldn't be everywhere or help every-one; all he could do was to ask debtors to pay up, and circular letters to that effect went out in January 1848.[13] Fatal 1848.

Nor had the Great Baron anticipated the wave of discontent that would sweep over the continent, toppling its hierarchies. In France it began with a series of protests by workers and students, followed by the defection of government troops; soon barricades were thrown up on major thoroughfares, the resolution heralded by the precip-itous flight of tired old Louis-Philippe. Perhaps one shouldn't be surprised at James's surprise; he hadn't witnessed a French rev-olution.

The king had fled to England; James sent Betty there—with their precious son Alphonse. (Constance Battersea had a childhood memory of that; it had seemed the dead of night when she was carried downstairs in her home on Grosvenor Place to greet the Rothschild refugees, who had arrived "in a sad state of misery and depression"; Constance's nursery was one of the rooms taken over for their comfort.)[14]

In fact the rebels of 1848 would prove to be reformist and reasonable, once they had their way. Their leaders included poet Alphonse de Lamartine and scientist-turned politician François Arago; the republic they proclaimed on February 25 abolished slavery and instituted universal suffrage but did not savage property. The choice of a Jewish banker, Michel Goudchaux, as minister of finance was reassuring.[15]

Then a young stockbroker's assistant, the writer Ernest Feydeau—to be the father of a more famous comedy writer—was serving as a junior officer during the street fighting; on February 24, as shells ripped across Rue de Rivoli, he recognized Baron James, walking nonchalantly toward the Tuileries gardens. Feydeau approached respectfully, suggesting that the baron cease to expose himself to the constant gunfire.

"My young friend," he remembered Rothschild replying in that accent thick as a loaf, "I tank you for your adfice. But dell me, why are *you* here? To do your duty, is it not zo? Vell, de paron de Rotchild game here for de same ding. . . . My duty is to go to de Vinance Ministry to zee if dey need my exberience und adfice."[16]

But as pillars of Louis-Philippe's kind of France, the Rothschilds were indeed symbols of what had to go. "The Rosthcild [*sic*] mansion at Suresnes was burned down," Balzac reported to Anna Hanska (in fact the house belonged to Salomon of Vienna, who spent much time in the French capital). James's biographer observes that the Rothschilds and the royal family had been the only targets of mob violence.[17]

Another tense moment: the meeting of James and Marc Caussidière, the fiery political leader who moved from the barricades into the office of prefect of police; he would later say that he persuaded the baron to remain in Paris in the higher interests of the nation. Caussidière had heard a rumor that James was smuggling gold out of the country in dung carts, so as to be able to declare himself bankrupt. Even if one couldn't believe such stories, one had to recognize that public opinion was aroused against bankers, and so the banks—particularly Rothschild's—was kept under police protection, while the prefect assigned a plainclothes agent to watch over the baron. "They think I'm covered with gold," Caussidière remembered James telling him; "but I have nothing but paper. My wealth and my cash are now all in stock certificates—which at the moment are worthless. I have no desire to declare bankruptcy, and if I have to die I'm ready. But I'd consider it cowardice to leave." He had asked family members in other banking capitals to send him funds so that he could meet his commitments. Prefect Caussidière assured him that he had nothing to fear from the poor but honest people of Paris.

Soon James was back with a cash donation of 2,000 francs to be disbursed for worthy causes.[18] The daily press would make much of James's resolve to stay; one paper, so close to the Rothschilds that it was generally taken to be in their debt, announced, "Mr. de Rothschild, who was told to leave the country, has given an example of his confidence in the people and in the provisional government. He has refused to go." True or not, the press let it be known that the house of Rothschild had given not 2,000 but 50,000 francs for the wounded and for workers in need.[19] The presence of Rothschilds unstained by scandal was an asset even in that revolutionary year.

Agitation diminished, but the financial crisis worsened. Rothschild stood firm; archivist Gille finds evidence that his bank was still honoring commitments when even the Banque de France had shut its windows.[20] But with government itself in virtual suspension of payments, where to turn? In the absence of the will or the wherewithal to meet the demands of workers and farmers, the revolt spread.

It was during a lull in the agitation, or what he took for a lull, that James accepted the offer of his wife to return to Paris, although not to stay. "One never knows what to expect from a republic," he warned Betty. For the time being, all was calm, but he considered the situation "still very dangerous." As for the bank, all they could do was to meet its obligations; new business was impossible.

If Betty did return from London, her husband beseeched her to obtain a passport in another name. "If you expect to bring Alphonse with you, he must also have a passport in another name, for I don't want the papers to report that 'Madame de Rothschild has returned to England. . . .' " He had reached the point, he said, of wishing he could give up working, to live quietly. "Come, bring Alphonse with you, although I wonder if we shouldn't prevent him from getting involved with politics. If they see him he will be required to enroll in the national guard. If he doesn't show himself too much, he can come. . . ."

Betty did return, accompanied by Alphonse, and soon his younger brother Gustave would join them. "The workers are our masters, we have to resign ourselves to that," Alphonse reported back to his London cousins.[21] And indeed, the agitation had paralyzed production. For his part, Baron James froze credit and nurtured his railroad while letting less promising affairs lie fallow. Help from London took the form of silver ingots.[22]

The pivotal month of March (pivotal because it formed a bridge between disorder and order, although a short-lived one) can be followed in the punctilious correspondence of the industrious Honoré de Balzac, never too busy to write reams to Anna Hanska. Compagnie du Nord railway shares were low? It was a time (March 12) to buy (Honoré asks Anna to send him money for that). Rothschild was afraid, said Balzac; Balzac himself feared for his dividends (and yet he wanted to purchase more stock). March 17: Civil war may begin today; Rothschild has already left Paris. (Actually he hadn't budged; perhaps he simply didn't wish to listen to Balzac's whining.) March 21: Balzac worries that the banker won't survive the fall of Metternich and the Austrian monarchy. March 25: Another decline in Rothschild railway shares. March 29: A letter received from Rothschild—who is taking money the writer intended to invest to reduce Balzac's debt to the bank—convinces Balzac that the crisis has become still worse for the railroads. In early April, Balzac shows up at the bank again, to hear the baron complain of a further decline in government bonds. Employees he

talks to are dismayed, and Balzac understands that Rothschild's
entire fortune is threatened. . . .[23]

As James had feared, his oldest son, Alphonse, was taken into the
national guard; Gustave was to follow. "Every time I hear the call
to arms I tremble for the lives of Alphonse and Gustave," James
confessed to his London family. "My Alphonse, with a rifle on his
shoulder, fighting for the Republic." There was something he could
do about that—between calls to arms. He'd simply send Alphonse
on a mission to the United States, young as he was (twenty-one
then). "I wish him to leave Paris rapidly," he wrote on May 5, "and
I also want him to set to work seriously and become a man."[24]

Just in time, for the worst did happen in June 1848, when the
failure of the moderates to alleviate the crisis affecting the working
class first of all led to renouncement by the former, and violent
protest by the latter; the bloody "days of June" left a thousand dead
on the streets of Paris and led to 12,000 arrests, while the tough
general who achieved all this won promotion to the office of prime
minister. The way was paved for a new, less affable republic, a
party of Order, a president (Louis-Napoleon) with imperial ambitions. James de Rothschild survived.

Indeed, Balzac saw him in July at a popular cabaret theater, got
himself invited to the baron's table. In August, Balzac was able to
report to Madame Hanska, "The Nord railroad won't need a loan
until the end of next year and its revenues are superb."[25] Business
as usual for the Rothschilds didn't please everyone, as suggested
by an open letter to the great baron circulated by street vendors:
"You are a miracle. . . . Louis-Philippe falls . . .; both the constitutional monarchy and parliamentary debate disappear, but you
survive. . . . Alone, amid so many ruins, you don't falter. The Jew,
king of our times, has kept his throne!"[26]

Until now the Rothschilds had maintained their low profile on
the far side of the Atlantic, leaving it to the eloquent August
Belmont to speak for them. Alphonse, as his letters home show,
was all for expanding the American side of the business. "The
generosity with which space was granted this country," he writes to
his mother, "assures it in the not distant future of prodigious

commercial development." Belmont was found to be living as "a true lord," and a man not easy to deal with—especially if one asked to see the accounts. He had been independent of the Rothschilds for too long, noted the perceptive young man. (Perhaps part of the fault was the Rothschilds', he dared to add.)

Then as today, London and Paris Rothschild banks were associated in American operations, so Alphonse lobbied his London cousins too. He described the promise of California—not so much for its gold mines as for its geographic position, the access it provided to nations across the Pacific. He was equally perspicacious about the United States as a market. "The country possesses such considerable assets that one must be blind not to recognize them, and one can't help admiring the energy and intelligence with which people go about exploiting them." He pleaded for the establishment of a full-dress House of Rothschild in the United States; everybody who counted in business wanted them to come. There was ample room now; later the competition would make it more difficult.

Alphonse did a grand tour of sorts, notably to New Orleans, base of the family's lucrative cotton trade; he pushed as far as Havana, pummeling his parents with reasons to implant themselves in the New World. Without success. Archivist Gille wonders if this failure of nerve was due to the unavailability of a family member— Alphonse apparently being considered too young (though already older than his father had been when he waged economic war against Emperor Napoleon). Or was James simply exercising caution about something so far away, so new? America with its volatile economy, its market highs and lows, was a bronco needing a tamer; the Rothschilds had horses enough to tend.[27]

ANOTHER EMPEROR

he Rothschilds had not been on the best of terms with Napoleon Bonaparte. Louis-Napoleon, Bonaparte's nephew, seemed willing to overlook that; while still imprisoned during the restoration monarchy he actually tried to interest Baron James in putting money into a canal project in Central America. Later, when the events of 1848 had cleared the way for Louis-Napoleon to rule as "prince-president," and still later (after his coup d'état in December 1851) as the least credible emperor one could imagine, he often turned to Baron James for both personal and official needs. More businessman than monarch, Napoleon III couldn't help wanting to be friendly with the country's leading banker; for his part, James appreciated having a head of state who could assure civil peace, and if he participated in a public bond issue it was to demonstrate, so he wrote to his London family, that "we don't reject the government nor do we wish to make things difficult for it."[1]

But James neither liked nor trusted Louis-Napoleon, and the distaste seemed to be mutual. In the end the emperor would find more pliable bankers, and the Rothschilds would cease to be the privileged financiers of the French state.[2] The Austrian ambassador reported another possible reason for Louis-Napoleon's antagonism: General Nicolas Changarnier, in charge of the Paris garrison and a declared enemy of the prince-president, was thought to be carrying on a flirtation with the lovely Baroness Betty, who turned up at one too many of the dashing general's parades. (After the December 1851 coup, the new emperor simply exiled the troublesome soldier.)[3]

No question of anti-Semitism here, for the Rothschilds would be replaced in the emperor's heart by another Jewish banking family, the Foulds, with Achille Fould as finance minister and intimate adviser; Napoleon III was also to give his blessing to the ambitious Pereire brothers, without doubt James's most troublesome competitors of the Second Empire. The ideological Pereires—making money in the name of Saint-Simonian socialism—seemed predestined to dethrone the Rothschilds as the right men for their time, offering France's new regime both the means to free itself from the tyranny of the merchant bankers and a way to mobilize immense amounts of capital—more than the merchant bankers were ready or willing to offer—for the needs of the industrial revolution.

The chief contribution of Emile and Isaac Pereire to the new order of things was the Crédit Mobilier, an investment bank whose assets would come from its shareholders, a truly magic formula for draining funds from rank-and-file savers, small sums that quickly grew into a substantial treasury. A people's bank, in other words, which in theory would result in a more equitable distribution of goods.[4]

Volumes have been written about the Pereires and their victory (temporary) over their mentor James de Rothschild, with some of the writers reducing the clash of banking and social philosophies to a quarrel of persons: James de Rothschild vexed that his protégés had found their own path to success, the Pereire brothers anxious to free themselves from a paternalistic sponsor. How could they fail, with the emperor on their side?[5]

The Pereires' revolutionary bank was launched by presidential decree—Louis-Napoleon was not to become emperor for another fortnight—on the eighteenth of November, 1852. It did seem that everybody in banking, and many of the most influential personalities of the Second Empire, had combined forces in the Crédit Mobilier—everybody except the Rothschilds.[6]

* * *

Modern businessmen on one side, an old money merchant on the other—so the Pereire-Rothschild duel would be summed up.[7] (Although it was a bit premature to see the conflict uniquely in terms of old and new generations, for the Rothschilds were hardly on the decline.)[8] One witness to the feud was the young broker's clerk Ernest Feydeau, who (at least when recollecting in tranquillity) gave the advantage to James, first because he knew how to mock his enemies, "to make people laugh at their expense, even while ruining them." And then Rothschild was working with his own money, the Pereires with the public's.

Feydeau would see James, just as he was seeing the Pereire brothers, several times a day in the course of soliciting their orders for stock. He remembered one such time, when James received him in the large mezzanine office on Rue Laffitte that he shared with sons Alphonse, Gustave, and Salomon. (Feydeau also spotted one of James's daughters-in-law endorsing notes in a corner—one of the rare glimpses we have of a Rothschild wife at work!) To Feydeau's surprise, Baron James asked him to buy one thousand shares of Crédit Mobilier stock—an absurd order as seen by the clerk, who asked the baron please to repeat it: Did he really mean buy and not sell? The same order was repeated the next day, and the next; before his buying spree was over, the baron had amassed five thousand shares. Feydeau also noted that the Pereires were selling as many shares as James was buying—showing the little confidence they had in their own business. "I recret only one ting," the baron told the broker's assistant, "und dat iss not do be able to giff all my capital to zuch intellichent men." But of course the day came when James began to sell Crédit Mobilier as readily as he purchased it—at the precise moment that he could inflict the most damage.[9]

When necessary to prevent the extension of the Pereire formula to other European nations, the Rothschilds were perfectly capable of setting up their own Crédit Mobilier clones, or to join partners in creating one. They did it in France with the Réunion Financière, a coalition of Pereire's enemies in the banking establishment. On their side, the Pereires scored one victory after another in luring

Rothschild partners into their system—weakening the legendary network on which much of the older bank's prosperity depended.

The battle was engaged elsewhere—in railroads, for instance. For if the Pereires had inspired James's original investments, and James had backed the Pereires in some of theirs, from now on they were to compete for concessions of new lines, with the Pereires having the advantage of the emperor's favor. While the Rothschilds weren't totally cut out of new projects—the Paris-Lyon route, for instance—they couldn't hope for more than a minority share; the Pereires always seemed a length ahead.[10]

A book remains to be written—not this one—on each of the major battlefields where the Pereires and their allies were pitted against the Rothschilds. In Spain, for instance, rival combinations of investors fought for strategic railway concessions between Madrid and provincial capitals providing access to new industry and mineral wealth, and then from Spain north to France. Each rail link involved a bidding strategy, a trade-off; the point was to secure a route that could be added to other routes, in regions of this still-to-be-developed country whose resources could be profitably exploited with better transportation. The Pereires won an early battle by establishing a Spanish version of their French bank, Crédito Mobiliario Español, an instrument for investing not only in new rail routes but in coke and iron mines, brickworks, shipping, and utilities.

Indeed, as a historian of the Pereire dynasty tells us, Spain's railroads were virtually a gift from France, built with French capital, encouraged by Second Empire foreign policy. Yet in their pitched battle with the Pereires, it was the Rothschilds, headed by paterfamilias James, who won in the end. A link between Spain and France was opened only in 1865—a Pereire initiative; Rothschild revenge would come with the failure of the Pereire banking empire, and by 1880 the Rothschilds dominated the Spanish rail system with some 1,400 miles of track.[11]

The railroad war spilled over into Austria, Switzerland, and the still-to-be-assembled Italian states; the same adversaries fought for dominance in government bond issues. At one point both James and eldest son Alphonse took to the road, each in turn engaged in winning over Count Camillo di Cavour, finance minister, then prime

minister of the Kingdom of Sardinia, chief architect of Italian reunification. It was the Rothschilds who won this fight, apparently
because they convinced Cavour that their system allowed more freedom of action. But it was also true that Cavour used the French
banking feud to get the best possible terms for his state loan.[12]

The Rothschild family archivist dates the apex of the Rothschild-
Pereire rivalry as the years 1855 to 1857, set off by the invasion
of a traditional Rothschild stronghold, Austria, through Crédit Mobilier's purchase of that nation's railroads. A contemporary witness, the financier Jules Mirès, paints the portrait of a James
isolated in his milieu. Now it was the Pereires and their allies who
ruled the roost; it was their receptions that drew distinguished
Parisians, while James's drawing room emptied.

So James counterattacked. He did it by forming new alliances,
challenging Crédit Mobilier on its own terrain. He secured Austria
in 1855 with the establishment of a Pereire-type financial institution in Vienna, the Creditanstalt.[13] In time it would become Austria's biggest bank, still thriving when the Pereires were forgotten.
Using the new bank, the Rothschilds could beat their rivals at their
own game in financing new railroad routes in Austria.[14]

The contradictions in James's strategy were remarked at once by
Duke Fialin de Persigny, France's ambassador to London, when in
September 1855 James called on him in the company of his British
nephews Lionel and Anthony (sons of long-deceased brother
Nathan). As Persigny reported the London visit to Napoleon III,
Baron James showed inconsistency in attacking Crédit Mobilier,
for he warned both that its fragility threatened public finances and
that it was becoming so rich and powerful that it could dictate its
terms to the government. At that point, so Persigny told his emperor, Lionel broke in to say: "You do realize that my uncle, who
says the worst about Crédit Mobilier, dreams of only one thing—to
create the same sort of institution in Austria—and he's come here
to ask us to join him as partners."

Equally revealing were Lionel's confidences to the French ambassador after his uncle James's departure for Paris, when Lionel
confessed that James's opposition to the Pereires was not founded

on differences in philosophy but on irritation against these bankers who had been trained by Rothschild and had then turned against him. The Great Baron was particularly peeved at the Pereires for their purchase of nearly 20,000 acres of forest adjacent to the castle he was then building at Ferrières, preventing him from expanding his own estate.[15] Later the story went around (the Goncourt brothers jotted it down in their diary) that at the railway station serving both the Rothschild and Pereire estates "the stationmaster looks through the windows to be certain, before Rothschild boards the train, that there is no Pereire in the compartment. Rothschild was so furious that the Pereire castle was finished in two years that he wanted to be able to sleep in his own that very day."[16]

Decidedly, the king of the Rothschilds would never be an intimate of the emperor of the French, although he once came close. James happened to be on the best of terms with a young lady of the Spanish nobility, Eugénie de Montijo. He had been banker and adviser to Eugénie and her mother during their Paris years, and it was on James's arm that Eugénie first appeared at the imperial court in the Tuileries palace in January 1853. Unable to arrange a marriage with the daughter of a reigning family, Napoleon the Little—as Victor Hugo called him—threw himself at the feet of this attractive and intelligent lady of lesser lineage. In an oft-told tale of that Tuileries ball (the teller was the Austrian ambassador), when James offered seats to Eugénie and her mother, a minister's wife observed sharply that the area was reserved for ministers' wives. Witnessing the episode, the lovestruck emperor rushed over to escort the distressed women to a seat close to his own.[17]

The emperor and his advisers could also compare the unbending solidity of the Rothschild bank and the febrile Crédit Mobilier, whose speculative behavior was beginning to alarm even aggressively business-oriented leaders of the Second Empire. Napoleon III began to see James more frequently; European political tensions as well as finances were on his mind and on their agenda.[18] More war was brewing: a war for Italian independence, with France allied to the Sardinian throne against Austria, the threat of Prussian intervention on Austria's side. Who could better provide

Napoleon III with the moral and financial support, the political intelligence desperately needed, than the de facto head of the Rothschild empire?

In James, of course, Napoleon the Little had met an equal. This is James at the summit of his powers, sharp but not malicious, ironic without cruelty. His gibes were legendary, given added zest by the eminence of the speaker. In one story an acquaintance wonders why the price of government bonds has fallen. "Can I know why there are highs and lows?" James is quoted. "If I knew I'd have made my fortune."[19]

Ernest Feydeau was surely the author with most access to Baron James at the workplace, for, unlike Heine or Balzac, he was himself part of James's world. The baron played with business (thought Feydeau) like a cat with a mouse. At the time, Feydeau was still employed as intermediary by a leading stockbroker; as he passed from one bank to the other he could compare the good-humored Rothschild to the men of Crédit Mobilier, "icily polite, distorted by hatreds, ever concentrated, as taut and unbending as iron bars, inflexible in their ideas, immersed in self-esteem."

James easily accepted the constraints of his exalted position, receiving each of the brokers who called on him to submit stock quotations, even if he had no intention to buy; he wasn't at all a speculator (as the Pereire brothers were speculators), but "simply a solid, intelligent, oh so wily merchant capitalist." His environment was "deafening," "the incessant racket produced by slamming doors, the constant movement of employees carrying dispatches or asking for signatures." It was a Tower of Babel, with every language spoken including Hebrew. The baron, Feydeau observed, received visitors "of the three sexes": masculine, feminine, beggar. Jewelers unwrapped precious stones under his weary eyes; art and antique dealers surrounded him, and pretty women.

To believe Feydeau, James couldn't even enjoy his breakfast in peace, for the world turned up at his door as early as five each morning; his valet at the Rue Saint-Florentin obligingly ushered in solicitors and petitioners, one at a time. Later, in the bank on Rue Laffitte, the baron might lunch with his family in a small room adjoining his office—while the procession of uncaring visitors continued. James's best weapon was silence.

If necessary he could be even tougher than that, turning away an importunate solicitor with sarcasm; to those who observed only that side of his personality, he was a villain. Feydeau saw the baron's sizzling retorts as self-defense. Sometimes he'd turn an unwanted visitor over to one of his sons—Alphonse, for example—while in another corner of that same large room the Great Baron pursued a more important meeting with a minister or an ambassador.

"We must remember that the entire universe was his domain," recalled Feydeau, "that he had offices everywhere, in China, India, even in the least civilized places . . . , that his ships sailed on all the seas; that he was everywhere considered the highest expression, the support and the defender of his fellow Jews; that during all his long life no important deal could be put together anywhere, in any corner of the planet, without his being consulted and invited to take part."

He had the gift—still Ernest Feydeau recollecting—of being able to see and do everything himself. Of course he had the benefit of an intelligent (and docile) staff, of obedient, respectful sons— sons who wouldn't initial the most trivial agreement without consulting father. "Ask Papa," was the usual response of these forty-year-old sons. (Feydeau, sensitive to differences between Jews and Christians—he was sure the former were more tenacious in business—felt that this Jewish household, in which sons respected parental authority, could serve as a model to Christian families.)[20]

James himself was a model; the founder of the Morgan banking dynasty, the father of J. Pierpont Morgan, would have liked to be an American Rothschild.[21] Yet for Frenchmen brought up in traditions hostile to Judaism, the new class of successful Jews sparked a no less pernicious type of anti-Semitism, one that in times of economic crisis could be as violent as the old kind. This transformation of ancestral, quasi-racial Jew hatred into a modern form of anti-Semitism inspired by social tensions leaps from the pages of a contemporary tract by the polemicist Eugène de Mirecourt. He compared the character of contemporary Jews "covered with gold" to the "stinginess" of their medieval ancestors, finding "two distinct natures" in Baron James: he was both the "traditional rapacious Jew, a function of two thousand years of ostracism, servitude, and hate," and the intelligent financier "who knows when to sacrifice a million francs if the sacrifice brings many more lucrative deals. . . ."

Mirecourt describes—though he says "everyone in Paris knows it"—the bank's palatial home on Rue Laffitte, all of marble and gold, especially gold. For Mirecourt, James is "this curious man who for the past forty years, to the shame of intelligence, wit, and good taste, has shaped our times by the sheer weight of his millions."

Nor does this writer spare Baroness Betty; he portrays her running over an old man with her coach and, without stopping, simply tossing the victim a purse filled with gold, unwilling to offer first aid "out of fear that the blood will stain her cushions." As for her husband, he simply despises humankind. The baron, concludes Mirecourt, is now sixty-three years old, although the precise date of his birth isn't known; "the reader will understand that we have not been able to obtain a copy of his baptismal certificate."[22] A line that would be repeated more than once.

THE NEXT GENERATION

Before his thirty-eighth birthday, Baron James de Rothschild had the good sense to pounce upon another abandoned possession of Napoleon's police chief, Joseph Fouché. This time it was an estate at Ferrières, less than twenty miles east of Paris, which with later acquisitions grew to include nearly ten thousand acres of farms and forests. He'd build a fairy castle there, designed to his taste by the horticulturist and self-taught architect Joseph Paxton, already famous for the extravagant glass and iron Crystal Palace erected for the Great Exhibition of 1851 in London. (Paxton had previously designed a similar fantasy in the English countryside for James's nephew—and Nathan's son—Mayer Amschel.)

Paxton's French incursion, turreted Ferrières, was built in record time (from 1855 to 1859), and would prove to be suitable lodgings for emperors; then and later it was an honor to be invited to hunt on its grounds. Built as a square, with a pinnacled tower at each of the four corners, which seemed to accord it the authority of a royal domain, the castle faced a formal park and lake through colonnaded windows; inside, the immoderate dimensions of drawing rooms below, bedrooms above, also suggested regal pretensions. Austrian ambassador Rudolf Apponyi seemed particularly impressed by its "model laundry room, a veritable masterpiece of its kind, elegant, picturesque, and most practical. It can handle eighty thousand items per year, which is the normal consumption of the house." He found all the other furnishings of excellent taste, and went on to describe the armor, the statuettes, the goblets of vermeil, ivory, gold, covered with pearls or precious jewels, the chests of bronze or even silver. . . ." The account books show that at one time the stables held twenty-four horses.[1]

Faced with the cream-white limestone which was the hallmark of Renaissance royal architecture, the Never-Never Land castle was built around a high-ceilinged and skylighted ballroom known as the Grand Hall, covering 2,800 square feet. All the drawing rooms and dining rooms, the reception and game rooms, branched out from it; sleeping quarters were upstairs. Inside and out, and for all its English parentage, Ferrières was pure (or impure?) Second Empire, the nouveau-riche style through which the new bourgeoisie, like the new nobility, sought to enhance the ancien régime by building everything bigger and decorating it more garishly. Guy de Rothschild quotes an anonymous description: "Napoleon III clothing draped over a Victorian house built to Elizabethan specifications."[2]

"We are back from Ferrières," the Goncourt brothers confide to their diary one evening in 1858—not as guests, but as part of the crowd of curious Parisians with sufficient time on their hands to do the trip uninvited (by then a rail line made that easy). "Trees and ponds created by money, surrounding an 18-million-franc castle extravagant in its stupidity and ridiculousness, a pudding of styles, the stupid ambition to possess all monuments in one!" Not long after this the Goncourts read a press account of a Rothschild marriage with no fewer than seventy-four members in attendance; it calls up for them a Rembrandt painting, as they imagine "all these heads green with the patina of millions . . . Pariah-kings of the world, reaching out for everything and possessing everything, the press, the arts, the writers, the thrones, disposing of the Vaudeville theater and of world peace, owning states and empires. . . ." They also think that the Rothschilds "own" the ballet corps at the Opera—which meant having privileged access to the young women who danced in it. To the point—so the Goncourt brothers scribble maliciously—that one ballerina was surprised to encounter an uncircumcised male: "It was the first foreskin she'd ever seen."[3]

One marriage that assembled all the Rothschilds was held in London in 1857, when James's eldest son, Alphonse, heir apparent, took as his bride the daughter of his British cousin Lionel, in an extravagant (and traditional Jewish) ceremony captured in an engraving that made the public prints. It was one more marriage within the family, and not the least. Soon Alphonse and Leonora were installed in the former Talleyrand mansion on Rue Saint-Florentin with its view of the Concorde and Tuileries; James and his Betty would be as comfortable in the living quarters attached to the bank on Rue Laffitte.[4]

This matter of being a Jew in France preoccupied even the very rich Rothschilds during the reign of Baron James, as it would in Alphonse's time. Very rich Christians didn't necessarily wish to share their privileges with very rich Jews. Thus James had been one of the earliest members of the Jockey Club, but when it came time for Alphonse to apply, he was twice turned down before being accepted in 1852, and it was not for lack of good horses.[5]

Each of the Rothschild children received a Jewish education—though compared to their orthodox cousins of Frankfurt they were arrant pagans (they had all the right utensils needed to prepare kosher meals but seldom used them, and had to scramble to put things in order when more orthodox German cousins were announced). Importantly, James was de facto leader of the French Jewish community; when money was needed to build a charitable institution, or a synagogue, everyone knew it would come from him.[6]

For if there was now a Jewish bourgeoisie in Paris, coexisting when not cohabiting with its Gentile peers, the percentage of truly poor Jews remained stable (representing nearly a third of the Jewish population of the French capital in 1860).[7] Here the Great Baron could be effective: Rothschild contributions to the Jewish community amounted to half those of the government (in its customary allocation to religious congregations); James also subsidized the settlement of immigrants from central Europe. The construction of a Jewish hospital on the Rue de Picpus endowed by the Rothschilds was a landmark in the community's history; its inauguration in 1852 was attended by a minister and a prefect, as speakers acknowledged, to quote the report in L'Univers Israélite, one of the principal organs of the French Jewish community, "everything Jews owe to the great house [of Rothschild], which, thanks to its exceptional integrity and eminent virtues, has contributed so much to our moral emancipation."[8]

Of course there were dissenters; no act of this very public family went uncriticized. Thus a generally sympathetic nineteenth-century biographer suggested perfidiously that "Baron James displayed remarkable skill in being charitable at the expense of others." He explained that after having been chastised for not giving deprived Jews the benefit of his stock market successes, James carried out a coup that earned a profit of 850,000 francs—which he promptly applied to his hospital project.[9] There was also the reproach that a hospital devoted exclusively to France's "Israélites" reinforced apartness—something no forward-looking French Jew now desired.[10]

Perhaps the most moving recognition of James's benevolence has come down to us from an unexpected source, that diligent historian of Parisian institutions Maxime Du Camp. He justified the implied segregation of a Jewish institution: "Jews enjoy proper care in regular hospitals, but they commit more than one involuntary sin there, reduced to sharing the regular meals given to patients."

It's from Du Camp that we learn that this hospital—to which not only Rothschilds but other Jewish community leaders had contributed, with beds duly labeled with their names—willingly cared for non-Jews in emergencies. "Besides, neighborhood people flock to its consultations; each year some ten to twelve thousand of them see a doctor there; need one add that consultations and medicines are free?"[11]

The record shows that beyond French frontiers the protection of Jews continued to preoccupy the Rothschilds of France. They had been bankers to the Holy Office since 1831, often acting as surrogates for a French government concerned by Austrian influence on the Papal States, and anxious to counter it. Hardly viable as economic units, suffering from a paucity of industry and from backward, unproductive agriculture, the Italian territories then subject to the Pope's authority were also handicapped by an antiquated bureaucracy; they counted more than they should on what the faithful of other nations might contribute. Rothschild loans were useful, when not vital.[12]

At least once Baron James ventured to capitalize on this dependence. The occasion arose in 1848, when local rebellion linked to Italian aspirations for reunification and independence drove the Pope from his Roman states, and the Church needed exceptional sums at affordable interest rates in order to reestablish the papal residence in Rome. The loan from James and his family came with conditions: a relaxation of the severe restrictions suffered by Rome's Jews, then confined to a walled ghetto. At papal insistence the status of Jews under Church rule was not specifically written into the loan agreement, and indeed little was to change quickly. But henceforth the Church knew that Rome's Jews had a strong advocate *extra muros*.[13] The situation in Austria, where a relaxation of anti-Jewish measures was often followed by new restrictions, also brought the influence of family hierarch James to bear, often discreetly, and through the diplomatic pouch—but effectively.[14]

Henceforth, in waging battle against financial rivals in France and abroad, in maintaining European peace in the interests of market expansion, Baron James de Rothschild had a strong right arm in Alphonse, this first son who would assure the house of Rothschild a smooth transition after the Great Baron's passing. His education had been the best possible—tutors, then the Collège Bourbon (where a fellow student was Léon Say, later an outstanding finance minister). After studying the organization of Britain's railroads, Alphonse was given a responsible position at the Rothschilds' principal railroad holdings, the Compagnie du Nord, which ran the strategic northeastern network; later he would be its president. There was also Gustave, only two years junior to Alphonse, but the Rothschild succession all but forgot second sons. So what to say of third son Salomon, who followed Gustave six years later, or Edmond, ten years after that, and who was only twenty-three years old on his father's death?

All of James's sons were men about town, rich young men who followed their pleasures. Both Alphonse and Gustave were observed in the company of celebrated courtesans—Alphonse with La Païva (who happened to be of Russian Jewish origin), Gustave with a sometime mistress of the emperor, the countess of Castiglione.[15] During business hours these men were serious; only Salomon seemed unable to separate profligacy from the workday. In 1859 he was sent off to the New World; the Goncourts heard that it was because of the young man's unwise plunges on the stock exchange.[16] Salomon's contribution to family history was a succession of reports from the United States on the eve of Civil War, and then as the first guns thundered.

To Salomon, the abolition of slavery signified social revolution, never a very good thing for business. So the Rothschilds (according to Salomon) should do what they could to obtain French recognition for the Confederate states. But this meddling in a foreign civil war was not going to sit well with devoted Unionists. "Will we have a dishonorable peace," asked an angry editorialist in the *Chicago Tribune*, "in order to enrich [August] Belmont, the Rothschilds, and the whole tribe of Jews, who have been buying up Confederate bonds, or an honorable peace won by Grant and Sherman at the cannon's mouth?" In truth, despite Salomon, the Rothschilds bought no Confederate bonds, and August Belmont was an ardent supporter of the Union.[17]

Back home in France, young Salomon married cousin Mayer Carl's daughter Adele Hannah in March 1862. Two years later, at twenty-nine, he was dead—a rare example of a member of the tough-skinned Rothschild tribe dying before his time. It was said (and of course repeated by the Goncourts) that the excitement of a stock speculation had killed him.[18] He'd be mourned, but his absence would hardly make a difference for the business of the bank.

Alphonse was one of the survivors. His father put him to work on the difficult jobs; he proved to be as opinionated as his father, as peremptory in expressing his opinion. Count Corti (author of the most complete history of the Rothschilds up to modern times) found a choice example in the State Archives in Vienna—Alphonse writing to his uncle Salomon at a time (October 1850) when Prussia's attempts at unification of the German states clashed with Austrian hegemony. Alphonse warned his uncle that Persigny, then France's ambassador to Prussia, hoped to push Prussia into a declaration of war against Austria, after which France would intervene, all this in the interests of imperial ambition. It was Alphonse's job to see that Salomon in Vienna reassured Austria that plotting of the kind Persigny was up to enjoyed no support in France. Should Louis-Napoleon dare to try such an unworthy move, neither the French political class nor Parliament would follow. "So you can be tranquil," wrote this peace-loving son of a peace-loving father. "The government will follow a totally conservative policy."[19]

It was secret messages like this one, conveyed by Rothschilds to host governments, that dampened incendiary sparks. Later James would send his dependable heir all the way to Constantinople to counter an offensive by their Pereire rivals to establish a Crédit Mobilier in Turkey, a project favored by the French government. Alphonse managed to parry the Pereire thrust without committing the family to setting up its own bank; he showed himself to be a seasoned diplomat, unintimidated by financial warfare on distant battlefields.[20]

The same Alphonse, if we believe his cousin Constance (later Lady Battersea), was a serious student of history and politics, equally enamored of culture. His beautiful wife, Leonora, remained terribly English, visiting her London family and friends regularly; a "plucky horsewoman," at least once she organized an English-style stag hunt at Ferrières. In her will Alphonse's wife asked to be buried on English soil, and although she died in Paris her will was obeyed.[21]

In December 1862 the emperor of the French consecrated his reconciliation with James, inviting himself (or accepting an open invitation) to the Great Baron's domain at Ferrières. The event was captured for history by a trainload of chroniclers, from the arrival of Napoleon III and his party at the local railroad station, where they transferred to the imperial horse-drawn coaches that had made the trip from Paris empty. The emperor was properly outfitted for the country, so an ecstatic French journalist recorded, in an outfit resembling the typical costume of Brittany.[22] "At a quarter to eleven," *The Times* of London told its readers, "the Emperor arrived at the Château, and the Imperial flag was at once raised on one of the towers. After looking over the interior of the edifice, the

Emperor took a walk in the park, where he planted a cedar to commemorate his visit."[23] Tradition adds that at this point the emperor took the arm of Baroness Betty, declaring, "Madame, you would not visit me, so, as I much wished to make your acquaintance, I have been obliged (happily for myself) to be your guest."[24]

And so to breakfast. "The service of silver plate," noted *The Times*, "made from models which were immediately destroyed to preserve it unique, was accompanied by the celebrated service of Sèvres porcelain, every plate of which bears an authentic picture by Boucher." Then to the hunt, in the forest covering 3,700 acres; the correspondent reported that a thousand head of game were killed.[25] Afterwards the imperial party returned to the château to find the illuminated courtyard crammed with inhabitants of nearby villages. During supper a chorus of singers from the Paris Opera sang an ode to the pheasant shoot by Rossini, directed by the composer himself. Then the departure, the road to the station illuminated by Rothschild personnel bearing torches, bushes adorned with candles.[26]

After the fête, the reckoning. A historian of the Second Empire economy noted the choice of guests that day (although it isn't clear whether James or Napoleon III drew up the list): Achille Fould, the finance minister, as well as both the British and the Austrian ambassadors. Financial reconciliation first of all—an indication that the speculative fever symbolized by the Pereires was being replaced by a return to the old wisdom of the merchant bankers, perhaps also a sign that the empire's dangerous foreign adventures were coming to a close.[27]

So it was going to be easier for James's successor. Henceforth Alphonse had only to prepare himself for his obligations to high society, although that was not always as simple as it seemed. In a letter from Paris in September 1863, by Lionel de Rothschild's wife, Charlotte, written to sons Nathaniel and Leopold, we catch a touching glimpse of this banker's son making his way: "Alphonse wishes you, my dear Natty, to purchase some good brood mares for him, but Laurie [the diminutive of Alphonse's wife, Leonora] is of the opinion that her husband could never possess a really good

racing establishment, as he is utterly unable to attend to it himself." (Surely Alphonse would be the last Rothschild of whom such
a complaint could be made.) In another letter Charlotte told her
youngest son, Leopold, of the visit of Alphonse and Leonora to
Compiègne, invited by the emperor for a hunting weekend; before
Saturday morning was over, "1,250 feathered or furred innocents
were slaughtered by the gentlemen." But none by a Rothschild.
"Alphonse could not join the sportsmen," Charlotte explained,
"owing to the sanctity of the Sabbath—so he wandered in the
woods with Laurie, and on Sunday there was an immense and very
frolicsome walking expedition, which their Majesties joined, or
rather led."

If he was neither the compleat breeder nor a Saturday hunter,
Alphonse, we know from these letters, was a knowledgeable collector of art; he could also be good company for crowned heads.
Again, Lionel's Charlotte to London: "Alphonse, who took the
Emperor and Empress from Paris to Compiègne, was much pleased
by their conversation, although Her Majesty wanted to know too
much about the Jews."[28]

Goncourt venom, always ready to flow when Jews were concerned, was soon directed against the Rothschild heir apparent.
They record a story of Alphonse at dinner, where a fellow guest
asks him why, being so rich, "he worked like a slave to become
more so." Alphonse supposedly replied, "Ah! you can't imagine
how thrilling it is to feel a heap of Christians under one's boots!"[29]
However unlikely it is that a Rothschild or anyone else would say
such a thing, the anecdote serves wonderfully to illustrate the
twisted perceptions of pathological anti-Semites.

Indeed, the Goncourts had never come face to face with a Rothschild, although on occasion they'd have to put up with other Jews
at the receptions of Princess Mathilde, the emperor's cousin and
perhaps the brightest star of that dynasty. Now, on January 21,
1863, in Mathilde's grand drawing room on Rue de Courcelles,
where one was sure to encounter both the cultural and the social
elite of the time, they behold the Great Baron himself—"a mon-
strous figure," the Goncourts will tell their diary that night, "the
flattest . . . most ghastly toad face . . . a mouth like a cash drawer
and drooling, a kind of satyr of gold. . . ."[30]

*   *   *

A more reasonable portrait of James in old age has come down to us in the report of an interministerial committee that took testimony from leading members of the financial community on French monetary policy. In it one hears the voice of an ailing James, James in his final years (the date is October 31, 1865, when the baron has passed his seventy-third birthday). Accompanied by Alphonse, he has been invited to expound Rothschild philosophy to a panel presided over by his longtime antagonist Achille Fould; sometimes, because his son is now more competent on many matters, he yields to Alphonse, who had in fact been appointed to the board of directors of the Banque de France a full decade earlier.

Because of illness, James explains, he hasn't been able to study the panel's questionnaire; nevertheless he'll do his best, "making use of the financial experience I have been able to acquire." He recalls the time when, as a young man, he accompanied his brother Nathan to the Bank of England, to which he had been summoned to help solve a payments crisis. He argues for a strong currency, protected when necessary by a rise in interest rates. Did that mean having a central bank sufficiently powerful to guarantee the convertibility of the franc? Indeed it did, declared this pillar of the Banque de France. "I never hide my opinion," he added (as if a Fould could doubt that), "I say what I think." Why encourage a multitude of lending institutions in a country whose economy was sound? "In no country in the world is commerce more solidly grounded, does one find fewer bankruptcies, or is business better."[31]

So there was still life in the old boy. In his last decade, James was to preside over further development of the Rothschildian universe, which now extended from the American continent across Russia, with James (the only surviving son of the Frankfurt ghetto) as head of the clan. Often his chief or only competitor in a potentially lucrative market was financial nationalism, inspiring (as in Italy) the creation of local banking institutions.[32] The firm remained a force to reckon with in international trade, in cotton, tobacco, minerals, metals, and now oil—increasingly oil, from the rich fields of the southern Russian empire. In this context the once primordial railroad empire seemed less overwhelming, representing an undesirable immobilization of capital at a time when money placed elsewhere could make more.[33]

New powers, when they broke surface, would know where the old power lay. After Metternich and Cavour came Bismarck; the Prussian chancellor who was to be the architect of German reunification was an early recruit to the ranks of Rothschild debtors. Otto von Bismarck had a direct line to Baron James through Gerson von Bleichröder, who, like Rothschild, was born of a ghetto family, and was both a Rothschild agent and Prussia's banker; the legendary courier network that served Bleichröder in his dealings with the Rothschilds also became a source of intelligence for Bismarck, and a discreet channel for French-German contacts. It could help keep the peace when both sides wanted peace.[34]

When in 1865 Bismarck came to France to rally Napoleon III to his side during a dangerous Austro-Prussian confrontation, the Prussian made it his business to enlist Rothschild in his cause; it happened during a hunt at Ferrières. James would not furnish money for war between Prussia and Austria, or indeed for any war; that he made crystal clear.[35] The war was fought all the same, Bismarck feeling that he had to reduce the influence of the Austrian empire in order to guarantee Prussian hegemony in the German states. That the Prussian leader held no grudge against James for his defection is suggested by Alphonse's letter to his London cousins after still another Bismarck visit in 1867 following Austria's defeat. Bismarck brought a gift for James: the Great Ribbon of the Red Eagle, his country's highest honor. "No other Jew has received this in Prussia," Alphonse reported with evident satisfaction.[36]

Before passing on his mandate to the next generation, Baron James lived to see the rout of his domestic enemies. However astute they were, however rigorous in their application of good and proper theory to the ways of the marketplace, the brothers Pereire and their allies could not manufacture profits in the teeth of economic recession, nor could they anticipate the depreciation of values in an Austria diminished on the battlefield. In 1866, the year of Bismarck's victory, Crédit Mobilier racked up steep losses; with its stock in a free fall, it was obliged to pay dividends to shareholders out of capital: the straight road to disaster. In the

absence of government help in 1867—for that, in the opinion of
the emperor's advisers, would have been to throw good money after
bad—the Pereires could only look on as their brainchild died. (An
institution called Crédit Mobilier survived, but sans its creators,
with their once impressive web of corporate ties.)[37]

No one doubted that the Rothschilds were among the hands that
gave their arch rivals a final push.[38]

So Baron James could give himself a present; it took the form of
one of Bordeaux's best vineyards. He wasn't the first of the Rothschilds to invest in French wine; that honor belonged to Nathaniel,
his brother Nathan's son, after a hunting fall crippled him and he
settled in France (he had married James's daughter Charlotte in
1842). In 1853, when he was forty-one, Nathaniel had the good
sense to buy Château Mouton, then rated as one of the region's
second growths but then and later an astounding wine all the same.
(His choice was ratified as Château Mouton-Rothschild, which
rose in prestige over the years, eventually to be transformed into a
famous label by wine impresario Philippe, Nathaniel's great-great-
grandson.)

Not that he was emulating, but James now knew that a Rothschild could make good wine—and sell it for profit just like everybody else. James's vineyard was an already prestigious first growth
called Château Lafite—and nothing tells us that he bought it (in
August 1868, for what seems to have been the record price of over
four million francs) because its name recalled the street (with two
_f_'s and two _t_'s) on which his bank stood.[39]

James was never to set eyes on his vineyard, or dwell in the
manor on the grounds; three months after purchasing the splendid
property he was dead. A man of seventy-six was verily old at the
time, yet James combated illness as tenaciously as he had the
upstart Pereires. Letters tell of travel to thermal baths, perhaps for
the acute rheumatism with which he was afflicted; he had long
suffered from painful gallstones, and his fatal illness was diag-
nosed as jaundice.[40]

He had asked for a simple funeral, in the face of tradition calling
for a parade to honor those decorated with the Grand Cross of the

Legion of Honor. But half of Paris attended the funeral, with the envoys of kings and emperors (the president of the United States dispatched a telegram). A reporter for *The Times* of London had never seen as many people on the streets of Paris, as the cortege made its way from the family bank on Rue Laffitte to the baron's final resting place in Père-Lachaise cemetery. There the rabbis said the prayers of committal, tribute was paid by associates, but there were to be no official speeches at the simple tomb marked with an *R*.[41]

"By race and religion, by the dimensions of his activity, Mr. de Rothschild escaped to a certain point strict confines of nationality, and could be seen rather as a citizen of the world," declaimed Lucien Prévost-Paradol, a politician and author. "But it was easy to see that his heart was truly French."[42] The eulogy appeared in *Journal des Débats*, a newspaper close (and surely indebted) to the Rothschilds. "Thanks to him, the Banque de France and the House of Rothschild remain the two financial pillars on which the nation's credit rests," one could read in *Journal de Paris*. "For long years nothing in France or Europe, in the world of high finance, was done by anyone else but him, or at least nothing was done without him." That in a publication called *La France*.[43]

In a eulogious pamphlet the editor-in-chief of the popular *Figaro* declared (and there is no way to know to what extent he was encouraged, or subsidized), "Thus there is only one less Rothschild. The Rothschilds remain." The author adds, almost too gently for his time and place, "Thanks to their will and to social progress, Jews have ceased to be foreigners to us. They are no longer simply *intendants*, but the reasonable and hardworking children of the French family."[44]

FRENCH BARONS

*N*o one knows who first cried out, "Rothschild is dead; long live Rothschild!"—an expression heard at the imperial court;[1] but it is so obviously the thing that had to be said. Everything was in place for an orderly succession in the dynasty, even if in slight, soft-spoken Alphonse it was difficult to perceive a second James. He lacked, among other things, what another suave Parisian-born-and-raised Rothschild called "the ruggedness of the ghetto."[2]

By family tradition, his coming to power was ordained. But Alphonse was not only the eldest of the French Rothschilds; he may also have been the most competent of his generation. Gustave felt a kind of hero-worship for his older brother, and seems never to have disputed his preeminence. On his own, Gustave engaged in stock speculations (and didn't always win). But as far as the family bank was concerned, he could almost be described as a sleeping partner.[3]

Certainly Alphonse possessed the financial power. On the death of the Great Baron in 1868, his one-fourth control of the combined Rothschild banks of Frankfurt, London, Vienna, and Paris passed to Alphonse and his brother Gustave. (Their brother Salomon was dead, while Edmond was still too young to be counted.) Working with every scrap of surviving document, archivist Bertrand Gille succeeded in quantifying the legacy of the King of the Rothschilds. In 1863, five years before James died, the total value of the four surviving banks came to 22,312,864 pounds, or, at the going rate of twenty-five French francs to the pound, 557,821,600 francs— well over ten billion of today's francs.[4] No other credit institution was worth as much. The next revealing figure is a balance sheet drawn up in February 1874 on the death of cousin Mayer Carl of Frankfurt; it provides a breakdown of the capital of each of the Rothschild banks then operating, with Paris strikingly dominant:

Paris	£20,087,652
London	£ 6,509,208
Frankfurt	£ 4,533,096
Vienna	£ 3,228,562
TOTAL	£34,358,562[5]

Alphonse kept an even keel. He had the benefit of long years of association with peers also raised in the best French circles, such as his schoolmate Léon Say. Thanks to Alphonse, Say began his career as a Rothschild manager; it didn't hurt that he happened to marry the daughter of the publisher of the "Rothschild" newspaper, *Journal des Débats*. Say was to become one of the brighter stars of that Third Republic built on the ruins of the Second Empire, an outstanding finance minister, effective advocate of free trade in an unfettered domestic economy. "Rothschild's man," he'd be called, usually without prejudice.[6]

Had Alphonse de Rothschild and his brothers counted on stability during the years required to transform the Great Baron's one-man show into an institution, they would have been disappointed. Until now the great powers—France no less than the others—had been playing games on the European chessboard, trading zones of influence, the sovereignty of smaller peoples. But in the 1860s there was an Iron Chancellor to challenge Napoleon the Little, and the stakes would soon be raised beyond manageable proportions. With a Bismarck looking for ways to test his strength, convinced that Napoleon III was determined to challenge his ambition to unite the German states in a powerful new empire, war became inevitable; the only question was when and on what pretext.

The pretext was found, improbably, not on the Franco-German border but in Spain, where another contest for the royal succession gave the bellicose Bismarck an opportunity to challenge the French in a territory considered to be under their protection. For the heir to the Spanish throne was a Hohenzollern prince (who happened to be married to a Portuguese princess); with a German as king of Spain, France could well feel surrounded. Soon even rank-and-file Frenchmen were in a fighting mood, while their emperor seemed as eager for war as Bismarck was.

During this troubled period the man in the middle was Alphonse de Rothschild. He had his emperor's undivided attention now, and through his German financial correspondent Bleichröder had Bismarck's too. Alphonse believed as strongly in the need for peace among nations as his father had; more, he believed in France. Surely Napoleon knew all that. He could use this man of goodwill, during the crisis of early July 1870, to convince the British that France could not accept a Hohenzollern king in Spain. So it was Alphonse, employing a Rothschild code, who relayed the French emperor's message to Britain's prime minister, William Gladstone.

The British, alas for France, alas for the Rothschilds, were not prepared to oppose Spain's choice of a king; hostilities seemed even closer. Then on July 12 there was a respite, Leopold von Hohenzollern-Sigmaringen having chosen to remove himself from the contest. Alphonse wired Gladstone: "The Prince has given up his candidature. The French are satisfied." No more *casus belli*, or so it seemed.[7]

But Bismarck was not to be robbed of his war. "Politically," he had confided on July 10, "a French attack would be very beneficial to our situation." "Until just now," he said when he learned of the Hohenzollern defection, "I thought I was standing on the eve of the greatest historical events. . . ."[8] The conflict he needed to unify Germany under Prussia's banner would take place all the same, thanks to Napoleon's blunder. He asked Kaiser Wilhelm for a guarantee that the Hohenzollern candidacy would not come up again; Wilhelm's reply, the famous Ems dispatch, was cleverly reworked by Bismarck into a humiliation the French could not ignore. Grabbing the bait, on the nineteenth of July, France declared war against an enemy stronger and more determined.

There is evidence that during the brief hostilities the French Rothschilds behaved as Frenchmen, refusing, for example, to continue to deal with Bleichröder, their agent but also Bismarck's banker. Alphonse also made it a point to resign his charge as Prussia's consul general in Paris, a title that had proved useful.[9] Meanwhile the Prussians were overrunning eastern France in the first of the lightning wars that would span seven decades. By September 2 they had taken the surrender of Napoleon III at Sedan, and could move on to Paris (a Paris that lost no time before proclaiming the end of the empire, the birth of a new republic).

In an earlier crisis, Baron James had packed Alphonse off with his mother to London. This time Alphonse sent Leonora away with their children (twelve-year-old Bettina; six-year-old Charlotte Béatrix; two-year-old Edouard Alphonse James, born February 24, 1868). A contemporary portrait of Leonora at her parents' home in London, following Napoleon III's defeat, the fall of the empire: "She was dark crimson with excitement and her voice trembled so that she could hardly speak. After a few moments her children came screaming and shouting into the room. They were allowed to make a fearful noise as no one seemed to mind them. In the midst of their childish voices came the muttered doubts and fears concerning the Empire. . . ."[10]

James's widow, Baroness Betty, who was now sixty-five years old, wrote the French war minister on August 12 that she was placing her estate at Boulogne-sur-Seine at his service for treatment of the war wounded; she would also endow a twenty-bed hospital on the grounds. Betty added (so the authoritative *Le Temps* reported) that she was also opening the Ferrières estate as a military hospital.[11] "I can't accept the idea that France won't beat Prussia all along the line!" the granddaughter of Prince von Metternich heard her exclaim.[12]

Soon Paris was surrounded, in a siege to last nearly four months—months of fright and despair, as blockaded Parisians were cut off from vital sources of food; in the end they'd slaughter zoo animals, and the least privileged devoured cats and rats. Heroic months, when messages and even properly posted mail went out by carrier pigeon, by balloon—even by submersion in the Seine; of lethal conflict, when the Prussians bombarded the capital, and the capital—now in republican hands—fought back. Vignette: the Rothschild brothers—Ernest Feydeau saw them—spending their nights on the ramparts, firing at the besiegers.[13]

To direct the siege of Paris and settle the fate of France, Kaiser Wilhelm, Chancellor Bismarck, and victorious general Helmuth von Moltke chose as a convenient field headquarters the Rothschild château at Ferrières. Contemporary accounts tell of the surprise of the conquerors on exploring that splendid house surrounded by a dense population of deer and pheasants for hunting, ducks and swans for decoration. The Kaiser was heard to exclaim: "Only a Rothschild could own all that."[14] "Here I am seated under the portrait of old [James de] Rothschild and his family," Bismarck wrote to his wife on September 21. ("We're suffering from hunger," he added, "because His Majesty has forbidden us to requisition anything.")

To his son Bismarck revealed that the Prussians would not simply starve Paris, but would eventually launch an attack against the capital. By September 23, still in Ferrières, the chancellor received French emissaries led by Jules Favre, foreign minister in the hastily improvised government of National Defense, but the negotiations led nowhere, as Bismarck reported it to his son. "The Alsatian question gave them such a stomachache that we had to stop there. They think they can settle for five billion francs and keep Strasbourg, but I told them that we'd talk of money later; first we must map out defendable frontiers." The fate of Alsace and Lorraine was already settled in his mind at least.

It was château life, all the same, and Bismarck didn't really go hungry. "It's now two weeks that I've been dwelling among the green damasks of old Rothschild," he wrote to his wife on October 1. "Yesterday we celebrated His Majesty's birthday with . . . a ceremonial dinner, all the princes sporting their medals. . . . Three days ago I shot a number of pheasants."[15]

The stay of the Prussians at a Rothschild castle gave rise to a legend. Thus Bismarck's faithful scribe, after recognizing that the Prussians had entered the domain in the absence of the proprietor, noted with regret that Alphonse had left the house in the hands of a caretaker and a few women servants. Soon, reported the indignant scribe, they had a "specimen" of the hospitality of Baron de

Rothschild, "who had the honor of being the host of our king and whose estate was treated with the greatest respect in consequence." He explained: "Mr. de Rothschild, a millionaire a hundred times over, and who until recently was the Prussian consul general in Paris, refused, through his caretaker, to allow us to drink his wine—even if we paid for it." When the Iron Chancellor heard about that, he summoned the caretaker, who maintained his refusal, first claiming that there was no wine on the estate, then conceding he had about a hundred bottles of ordinary Bordeaux. The Prussians began a search, and found that there weren't a hundred but 17,000 bottles in the cellar. Bismarck declared to the hapless estate manager that Rothschild's behavior was both mean and discourteous, that one didn't act that way when one's guest was a king. When the caretaker pretended not to understand, Bismarck demanded where he could get his hands on some bundles of hay; this time the manager seemed to realize the peril to his charge. Rather than see everything burn, the manager let the wine flow. And the wine flowed.[16]

Then, when Alphonse found out what was going on at Ferrières, he told his own stories, for example that the Prussians wanted to punish his caretaker because Rothschild pheasants didn't fly about already stuffed with truffles. Thanks to intercepted mail, Bismarck discovered what his absent host was saying, and this did not exactly cement their relations.[17] Later it became known that the boorish Prussians, finding the initials *J.R.* (for James de Rothschild) in heraldic emblems, mocked the deceased builder of the castle as "Judaeorum Rex"—King of the Jews.

All this while, Foreign Minister Jules Favre was shuttling between besieged Paris and fairyland Ferrières to negotiate with the invader. Otherwise Paris remained cut off from the rest of France, and only at the end of January 1871 was Favre able to initial the city's surrender in a meeting with Bismarck at Ferrières; just to free Paris, the French were to pay out 200 million francs (some 3.5 billion today). The Rothschild role in advancing funds for a rapid end to the siege created a surge of popular sympathy, and both Alphonse and Gustave were urged to run for the legislature in the special elections called for February 8 (for Bismarck insisted on negotiating with a legitimate government). "As flattering as this spontaneous nomination may be," prudent Alphonse was to tell the press, "and however appreciative we are of this testimonial of confidence, I regret to say that we cannot accept the candidacy with which we have been honored."[18]

Now the stage was set for a formal peace, with veteran politician Adolphe Thiers as chief of the executive of the new Republic, empowered to represent France in the talks. A moderate liberal in the face of monarchy, a conservative in the face of worker rebellion, Thiers had been a reformer opposed to Napoleon III and his Second Empire. Now, at the age of seventy-four, he was a French patriot in the presence of the conqueror. Meanwhile the scene had switched from the Great Baron's Ferrières to the Sun King's Versailles, and there Prussians and French came to terms. In return for an end to Prussian occupation, France was obliged to cede the cherished provinces of Alsace and Lorraine, *and* to pay an extraordinary indemnity of six billion francs (the equivalent of 105 billion now). To French protests about the enormity of the sum— for if one had begun counting out francs at the time of Jesus, one would still be counting—Bismarck replied that he was prepared for that, having brought along an expert who had begun counting at the Creation (his Jewish banker Bleichröder).[19]

Bleichröder on the Prussian side, Rothschild with the French. For Thiers realized that he required the assistance of France's best and most powerful money man, and asked to be allowed to summon him to Versailles. If the Prussian warlord didn't enjoy the prospect of a confrontation with the owner of Ferrières, he couldn't reasonably reject it. Alphonse got the call on February 25 and showed up in Versailles that very evening. The first explosion came when the bantamweight banker addressed the Prussian giant in French, as if unable to speak German; Bismarck couldn't take that from the son and grandson of Frankfurt Jews. Witnesses observed that Bismarck treated Alphonse less kindly than he did the other Frenchmen present. The chancellor became even angrier when he discovered that Alphonse wasn't ready to say yes or no to anything, objecting that he hadn't been given all the details.

By now the amount of the war indemnity to be paid to the

Germans had been reduced to five billion francs. Alphonse and associated bankers took responsibility for raising the money, as well as to finance supplies for starved Paris. Temporary peace terms were signed in Versailles on February 26.[20]

It was only the beginning of the reparations crisis. The ways of raising the money, the means of remitting it, were questions that would not be resolved in a day. Bankers involved in the "liberation bond" issues (referring to the brutal truth that Prussian occupation troops would stay in France until the war indemnity was paid)— bankers motivated by patriotism but also by high commissions— included both the Rothschilds and their merchant banking peers and a new generation of challengers. But it was the Rothschilds— ever the Rothschilds—who headed the syndicate.

It was a race against the clock. To reduce occupation costs—for the French were also obliged to pay for the maintenance of the enemy troops who held their soil—the second of the two major loans was paid by September 1873, eighteen months ahead of schedule. After that the Prussians went home.[21]

A brief period of euphoria followed the negotiating of the peace treaty in February 1871. By then the frustrations of the siege, the hardships that fell first of all on the least privileged, the all-too-evident conservatism of a republic as distant from the concerns of the laboring classes as any empire, had built up to explosive force. The spark ignited during the night of March 17–18, when Thiers moved to recover guns purchased during the siege with funds contributed by the citizens of Paris. The national guard, siding with the insurgents, arrested two generals and promptly shot them; it was war, war between the Thiers government based in Versailles, then a safe distance from the streets of Paris, and the self-proclaimed Commune whose people's army was drawn largely from working Paris.

Alphonse lived out the insurrection in Versailles, occupying a room at the best place in town, the Hôtel des Réservoirs facing the palace; not being the only refugee from the civil war, he had to make do with a single room, using screens to divide it into living and working space.[22] Legend has it that his anxiety was such that his hair, formerly jet-black, turned gray overnight.[23] For Paris was burning—the Tuileries palace, the Hôtel de Ville, or city hall, along with other conspicuous symbols of the old order.

Much was made—by their enemies—of the apparent immunity of the Rothschilds, who lost neither their bank nor their stately homes during the months insurgents ruled the streets. The arch anti-Semite Edouard Drumont, sowing hysteria to be harvested in the years of the Dreyfus affair, claimed to have a witness who could prove that the Rothschilds had financed the Commune.[24] There is also a story concerning Alphonse's mother, who continued to live in the princely house on Rue Laffitte; going through the Bois de Boulogne one afternoon, Baroness Betty was stopped by an angry crowd, who asked her how she could drive about when people were starving (her horses would make excellent food). She replied, "Yes, take my horses if you will have them, but I am as good a patriot as any of you. Come and see my hospital in my own house. . . ." She mentioned her sons who had fought for their country. The mob cheered, then formed a bodyguard to march alongside the carriage, ushering James's widow safely home.[25]

The Commune came to a bloody end in May 1871; the government regained Paris after an easy victory. And Alphonse de Rothschild found an old friend at the Hôtel de Ville: Léon Say was Thiers's choice for governor of the district. Soon the first Rothschild-managed bond issue to pay the war indemnity was launched, amounting to two billion francs, and it was successful. Meanwhile another merchant bank consortium led by the Rothschilds managed a loan for the city of Paris.

But there was a new banking generation now, grouping outsiders such as Banque de Paris et des Pays-Bas (a merger of two existing ventures that would become known as Paribas) with established institutions such as Crédit Lyonnais, and the newcomers were ready to challenge the domination of established merchant bankers over state finances. It became a struggle between "bankers" (the traditional ones) and "banks" (the new investment and deposit institutions). The upstarts felt that they had not been given a fair share of the original two-billion-franc bond issue, or the city of

Paris loan; they'd score their first victory in the final indemnity loan of three billion francs in July 1872. "A struggle is under way against the powerful baron," was how the director of the Crédit Lyonnais put it. Before it was all over, the new boys, led by Paribas, came out with better than a one-third stake in the loan for the final billion-franc installment of the indemnity. The Rothschilds had won, but each subsequent victory over the new credit institutions would be harder.[26]

The war left other traces. At one point, nearly the entire network of the Rothschilds' Compagnie des Chemins de Fer de l'Est— tracks and depots both—was in enemy hands. Then the surrender of Alsace and Lorraine signified giving up 430 miles of railroad; the Treaty of Frankfurt, which spelled a formal end to the war, obliged France to cede both its Belgian and Luxembourg lines to the conqueror.[27]

We can believe with Count Corti that the Rothschilds would never forgive Germany.[28]

THE BROTHERS ROTHSCHILD

They hadn't really lost much, certainly not their style. Later a Marxist historian, Jean Bouvier, discovered precisely how the "old" Rothschilds—Alphonse was forty-eight years old in 1875, Gustave forty-six—were perceived by the new bankers, who still couldn't beat them, but occasionally would join them in underwriting a major loan. He found his evidence in the archives of Crédit Lyonnais, one of the financial institutions that collaborated with Rothschild in floating a bond issue for the Ville de Paris. "The negotiation has been placed in the hands of [Alphonse de] Rothschild," notes the Crédit Lyonnais director, "who brings to these matters a kind of dignity prejudicial to a successful outcome. He never leaves his desk; he waits for others to come to him."[1]

Prejudicial to success? Alphonse, with Gustave, seconded by Edmond, was still very much on top of the heap in the final decades of the century, challenging the new French banks in foreign territory—in Spain, for instance, with the mines of Almaden, Peñarroya, and Rio-Tinto that were extracting the raw materials of the industrial age: copper and iron, lead and zinc. By arrangement with the Spanish government, the brothers also held a monopoly in the exploitation of mercury from that country, soon to represent over 40 percent of world production. "Rothschild, given his dominant position on all exchanges, can deal with governments on very special terms," noted a despoiled competitor (the same Crédit Lyonnais man).[2]

The new emphasis on strategic materials—diamonds (with De Beers in South Africa), nickel (with Le Nickel in New Caledonia), and Russian oil—was seen as a fair exchange for earlier Rothschild dominance in state bond issues, in which they were now often outgunned by those strong new credit institutions drawing their resources from a mass of shareholders and depositors. Railroads were also a field in which Rothschild know-how and dash still counted: owning and operating a line such as Südbahn, linking the Austro-Hungarian Empire to Italy, or the Saragossa crossing Spain, signified that one prospered in proportion to the expansion of trade and industry. The family also knew that even if it no longer swept the field in banking Paris, it could remain dominant in a less sophisticated business environment, in still-developing Italy, for instance.[3]

On one occasion, if we trust family legend, Alphonse and his brothers seemed to have had an opportunity to play a pivotal role, but let it pass. In 1875, Khedive Ismail Pasha, the viceroy who ruled Egypt in the name of the Turkish Ottoman Empire, let it be known to Alphonse that he wished to sell his substantial stake in the Suez Canal, an already strategic passage built by another Frenchman, Ferdinand de Lesseps, inaugurated only half a dozen years earlier. Armed with what amounted to an option on the khedive's shares, Alphonse marched into the office of his friend Léon Say, then finance minister, who told him that an outlay of such importance would require a vote of Parliament; there wouldn't be time for that. So Alphonse alerted his London cousin Lionel de Rothschild; Lionel got in touch with his friend Benjamin Disraeli, then the queen's first minister. The British grabbed the shares, and with them historic control of the Suez Canal. "You have it, Madam," Disraeli exclaimed to Victoria.[4] (They had it until 1956.)

A neat account, endorsed by the French historian Charles Lesage, who insisted that French bankers not only had the first option on the khedive's shares, but would have gotten a better deal than the British eventually did. The French, in this account, did not wish to alienate London, needing Britain's goodwill in a Europe under Bismarck's shadow. When the French foreign minister queried Disraeli, Disraeli pounced on the opportunity to buy. . . .[5]

The fact—contemporary documents make this clear—is that the British were the first to know that the khedive was ready to sell his interest in the canal, and seized the chance—thanks to that ever-ready source of funds, the local Rothschild bank. "Our friends, the Rothschilds, distinguished themselves," Disraeli informed the Prince of Wales (later to become King Edward VII, a friend and a debtor of both the London Rothschilds and Alphonse in Paris). "They alone could have accomplished what we wanted," Disraeli explained to Edward, "and they had only four and twenty hours to make up their minds, whether they would or could incur an immediate liability of four million [pounds]. One of their difficulties was that they could not appeal to their strongest ally, their own family in Paris, for Alphonse is *si francese* that he would have betrayed the whole scheme instantly."

The facts—for these are the facts—come to life in the description of how Disraeli's private secretary made his way to the Rothschild bank in New Court, just down the street from the Bank of England, to find Lionel de Rothschild at table, eating grapes. The banker was informed that Disraeli needed 4 million pounds by the next day. He took a grape, spat out the skin as he asked, "What is your security?"

"The British government," the aide replied.

"You shall have it," said Lionel.[6]

The reward took the form of a reasonable two-and-a-half-percent commission (rumors circulated that the Rothschilds had gotten more than twice as much).[7] All the rest is fable.

Tamper-proof evidence of this version of events is found in the daily reports that Alphonse in France sent to his British cousins and associates (just as they reported each day to the Paris brothers). Lionel asks Alphonse to contribute to the cash advance to the khedive, against a proper fee. "We accept with great pleasure the participation you offer," Alphonse replies in a letter preserved in the archives of the London bank, "and shall place the payment at your disposal at the times you indicate." He avoided encounters in Paris, adds Alphonse, so as not to have to reply to questions. "It seems certain that in high circles there is fear for the future. . . . Above all we must seek to maintain peace and tranquillity in the world, and any matter of a nature to cause a conflict between the powers can only harm us." (He worried that other states would exploit the khedive's patent weakness, dividing Turkey among themselves, "and once again modify the map of the world.") In subsequent letters to London, the Paris brothers conveyed their feeling that the British acquisition of Suez was a step for peace, since Britain desired only to guarantee freedom of passage through the canal.[8]

It didn't matter to the world, of course, which Rothschild rescued Suez from Middle Eastern turmoil. "I am of the opinion, Madame," Disraeli remarked to Queen Victoria with a smile, "that there never can be too many Rothschilds."[9]

The historian who seeks to follow a nineteenth-century phenomenon from a distance of well over a century picks up every track he can. One source should be the police, for the yellowing dossiers of the Paris prefecture are diligently preserved. And the files show that much of what the Rothschilds did and said outside their homes was observed and recorded, thanks in part to a legion of informers, not all of them reliable or unbiased. Thus a report in May 1873: "Mr. Rothschild [no "de" from this informer], who had promised 10,000 francs to Mr. Queyriaux, publisher and owner of the newspaper 'l'Assemblée Nationale,' gave him only 2,000." (Should that be taken as a tribute to Alphonse, who had given only a fifth of a promised hidden subsidy to the press?)

The police files on the Rothschilds are cluttered with messages such as this one of June 4, 1874: "Seven hours ten minutes—Mr. the baron de Rotschild [sic], accompanied by his mother coming from Férère [sic] arrived at the Gare de L'Est at 6 in the evening." Again (also 1874): "The Turkish ambassador and Mr. and Mrs. de Rothschild came to call on the Empress of Russia [then in Paris] at 10:50 A.M." In February 1875 an informer reported that "the left-wing parties have just had a clever idea. They are placing Mr. de Rothschild at the top of the ballot for the senatorial election. . . ." In July 1876 the police made sure to clip and file a press account of Alphonse's promotion to commander of the Legion of Honor.

In 1877 the French voted in one of a series of elections that was to shape the Third Republic; modestly, Alphonse de Rothschild offered himself as a candidate for the Conseil Général (a regional assembly)—and was defeated. The alleged reason delighted a police informer:

> A pretty story.
> Mr. de Rothschild wasn't elected because during a meeting he was said to be on the side of the Catholics!
> "Le Pays" published this, thinking it a joke. In fact it is perfectly true; I have it from an eyewitness.

Another police informer had heard that Alphonse was deeply hurt by his failure to win election, not because he desired the office but because of the slanders that accompanied the campaign. The Rothschilds, said this source, were feeling very negative about France; Alphonse was even thinking of abandoning Paris.

Occasionally the police kept track of what went on inside a Rothschild home as well. A report dated May 11, 1878, noted that Alphonse and Leonora had given a ball at Rue Saint-Florentin that lasted until seven the next morning. There had been 270 carriages, seven hundred guests, among them the Prince and Princess of Wales, the Danish royal prince and princess, Prince Amedeo of Italy. . . .[10]

These bankers who dined with future kings were (virtually by birthright) heads of the nation's Jewish community. In 1808, pursuing his policy of organizing and codifying everything that could be, Emperor Napoleon decreed the establishment of a Central Consistory, with separate consistories for each district, to supervise local Jewish communities and the education of rabbis. The consistories would have a role to play in schools, charity, and burial of the dead; obviously they were to be headed by the most respected—and the wealthiest. Alphonse succeeded his father as president of the Central Consistory; to Gustave fell the presidency of the Consistory of Paris (he was elected as early as 1858, when he was only twenty-eight years old). Both brothers were to serve for what amounted to lifetime tenure.[11]

It goes without saying that they and their cousins were expected to be the leading contributors to the community's needs, as well as for ambitious projects such as the construction of the grandiose synagogue on the Rue de la Victoire. Alphonse was to add a sizable extension to the hospital his father had endowed on the Rue de Picpus, to allow treatment of contagious patients at a safe distance from the main wards. His mother built an annex to serve as a home for the chronically ill.

Maxime Du Camp, chronicler of Paris charity, noted with admiration that Baroness Betty's hospice was finished just in time for the war of 1870, and served as a French military hospital before it saw its first civilian patient. "Israel flew the Red Cross flag and didn't spare its energies," as he put it. James's widow had also contributed a large sum to welfare authorities to help poorly paid workers meet rent payments.[12] The "exceptional situation" of James de Rothschild had made him the natural protector of fellow Jews, so Du Camp informed his contemporaries. And James had transmitted that role to his children, "who have not repudiated the responsibility."[13]

With a father like the Great Baron, it would have been hard for the sons to innovate—to carve out new areas of philanthropy, or even to be better collectors. One could be a *worse* collector, as the ill-disposed Edmond de Goncourt seemed to feel, paying a call on the youngest of Baron James's children, Edmond, in June 1874 (when the Rothschild Edmond was twenty-nine and the Goncourt Edmond over fifty). "Truly, it is in these dens of wealth that one touches the depths to which money can sink," reflects the diarist, as "the young baron, with the air of a victor, had us inspect some twenty gouaches not one of which was authentic." His host actually dared to defend one of the works rejected out of hand by Goncourt, who concluded, "At bottom, these people can reach beauty only in the industrial arts."[14]

They'd get the last laugh, "these people": their collections would be envied by the world's great museums, and some museums would manage to obtain a few of the masterpieces. But this is to anticipate.[15]

*   *   *

The balance sheets suggest that a Rothschild could prosper as well under a republic as under a monarchy. It helped that Alphonse's school chum Léon Say stood at the helm of state finances at a time when the state still led the way in investing for infrastructure. But the funds for these investments had to come from the banks, and here, as a rule, the Rothschilds continued to be first among equals.

Not even Léon Gambetta—that flagbearer of progressive France—could ignore the power of the banks in general and of the Rothschilds in particular. A witness (the dramatist Ludovic Halévy) recorded a dinner meeting of Gambetta and Alphonse de Rothschild in April 1881, when the politician was president of the Chamber of Deputies, kingmaker rather than king. Reproached by the politician with responsibility for the defeat of conservative leader Adolphe Thiers eight years earlier, Rothschild was heard to reply, "That isn't true. I obviously did have some influence on a large number of legislators, and I kept Thiers in office six months longer than he'd have lasted without me." He had told his "friends" in Parliament, "Wait until the loan question is settled; France's good name and fortune are at stake here."[16]

Abroad, the family name still counted for much. In 1878, Alphonse and his brothers, with their London cousins, joined as chief sponsors of a major loan to Egypt's hopelessly indebted khedive, guaranteed by some 620,000 acres of fertile Nile delta soil. Thus the Rothschilds, albeit with the tacit approval of the British and French governments, had a lien on a full twelfth of that nation's cultivated soil. A Marxist historian would see in the arrangement—beneficial to European foreign policy as well as to its financiers—a consolidation of the colonial grip on Egypt (Britain's grip, let it be said).[17]

But it was clear that Alphonse de Rothschild would not do business with an enemy of his country. A test case arose in January 1882 when Italy—a Rothschild client—took strong exception to France's occupation of Tunisia, the first step toward turning that country into a French protectorate. Under the circumstances, with a colonial conflict in the making, Italy's attitude was "certainly not of a nature to encourage us to offer a hand and to facilitate a loan designed to purchase arms directed against France," as Alphonse told his English cousins.[18] And just to be sure, Alphonse called on French foreign minister Charles Freycinet a few days later to hear him agree that a loan to Italy would be inopportune; this was all Alphonse wanted to know.

Sometimes the Rothschilds would make their own foreign policy, especially in the cause of persecuted Jews. The family had long been involved in developing Czarist Russia's nascent industry and banking system, while that country's growing network of railroads was largely financed by Rothschild-managed loans. Although their dominant position was to be challenged by the same banks who fought them in France, the chief inhibition to a Rothschild monopoly was now going to be the Rothschilds themselves.[19]

An early sign of Alphonse's concern with officially inspired attacks on Jews appears in a report to his London banking family in September 1881: "The rumor spread that the [Russian] government had negotiated a loan from us, because Mr. Gunzberg [Horace de Günzberg, a Russian banker] was seen in our company; what we talked about was the plight of our unhappy fellow Jews in Russia."[20] By then the reformist Czar Alexander II had been assassinated, succeeded by his son, a rabid nationalist whose "Russification" included deliberate encouragement of attacks on Jewish villages—the infamous pogroms. "We shall therefore cease to work with Russia and attempt to stir up a movement of sympathy in France on behalf of our poor fellow Jews," Alphonse wrote his cousins.[21] As he saw it—as his advisers persuaded him to see it—the Russians had to be won over by behind-the-scenes contacts, subtle pressures. Public rallies could only irritate, although Alphonse was not averse to inspiring newspaper editorials or even to financing the emigration of Russia's Jewish population.

Initially the lobbying from Paris seemed to work. Alphonse won the ear of Dimitri Tolstoi, the Czar's representative on the Holy Synod governing the Orthodox church, soon to become minister of the interior. It was understood that the Czar's advisers would rein in anti-Jewish agitation, while the West was to desist from criticizing Russian policy so as not to aggravate tensions. (Alphonse, so he reported to London on June 22, 1882, had agreed to call off an anti-Russian rally.) Within a week Alphonse was telling his cousins that he had received confirmation of Russia's readiness to discourage further outbreaks; that had something to do with Russia's need for money. Unfortunately, this was not the right time to go to the public for money, he explained, and Russia's credit was far from good. Rather than float a bond issue, he thought it would be easier to provide Russia with an advance of funds. "If I speak of it today, dear cousins, it's only to warn you and give you time to think about this matter, which can be important both from the political and humanitarian point of view."[22]

By October 1882 the Russian finance minister had an emissary in Paris to sound out the intentions of the Rothschilds (so Alphonse informed the London bank). Alphonse was to reply that they'd like nothing better than to work with the Russian government, "but that unfortunately they make that impossible by the persecutions of our poor fellow Jews in Russia." He was being advised by banker Günzberg that this kind of argument could lead to significant improvement in the lot of Russia's Jews.[23]

Often enough, international tensions interfered with well-thought-out plans for development. There was that dream of a tunnel under the English Channel, linking sometime enemies, occasional friends. Plans were drawn up for such a tunnel at the beginning of the nineteenth century (when neither the engineering nor the political will existed to realize it). Before the Second Empire faded, a Franco-British commission undertook a feasibility study, and now both the will and the science were ready for a railroad under the sea. In 1875 both Britain and France approved the project, the actual digging and laying of tracks to be carried out by private enterprises. A French Tunnel Society was founded in February 1875, half of its capital subscribed by the Compagnie du Chemin de Fer du Nord, still the principal Rothschild holding in railroad development, another fourth by the family bank. The balance of the shares went to banking partners, industrial establishments, and prominent individuals such as Léon Say. The French investors received an exclusive concession to build and maintain a line connecting to existing track, extending it under the Channel to link up to a similar British venture. For its part, the Rothschild company would be responsible for exploration of the soil and channel bottom.

In all, a sum exceeding two million francs was invested in preliminary works, including the digging of a tunnel running over a mile under the sea in the direction of England. A corresponding effort on the British side was carried out not by an exclusive concessionaire but by a succession of entrepreneurs (the first of them, the Channel Tunnel Company, included the participation of the London Rothschild bank).[24]

But it was not to be—not then. Britain wasn't ready to give up its protective isolation, while neither Britain nor France had renounced the exploitation of its own interests—often divergent or conflicting—in continental and colonial arenas. By 1882, Franco-British differences concerning Egypt had reached the boiling point, at which time the War Office actually suspended the activity of the country's tunnel company. The anti-tunnelists captured the London press, including the influential *Times*. A pamphlet raised the specter of French soldiers, disguised as tourists, springing from a tunnel train to seize strategic objectives on British soil. Leading personalities joined in signing an anti-tunnel manifesto, whose arguments centered on security.

The French continued to pursue this project hailed by Victor Hugo as "a labor that will be the consecration of the unity of mankind and fraternity among peoples." (His Victorian counterpart, Alfred Lord Tennyson, was among prominent opponents of the project.)[25] But when a British parliamentary committee concluded that the tunnel did indeed endanger the nation, the scheme was abandoned, to be picked up again and again before the final and successful attempt a century later.[26]

"JEWISH FRANCE"

*S*ometimes it takes only a spark to destroy a forest, and one can't always trace it; all we know is that the timber was very dry. Those who inspired French anti-Semitism in the century's final decades were nourished on the works of visionaries who equated capitalism with evil, and so much the worse for Jews in the middle. Jews so often *were* in the middle, since handling money was one of the only trades permitted to them.

Eugène Bontoux was another visionary, who (like the Pereire brothers) saw banking and industry as instruments of social advance; he happened to be a practicing Catholic. And when he left the service of the Rothschilds—for this gifted engineer had held responsible positions in both their French and Austrian railroads (ending as director of the all-important Südbahn)—it was to join like-minded investors, political conservatives and monarchists, including members of the Church hierarchy, in an ambitious banking venture called the Union Générale. But these were republican years, when the Catholic Church was a political underdog. And the Union Générale, which drew its strength from militant churchgoers prepared to challenge the existing banking structure, was to place Bontoux in conflict not only with his former employers but with other leading bankers of the time.

In an "Appeal to Catholics" issued in Lyon in 1875, the founders of the new bank had made no effort to hide their bias: "To unite the financial strength of Catholics, thus giving them a power they lack, and which is entirely in the hands of adversaries of their faith and their interests." Another statement stressed the importance of combating "capitalist power associated with . . . Jews and Protestants."[1]

Rhetoric so highly charged with passion, when applied to a financial institution, demanded of its management truly inspired (if not to say blessed) leadership; a favorable business climate was also essential. Although not born to banking, Eugène Bontoux was that good manager, but he couldn't fight his times. And in January 1882, the alarming plunge of Union Générale shares, revealing a dangerous shortage of liquidities, came in the context of a falling market. In a previous phase, speculation had been frantic, and Bontoux's Union Générale had been as reckless as the worst of the gamblers. When a run on the bank began, it couldn't meet demands for cash because of the enormous sums it had committed to the purchase of its own equities. All major stocks were falling (Suez, notably), and at least one sister bank in Lyon had already closed its doors.

Later, militant partisans of the Bontoux bank, cheered on by radical anti-Semites, were to accuse Jewish bankers of leading a cabal against the Union Générale, and no matter that no one, including government investigators, was ever able to find evidence of a plot. In the end it was Bontoux who would be indicted for fraud and breach of trust after his company was declared bankrupt.

In fact the Rothschilds and other merchant bankers advanced funds to Eugène Bontoux during the panic—not to protect him, surely, but to stave off a market crash triggered by his fall. So there hadn't been a vile scheme to destroy Bontoux and his bank, though plenty of people were happy to see him go. Sentenced to five years in prison in December 1882, he fled to Spain to avoid incarceration, returning only when it seemed safe to do so.[2] He'd write a book about the experience, attributing his bank's demise to "the coalition of Jews and Freemasons."[3]

But by then his voice was all but drowned out by more violent partisans; more than once the leading pamphleteer of the anti-Semitic *fin de siècle*, Edouard Drumont, reproached Bontoux for failing to pin the blame squarely on Rothschild.[4]

Even that anticapitalist historian Jean Bouvier had his doubts; it was "possible—should one say probable?—that the Rothschilds, and others, contributed to sink Bontoux in selling shares to lower the value of his stock."[5] But Bouvier didn't have access to what we can hold in our hands today: the private correspondence of Alphonse with his London cousins and banking partners. In a letter to London on January 23, 1882, Alphonse reveals his part in an advance of funds made to the Union Générale to save it from bankruptcy; on January 27 Alphonse is still looking for ways to keep Bontoux afloat, deploring the news that "Poor Madame Bontoux has gone mad and her husband doesn't have much of his reason either." Next day he tells of a request by Bontoux, "with his habitual cynicism," for another large sum to reimburse urgent calls on capital.

Bontoux was actually offering, among other things, a new issue of Union Générale stock—something Alphonse would never accept, "not wishing under any pretext to involve ourselves in their affairs." He did regret the Union's bankruptcy, when it came, after all the efforts that had been undertaken by the Rothschilds and associated banks to avoid it. They had banded together to limit the damage, Alphonse explained, yet without receiving the gratitude or the cooperation they might have expected.

On March 7, after hearing that the Union Générale might be revived with new funds raised by Bontoux, Alphonse tells his cousins: "I wish these gentlemen much success; we're not the ones who will seek to block their plans, but I doubt that they will find brokers ready to help them speculate on their own stock."[6]

It seems worth taking the space to examine these documents, for they offer a historical corrective to what is to follow. France was now to enter into its most destructive period of anti-Jewish hysteria, inspired by (and inspiring) a legion of polemical periodicals, shelves of tracts and pseudoscientific volumes. Even the arrest in 1894 of a French army captain who happened to be Jewish on fabricated treason charges was only one episode of the ongoing crusade, and was so treated in the anti-Jewish press.

That consummate student of the subject, Léon Poliakov, is convincing in his demonstration that modern anti-Semitism—a conspiracy theory that sees Jewish plotting as the key to universal history—was born in France, even if the term itself had been imported from Germany.[7] Certainly anti-Semitism was to find an easy target in the conspicuously rich Rothschilds. The new capitalism of the merchant bankers seemed a threat to the old aristocracy, already virtually deposed by the bourgeoisie. It also frightened small landowners, traditional artisans, and tradespeople. This was a world they couldn't grasp, except through the vague feeling that their status was threatened.

Their anxieties were fed by a specialized press, with titles such as L'Anti-juif (The Anti-Jew) and L'Anti-sémitique. A student of that unhappy era found no fewer than three novels describing the crash of the Union Générale as a Jewish plot (one of them was called La Comtesse Schylock—Schylock [sic] identifiable as Alphonse de Rothschild).[8] Later the scandal would be elevated into literature in Guy de Maupassant's Bel-Ami, Emile Zola's L'Argent. "Down with Rothschild, down with the Jews!" right-wing polemist Maurice Barrès summed up the battle cry. "It's the formula that sums up the resentment of he who doesn't have enough against he who has too much."[9]

Of course the tendency of anti-Semitic Socialists to equate Jews with capitalists had begun earlier in the century with the followers of Fourier and Proudhon; after the banking scandals and the recession of the 1880s, the habit tended to spread.[10] It took the crying injustice of the Dreyfus trial to bring the Socialists to their senses.

They were a very big target, the French Rothschilds. Already the stuff of myth. One indication of their popularity is police files, which at Paris headquarters grew fat with whispered rumor centered on Alphonse—that, for example, he was plotting for a restoration of the monarchy (which meant the Orléans dynasty personified by Philippe, Count of Paris). One informer described a manuscript that was making the rounds, written by the founder of L'Anti-sémitique. Insisting that the allegations in the book were true, the police agent explained that Alphonse de Rothschild had impregnated a young woman and then failed to keep his promise to marry her. When she had committed suicide, Alphonse had put their daughter in Paris's

Jewish School, abandoning her at twelve; she had become a prostitute and Alphonse had been her first customer.[11]

Edmond de Goncourt was as good as a police file. In November 1883 he reports on a soirée at the home of Princess Mathilde: "Like all the salons of Paris," he grumbles, "the drawing room of the Princess has become a veritable salon of Jewry. . . ." On this particular day he ran into Emile Straus, who was whispered to be the natural son of the late Baron James. "For a novel," says the diarist, "this would be the perfect physique of the satanical merchant, with the bestial paralysis of his eyelids and his wrinkled forehead." Guy de Maupassant tells Goncourt that at Ferrières the Rothschilds and their guests, having exhausted every species of animal that might be hunted, now found it more chic to drag a deerskin through the woods, and then send the dogs to follow the odor. "Then, as Madame Alphonse Rothschild [Goncourt omits the *de*] jumps very well, the obstacles are prepared in advance and the grass is watered, so that if the Jewish huntress falls she won't get hurt."[12]

The times were ripe for a newspaper called *Le Rothschild,* subtitled "Journal Financier Populaire," and although it presented the family with respect and approval, one can be certain that the very grossness of the title precluded financial support from Alphonse and his brothers. The first issue, published on October 20, 1883, included an article under the heading "Anti-Semitic Fury" telling how the writer Octave Mirbeau had been given a start in business by Rothschild (presumably Alphonse), yet when he failed to get more help from the same source, he "swore eternal hatred to Rothschild and the whole Jewish race."[13]

There was hardly more coherence in *La France juive* (*Jewish France*), but this inflated pamphlet, which filled two ponderous volumes, was to mark its time. Its author, Edouard Drumont, had until then been a minor journalist; this book, written in his forty-second year, was to make him a celebrity. His approach was inspired both by traditional racist, militantly religious anti-Semitism and by the new fear that Jewish financiers (with their Protestant and Masonic allies) had become the occult rulers of France. From his first pages Drumont spelled out his obsession: Jewish domination of the economy, to the impoverishment of rank-and-file Frenchmen—"a whole people working for another that appropriates, by a vast system of financial exploitation, the profits of the labor of others." Jews amassed their fortunes without performing any effective labor, producing nothing, so he explained to readers surely as unable to grasp the fundamentals of modern economy as was he.

His chief target, of course, was the Rothschilds. "It is certain . . . that the Rothschild family, that now seems to possess three billion francs in the French branch alone, didn't have that money when it arrived in France; it invented nothing, discovered no mine, cultivated no soil; it therefore levied these three billion from Frenchmen without giving them anything in exchange."[14] He was to recall a considerable number of tales told to the disadvantage of the Rothschilds—and make them worse in the retelling. After repeating the fable of how the Rothschilds became rich thanks to early news of Napoleon's defeat at Waterloo, Drumont alleged that the Rothschilds got this information from fellow Jews who killed and robbed wounded soldiers.[15] Mocking the social pretensions of the family, he attacked aristocrats who "lower themselves" by being courteous to Jews. He expressed indignation at Rothschild winemaking: "Our wine, in which the national spirit dipped in olden times, now belongs to Jews along with everything else."

Even in appearance, Drumont's Rothschilds are inferior: Alphonse, "so small, with his whitened sidewhiskers, thinning hair . . . , "absent stare," "perpetual blinking of the eyes"; at the age of fifty-four, says Drumont, Alphonse "personifies the decrepitude of his race." (In fact Alphonse was fifty-nine when La France juive was published.) The Rothschild estate at Ferrières was described with an abundance of detail; clearly Drumont, like his fellow anti-Semite Goncourt, had walked its floors, for he remarked Marie-Antoinette's harpsichord there—a shocking thing to find in a Jewish household, along with inferior literature and vulgar bindings in the library. In Paris, he observes, the Rothschild houses are fortified—but will they have time to pack when the day comes?[16]

All petty, and nothing new? But people had more time to read in those days. The combination of superficial social criticism and newspaper gossip appealed to motivated book buyers. At the outset, *La France juive* was published at the author's expense, and only because Drumont's friend, popular storyteller and visceral anti-Semite Alphonse Daudet, had vouched for him. Its fortune was made when the publisher of *Le Figaro*, at Daudet's urging, hailed the book on his front page. The first printing of 2,000 copies was rapidly sold out, and edition after edition followed; within a year it had found 65,000 buyers—a best-seller for the time.[17]

Within days of publication, Edmond de Goncourt had Drumont's exposé in hand, and told his private diary that it made him sit up and think about Rothschild omnipresence. "To us, who for twenty years have been crying out that if the Rothschild family isn't dressed in ghetto yellow, we Christians will soon be . . . reduced to servitude, Drumont's book was frightening in its statistics and documentation of their occult powers."[18]

La France juive inspired a new press, some of it wholly devoted to anti-Jewish polemics, as well as a stream of sequels, many written by Drumont himself. A student of modern anti-Semitism calculated that though no more than one anti-Jewish work had been published each year before the appearance of *La France juive* in 1886, there were fifteen that year, fourteen the next, nine in 1888, twenty in 1889.[19] Soon the leading Catholic organ, *La Croix*, would be proclaiming itself "the most anti-Jewish newspaper in France," while another short-lived periodical gave itself a title one can translate as *The Anti-Kike*.[20]

Drumont's first attempt to capitalize on his own success, *La France juive devant l'opinion* ("Jewish France" and public opinion), was ready seven months after publication of his magnum opus—and became another success, selling more than thirty thousand copies in under six months.[21] In the new work he accused the Rothschilds of collusion with the French government, while demanding that misappropriated funds be reclaimed from the Jews (peacefully if possible—but inevitably). Making common cause with the working class, and with small businessmen said to have been ruined by Jewish competitors and reduced to the status of laborers, Drumont predicted the prosecution of the Rothschilds (because he couldn't have predicted a Dreyfus affair) as the "great event" (he uses the English phrase) of the end of the century, just as the trial of Louis XVI had closed the previous century.[22]

Such violence, even if only verbal, bred violence. Within weeks of the appearance of *La France juive,* the Socialist militant Jules Guesde, speaking at a public meeting in Paris, threatened Alphonse de Rothschild with prison or the firing squad. "When the revolution comes, we'll make use of the liberating rifle." A trial followed, with Guesde and fellow speakers at the rally accused of incitement to murder (Guesde was to insist that he had only wanted to see Rothschild in jail). As the verdict was reported in *Le Socialiste,* organ of Guesde's French Workers Party: "The Seine district jury, composed of ten good men, merchants and manufacturers, proclaimed that the Socialists accomplished a social obligation in denouncing the financial thieves, in demanding their imprisonment and the confiscation of their wealth stolen from the nation. The Revolution will execute this verdict."[23]

The best evidence is that the Rothschilds did not let themselves be moved by local manifestations of anti-Semitism, even as they participated in efforts to help Jewish victims abroad—close by in neighboring Germany, farther away in Russia and Rumania.[24] As head of the family, head of the bank, Alphonse was surely the most stoic, the least vulnerable to pressures; he'd be accused of timidity.[25] Yet in each generation there was at least one Rothschild at a remove from the family bank and its industrial interests, available and willing to deal with charities and other good works. Edmond was the Great Baron's youngest son by far; only twenty-three when James died, he could never be his brothers' peer. But he could mount his own hobbyhorses and ride them hard. In addition to art— buying it, befriending artists—he devoted himself to industrial applications of science, notably the transmission of electrical energy, and new uses for the recently discovered Russian oil.[26]

But what he chose as his great cause surprised everyone, certainly his brothers. Edmond found a solution for Europe's uprooted Jews—his persecuted coreligionists of eastern and central Europe—in Palestine settlement, and then proceeded to organize and to finance such settlement in painstaking detail, and with much treasure, all the rest of his long life.

When Edmond de Rothschild is spoken of, one tends to forget the Rue Laffitte (and Château-Lafite). In Jewish Palestine he became known as *Ha Nadiv,* Hebrew for "the benefactor," but (as Israeli

statesman David Ben-Gurion remembered him) he was not only a
benefactor. For if he did more for Jewish settlement than anyone
else ever had, perhaps more than all Jews together in the years before independence, he was above all a bold planner, a stubborn
manager. Ben-Gurion found it a "miracle" that a French Jew, an
assimilated, all-but-nonexistent Jew who had never himself suffered
from anti-Semitism, had nevertheless been "touched by grace" to
the point of devoting himself, and his fortune, to the cause.[27]

Scholarship has been applied to Edmond's case—to the reasons
behind his momentous option in the face of older brothers remaining "fastidiously aloof" (in Simon Schama's phrase) to Palestine
settlement. Like his brothers a French patriot (who had served
under French colors to defend Paris in 1870), he could also be a
supporter of Jewish nationalism, of tilling the soil (and what heartless soil); another Hebrew name given him was *Avi Hayishuv*,
"father of the settlement." All the sons of Baron James and Betty,
it has been pointed out, were introduced to Judaism by the same
tutor, the scholar Albert Cohn, who was responsible for Rothschild
charities both in France and in Palestine—and a true believer in
a return of the Jews to their lost land.[28]

For 1882 wasn't only the year of the crash of Eugène Bontoux's
Union Générale. Elsewhere in Europe it has been seen as a turning
point in Jewish history, with the pogroms unleashed against Russia's Jewish population by Czar Alexander III. It was the year of an
international congress of anti-Semites in Germany, but also of the
arrival of a small group of Russian students in Palestine, dedicated
to nothing less than the rebuilding of a Jewish nation.[29] In France,
Alphonse de Rothschild had gone so far as to set up a relief
committee for the Jews of Russia; Edmond signed its manifesto,
while his twenty-eight-year-old wife, Adelheid, became head of a
similar organization of Jewish women.[30]

The moment of decision for Edmond may have been his encounter in September 1882 with Rabbi Shmuel Mohilewer of Bialystok
(then in Russian Poland), who informed him of the plight and the
flight of eastern Jews. Mohilewer, a spokesman for the Russian
precursors of the Zionists (to be formalized as a movement by

Theodor Herzl a decade and a half later), made a case for the establishment of agricultural settlements in Judaism's ancestral home. The best evidence (and it is legend rather than evidence) is that Edmond was quickly convinced of the urgent need of assistance to refugees, but not by the ideology. "Rabbi," he supposedly said, "if you have come to me to ask for money to support this work [of colonization], mention the sum and I will give it to you. But if you have come to win my soul, then I must first consult my own self. . . ." After a second meeting, when Edmond agreed to resettle a small group of Polish farmers in Palestine, Rabbi Mohilewer was sure that he had won the baron's soul as well.[31]

Events were to move quickly after that, for there were preexisting settlements on the soil of the ancient Jewish homeland, notably near Jaffa. Edmond's meeting with an emissary from the failing colony of Rishon Le Zion, shortly after his second encounter with Rabbi Mohilewer, has been called even more decisive, for here was a specific community whose material needs could be defined.[32]

It must have been discouraging to ardent Zionists—this chaotic land subjected to the decadent Ottoman Empire, and whose Jewish population, for the most part, was pious, unproductive, dependent on donations from Jewish communities the world over. The Rothschild commitment faced a different sort of challenge, its pragmatic insistence on viable agriculture—produce that could be sold for cash to assure both survival and growth—clashing head-on with ideological Zionism and the collectivism of agrarian socialism, later with religious interdicts as well (when settlers insisted on following biblical preachings to the letter by abstaining from physical labor every seventh year). The very fact that Edmond's contribution was philanthropic made it next to impossible for true Zionists to accept; the pioneer spirit and the baron's stress on good management—seen by his critics as paternalism—were not to mix well.[33]

The irony is that if the Zionists were never quite reconciled to the Benefactor, neither were the Benefactor's brothers, Alphonse and Gustave. Frenchmen first, they feared that their younger brother's engagement could be interpreted as alienation from their national loyalty, creating a distinction between French Jews and France they did not wish to see.[34]

ELEVEN

RUSSIA AND PALESTINE

It should be clear that there was more than a little of the paranoid in Edmond de Goncourt. Literary historians tell us that both he and his brother (whose premature death was attributed to syphilitic brain damage) were convinced that the world had it in for them, or at the very least failed to understand and appreciate their talents. They responded in kind. Edmond de Goncourt, who recorded everything but didn't necessarily remember everything, told his diary of being introduced to Edmond de Rothschild in December 1887 (having forgotten that he had not only met Edmond, but had examined and despised his art collection, a dozen years before). The second occasion was a reception in the grand salon of Princess Mathilde on Rue de Courcelles; it was Madame Emile Straus, a model for Proust's Duchesse de Guermantes and the wife of the man Goncourt saw as the bastard son of James de Rothschild, who made the introduction. Of Edmond Rothschild—always without the *de* in the contemptuous Goncourt way—the diarist notes "a horselike head of unintelligent ugliness." (Presumably he had in mind persons whose ugliness accompanied brilliant minds.) Edmond and Edmond speak of French engravings, but Goncourt decides not to admire anything a Rothschild could like. "Rich people," he tells himself, "can become art-lovers; they will always be poor art-lovers."[1]

There was no law that said a Goncourt had to be consistent. After his condescending comments on Rothschild bad taste, he was to work himself into a fit for the opposite reason. Again the scene is Mathilde's salon: Goncourt hears that a Rothschild is to acquire a collection of drawings by the well-known caricaturist Eugène Giraud. He loses no time in telling his notebook what he thinks about that: "It's certain that if the Rothschilds aren't intimidated and fail to restrict their purchases in the face of whispered grumbling about their pillaging, this family will soon own everything beautiful that is still to be sold." To conclude: "For there isn't an art object of any kind in any corner of the earth whose owner or dealer isn't trying to offer it to the Rue Laffitte."[2]

Goncourt was closer to the mark here: Edmond's acquisitions, which included drawings by Michelangelo and Rembrandt as well as Fragonard, Boucher, and Watteau—eventually to number 600,000 items—would become the cornerstone of the Louvre museum's collection.[3]

The diarist's second introduction to Edmond de Rothschild followed the baron's landmark visit to Palestine in the spring of 1887, an inspection tour of his extensive good works there, but also a good and proper sightseeing trip, allowing time for indulging his interest in history and archeology. Simon Schama describes the precautions taken to protect the visitor's identity, for until then Rothschild's role in developing settlements in the ancient Holy Land was kept secret—from the Turkish masters of the region first of all. So he and Baroness Adelheid traveled to Jerusalem in a closed carriage, their legion of servants kept at a distance. (There was another reason to protect the visitors' identity on visits to Christian religious landmarks, such as the Holy Sepulcher Church: Jews were not to enter such places.) The visit had its emotional high points, as when Edmond sought to buy the surviving western wall of the Second Temple, popularly known as the Wailing Wall—an acquisition apparently stymied not by Muslims but by local Sephardic Jews, wary of control of this holiest of places by European Jews—the Ashkenazi.

There were practical reasons for the trip, of course. Edmond remained heavily committed not only to funding but to close supervision of his agricultural colonies, which, like all institutions

run by man, had proved vulnerable to human frailty, taking the
seemingly self-excluding forms of lax management and overly dom-
ineering managers. Fully expecting that his pioneer farmers would
experience difficulties on the way to self-sufficiency, Edmond resolved to nurse the settlements until they could fend for themselves. He was convinced that Jews would continue to be
persecuted in Eastern Europe, so a safe, self-supporting refuge in
Palestine was essential. Moreover, Edmond wished to prove that
despite the scoffing of the anti-Semites, Jews could be credible
farmers, could grow olives and peaches and almonds, could cul-
tivate grapes and press them for wine. He did *not* intend to sub-
sidize the settlements all his life.[4]

The settlements grew, new settlements were born of the pioneer
villages; the choice of land (and of managers) would not always be
happy. And then the Rothschild method came up against the militant Zionism of Theodor Herzl, whose blueprint for *The Jewish
State* put ideology ahead of bookkeeping. Seen by Herzl, the baron
was "a decent, good-natured, fainthearted man. . . . I believe that
he is now aghast at having got himself involved with Palestine, and
perhaps he will run to Alphonse and say 'You were right, I should
have gone in for racing horses rather than resettling Jews.' "[5] The
two men were to meet in 1896, Herzl to put forth his proposal for
massive immigration of Jews to the Holy Land, Edmond to resist in
the name of step-by-step growth.[6]

Did his wealth explain Edmond de Goncourt's otherwise inexplicable attraction to Edmond de Rothschild? For the Edmonds were
to meet again at Princess Mathilde's, the Goncourt Edmond finding
the Rothschild Edmond particularly friendly ("One would really
imagine that he wants to borrow some money from me," Goncourt
jokes to himself). Rothschild speaks not of Palestine but of Sam-
arkand in Asia, where he had encountered homosexual courtesans.
("The Jew speaks of dirty things in a more disgusting way than
other races do," Goncourt decides.)[7]

Some months later, a seemingly mellowed Goncourt actually
accepts an invitation to dine at Edmond's (who gets the *de* at last).
"The most princely house I have ever seen in Paris," Goncourt will

note with astonishment; in fact it was an ancient mansion totally renovated for the youngest Rothschild on Rue du Faubourg Saint-Honoré, which in our own time became the residence of the American ambassador. "A staircase worthy of the Louvre," observes Goncourt, "guarded on the landings by legions of servants in cardinal's livery. . . ." Princess Mathilde is the guest of honor, a Duchesse de Richelieu is present, a Prince de Wagram. . . . But Goncourt will tell a friend that the food was mediocre—compared to what he'd been served at the home of Madame Nathaniel de Rothschild (James's daughter Charlotte). He would also have a closer look at Edmond's famous art collection, only to dismiss it for its "falsity."[8]

As for Edmond's brother Alphonse, he continued to fight the scourge of anti-Semitism with the weapon available to him. There could be no breaking of financial relations with Russia—for then the Rothschilds would no longer hold a trump card. And indeed there is evidence that when threatened with exclusion from the Russian loan business in 1889, the Paris bank fought to be brought back in—and won.[9]

That made it possible for Alphonse to direct a personal appeal to the Russian finance minister, I. A. Vishnegradski, in August 1890. Russia's credit, the senior Rothschild declared bluntly, would be damaged by further persecution of Jews, rumors of which "have already created painful emotions in political and business circles." The new measures, he added, "will have the effect of reducing to misery, despair, and perhaps even to death, a population of several million souls. . . ." A population "active, industrious, devoted to its emperor. . . ."

Vishnegradski quickly reassured the baron: There was no plan for further restrictions against Jews. Perhaps there *had* been a plan—but the protest was effective.[10]

Yet by the spring of 1891 it became clear that the condition of Russia's Jews had not improved; if anything, it was worsening. How to use the money weapon against a tyrant seemingly indifferent to Western opinion and pressure? Which was the wiser course of action, the Rothschilds wondered—to pursue relations with Russia or to break them? They'd rather be done with it, but what *then* would happen to Russia's poor Jews? On April 22, in a letter to Adolphe Rothstein, a prominent Jewish banker in the Czar's capital of Saint Petersburg who served as a discreet intermediary with the finance minister, Alphonse warned that the situation was alarming, and pressure was being brought on the Rothschilds to do something about it. Surely Minister Vishnegradski must be aware of public feeling. "By no means do we wish to sound imperative; but we tell you in all sincerity that if the minister rejects our plea, we won't be able to guarantee the success of your important loan concerning which we had planned to engage all our effort, all our devotion."

That letter to Rothstein was actually written for Minister Vishnegradski's eyes, as Alphonse made clear in a covering note. And Vishnegradski took only a few days to reply. Questions involving Jews were not in his domain, said he, nor could he do anything to alleviate the persecutions. (Speaking privately to Rothstein, the minister added that this was hardly the moment to approach the Czar on the matter, for he was "in a state of extreme irritation.")

So the Rothschilds broke their contract with Russia—invoking an "act of God." Alphonse knew full well that his decision would create "a great explosion" in Saint Petersburg, and at Rothstein's request agreed not to reveal why he was rescinding the agreement. Otherwise "the Czar's anger would be ferocious and it would fall on the poor Jews we are trying to help."

Alphonse was as good as his word. "The steep decline of the market in recent days" made it impossible, so he told the Czar's minister in a white lie, to guarantee the success of the Russian bond issue. Vishnegradski also knew the rules of the game. Thanks to the Czar's wise rule, he replied to Alphonse, Russia could do without the money.[11]

All that for the public ear. Separately Alphonse wrote to his intermediary Adolphe Rothstein—the message if not the letter was meant for Minister Vishnegradski—to tell him ("most politely," as Alphonse explained to London) that in future Russia couldn't count on the Rothschilds if persecution of Jews continued.

Soon Alphonse was having second thoughts; it would be better, he suggested to his cousins, to let the Russian finance minister believe that he would have Rothschild support for a loan at a later date. Otherwise he'd simply abandon Russian Jews to their fate.[12]

It is no small irony that diplomatic observers refused to believe the Rothschilds had given up on the Russians for so trivial a matter as the persecution of Jews. They were convinced that this was only a pretext; in their convoluted reasoning, the Rothschilds were really acting as instruments of the French government, which was seeking to make the Russians more attentive to its pivotal position in Europe.[13]

It wasn't easy to be a French patriot and an enemy of Russia, as Alphonse and his brothers were to learn. In the European power struggle it was in France's interest to have the Czar on its side. Soon after the breaking of Rothschild-Russian relations the French fleet made a historic call at the port of Kronstadt, a prelude to the signing of a Franco-Russian defense alliance on July 23, 1891— guaranteeing a sympathetic French ear not only to Russia's foreign policy goals, such as a stake in the Mediterranean, but to the Czar's seemingly inexhaustible need for credit both for arms and to come to terms with an unprecedented famine.[14]

So Russia would get its loan after all, the Rothschilds replaced by a consortium of banks led by Crédit Lyonnais, with the participation of the government's own Crédit Foncier; the bonds were issued on October 15, 1891.

But the terms were too tempting, and subscribers to the Russian obligations found it all too easy to make money by a quick resale; as everybody unloaded, Russian bond prices tumbled—and with them *other* bond prices. It seemed to those raised on conspiracy theory that international bankers—and why not Jewish banks, and why not the Rothschilds?—were working behind the scenes to sink Russia's credit. Rothschild at once called on Maurice Rouvier, then French finance minister, to protest the accusation; Rouvier knew quite well that Rothschild had been up to no mischief.[15] It was agreed that a formal statement would be made to deny the rumors. As the Havas press agency reported it, "these calumnies have no other motive than to help those speculating on a fall in bond prices. At no time has the house of Rothschild opposed an operation concerning a government with which it has always maintained excellent relations. . . ."[16]

It was also true that the Rothschilds had become heavily committed to a Russia far from the Czar's capital. For something important was happening at the southern extremity of the empire, in the mountainous Caucasus, inhabited by a congeries of non-Russian peoples. There the brothers of Sweden's dynamite king, Alfred Nobel, were pumping oil for the lamps of Europe. Soon illuminating oil from south Russia was to challenge what had been America's virtual monopoly, and the French Rothschilds were financing a railroad—the kind of investment they did so well—to move the precious crude from Baku across the mountains to Batum, a Black Sea port open to the Western world. From railway tracks the Rothschilds went on to storage and marketing facilities (and their management); by 1886 they had become a force to reckon with in Russian and world petroleum, working through a company they founded called the Société Commerciale et Industrielle de Napthe Caspienne et de la Mer Noire, known by its Russian name Bnito. Between Bnito and the Nobels, Russian oil accounted for nearly 30 percent of the world market at the beginning of the 1890s, the balance coming from John D. Rockefeller's Standard Oil.[17]

It seemed worth another attempt to bend Alexander III when a new finance minister was appointed in Saint Petersburg in 1892; in that authoritarian climate, Sergei Witte appeared to be a flaming liberal. It was even suggested—by Count Georg von Münster, Germany's ambassador to Paris (writing to his chancellor, Count Leo von Caprivi)—that Witte's wife, "an intelligent and conspiratorial Jewess," might serve as a link to the Jewish bankers Russia so much needed. According to Münster, reporting from Paris on October 23, 1892, the French Rothschilds were then negotiating a new Russian bond issue. "The expectation of profit and, as Alphonse Rothschild claims, the hope of obtaining better conditions of existence for Russia's Jews, have led the Paris Rothschilds to participate in talks concerning the loan." He added a malicious comment: "The fact that the London Rothschilds are staying clear of the operation shows how these famous Jews are wily and know how to save a way out for themselves. . . ."[18]

But it was a question of patriotism—of serving what France considered to be its higher interests. Soon Alphonse had contributed 10,000 francs to finance a Franco-Russian celebration during the visit of a Russian fleet in autumn 1893; the instigator of the fund appeal was a French Jew who announced that as "adopted sons," Jews had to show they were "twice as French as everyone else."[19] The organ of the indefatigable Edouard Drumont would report slyly that on the unexpected death of Czar Alexander in November 1894, flags flew at half mast over the Rothschild bank on Rue Laffitte.[20]

Rothschild archives do show a return to business as usual, with a loan in the very month of transition between the oppressive Alexander and his seemingly amiable successor, his son Nicholas II, launched by a consortium headed by the Rothschilds of Paris, London, and Frankfurt (and Bleichröder in Berlin), another in July 1896 (again with the Paris Rothschilds leading the way).[21]

"The press has announced the Great Cross that Alphonse received from the Emperor of Russia," Gustave announced proudly to his London cousins in September 1896. "This is an indirect response to the latest attacks against us by Mr. Drumont. . . ."[22] Then it was Alphonse's turn to report the October visit of the Czar to Paris, during which he had two opportunities to approach Nicholas, once at the Elysées palace reception to which Alphonse had been invited as president of the Consistory, later at the Opera, with France's president of the Republic Félix Faure. He found the Czar dignified but reserved, with no particular grudge against a Rothschild. Further letters echo this favorable impression, confirming Alphonse's high hopes for Franco-Russian alliance.[23]

Alas for Alphonse, and for Russia's Jews, Czar Nicholas was to show himself no less oppressive than his fierce father had been, although perhaps less obviously so.

It was a time of reshuffling of the European deck, the forging of new alliances, the dissolution of old ones, and almost always finance was a weapon. Thus in the last years of the 1880s, when Italy seemed to be moving ever closer to the Austro-German coalition, French banks at the behest of their government unloaded their Italian securities, creating havoc in that country's economy; the Rothschilds, as the dominant force in Italian bond issues, were implicated.[24]

In France itself, the race to corner strategic metals in colonial territories, notably copper and nickel, was creating a new hierarchy in the banking community, with dizzying ascensions—and thunderous falls. One of the victims was a bank called Comptoir d'Escompte de Paris, whose director, Eugène Denfert-Rochereau, before shooting himself, allegedly informed a friend that it was all the fault of the Rothschilds and he could prove it. In fact, the fault was poor management of investments; no one outside the anti-Semitic pack took the Denfert-Rochereau story seriously.[25] There was scandal enough in the colonies, where strategic metals were being mined by hard-labor convicts, later by coolies, and no venture capitalist came out of the Pacific territories with clean hands. The Rothschilds had the good sense to keep their distance from the major financial scandal of the last years of the century, the collapse of the Panama Canal Company, in which a number of prominent French Jews were implicated.[26]

And yet so little seemed beyond their range. That Americans were mining and coining silver and using it for trade was upsetting to gold-minded Europeans like the French Rothschilds, and was the subject of anxious exchanges with their British cousins. This from Alphonse to London in December 1890: "I hope that the present crisis will be a lesson to the Americans, and that these gentlemen will understand that they cannot do without Europe as they had insanely imagined they could, and that they will have some consideration for citizens of the old world."[27]

When Alphonse and Gustave won the Derby in 1890 with a horse named Heaume ("Helmet"), a Paris paper took the opportunity to write a brief "Man of the Day" profile of Alphonse. Peasants got his name wrong, the article began, and called him Roi de Childe— King of Childe; there was no such kingdom, of course, but the story did indicate the extent of their respect for this financial monarch. When Heaume came in first, grumbling was heard among losing bettors that water always goes to the river. This was unjust, said the

author of the profile, for the family stable at Meautry (near Trouville on the Seine estuary) hadn't enjoyed much success up to now.
As for Alphonse, he was a banker but he'd like to be known for
other things—art collecting, for instance. He was also a famous
philanthropist, in private life "charming, and most courteous, even
if somewhat dry, a bit rigid."[28]

Even a police informer could be mellow about Alphonse. The
baron took a holiday on the Riviera in the autumn of 1891, his
movements there, as everywhere, observed and reported. The agent
noted that Alphonse boarded the 10:47 train from Nice to Monte
Carlo each morning, although he did little gambling at the casino
there. "At the Nice station he is known for his simple behavior,"
he reported—as if expecting more. "He waits for his train seated
on a bench, like a common mortal, while smoking a cigar. But he
is watched carefully by the train conductor, who follows his every
movement, always ready to open the reserved compartment when
Mr. de Rothschild decides to climb aboard."[29] (Of course, this *was*
the Paris-Lyon-Méditerranée line, a Rothschild company.)

We can catch the baron at home, thanks to Elisabeth de Gramont, daughter of Agénor, Duc de Gramont, and Margaretha Alexandrine von Rothschild (herself the daughter of Mayer Carl of
the Vienna family). Just seventeen, Elisabeth owed her presence at
one of Alphonse's Tuesday evenings to her mother's migraine;
instead, her father took *her* along to Rue Saint-Florentin (the Talleyrand house on Place de la Concorde, which James had acquired
as a residence). And she got to sit at Alphonse's right; it was he
who had the Tokay and the Romanée-Conti poured for her. This
remark was addressed to her: "I don't know if you agree with me,
but I only like carp when they've been marinated in spirits for
three days." Young, she could be astonished by nothing; she remembered feeling the distance that separated the privileged few
from the guests consigned to the lower end of the table. Guests who
that evening included Léon Say and other old friends, some of
them racetrack familiars, fellow clubmen, pretty women, in a setting of Sèvres porcelain, paintings by Raphael and Gainsborough.
Through the windows facing Place de la Concorde, "the rare
coaches and cabs sliding by accentuated the silence."

Alphonse himself she found "somewhat diminished by age,"

though affable, even charming. If the style of the house was voluntarily sophisticated, a bit playful, it was thanks in part to Baroness Laurie (Leonora), and their daughter Béatrix Ephrussi. Austere director of the Banque de France he might be, Alphonse seemed a man of worldly pleasures first and foremost. His young cousin thought she could read "nobility of character" in his features; it added to his authority.[30]

Surely there had never been a benefactor possessing both his means and his will. Thus when the founders of the Institut Pasteur—a groundbreaking center for research and vaccination—approached him with their revolutionary project, he had to be the first contributor. National causes, disasters affecting workers and peasants, never failed to draw an appropriate response. He also had his list of artists and musicians who received regular subsidies.[31]

Gossip—stimulated by Drumont—continued to insist that the Rothschilds subsidized newspapers favorable to them as well as potential troublemakers (such as the anarchists).[32] It must have been hard to miss the flamboyant posters covering the walls of Paris in May 1892, on the day Alphonse's niece Juliette, Gustave's daughter, married Baron Emmanuel Leonino. "Long live Rothschild!" the broadside declaimed, in language as flamboyant as its typography:

> Long live Rothschild, who had the genius to accumulate the century's most prodigious fortune!

Should this be mistaken for irony, the message continued:

> Long live Rothschild, whose hand is so often outstretched to the disinherited . . . !

The poster comes with a story. The text had been written by a certain Léon Hayard, publisher of polemical tracts, whose specialty of the moment was satirical treatment of the Panama Canal financial scandal. On May 25, according to a police report, Alphonse de Rothschild received the visit of an "individual" who asked him to pay for the "Long Live Rothschild" poster. Alphonse refused to do so. So printer-publisher Hayard hired twenty street vendors to sell a broadside headlined "Down With the Jews!" and himself made his way to the synagogue on Rue de la Victoire for the marriage ceremony. Standing on the opposite sidewalk, Hayard shouted "Down with the Jews!" until he was arrested.[33]

For a man who preferred to stay out of the papers, Alphonse was soon to get himself very much in. It was summertime, Alphonse and family were vacationing on the north shore of Brittany at Dinard, then a fashionable beach resort. They had rented a manor with a clifftop vista, and there an earnest writer named Jules Huret found him. As Huret was to remember, he had climbed a circling path, opened an unlocked if imposing gate, and given his card to "a colossus" of a white-gloved servant. He was about to meet "Rothschild"! "Even if you hear the name a hundred times a day," he reflected, "even if Mr. Drumont spends his time cursing it, it still rings out with an echo of distant legend, something mysterious, immense and fantastic like other dazzling names evoking grandeur, Croesus, Golconda [fabled diamond center of India], gold mines, bullion . . . Rothschild!" He remembered that the name was one of the first that struck his infant's ears, along with childhood fairy tales; when he demanded an expensive toy, his mother would reply, "Do you really think I have Rothschild's money?"

Now, in Dinard, the servant ushered him into a smallish room facing the sea. And there was the baron himself—dressed more for town than for a bathing beach. "Of average height, slender," Huret was to remember. "Silvered hair, rather long, . . . whitened sidewhiskers, fluttering, a white mustache too, shaved chin, pink complexion, prominent cheekbones, a long nose a bit flattened on the bridge; only the lively blue eyes, prominent, recall his race." The visitor decided that "his features taken as a whole show strong will, energy, gravity."

Huret told Alphonse that he was doing a series of articles for *Le Figaro* on labor and the Socialist movement. Straight off, Rothschild dismissed the very idea of working-class dissension, of conflict between capital and labor. "I am certain that workers—I speak in general terms—are quite satisfied with their condition, that they're not complaining and not interested in socialism," so Jules Huret quoted him. Of course there were agitators, said the baron, and one had to distinguish between good and bad workers. "So it is absolutely false to think good workers are demanding an eight-hour day; those who want it are the lazy and incapable. . . ." The others were quite prepared to work ten or twelve hours a day, "the time they judge necessary for their needs and those of their children." And if they worked only eight hours—"Do you know what most of them would do? They'd drink!"

Alphonse said these things simply, in flowing speech, remarked Huret, with a high-pitched voice, a trace of an English accent in the pronunciation of certain consonants. As he spoke, the interviewer noted "the crossed legs, black socks rolled under his trousers, thick half-boots loosely laced." He smoked a bad cigar that wouldn't burn; from time to time, a bit of ash dropped onto his vest all the same.

There would be more probing questions. Didn't the accumulation of capital in the hands of a small group, the merchant bankers for example, threaten a social revolution that would mark the end of capitalism?

What "merchant bankers"? "Some people are richer, some less rich, that's all!" declared his host. "Some are richer today and will be poorer tomorrow; everything varies." Huret could not have been surprised to hear Rothschild's praise of capital, or even his conviction that as a rule everyone had the wealth his intelligence and energy had earned for him, no more and no less. (The baron also pointed out that it was the socialist Saint-Simon who had said, "To each according to his ability, to each according to his achievement.") For injustice Rothschild knew a remedy: the strike. He was all for that right.

Anti-Semitism? He saw it as on a par with anticapitalism, and the work of the same people; whether directed against Jews or not, anticapitalism would ruin the nation.

As for Rothschild wealth—he had seen the references to his three billion francs—"It's madness!" Real happiness, all the same, derived from work. But what about those who hadn't worked and were rich all the same, through inheritance? It was to be the interviewer's final question.

"Are you married?" Alphonse countered.

"Not yet," replied the twenty-eight-year-old writer.

"Well, when you marry and have children, you won't allow them to attack the idea of inheritance." He smiled. Huret took his leave.[34]

The interview would not appear in Le Figaro until mid-September, in a three-column story at the top of that popular daily's front page, but its explosive charge had lost none of its force in the interim. The austere Le Temps was one of the first of Figaro's sister papers to express alarm over the "singular" nature of the interview process, the likelihood of "unfortunate consequences" to interviewer and interviewee both. For Jules Huret, Le Temps's editorialist warned, did not portray the Rothschild they knew, a man with "a judgment subtle enough to understand public opinion, and especially, given his financial position, a keen sense of caution." Could he have said, "with blissful optimism," that work is the only true happiness (which was more or less what Huret said he heard Rothschild say)?

The only certain thing, concluded the editorialist, was that the baron smoked a cigar that wouldn't burn.[35]

Alphonse also saw the problem. He sent off a letter to Figaro's editor-in-chief. Of course he had received the journalist. "He found me, as he himself said, smoking a bad cigar, not a very favorable condition for resolving complicated social questions." There had been a relaxed conversation; reported a month later, one can understand that the writer's memory proved faulty—without this reflecting on his good faith. For the baron hardly believed that all was for the best in the best of all worlds—not when there was "so much suffering we overlook no opportunity to alleviate."[36]

Edouard Drumont, whose bête noire (and whose bread and butter) remained Rothschild, was not going to let that pass. In a front-page editorial in La Libre Parole, the daily newspaper he had founded in April 1892 largely as a vehicle for his Rothschild fixation, he quoted extensively from Huret's text, exclaiming with irony that he and his friends must have been wrong to launch a newspaper in behalf of exploited workers—since Rothschild says there is no social problem, that everybody is happy.

Then Drumont became the real Drumont. "One finds it hard to imagine . . . a Frankfurt Jew dismissing with such insolence the workers before whom he will tremble when the people, betrayed for so long by false democrats in the pay of Israel, at last comprehend the nobility and the justice of the work of liberation undertaken by us."[37]

DREYFUS?

*E*ven a hunting accident that was to cost Alphonse an eye provided an opportunity for Edouard Drumont, whose daily newspaper and constant stream of books owed so much to the existence of the Rothschild family; Drumont was the parasite that lives only thanks to a particular host organism. The accident occurred on December 19, 1892, a day of heavy fog over Ferrières, but some thirty hunters went out all the same. In midafternoon, when the hunt was drawing to a close, a shot ricocheted, striking the host in the left eye; in an instant his face was covered with blood. "Nothing to worry about," Alphonse told his fellow hunters—or words to that effect. They escorted him to the station, where they boarded the regular train for Paris. By ten that night an announcement was handed out at the Rue Saint-Florentin: the victim's condition was "satisfactory."

Next morning the doctors were less optimistic. A small pellet of shot had caused a hernia of the iris, and although the iris had been removed, the pellet had not been recovered; apparently it was lodged deeper still. And the optic nerve had been affected; Alphonse had lost sight in that eye.[1] Family legend had it that Alphonse could have identified the inexperienced hunter whose shot had destroyed his eye, but that he would never say that he knew (and remained on friendly terms with the involuntary aggressor).[2]

So, commented *La Libre Parole,* the "king of the Jews" had gotten lead in his eye. "Decidedly, Jews ought to give up playing gentlemen," the writer snorted. "Aristocratic sports don't suit them, and they'd be better off sticking to their age-old role of money-lenders, the only one in which they are in their place and at ease."[3] A month later Drumont's paper quoted a press report on the victim's progress: "The baron goes out for an hour each day, either by coach or on foot; a bandage covers his entire head, except for his right eye, which is absolutely intact."[4]

This only a day after an appeal published in *La Libre Parole* against the reelection of Alphonse as treasurer of a farmers' organization, the Société des Agriculteurs de France. ("Don't vote for the Jewish baron," a member of the association was quoted.) Gleefully the paper was able to report in February that although officers of the society were traditionally reelected without incident, this time Alphonse had gotten only 2,500 votes, 500 fewer than fellow members of the executive.[5]

Edouard Drumont is only partly responsible for the anti-Semitism of the final decades of the nineteenth century, and of course he was also its product. He was a singular character all the same. Thanks to Edmond de Goncourt's precise note-taking, Drumont can be examined in close-up, so that we need not depend on bundles of yellowed newspapers to figure him out. At a dinner Goncourt hears Drumont wishing he had enough money to organize a "mutiny" against the Jews. "Yes," explains Drumont, "after some days of whipping up the crowd, on a particularly feverish day, there'd be a rallying point on Place de la Concorde"—near the Rothschild house, in other words. "And from there . . . the smashing of windowpanes and breaking down of doors; and if by chance Alphonse de Rothschild is caught . . . you know what I mean!"[6]

Another time Goncourt encounters Léon Daudet, son of the novelist, who has just been with Drumont, and finds him complaining that he has been poisoned by Jews: Drumont and the Marquis [Antonio] de Morès, another professional anti-Semite, have become ill after drinking water at an electoral meeting. Drumont tells Daudet that he expects to go to prison soon, for he has sworn to join a crowd of militant anti-Semites demonstrating on May Day in front of several Rothschild houses. Truly Drumont was obsessed, and it hardly mattered that he failed to demonstrate on May Day, although in the privacy of his journal Goncourt was to mock him for his timidity. Léon Daudet did tell Goncourt that the army was now protecting Alphonse's home on Rue Saint-Florentin.[7]

"This Jewish race is really a contemptible race"—thus Drumont began a typical front-page editorial about "these lousy Yids." This time Drumont alleged a Rothschild plot to have him assassinated, named a Rothschild bank official who allegedly paid off journalists to defame him, and dared his targets to fight a duel. In "the great Jewish families," he concludes somewhat incongruously, "all the women are whores and the men cowards. . . ."[8]

The hysteria had been building ever since *La France juive.* Drumont fed the flames with successive books, with a daily newspaper dedicated to his prejudices. To Drumont, the Eiffel Tower, which had just been erected in Paris, was the symbol of these detested times, the new monument having "as its mission to be as insolent and idiotic as modern life is, with its stupid height to crush the Paris of our fathers, the Paris of memories, the old houses and the churches, Notre-Dame and the Arch of Triumph, prayer and glory. . . ."[9] That from a book appropriately titled *La fin d'un monde.* The very next year, in *La dernière bataille,* Drumont described Alphonse as a "white rat." "This rodent takes advantage of the situation, making himself into a water rat to chew up an entire fleet, then undermines a whole city in racing through the cellars and climbing through the attics." To do him in, one would have to demolish the house or sink the ship.

He sees anti-Semitism gaining (the year is 1890). Alphonse's son Edouard was turned down when he applied for membership in the Jockey and Union clubs; ten years earlier he'd have been received with applause. But Drumont seems to be contradicting himself when he goes on to demonstrate that Alphonse is more than ever the master of government and finance. Jews, he concludes, were preparing the destruction of France "with a kind of mathematical precision."[10]

That same year a reporter called on Alphonse de Rothschild and Zadoc Kahn, the new grand rabbi of France (appointed by decree of the President of the Republic, read out at the Rue de la Victoire synagogue by Alphonse as president of the Consistory). What did they think of the current wave of anti-Semitism? "I am in no way affected by the outpourings of Mr. Drumont," Alphonse told the reporter. "You tell me that in this book he accuses me, or rather the whole Rothschild family, of having gotten away with three billion francs. I can only shrug. It's as if I were accused of stealing the towers of Notre-Dame. Do such accusations merit a reply?" He trusted the good sense of the public. As for Zadoc Kahn, he didn't feel authorized to say anything at all, preferring to avoid a discussion that might create "bitterness."[11]

Violence became frequent. Even Alphonse's son Edouard, not quite twenty-two years old, fought a duel (with a former classmate, then a count), coming out of it with a superficial cut.[12] The quarrel of the young men dated back to schooldays, Alphonse was to explain to his London cousins. "His behavior on the field, I'm happy to say, was excellent, and for a youngster he showed lots of cheek. . . . Personally I spent rather a bad quarter of an hour but the affair in itself was both useful and honorable for Edouard, for in France at his entry into society it's good for a young man to show that he doesn't lack nerve."[13]

More precisely to be laid at Drumont's doorstep was the death of a French officer, Capt. Armand Mayer, who in protest against Drumont's campaign against Jews in the army had issued a challenge in June 1892. It was one of the three separate duels that came out of Drumont's campaign; in this one the cause of the anti-Semites was taken up by the half-crazed Marquis de Morès, then chief of a band of anti-Jewish toughs whose improbable uniform was cowboy dress. In the duel Morès killed Captain Mayer, to the applause of fellow anti-Semites but apparently not to public acclaim.[14]

Drumont descended still another notch. In an article in *La Libre Parole* a Drumont associate observed menacingly that the workers of Paris, descendents of earlier revolutionaries, already had their eye on the Rothschild bank on Rue Laffitte; they were also watching some other buildings, and here the writer listed Alphonse's home on Rue Saint-Florentin along with twelve other Rothschild residences in Paris, in each case specifying the house number (just as Nazi collaborationist journalists would do in occupied Paris half a century later).[15]

Police files contain further evidence of how conspicuous a target a Rothschild could be. There were attempts at blackmail (otherwise "the citizen Rothschild . . . will be punished with one or several bombings," as one such threat—signed "The Committee"—expressed it).[16] In April 1894 the Paris police investigated a rumored plot to assassinate the baron.[17]

Later—two decades later—a Drumont collaborator, with twelve duels and half a dozen court convictions to his credit, withdrew from the crusade and decided to confess. Raphaël Viau described how he had left his native Brittany for Paris expressly to join Drumont. He tells how Drumont's fanatic ally Morès plotted to abduct Alphonse de Rothschild, then to demand a ten-million-franc ransom for the benefit of workers; if their emissary had been arrested, Alphonse would have been killed. As for Drumont, his contribution to violence was a suggestion that Viau challenge one of the Rothschilds to a duel.

Then when a poacher was killed on the estate of Henri de Rothschild (descendent of Nathaniel, the London Rothschild who settled in France), Drumont assigned Viau to write a series of "sensational" anti-Rothschild exposés. Although Viau discovered that the poacher killed by the Rothschild guards was a violent drunkard who made his living from petty thefts, he wrote the articles Drumont's way. For a period of four years, Henri de Rothschild was "assigned" to Viau, as Drumont assigned other prominent targets to other staff members. On one occasion Viau's Rothschild target sued, and won.[18]

With a foil like Edouard Drumont dominating center stage, the quotidian anti-Semitism of less violent writers seemed almost banal; the banality opened the door to the utilization of anti-Semitism in politics. Church-sponsored publications designed for devout Catholics raised their pitch; Le Pèlerin joined La Croix in emitting a constant flow of anti-Jewish news and views, while a caricature of a Rothschild, in La Croix, anticipated what the Nazis would produce.[19]

Banalization by contrast (contrast with the gratuitous violence of the Drumonts) made it possible for a Maurice Barrès, author and political militant, to be hailed as a patriot despite his introduction of anti-Semitism into otherwise respectable political discourse; one could, with Barrès, express fear of "the kingdom of Israel," "the Jewish genius," and Rothschild himself ("Everything ends up each morning on the table of such a man") without being a raving lunatic à la Edouard Drumont.[20]

In the agitated climate created by the self-proclaimed anti-Semites, even the arrest of a Jewish army officer on treason charges could only seem another episode. When Jews were *already* being blamed for all of the nation's ills, how could the crime attributed to Capt. Alfred Dreyfus be worse? The skeptical reader need only refer to the public prints of the time, to see how imperceptibly the temperature rose between the day before and the day after the announcement of Dreyfus's arrest. In Edouard Drumont's own daily newspaper, a Dreyfus could hardly be guiltier than a Rothschild: "Jews like Dreyfus," he told his readers, "are probably only second-rate spies who work for Jewish financiers; they are wheels of a great Jewish plot that would deliver us body and soul to the enemy. . . ."[21]

For the shock troops of the anti-Jewish crusade, in other words, a Dreyfus affair was only another aspect of an unending Rothschild affair. And so the gutter press that flourished in the wake of *l'affaire* felt it necessary to link the army traitor to the banker; in the popular mythology, Dreyfus had to be a protégé if not a relative of Rothschild.[22]

"You know very well"—Drumont again—"that in this era when the Jews are our masters, one doesn't shoot a coreligionist of Rothschild in the back." Apparently some readers of *La Libre Parole* did want to see Dreyfus shot in the back.[23]

On October 13, 1894, French army captain Alfred Dreyfus, assigned to the general staff in Paris, was called to the War Ministry for what he understood was a routine matter. There he was asked to copy a dictated text in his own handwriting—in fact a list of reports on French military movements and equipment. The original list happened to be a spy's offer of intelligence information to the German military attaché in Paris (torn up and simply dropped into a wastebasket by the imprudent German officer). When his fellow officers decided that Captain Dreyfus's script resembled that of the spy message, he was arrested, accused of high treason. *L'affaire* was under way.

It would turn out, of course, that someone else had scribbled the original message, and that Dreyfus was innocent. But before that could be established, he was banished to the harshest, most desolate of penal colonies—Devil's Island, off the coast of French Guiana—while bad faith and prejudice led to a succession of forgeries by high-ranking officers. Defending Dreyfus, the already famous novelist Emile Zola was himself convicted of defaming the army. The officers who suspected and condemned Dreyfus, those who fabricated or covered up evidence to support their case, were motivated by anti-Semitism; in the dozen years that elapsed between Dreyfus's arrest and his pardon, France would be torn by religious and political strife on a scale not known since the Revolution a century earlier.

But in those first weeks of that affair, how could a French patriot believe Dreyfus innocent, how not trust the army? Alphonse de Rothschild was a French patriot, a respecter of French institutions—"more French than the French," a grandson would call him.[24] So his reaction should not surprise. "A very regrettable event has just taken place which is causing great grief to Jewish society as a whole and especially to Jews in the army," Alphonse informed his London cousins on November 2. "A senior Jewish officer, a Mr. Dreyfus, has been arrested for treason. The behavior of this officer is all the more inexplicable because he is considered a person of great merit, he has no money problems, and he is not known to be a gambler or a libertine. To what motive [can one] attribute this criminal turn of mind?"

No explanation had been furnished by the War Ministry, explained Alphonse; one could only guess what might have happened. Some said there had been a plot against Dreyfus; that would be good news, "but meanwhile the event is no less deplorable and is reviving anti-Semitism—which was dying out. We aren't lucky with our fellow Jews, for the day doesn't go by without someone asking us for money in order to suppress another scandal."[25] Historians of that time make it clear that the Rothschild reaction was typical of the Jewish establishment, and indeed of the public as a whole, for there was as yet no reason to doubt Dreyfus's guilt. Prudence dictated silence.[26]

The court-martial opened on December 19 in Paris. There was little to hold against Captain Dreyfus apart from the apparent similarity of his handwriting to that found on the list of intelligence reports, but that was enough for a conviction. Dreyfus would be stripped of rank, sentenced to a life of hard labor. Alphonse summed it up for his cousins in London on December 24: "One can only bow to the sentence pronounced by a group of officers whose impartiality must be considered above suspicion despite the absolute secrecy of the hearing. It is no less a most unfortunate affair, not only for the captain, but for all Jews in the army."[27]

Given the feeling that the army could do no wrong, the task of Dreyfus's defenders was Herculean. The condemned officer's luck was that an honest officer not blinded by prejudice found the real spy, and was willing to fight for truth. On its side, the Dreyfus family lobbied incessantly for a new trial, and soon political liberals were openly defending the convict. But in the political climate of the last decade of the century—a climate largely prepared by the Drumonts and their allies both less respectable and more respectable, each piece of evidence uncovered by the Dreyfusards was promptly countered by anti-Dreyfusards.

Then when Maj. Georges Picquart—one of the original investigators—stumbled on evidence proving that the real German agent was Maj. Ferdinand Esterhazy, even the Rothschilds knew a thing or two about this prodigal man-about-town. In 1892, following the *Libre Parole*'s campaign against Jews in the army, Edouard Drumont was challenged by one of them, Capt. Ernest Crémieu-Foa; Esterhazy agreed to serve as one of the Jewish captain's seconds. (The Marquis de Morès provided the same service to Drumont, before going on to kill Captain Mayer in another duel.) The combat was violent; Drumont's doctor stepped in to suspend it. And the spendthrift Major Esterhazy proceeded to ingratiate himself both with the Drumont crowd *and* the Rothschilds.

In June 1894—four months before the secret agent's message to the German embassy—Esterhazy had written both to Alphonse de Rothschild and his youngest brother, Edmond (who had been his lycée classmate). He was desperate for funds, he said; because he was considered friendly to Jews, his in-laws refused to help him, and so he could no longer support his ailing wife and small daughters; he'd kill them and commit suicide if no one came to his rescue. "I'd go as far as committing a crime rather than allow them to die of hunger."

He attached another letter—later proved to be a forgery—supposedly written to him by his uncle: "You defended Jews and you are a victim of money. It is the finger of God." The Rothschilds decided to help this impossible man—because he had seemed a friend to Captain Crémieu-Foa, and of course had been a classmate of Edmond (who had helped him with money more than once).[28]

Soon after writing the Rothschilds, Major Esterhazy paid his first call on the German military attaché in Paris. To save his wife and children from starvation, said he, he wished to sell military secrets to the Germans.[29]

FIN DE SIECLE

In 1894, at the beginning of that first Dreyfus year, a Paris daily published one of those eulogies of Baron Alphonse that readers of the conservative press had learned to expect. "Early risers drawn to the boulevard by chance or habit have often observed, almost always walking alone, a gentleman with slender features framed by white sidewhiskers, lip hidden by a mustache just as white." His "simple clothing," his "modest bearing," would make it difficult for passersby to divine the importance of the man sharing their promenade. Then comes the moment when "he leaves as if regretfully the street on which he feels more at home than in a building where in a short while hundreds of visitors, employees, bankers, spongers of all sorts will be besieging him."

The bank on Rue Laffitte, wrote the journalist Jules Meulemans, was a door open to everyone. Each gesture of the baron was remarked, the slightest error forbidden him, for immediately it would be seized upon by "the cohort which, under the cloak of anti-Semitism, has declared war on all those who through their intellectual capacity have raised themselves above the level of their fellow citizens."

The writer went on to enumerate the baron's titles: member of the board of the Banque de France and commander in the Legion of Honor, he had also been elected to the Academy of Fine Arts, an honor of which he was proudest, the learned assemblies of this body representing for him both engagement and relaxation. For truly Rothschild cared about art, encouraged contemporary painters by buying their production. His salon was a forum for those distinguished in the arts and letters. As for good works, would that everyone gave the same proportion of his income to charity. "If this would not by itself abolish poverty, it would at least be good socialism."[1]

He was a very accessible person, this man who walked the boulevard alone. Everybody knew where he worked, where he lived (if they did not, they could always find out in *La Libre Parole*). Everybody didn't necessarily know, in August 1895, that the baron and his family were on holiday at their favorite hotel in Trouville, the grandiose Hôtel de Paris facing the beach, walking the boards, occasionally driving out to the racetrack. So when a strange packet was delivered in the mail on a Saturday morning— delivered not to the bank but to the Rothschild residence on Rue Saint-Florentin—it was forwarded to Rue Laffitte, to be opened by one of the baron's trusted managers. He hesitated because of the words *Personal* and *Please Forward* on the plain white envelope, but its rigidity suggested that it contained nothing more personal than an invitation.

The bank officer inserted his steel letter opener, found two stiff cards, and began to remove them, upon which the packet exploded. He was struck full-face, and was to lose an eye. Investigators identified the explosive as mercuric fulminate, a product not easy to obtain; the letter bomb was the work of an expert. Was he also an anarchist, an anti-Semite?

Police files show that no effort was spared. One agent had been infiltrated onto the staff of *La Libre Parole,* and turned in reports under the code name "Aspic." He listened as Drumont's staff discussed the event, telling one another that the bomber was either clumsy or stupid—to think that Alphonse de Rothschild opened his own mail.

Soon the letter bomb had given birth to imitations, packets with explosives, even a farce—an envelope containing little else than fragments of a cigarette. A police agent in the anarchist movement heard some of the "companions" attribute the bomb to another anarchist—and approve what he had tried to do. The informant noted that some time earlier an anarchist had preached the efficacy of letter bombs to younger men looking for action. But another companion was heard to say that it wasn't a letter bomb that would get Alphonse, "but a revolver and a dagger at close range." We know from police reports that protective surveillance of all the Rothschilds was stepped up. And although the hunt was widened—as far as anarchist circles in Geneva—no one was heard to boast that he had done the deed.[2]

Alphonse lost no time in getting back to Paris, to help care for his unlucky manager, "telling him over and over again," says Constance Battersea, "that he, his chief, ought to have been in his place."[3]

After Alfred Dreyfus was convicted and dispatched to the desolate, debilitating South American penal colony in December 1894, the case seemed forgotten. His name vanished from the incendiary pamphlets and journals of the lunatic fringe—but Rothschild's did not. In March 1896, Drumont's daily was to cheer the defeat of Alphonse de Rothschild for reelection as treasurer of the Société des Agriculteurs de France (by a vote of 2,782 to 1,949). "It's not the slaughter of the Jewish Hydra," the editorial said, "but it's the slicing off of one of the tentacles of the octopus; the others will follow."[4]

There were anti-Rothschild demonstrations outside the offices of La Libre Parole, and in front of the Rothschild bank. Once, when police got wind of the plans of anti-Semitic students to march on the house on Rue Saint-Florentin, they quickly blocked the route. Drumont published a sketch showing a detachment of police agents protecting Alphonse's home at night, and offered a detailed description of the activities of the special squad assigned to escort Rothschild and to watch over his mail.[5]

In November 1896, Drumont's Rothschild hachet man Raphaël Viau published a mocking report on the opening of a small police station at the Rothschild house, to which forty officers had been posted for round-the-clock surveillance. The facility was inaugurated, according to Viau, at a banquet offered by the baron and in his presence. "At two [in the morning], these gentlemen were so merry that they suggested nothing less than to rush off to attack the editors of *La Libre Parole*. But they were told gently that for the moment their job was to watch over the sleep of their host."[6] It was the very moment that Commandant Picquart, now in charge of the army's intelligence department, became convinced that the author of the famous spy list—the document on the basis of which Drey-fus was convicted of treason—was actually Major Esterhazy. Pic-quart's discovery was not publicized; for his pains he was assigned to a post far from Paris.[7]

The man to watch remained Alphonse de Rothschild. Thus on November 20, 1896, on a satisfactory trading day at the Paris stock market, a rumor suddenly exploded on the floor: the baron Al-phonse had been struck by apoplexy, and was already dead. Bro-kers and their assistants rushed to their stations, unloading what shares they could, panic feeding panic. The point, of course, was to unload stocks with which the Rothschilds were involved, such as diamond and gold mines, South Africa's De Beers, and Ríotinto, but not only those; French state obligations also began to slide.

Brokers who dealt regularly with the Rothschilds dashed into the street and hopped cabs to bridge the 900 yards or so separating the Bourse from 19 Rue Laffitte—to find the sixty-nine-year-old baron at his desk; in a flash they were out on the street again, the fastest of them doing the round trip in ten minutes. The panic was dampened.

It was assumed that the false report had been a maneuver of those playing the market for a fall; as it was Friday afternoon, Sabbath eve for Jews, one could have assumed that the baron would not be found at his desk, and thus his good health could not have been confirmed. The rumor had been nailed quickly (the police commissioner responsible for the stock exchange would take credit for that). Press reports reminded readers that willful propagation of rumors was punishable under the penal code.[8]

Suddenly ex-Captain Dreyfus returned to the front pages. Long months of careful investigation by honest officers, parallel efforts by a growing legion of Dreyfusards, had made the indictment of Major

Esterhazy inevitable, and so much the worse for those senior officers who still insisted that Dreyfus was guilty, or that the honor of the army demanded confirmation of the original verdict, and never mind the details. The court-martial opened on January 10, 1898, in the same courtroom that had seen the disgrace of Alfred Dreyfus; the outcome could have been predicted by the respect shown Esterhazy and the mocking of Captain Dreyfus's brother Mathieu. "The verdict of the court-martial isn't yet known," Alphonse reported to his London cousins next day, "but one can only deplore these dissensions among soldiers of high rank which serve to discredit the general staff and cause great prejudice to military discipline."[9]

Not only would Esterhazy be acquitted, and by unanimous vote of the officer judges, but cries of "Death to the Jews!" would be heard from the select audience.[10] "The verdict pronounced yesterday will make you understand better than I myself could the state of mind of people belonging to the highest classes of society, nourished by devotion to honor," so Alphonse was to comment to London. "I wasn't surprised by the acquittal of Major Esterhazy, I was sure of it in advance. But I didn't expect the ovations accorded the hero of the hour. . . ." Two days later he was telling his cousins and associates, "We keep absolutely quiet, completely removed from politics and from the great men involved in them." He hoped only for an early end to the troubles—but didn't see that coming soon.[11]

Police informer "Aspic"—who had been watching the agitation from the Drumont side of the fence—turned in a report alleging that Alphonse had contributed to the pro-Dreyfus defense. The baron saw the campaign of the Dreyfusards as harmful to Jews but ceded to pressure, the agent added—although his contribution was small in monetary terms. "Aspic" 's information was certainly wrong.[12]

Even without the Rothschilds, the growing legion of angry men challenging the injustice of Captain Dreyfus's ordeal had now attained explosive dimensions. Credit Emile Zola for the detonation. By 1898 he was one of France's best-known authors, and one of its most prolific, with his suite of weighty novels exposing the secret (and not so secret) vices of French society; his reputation had long since spilled over France's borders. One of the novels was *L'Argent*, inspired by the collapse of Bontoux's Union Générale; in it Zola revealed considerable fear of Jewish bankers (his villain

Gunderman is a faintly disguised if implausible Alphonse de Roth-schild). But the developing anti-Semitism of the Drumonts brought a reaction from this deliberate thinker. In an article Zola an-nounced his growing realization that "these exclusive Jews, still badly assimilated into the nation, avid, racing after gold, are the work of Christians. . . . They have been shunted to infamous neigh-borhoods, as if lepers; it's hardly astonishing if in their ghetto prison they have consolidated family ties!"[13]

Nor is it astonishing that the desperate Dreyfusards sought out this man of goodwill; Zola's analytical mind did the rest. On Jan-uary 13, 1898, the daily *Aurore* opened its front page to a blistering "I Accuse" signed by Zola. In the guise of an open letter to the President of the Republic, the author identified high-ranking gen-erals as accomplices of the dishonest officers who had covered up the evidence of Dreyfus's innocence and Esterhazy's guilt—and in language that Zola said he knew made him vulnerable to indict-ment for libel. One general was an accomplice, "at least through weakness of mind, [in] one of the greatest iniquities of the cen-tury"; another had clear proof of Dreyfus's innocence in his hands—and had suppressed it.

The indictment would come. ("Mr. Zola will be prosecuted for the article he published yesterday," Alphonse reported, adding, "Busi-ness is suffering in this climate; the exchange remains inactive.")[14] For at last the Dreyfus affair—three years and a month after the captain's disgrace—had become a national affair; writing his cous-ins, the habitually calm Alphonse speaks of an atmosphere of crisis, although Paris was quiet, and the police were keeping it that way.[15]

Zola's trial opened in February, expected to take three days, "and then," wrote Alphonse, "I ardently desire that silence fall over this unfortunate Dreyfus affair concerning which nothing good can come at this tense moment. Once the Zola trial is over, perhaps one can go back to thinking about business."[16] So he followed the testimony closely, grateful that despite all the efforts of the judge, "the truth is coming out bit by bit." His instincts warned him that "whatever the outcome of the trial . . . the authority of our leaders will have received a great blow, French society will be divided into two camps ready to tear each other apart. . . ." The market con-tinued to feel the effects of it all.

Soon Alphonse was telling of anti-Semitic incidents on the streets, the looting of Jewish shops by gangs shouting "Long live the army!" A mob tried, without success, to enter a synagogue on the Rue de Tournelle.[17] Meanwhile the charade of a trial continued, the judge refusing to allow Zola's attorney to ask Esterhazy if he had been in contact with the German military attaché, on the pretext that he was protecting the "honor" of the nation. On February 23 Zola was convicted, sentenced to a year in jail; to the familiar cries of "Long live the army!" and "Death to the Jews!" one now heard a third: "Death to Zola!"[18]

In June, in the Paris city council, a letter from Alphonse and Gustave was read to the assembly: On the occasion of the first victory of their stable in the Grand Prix de Paris, the Rothschilds were donating a sum of 200,000 francs to be used in behalf of "the needy population of the city of Paris." At that a member of the council cried out, "What will the anti-Semites say about that?" One anti-Semite was sitting right there in the council; *he* called out, "It's just a lightning rod." But the gift was accepted.[19]

Another bombshell in the Dreyfus case: the suicide of Lt. Col. Joseph Henry, an intelligence officer accused of having fabricated a message purportedly sent by the Italian military attaché to his German counterpart—a message containing Dreyfus's name (and thus designed to be a convincing piece of evidence, used with great effect in the Zola trial). Henry was arrested at the end of August 1898, and next day was found dead—he had cut his own throat.

"In some ways," Baron Alphonse wrote to his London banking partners on September 1, "we can be pleased with the way this unfortunate Dreyfus affair is turning. . . . Obviously Jewish honor, since one has made a Jewish question of it, will be bleached of a stain, because a retrial of the case is now obviously called for." He foresaw more difficulties, although public opinion now demanded justice. But at what price? France was in "a veritable state of disarray, of total disorganization." Yet Alphonse was counting on the country's "elasticity."

Moreover, encouraging developments in the case gave the head of the French family an instant to reflect on its lessons. "The

Dreyfus affair is an episode of direct interest to Jews as well as to friends of law and humanity, but it is the pretext and not the true cause of the present agitation." The real issue was the struggle between partisans of "the ancient clerical regime" and "new ideals of religious tolerance and noninterference by the Church." Personally, Alphonse was certain that the liberal side would emerge victorious. That on September 19. But by September 23 he was attaching conditions to his optimistic appraisal. He feared that France was divided between the "military party" and the "republican party," the latter dominated by "socialists, partisans of disorder, declared enemies of bourgeois society." France sailed between Scylla and Charybdis, in other words, and who could know which was the more dangerous?[20]

There would be little time to think about it, with the anti-Dreyfusards having launched a wholly new campaign in Drumont's *La Libre Parole*, this time under the pretext of raising money for Colonel Henry's widow; there were thousands of individual contributions, and the opportunity for a new round of anti-Semitic attacks, if only in the letters accompanying the funds. In these letters Emile Zola was attacked thirty-six times, his editor Georges Clemenceau fifty-eight, Joseph Reinach (a leading Dreyfusard, and Jewish) 929 times. Even the Rothschilds, whose name appeared nowhere in the case and who were not even declared Dreyfus supporters, were cited in fourteen letters.[21]

An ominous note appeared in the society column of a Paris daily in November 1898: Baron Alphonse had stayed on in Ferrières for some ten days, "a touch of gout" having assumed worrying proportions. But the danger had passed, and the "chief of the powerful banking house" would soon return to Rue Laffitte.[22] Among the occasional rumors that punctuated the lives of the Rothschilds there was another report of the sudden death of Alphonse the following spring. "After investigation, the report proved untrue," a newspaper told its readers. "What is certain is that the great Jewish financier is very ill and that the state of his health is giving cause for alarm."[23]

EDOUARD

olonel Henry's amateurish forgery all but cried out for reexamination of the case of Alfred Dreyfus. The new trial was put on the calendar for August 1899 in the Breton capital of Rennes, and the ship bringing Dreyfus back from his tropical hell entered a Breton port. The proceedings took place in the presence of a convict diminished by years of inhuman confinement; surely this would be the final curtain on the Dreyfus affair.

This is to forget the continued reign of wrongheaded senior officers, those who had condemned Dreyfus and refused even to consider evidence pointing to the real culprit, senior officers who had punished honest colleagues who produced this evidence, condoning when they were not encouraging false witnesses and fabricated testimony. Fearing the confrontation, the real spy, Esterhazy, refused to testify and managed to slip out of the country.

Before the trial was over, Dreyfus's stubborn defense attorney, Fernand Labori, was gunned down in Rennes. And in this, his second court-martial, Alfred Dreyfus was once again found guilty, although by now the military judges had discovered "attenuating circumstances," reducing the sentence to ten years—to be served in a regular prison. French president Emile Loubet immediately issued a pardon, but only in 1906, seven years later, was the Rennes sentence actually overturned, restoring Dreyfus to his military rank; he could then retire, and in the grade of major. France moved into an uneasy truce.

At least once Alphonse's son Edouard, heir apparent to the Rothschild throne, experienced the bitter aftertaste. A certain Count de Lubersac issued a challenge to young Robert de Rothschild, Gustave's son, reminding him of a dispute they'd had in their school years, when both were too young for a duel. "But today have you not reached the age when one is personally responsible for his acts?" demanded Lubersac, himself then twenty-three years old. "To inform myself on this point," he added perfidiously, "I look in vain for your baptismal certificate in all the parishes of Paris." (Again that tired taunt.) Evoking "the disgust you and yours inspire me with," Lubersac demanded a duel. But if Robert was "too unworthy" to fight, then let him give 100,000 francs to the Ligue de la Patrie Française—a notoriously nationalistic, anti-Dreyfus movement.

When Lubersac's witnesses learned Robert's exact age—he had just turned twenty—they suggested arbitration rather than swords. Robert's witnesses rejected that, feeling that a twenty-year-old had a right to demand satisfaction (especially since Robert's father had asked them to serve the boy). Robert wrote the count: "When one finds a man old enough to be insulted, he's not too young to demand satisfaction."

Michel Ephrussi, Alphonse's son-in-law, entered the picture—but got no response from Lubersac. Then the hot-blooded count turned to Edouard, Alphonse's son, deciding that he was now head of the family. "I inform you of my contempt for you and warn you that whenever I meet you I shall throw my glove at your face."

So Edouard sent witnesses. The duel took place on the morning of April 12, 1900. Rothschild, now thirty-two, received a cut on the right forearm—a deep penetration some three inches long, according to the witnesses; it was described in the press as a superficial wound that didn't prevent him from having lunch at home or going out that afternoon.[1]

He was still at the center of things, old Alphonse. When Edouard Drumont's Rothschild specialist revealed that Rothschild had been laid low by an acute attack of gout—for Drumont's paper was "better informed and especially more rapidly informed about what goes on among the Great Jews than any gossip sheet in Israel's pay"—visitors mobbed the Rue Saint-Florentin, among them (said *La Libre Parole*) the whole French cabinet. There was a conference of Rothschild doctors, an official communiqué to announce improvement. If so, demanded the Drumont man, why the crowd at his bedside? The rumor was that Alphonse's heart was affected; he was, after all, seventy-four years old—an age that couldn't be reassuring to the entourage of the grandson of the famous Frankfurt "junk dealer" Mayer Amschel.[2]

He got better all the same. At the end of the year he could even take a winter holiday in London with the baroness. We know that from a telegram of December 23 sent by the special commissioner at the North station to the minister of the interior (and to the security services and the police prefect), reporting that the couple had boarded the train at 11:20 that morning.[3] Alphonse appeared to be living a normal life, a life whose high points could be followed in the pages of the polemical press. Thus *La Libre Parole* found Alphonse and his friends hunting on a Monday in January 1903, the day after the official closing of the season; they shot three hundred pheasants but couldn't eat all of them. ("The Jew, always a starver of the people, isn't always starving.") So Rothschild, of the "shopkeeping, swindling, mercantile" race, sent the birds to the central market, where a police officer had them seized and sent to a charity hospital. Rothschild, said Drumont's reporter, then grabbed the telephone to order the pheasants returned to the market, where they were put on sale again. Moral: "The Jew, poacher par excellence, who hunts, rapes, and plunders in a France that is not his, is above our laws."[4]

The Dreyfus affair was over, but not the Rothschild affair. A new police file was opened in August 1904 to deal with the discovery of a suspect package on a window ledge on the Rue de Mondovi side of the Rothschild residence on Place de la Concorde. It had all the signs of a bomb, with a cord that seemed to have been lighted; found at 3:30 A.M. by a policeman, it had been rushed to the municipal laboratory. There the package was found to contain herrings in an advanced state of decay.[5]

That year a pamphlet published by the Librairie Antisémite over the signature of one of Drumont's regular Rothschild reporters alleged that Alphonse was now worth ten billion francs (the equivalent of some 175 billion in our time). The author compared the sum to the billion francs declared some thirty-five years earlier on the death of Baron James. "Who would deny that the powerful baron, master as he is of the financial market, could without great effort double his fortune in ten years."[6]

Drumont and his men were less likely to comment when the Rothschilds *gave* money, but the event had a press all the same. The popular weekly *L'Illustration*, which was the *Life* of its day, published portraits of Alphonse, Gustave, and Edmond (the two oldest with white beards, the youngest with a black one) to accompany the announcement of a breakthrough in low-cost housing for workers. "A gift of ten million, something you don't hear every day," observed the reporter, "at least not in France, where the examples of American billionaires haven't taken root."

For the brothers were endowing a Rothschild Foundation for Social Hygiene, the money to be used to build low-rent housing. An enabling act had been voted as early as 1894, and many schemes had been drawn up; now the Rothschilds were to be the first to undertake a large-scale project. They would first sponsor a competition to find architects with new ideas in collective housing, then they would finance construction. The plan was to utilize the rent paid by low-income tenants for other nonprofit purposes.[7]

The Fondation Rothschild began with three lots in the eastern working-class districts of Paris, sinking unprecedented sums into planning and building; the program was pursued there and elsewhere until the outbreak of World War I, when tenants ceased to pay rent and maintenance became prohibitive. Henceforth the launching of new developments became the government's business.[8] But the pioneer work had been done, and these large-scale projects for workers' housing were to transform the Paris cityscape in the first half of the twentieth century. (In the second half, one can still come upon apartment compounds bearing the Rothschild name etched in stone.)

Still, in another of those tributes to Alphonse to which newspaper readers were accustomed, the coalition of anti-Rothschild forces was described. There were people who feared (and exaggerated) Rothschild power—these were the nationalists, the socialists, and the anarchists, as well as persons professing "intransigent Catholicism"; then of course there were the simple haters, said a writer in the popular *Gil Blas*. Through it all the Rothschilds remained serene, "an oasis of traditional and classic conservatism, once so dear to the French nobility." Approaching eighty, Alphonse had lived through many changes, and hoped to live long enough to see the end of the present agitation. The panegyric to Alphonse included his baroness: "Pleasant and charming, fair with all the beauty of Jewish women, manners of a rare distinction, captivating through an adorable nonchalance, good and kind, indifferent to her wealth. . . ."

The couple, the journalist went on, were now in semiretirement. When they entertained, it was to surround themselves with artists and scholars; their charity went to the likes of Louis Pasteur. Old Alphonse remained of "an agreeable approach, with a courtesy one seldom finds nowadays," with, "at bottom, a bit of the skepticism, half-mocking and half-tender, that comes to men who have lived a lot."[9]

They'd call it gout again; this time the attack took on more alarming proportions, and seventy-eight years *was* old. The illness that was to close Alphonse's life in the spring of 1905 was being followed as closely by *La Libre Parole* as by the police department; it was as if Edouard Drumont's existence depended on Rothschild's (and in a way it did). On the morning of May 20 the bulletin issued by the baron's doctors was succinct:

Notable improvement.
    The attack of gout seems to have passed. No further inflammation. Diminution of bronchitis. The night was peaceful.[10]

The wording would not have been different if designed to reassure a people about its chief of state.

He died quietly on the twenty-sixth of May, 1905, a Friday—Sabbath eve. The death made headlines. A visitor's book hastily opened at Rue Saint-Florentin filled up with the names of everyone who counted in Paris, including the President of the Republic, the prime minister, the chairmen of both houses of Parliament, ambassadors of the great powers.[11]

The police detachment assigned to Alphonse's home duly reported the removal of his body on Sunday evening, its destination the site of the family bank on Rue Laffitte: "No incident." Next morning, as the police observed, that street was mobbed as the funeral procession prepared to leave for the cemetery. A photograph captured the crowd outside the building draped in mourning, close family and friends top-hatted and on foot; one might recognize Alphonse's slender son Edouard wearing a handlebar mustache.[12] A poster entitled "The Paupers' Mourning" invited the poor of Paris to pay their last respects to this man who was the very "symbol of charity"; a newspaper reported that the appeal had been heeded, "and, among the dignitaries from the worlds of government and politics, diplomacy, aristocracy, and finance, one found so many of the underprivileged wishing to pay their last respects."[13]

Police headquarters had assigned ten inspectors to stand outside the offices of *La Libre Parole* on Boulevard Montmartre, to be ready just in case. But the commissioner in charge was able to report that nobody was even watching from the windows of that newspaper; "indeed the blinds were drawn." There were plenty of madmen as it was, including the author of a fake death notice sold by street vendors (printed at the shop of the late Léon Hayard, he who had shouted his denunciations on the sidewalk opposite the synagogue during the marriage of Alphonse's niece Juliette):

We have the immeasurable pleasure of inviting you to dance an enormous cakewalk [*sic*] of joy to celebrate the long-awaited croaking of the famous schemer

ALPHONSE DE ROTHSCHILD

EMPEROR OF GOLD, KING OF USURY

PRINCE OF BANKRUPTCY, DUKE OF SPECULATION

It was cruder than most such tracts. "The seven-branch candelabrum will be lighted. The candles will be made of wax from the single eye of the deceased."[14]

Edouard Drumont didn't wait for the funeral to publish another jeremiad in *La Libre Parole,* a rambling memoir of his own itinerary as the Rothschild flea. He couldn't have meant it that way, but in fact his front page was the most impressive tribute a public figure could receive, with its etched portrait (solemn, not caricatural) of the dead man, a view of Ferrières castle, other pictures on an inside page of the original Rothschild house in Frankfurt's ghetto and the town house on Rue Saint-Florentin. "The King of Gold" exclaimed the banner headline. Regular readers would know that the reference was to Alphonse de Rothschild, and the occasion was his passing.[15]

The procession arrived at Père-Lachaise cemetery shortly before 1:00 P.M.; the ceremony was brief before the family mausoleum in the Jewish section. Respecting the baron's wishes, there were no flowers, no military honors, no speeches. Entrance to the cemetery was by invitation only—but there were 5,000 guests all the same. Grand Rabbi Zadoc Kahn officiated; the parish priest of Ferrières was also present, prayer book in hand.

To mark the day, son Edouard sent 50,000 francs to the prefect of the Paris district, to be distributed to the needy.[16]

The press carefully noted the names and qualities of those who called on the family to express sympathy; one caller was overlooked. At that time the Catholic Church maintained the lowest profile possible in France, for a new wave of republicanism—in part a reaction to the Dreyfus years—had taken a hard line on church-state relations. After a formal rupture between France and the Vatican in July 1904, the papal nuncio had returned to Rome, leaving behind a lesser-ranking representative to watch over church interests, Monseigneur Carlo Montagnini. Later Montagnini would also be forced out, his papers seized, examined by Parliament—and leaked to the press. Among them was a telegram to Montagnini from Merry Del Val, secretary of state of the Vatican, asking the Paris envoy to offer condolences to the Rothschilds on the death of Alphonse.

Montagnini did as he was told. In his report—a copy of which was among the confiscated documents—he described his visit to Alphonse's brother Gustave on May 29—the day of the funeral. Gustave expressed appreciation for the sympathy extended by Pope Pius X. He added that he disapproved of the government's banning of religious orders, and deplored plans for separation of church and state, which he considered "dangerous for the Republic itself." Montagnini commented to Del Val that this opinion, expressed by an elderly gentleman who "retained a clear and remarkable intelligence," did not surprise him. Gustave, said the churchman, was more religious, less "vindictive" than Alphonse.

Soon after the visit of the Vatican's quasi-secret agent, he received cards from Gustave and brother Edmond, as well as one from Edouard. He reported that to Rome. "This note must be destroyed immediately," the message ended.[17]

It had been rumored that the long-awaited will of the deceased Rothschild chieftain would be disclosed immediately after the funeral; that was not to be.[18] The financial community, and a public always hungry for news of the dynasty, would have to wait until the following July for details of the reorganization of the house of Rothschild under Alphonse's successors. Half a dozen years earlier the Rothschild banks of London, Paris, Frankfurt, and Vienna had agreed to sever traditional links (that would save the Paris company from being seized at the outbreak of war in 1914, when the Rothschilds found themselves operating on both sides of the battlefield).[19]

Henceforth there would be a new firm, De Rothschild Frères, whose capital of 50 million francs had been brought in by Alphonse's brothers Gustave and Edmond and Alphonse's son Edouard, in equal parts. (Edouard's contribution was in cash; that of his uncles came in part from existing banking properties.) Each of the three associates had power of attorney; later Gustave would cede a token share of his capital—without powers—to his son Robert, Edmond doing the same for his son James Armand. But from now on Edouard was titular head of the bank, president of the Nord railroad—in keeping with the Rothschild tradition of primogeniture.[20]

That was the business side—known to those who needed to know. The public was to learn of Baron Alphonse's generosities, among them the donation of three million francs for a nonsectarian charitable foundation, more funds for the hospital on Rue Picpus, and the provision of dowries for daughters of Nord railway employees. There were grants to a Jewish charitable organization, to the poor of the commune of Ferrières, and for a biannual prize to be awarded in Alphonse's name by the Académie des Beaux-Arts.[21]

But soon enough the guns were sounding again in the Drumont camp. In *La Libre Parole*, Rothschild specialist Albert Monniot noted that while the government was taking inventory of church properties—one of the consequences of the breaking of relations with the Vatican and of a new law separating church and state—it was high time to investigate the investigators, i.e., those who were supposed to be collecting inheritance tax. "The most modest evaluations place the fortune left by the powerful king of the Jews at several billions," explained Monniot, who himself put the figure at five billion, meaning that at least a hundred million francs should have been paid in tax; where was the money?

What began as a bottom-of-the-page item soon moved to the top of the front page: Under the headline "Stolen Millions" the Rothschild specialist wrote of "colossal fraud," for (in his reading of the situation) the real worth of the defunct Rothschild had been concealed in the books of the family company. It was a matter, concluded Monniot, for the Chamber of Deputies.[22]

Not the Chamber but the Senate took up the gauntlet, in the person of a virulent anti-Semite, Dominique Delahaye, who quoted liberally from *La Libre Parole*. Finance Minister Raymond Poincaré was obliged to specify the precise amount of capital declared by the heirs: 250,942,332 francs—over 4.5 billion of ours—on which 11,377,944 francs (in 1905 value) had been paid in estate tax. "But then he was quite poor, Monsieur de Rothschild," replied the complaining senator (laughter in the assembly). To shouts of approval, Poincaré insisted that the estate had been assessed as carefully as the administration knew how.[23]

*   *   *

We know what Edouard got, or was to get; we can only surmise how Alphonse's only other surviving child, Charlotte Béatrix, was treated. The young wife of an old, unhandsome banker, Béatrix is remembered as "ravissante," partial to pink dresses, capricious and authoritarian; she'd build and tear down Riviera villas, move woods from here to there, plant gardens in the wind, or order up a train without bothering about timetables. She would forget that she had a house full of guests and rush off to Monte Carlo to gamble. . . . Or so a cousin would remember fondly.[24]

Indeed, it was in 1905—surely with money her father left her— that she began designing a domain suited to her temperament, perhaps the most bizarre on the bizarre Riviera, set on a narrow strip of the Saint-Jean-Cap-Ferrat peninsula. The grounds were as narrow as a ship, so she dressed her gardeners in sailor suits; to enlarge the garden she had a cliff dynamited.[25]

Some time would pass before Edouard sat in his father Alphonse's chair. He was a frail Rothschild, whose youth had been marked by tuberculosis. During his long convalescence in Switzerland, his uncle Edmond signed the mail. As soon as he could, Edouard let his London cousins know that "it is not without deep emotion that I have come back to the office, having made only rare appearances for the past year. It's with a heavy heart that I rediscover this place where I spent my youth, and which holds so many memories."[26]

Compared with the soft-spoken Alphonse, his father, James, had been sheer flamboyance; after soft-spoken Alphonse, Edouard seemed a wallflower. Alongside the portraits of James, the multitude of etchings of whiskered Alphonse, one finds it hard to come up with a sketch or a photograph of Edouard. "One didn't get into the papers," was his attitude. He treasured his privacy.[27] Perhaps it mattered that while Alphonse had grown up in the optimistic atmosphere of expanding empire, Edouard de Rothschild's adolescence and young manhood were the years of Edouard Drumont, then of the cataclysmic Dreyfus affair, when one did well to keep one's head down.

Even the authors of an iconoclastic and subtly anti-Semitic

sketch of the Rothschild dynasty found it hard to say anything unkind about Edouard, this man who "held an important place in society, thanks to his horses and his charitable works," despite the fact that he "at the same time played a significant occult role in our parliamentary life, thanks notably to his position as a director of the Banque de France, which allowed him to intervene in all negotiations dealing with the problems of the franc." This was almost the worst the critic could find to say, unless it was this: "Informed persons note that in the heyday of financial speculation—between 1920 and 1940—no cabinet was formed without Edouard de Rothschild being consulted."[28]

So quiet was he that the authors of this supposedly well-informed exposé seem to have ignored that for all his ostensible power, Edouard could not save the parity of the franc against the opposition of the Banque de France's governor in the 1920s, nor could this maker of French governments prevent a Popular Front cabinet in the following decade.

He'd be another paterfamilias and French patriot, aware of his responsibility both to family and nation, but he was not a builder of business; he'd be content to manage what his father and grandfather had built. In their day, clients had been governments, which left it to the Rothschilds to underwrite their loans. But times had changed; corporations replaced governments as borrowers, and there was a wholly new kind of client to go out for. But that would require throwing off tradition, a rethinking of Rothschild methods—an entry into the stock exchange, for example (for that was where the new corporations were going for their financing). Edmond couldn't see that—so others replaced the Rothschilds in this arena. Among the others were sons of another migration, descendents of Abraham Lazard, who had come from Bohemia to settle in Lorraine in 1792, and who as pioneers in the still-young United States, then in France and in Britain, were to make Lazard Frères a transatlantic institution geared to industry not as it had been but would be.

The Rothschilds could have been *the* bankers of modern business and industry, and in fact they already had their entry, thanks to pioneer investments in electricity and oil.[29] They could have moved forcefully into the United States; again Edouard was

hesitant. "Here we always have a respectful fear of the Yan-
kees," as he explained it to his London cousins shortly after sitting down in his father's chair at last in the spring of 1906.
"These gentlemen see and do things on the grand scale. If their
profits sometimes reach fantastic proportions, their failures cause
deep catastrophes."[30]

TIGHTENING CIRCLES

is son, Guy, remembered Edouard de Rothschild as "tall, slender, with delicate but pronounced features, an aquiline profile," and "an elegance all his own." Not only because of his traditional banker's uniform—those wing collars he never left home without (except for golf or hunting). He had his own idea of chic, neither outdated nor pretentious, but with which tradition had a lot to do. Later, when Guy began to pay attention, he'd remember Father riding around Paris in an old electric automobile long out of fashion (he was already forty-one when Guy was born).

Edouard married in March 1905, at the ripe age of thirty-seven—only two months before his father Alphonse's death. Married outside of the Rothschild clan, though into a family of French Jews of the best society. Germaine Halphen was sixteen years younger than her husband, small and dark, and with dark eyes; her children would remember learning good manners from her—manners seemingly imported from the English side of the Channel. "For my sisters and myself," recalled Guy, "parental authority was represented by our mother, our father being in our eyes an affectionate and distracted visitor."[1]

Guy's father was very much a *Jewish* Rothschild, conscious of his obligations, the presidency of the Central Consistory having fallen to him as if by divine right. In one of the first decisions called for during his mandate, Edouard demonstrated that active lobbying on behalf of the Jewish community could be reconciled with keeping a low profile. The problem (in April 1906) was proposed legislation to prohibit business activity on Sunday—patently unfair to Jews, whose Sabbath was Saturday. Edouard stood firm, but preferred that the case for exemption from the Sunday laws be founded not on religious arguments but on freedom of conscience, allowing everyone to choose his own day of rest. (In the end the Consistory's position was ignored by Parliament; the law as voted allowed no exemption for Jews, who, if religious, would now have to shut down their activities two days a week.)[2]

At home, as his son would remember, Edouard respected the spirit as well as the letter. On Yom Kippur eve, after the dinner preceding the twenty-four-hour fast, Guy would be invited to accompany his father on foot to the Rue de la Victoire synagogue, both of them—to the stupefaction of bystanders—in formal dress, with white ties and high hats. At thirteen, Guy was to celebrate the traditional bar mitzvah confirming his manhood. He'd be told, often enough, that the essential thing was to marry within one's religion; he'd remember that when he broke the rule.[3]

Edouard's phlegmatic nature—quite Edouardian—is apparent in a letter sent to London on May 1, 1906, after he had been sitting in his father's chair only a month; the streets had been noisy on the drive to Rue Laffitte that morning. "Here the first of May, instead of being a holiday, is taken as a day of revolution, which we await with calm and resignation," he explained. "Instead of revolution we have a military parade. . . . As for the house of Rothschild, it is guarded by soldiers; an armed sentinel stands at our door as before the homes of the great men of the world. This upsets me and I find such tactics somewhat exaggerated."[4] A few days later he was to greet the true Edwardian, family friend Edward VII, traveling in France incognito. When the British king left for London, Edouard was at the Gare du Nord to bid him farewell; he had been particularly amiable, Edouard hastened to tell his cousins.[5]

*   *   *

Counseled by his judicious uncle Edmond, and by an increasingly silent partner Gustave (who would die in 1911, at the age of eighty-one), Alphonse's cautious successor was obviously going to pursue traditional Rothschild peace policies, to the extent that they respected France's national interests. It just happened to matter less what the Rothschilds thought or did—since their power was no longer determinant. When loans to foreign governments were the main business of banking and they dominated that business, foreign leaders paid heed to a Rothschild's advice. They had even stopped wars in the past; they obviously were not going to be able to prevent the Great War, although they operated banks in each camp.[6]

It would be an exaggeration to say that the French Rothschilds had turned their backs on the financial rewards represented by major government loans—no longer on behalf of the Czar, perhaps, although they continued to handle Russian capital for the servicing of earlier loans. But without being the principal underwriter, they nevertheless committed themselves in Edouard's early years to significant foreign bond issues, notably on behalf of Japan and Brazil, while at any time regular customers of De Rothschild Frères could subscribe to a variety of current bond offerings at its counters. The family continued to manage substantial railroad investments in France, Spain, and Italy, while pursuing the exploitation of raw materials for nascent industries and precious metals through companies around the world. Not wishing to open their books to inspection as the law now required, they withdrew from active trading on the Paris stock exchange, but their role in the gold market remained considerable.[7]

One did hear less about the Rothschilds in the Belle Epoque—unless one listened to fanatics. In 1909, when Edouard had been running the bank in his own quiet way for three years, someone actually bothered to publish another of the long series of anti-Rothschild pamphlets. "Jews, the real enemy!" was the prefatory quote. For this author the zenith of Jewish triumph was the transfer of the body of Emile Zola to a final resting place in the Panthéon in June 1908, as "desired and demanded by the Jews."[8] Both Zola and Alphonse de Rothschild would have been surprised by that.

The accepted wisdom—and most historians go no further—is

that by refusing to underwrite major czarist bond issues, the Rothschilds had washed their hands of Russia. "The Paris house of Rothschild is hostile to Russia and keeps its distance from Russian operations," so Count Corti quotes a German ambassador who talked to Alphonse about it in August 1904.[9] Soon after Alphonse's death, a new wave of pogroms was launched against Russia's Jews, and the Rothschilds refused to participate in underwriting a major loan, this at a time when Russia desperately needed funds to stabilize a regime shaken by the country's disastrous war with Japan and the social and political unrest in its wake. More, they rejected out of hand a Russian offer to grant concessions to Jews in return for financial cooperation.[10]

In January 1906, Edmond's son James Armand informed the London cousins that French premier Maurice Rouvier—then also serving as foreign minister—had asked the Rothschilds to participate in a Russian bond issue. Rouvier was anxious to comply because the Russians were threatening to take their business elsewhere. After consulting his seniors, James Armand explained the difficulty of their position: the Rothschilds had just taken the lead in a fund-raising campaign for Russia's persecuted Jews; their conscience didn't allow them to come to the rescue of their persecutors just six weeks after that. How could they face fellow Jews in France, not to speak of Jews in the United States and Britain, after helping a government that had done nothing to stop the horrors committed in two hundred Russian cities and towns—and had even promoted the officials responsible? Finally the French government turned to the Hottinguer bank, a traditional Protestant institution, and the Hottinguers were aghast at the prospect of being involved with a czar whose tyranny had so alarmed their Rothschild colleagues. "They'd give a lot to be Jews right now!" James Armand reported with bitter humor.[11]

In April 1906 the Russians tried again—with the same result. (If the Czar wanted Rothschild help, Edmond told London, he knew how to go about getting it.) "The events now taking place in Russia are the shame of this supposedly humanitarian century," Edouard expressed himself to his London cousins in June.[12] Of course the Rothschilds continued to be very much involved with a different Russia. Thanks to their investments in the Caucasus, they were now one of the world's leading producers and distributors of oil. (In 1895 they had gone so far as to co-sign an agreement with rival producers—including America's Standard Oil—to divide up world markets. It never took effect, presumably because of the opposition of the Russian government.)[13]

In addition to their control of Bnito, the company that exploited the prolific oilfields of Baku, their Standard Russe (named for and modeled on the American Standard Oil) possessed seven fields in Georgian Grozny, with a huge refinery that could handle its own and other companies' production. Because of its privileged access to European markets, Rothschild Standard was the leader in that region.

In 1902, before the end of Alphonse's reign, the brothers entered into partnership with Royal Dutch and Shell (soon to become a single global company) to form the Asiatic Petroleum Company for exploiting the fields of southern Russia.[14] "Once we are combined with the Rothschilds," Royal Dutch's Henri Deterding confided to Sir Marcus Samuel, the British founder of Shell, "everybody knows that we hold the future, but we cannot do without their name."[15]

Their oil interests put the French Rothschilds at the center of Russia's turbulent prerevolutionary history. Daniel Yergin recalls that young Stalin himself led the agitation against the Caucasian oil industry in general, the Rothschilds in particular. Mass action by oil workers in Baku in 1903 was the spark that set off the first general strike across the Russian landmass. Then the poor showing of the Czar's military in the Russo-Japanese War in 1904 encouraged enemies of the regime, whose protests reached the Czar's doorstep; police fired on demonstrators marching on the Winter Palace in Saint Petersburg, the first shots of the 1905 revolution—the spontaneous one.[16]

A document from that agitated year shows how cooler heads could still prevail. Rothschild agents in the Standard Russe installation at Novorossisk on the Black Sea sent graphic descriptions of the insurrectionary strikes; De Rothschild Frères gave its local management full authority to grant material concessions. "If the movement is limited to workers' demands without spilled blood, the problems will be relative," Paris reassured Novorossisk (rather than the other way round). So the Rothschilds counted on the people at the scene, confident in "your tact, your sangfroid, and your firmness to avoid to the extent possible the unfortunate events that have taken place elsewhere."[17]

But by then it was too late. Labor conflict had aggravated ethnic differences in the Caucasus (pitting the same people against each other who would be fighting again at the collapse of the Soviet empire in our own time). Oil exports from Baku were virtually shut off; before the agitation subsided, an estimated two-thirds of the wells had been rendered inoperative.

Baku—already inefficient before the outbreak of violence, because of antiquated machinery—would never again be the same. And even if the agitation calmed, couldn't it start up again? The best evidence is that the Rothschilds were already looking for a way out of Russia at this time. Disaffection became a decision to sell by 1909; active negotiations with the logical purchaser got under way two years later. The divestment took the form of a sale of Rothschild holdings—80 percent of Bnito (the production and refining operation of Baku and Batum), the same share of the marketing company Mazout—to Royal Dutch, their partner in Standard Russe.[18]

Later it would be said that the Rothschilds had foreseen the approaching collapse of the czarist regime and moved to cut their losses. But the best student of that time and place sees the decision to withdraw as strictly financial. To Edmond de Rothschild, the family's senior oil expert, it would have made sense to let tested partners—Royal Dutch and Shell—take over the risk. Still later a Soviet historian with access to banking archives came to a similar conclusion. Oil was a growth industry, but the Rothschilds knew that they would never be able to compete with Royal Dutch experience in extraction and refinery operations, not to speak of its world market. Their real trade, after all, was banking. So they'd sell Russian Standard cheap (it was losing money), while they got more capital out of Bnito and Mazout than these companies were worth.[19]

The negotiations were exacting all the same, concluded only in December 1911, the final agreement to be ratified by all parties on February 21 of the following year. In the end the family was paid in shares—60 percent of the value of their holdings in Royal Dutch stock, 40 percent in Shell—thus giving them a sizable stake in the global operations of the merged giant, with a provision that they would continue to receive bonuses from their former Bnito fields in any year that production exceeded a given amount.

They remained friends, the Rothschilds and the Dutch. In 1913, when expanding operations called for a significant increase in capital, Royal Dutch went to the French market with its new shares; the syndicate of underwriters was composed of Banque de Paris et des Pays-Bas, Crédit Lyonnais, Société Générale—and De Rothschild Frères.[20]

They could not have known, cautious Edouard and his uncles, that in a very few years the fragile Russian leviathan was going to collapse. They might have been left with worthless stock; instead, their considerable equity in powerful and expanding Royal Dutch Shell would grow and grow.

The work in Palestine continued—the difficulties as well. Settlements had their bad years, settlers often proved disappointing, their pioneer spirit often dulled by the facility of employing Arabs for rough work. Rothschild subsidies removed an incentive for resourcefulness. From the turn of the century, Edmond himself was handicapped by poor health (not to improve radically until he underwent surgery in 1918). His older son, James Armand, who in the Rothschild tradition would inherit his father's responsibilities, was not quite ready to take over. Edmond's immediate solution was to confide the main burden of management of his philanthropies to a Jewish Colonization Association. He continued to oversee the management of his Palestine operations, and of course remained the sole source of new money.

As if human frailities had not caused enough trouble to this Benefactor, there was the increasingly aggressive Zionist movement, which saw Rothschild money as corrupting—a deviation of the spirit in which a Jewish state would be conceived. An irony, for Simon Schama notes that it was Edmond himself who demanded that his pioneers dirty their own hands in field labor. Disdain for the Benefactor seemed a personal vendetta on the part of Theodor

Herzl, who never got over Edmond's dismissal of his Zionist vision; only after Herzl's death in 1904 was rapprochement with the successors of Herzl possible.

By 1914 Edmond could say that he had never been at odds with the goals of Zionism, even when their tactics differed from his. In truth the Paris banker often appeared to have a better sense of economic and political realities than did many of the idealists who are given credit for having inspired the Jewish state.[21]

THE EXTENDED FAMILY

*A*fter the realignment made necessary by Alphonse's death, further changes in the Rothschild hierarchy would have been barely perceptible to all but a few privileged observers; again a Rothschild was dead, again "Long live Rothschild!" Alphonse's brother Gustave had taken pains to introduce his only living son, Robert, to the Rue Laffitte in 1909; Edmond did the same for his older son, James Armand. Each heir was endowed with a share of one million francs (about 20 million in our day), representing less than one-fifteenth of his father's equity in De Rothschild Frères. Two years later Gustave was dead, and by agreement Robert was authorized to buy up his father's shares.[1]

It was not to be the same for James Armand—almost always called Jimmy—educated in England, irresistibly attracted by things English. He would acquire an Anglo-Jewish wife and British nationality, returning his million-franc stake in the family bank to his father—this father who himself had never been an active director of the bank, preferring to pursue his own interests (in industry and science, in art collecting, philanthropy, Palestine). But Jimmy remained Edmond's spiritual heir, eventually taking on his father's good works in Palestine.[2]

* * *

So as the century grew older and Edouard did, his dominant position in the hierarchy became clearer. A dozen years his junior, cousin Robert was not a capitalist by divine right but a loyal second, even many years later, when, after further shuffling of family shares, he controlled a full 50 percent of the bank, to Edouard's 50 percent. A collector (of Modigliani and Picasso before they were fashionable) and a music lover, by training Robert was a mining engineer curious about scientific development and willing to sink money into it (a notable example being radio transmission of photographs, perfected by Edouard Belin). He was the "esthete" of his banking generation.[3]

A number of Rothschilds in France were not "French" Rothschilds at all—Adolph, for example, son of the founder of the Naples bank, who after the fall of the Bourbons of Sicily in 1861 had closed down the business, to retire to a sumptuous house on elegant Rue de Monceau. He might be encountered during his daily promenade in the Bois de Boulogne with the Queen of Naples, who, with the deposed king, lived in exile in Paris. Adolph was known for the huge sums he turned over to worthy causes, and for collecting objets d'art, as Rothschilds were wont to do. When he died in 1900 at the age of seventy-six, he left his widow, Julie (a Vienna cousin), with substantial wealth, superb art, and impressive properties, including "that admirable and prodigious castle of Pregny, whose immense white façade dominates the lake a mile or two north of Geneva," as a contemporary described it.[4]

Adolph's Julie, who was famous for puffing on big cigars, made the most of Pregny during her lifetime. Elisabeth de Clermont-Tonnerre (née de Gramont) remembered that she'd sail her yacht around Lake Geneva carrying boxes of her grapes to neighbors. Her good friend Elizabeth, empress of Austro-Hungary, spent the afternoon at Pregny the day before her assassination at the hands of an anarchist in Geneva.[5]

Julie was seventy-seven when she died in 1907. Having no immediate heir for her immense fortune, this Viennese Rothschild had been able to choose a favorite French cousin. Perhaps she understood that in her choice she was creating a second French Rothschild dynasty.

Nothing about Maurice de Rothschild, second son of Baron Edmond, predestined him to found a kingdom. A second son, he was not meant to sit atop a fortune, still less to exercise power; possibly this is what prompted aunt Julie to make the good-looking, suavely intelligent "Momo" her heir. Born in May 1881, only twenty-six when Julie died, Maurice was already famous for spending what others were earning, upsetting sterner Rothschilds by his womanizing (or by the reputation he had acquired for it). Worse, from the point of view of older and wiser cousins, he seemed to lack a desire to work—though he liked to play the market in his own way.

The art dealer René Gimpel enjoyed entertaining and apparently fruitful relations with Maurice, acquiring him as a customer when Maurice was still quite young but "already a rather bad sort." Maurice's father, Edmond, so Gimpel understood, had sent the lad off to hunt in Africa as a way of keeping him out of Paris and trouble—increasing the distance between him and those "costly embraces of the ladies of Paris," as his cousin Elisabeth de Gramont phrased it. So there would be costly embraces in Africa. Elisabeth tells the story of Maurice inviting an Ethiopian princess to his tent. His personal physician warned him of the possible consequences—but it was the good doctor who caught a disease from the princess's lady-in-waiting, and he died of it.[6] Later, because Maurice shied away from a desk job at De Rothschild Frères, his father turned him over to Nathan Wildenstein, in whose already famous gallery Maurice was to learn a good deal about buying and selling paintings (he enjoyed doing both).

At one point Wildenstein asked fellow dealer Gimpel to help Maurice find American buyers for part of his collection (undoubtedly part of Aunt Julie's). Gimpel never forgot his visit to 47 Rue de Monceau (once Adolph and Julie's residence, now Maurice's, a most private museum with its Jules Romain ceiling, Houdon sculptures, and paintings and drawings by Boucher, Nattier, Hubert Robert). The dealer was obliged to pass an unmade bed as he found his way, at his host's invitation, into the bathroom, entering just as the young baron was rising from his tub.[7]

Marcel Proust would tell a story that left Maurice looking good—but not Proust's friend Comte Robert de Montesquiou. The count had borrowed diamonds from the young Rothschild to wear at a ball. Outraged to receive a rather small brooch and the recommendation that he take good care of it as a family jewel, Montes-quiou replied, "I was quite unaware that you had a family, but I did think you had some jewels."[8]

All the way back in Baron James's time, there had been another branch of the family in Paris. The Great Baron had been a good host to his brother Nathan's son Nathaniel, providing him with a wife (his daughter Charlotte) as well as a desk alongside his, in the years when the founder of the French branch didn't have a son old enough to serve as his trusted number two. At the beginning of the 1850s Nathaniel, who was to remain a British subject, acquired a lordly manor at 33 Rue du Faubourg Saint-Honoré, until then the embassy of czarist Russia. He indulged in the usual Rothschild hobbies—art collecting notably—and then added one of his own, acquiring (in 1853) a vineyard in the Bordeaux region, an already celebrated second growth called Mouton, which under Nathaniel's descendents would become one of France's best-known wines, and one of the world's best-known French wines.[9]

Somehow Nathaniel lacked the rugged luck of his French cousins; severely injured in a hunting fall, he became paralyzed, totally blind, an invalid for the last fifteen years of his life (he died in 1870, at the age of fifty-seven).[10] "Each day," an obituary would recall, "he was taken on a promenade in an open carriage along the Champs-Elysées, while he slept deeply."[11]

Two sons survived him. James Edouard was trained as a lawyer, then trained himself as a bibliophile, in his short life building one of the foremost collections of French medieval and Renaissance literature, the catalog of which became a reference for all future work in the field. After his father's death he joined the bank under his uncle Alphonse, applying his legal knowledge to the administration of the northern, then the eastern railway line. He transformed the English branch of the family into a second French branch by applying for French nationality at the age of twenty-one, enlisting in the volunteer guard during the war against Prussia. Among his notable charities was a hospital for children's bone diseases at Berck-sur-Mer.

As if to adhere to Rothschild tradition, his younger brother

Arthur turned his back on business, helping out only during summer vacations, devoting the rest of a somewhat misanthropic existence to his yacht—the *Eros*—and to a mistress, cigars, and neckties; his nephew Henri would remember that he spent two hours each day between tailor and shirtmaker, and hunted at his mother's estate at Vaux-de-Cernay.[12] Arthur left no legitimate offspring; in 1872, James Edouard sired Henri. Henri, who in his time—the Belle Epoque and after—became the most visible member of the family, inheriting his father's love for books and medicine, along with his uncle's insouciance (*and* his yacht).

Yet it had begun badly. Henri's childhood as he remembered it was ghastly. Nine years old when his father died, he was raised by his mother, Laura Thérèse von Rothschild, a daughter of the strict Frankfurt side of the family; her intense dislike of brother-in-law Arthur's lifestyle made her stricter still. She resolved to make a doctor out of Henri, and starting at the age of ten he spent his summer vacations at the children's hospital endowed by his father at Berck-sur-Mer, living among the young patients, helping to care for them, obliged to watch operations.

Later Henri would say that this early initiation to medicine had been a failure; what finally got him involved was his mother's long illness, when their Paris home was transformed into a hospital. That didn't stop the authoritarian invalid from watching her errant son carefully. At eighteen he was still being escorted to school. But when at nineteen he was still being taken everywhere by a nurse, he decided to kiss her, and was soon in bed with her. After graduation from high school, Henri was dispatched to America (actually to get him away from another young lady). The baroness even recruited a guardian to accompany him. (This man quickly found a mistress on shipboard, and then took young Henri on a tour of the shady side of America's cities.)

At twenty-two, to free himself from tyranny, he decided to marry, proposing to the first eligible girl he met, his sister's friend Mathilde de Weisweiller (on the day following their first meeting). After eight arduous years he was ready to practice medicine (also to undertake and publish advanced research). Later he'd reflect that until the age of forty he had been "indifferent" to pleasure, so austere had been his growing-up years. Now he would alternate spells of work with hunting expeditions, sailing on the *Eros* (as far as Egypt and Syria, down the coasts of Africa). An early convert to what was then called *l'automobilisme,* he piloted his first vehicle in 1894; the permit he held bore the number 5. Being a Rothschild, he could also finance construction of the first factories for motor cars and trucks; as late as the 1930s he was using inherited wealth to save 1,500 jobs at a failing auto plant.

He was always good for a story, serious or otherwise. In 1902 the New York press made much of his cavorting at the Monte Carlo gambling tables with an American businessman (Charles Schwab, then president of U.S. Steel).[13] That same year he was photographed seated in an open car during a Paris-Vienna automobile race in which some contestants were clocked at over thirty miles per hour along the 740 miles of roadway separating the two capitals.[14]

Bankers being essentially indoor men, it was not terribly difficult for Henri to be the most kinetic Rothschild: man-about-town, man about Deauville, always good for a photograph in the popular prints. In August 1904, for example, a photographer for the country's leading pictorial weekly caught "a sympathetic tête-à-tête of two quite dissimilar personalities. One of them, thin and dry, with a jockey's shaved features"—that was the pitiless caricaturist Sem, who often focused his sights on Henri. "The other, of a certain corpulence, carries—with a good-natured simplicity as one can observe—a sonorous and magnificent name: Henri de Rothschild." Physician and fervent driver, notes the reporter, Henri was one of the first to apply the rapidity of motor transport to ambulances.[15]

In 1907 he acquired an old farm behind the beach at Deauville. Lying too low for a view, it was a piece of literary history, being the former property of Gustave Flaubert's family, sold by the writer to pay debts. Soon a Rothschildian villa went up on the land, though gadabout Henri seldom sat still enough to use it. (Its next owner was an American millionaire, whose son left it to Deauville; today it is at once a memorial to Flaubert, to Henri de Rothschild, and to the Strassburgers of Pennsylvania.)[16]

All the while breaking new ground with infant care, studying childhood stomach disorders, devising free milk distribution schemes, building a new children's hospital and running it for over three decades (treating not only children's diseases but syphilis and endocrinal disease), Henri also sponsored a soup kitchen. (After his wife's death, in 1926, he'd double the size of his children's hospital and name it for her.) Early in the century he began producing radium for treatment of cancer, eventually building a veritable factory just north of Paris at Saint-Denis for larger quantities of this precious medical tool; this facility, during the First World War, was to turn out luminous equipment for submarines and trench warfare.[17]

Until she died in 1931, his mother ("Baronne James" as Laura Thérèse was known) was probably his biggest competitor as a doer of good deeds, something she had perfected over fifty long years of widowhood. "Her home is a ministry," observed her niece Elisabeth de Gramont. "During the morning solicitors of small favors are distributed among the ground-floor reception rooms. If one calls on Aunt Thérèse at eleven in the morning, a servant escorts one to a room already crowded with three rows of women dressed in black. The valet opens a second door to reveal employees of the Northern Railway with their families. The Catholic clergy is in the third room. Hospital directors are a flight up. Members of the family are obliged to wait in the vestibule."[18]

Being a French Rothschild, even of the branch called "British," meant to be an object of curiosity; thanks to his energy, the diversity of his activities, and thanks also to his very conspicuous hobbies, Henri captured more newspaper space than any of his French cousins. At the height of the Dreyfus hysteria, the respected daily Le Temps had to print this disclaimer: "In the face of allegations repeated several times and already denied, according to which Baron Henri de Rothschild contributed a sum of money in connection with the Dreyfus affair, we are authorized by him to declare that these affirmations are in every way false and wholly invented."[19]

One of Sem's sketches of Henri graced the wall of the elegant smoking parlor of the Théâtre des Champs-Elysées inaugurated in 1913.[20] By then this indefatigable Rothschild was well launched on still another career, even more likely than the previous ones to claim attention. From the day he came into his birthright—and he inherited the collections of his grandfather, his father, and his uncle Arthur—Henri had been acquiring rare books and manuscripts, following the family vice (the manuscripts—6,000 of them—would go to the Bibliothèque Nationale). Even earlier he had begun to write; being a Rothschild, he could have his schoolboy travel diaries printed up for family and friends, and before graduation he was publishing a literary magazine. After 1898, with medical degree firmly in hand, he allowed himself to return to writing—scholarly work of course, but also entertaining pieces. During a convalescence at the Evian spa in 1906, he wrote a one-act play—he'd call it a "playlet"—which ran for three months on a real Paris stage. His first full-length comedy opened in 1909 and was also a success. The Rothschild name didn't hurt, but would not alone have accounted for its 117 performances, with another 300 abroad.

Everyone knew who wrote them, but Henri signed his plays "André Pascal," and before he was done there were thirty-eight of them, all but one of which reached the stage. He'd build an over-equipped theater, the Pigalle, publish a novel, a fictionalized biography, memoirs, even a book on stamp collecting. There are 277 items in this man's bibliography.[21]

In 1914, three months before World War I, the illustrated magazine that seemed to thrive on news of Henri devoted a page to his "scientific and hunting expedition" along the White Nile in Sudan. In one photograph he sits atop a slain hippopotamus, holding a parasol and smoking a cigarette. In another he stands with a rifle astride a crocodile measuring some ten feet from snout to tail. Henri and friends claimed to have shot 537 different animals, some of them shipped home for Paris's natural history museum.[22]

WAR AND PEACE

*H*enceforth—as a later head of the bank would put it—the Rothschilds survived on past success and present resources.[1] In a close-up portrait of the bank in the decade leading to the First World War, a German specialist, Eugene Kaufmann, discerned a paradox. True, De Rothschild Frères continued to enjoy a place of its own among private banks—but no longer because of the size of its business, now that it had abandoned the bulk of its foreign activities, concentrating instead on the management of the wealth of family and friends. What made Rothschild Rothschild was the amount of its disposable capital, and memories of past glory.

Not that a foreign observer found it easy to evaluate that capital. In his study, Kaufmann cited the declared value of the company for tax purposes: 50 million francs (over one billion of today's francs), observing that these funds weren't "working," they were only being "managed."[2] We can add a figure Kaufmann didn't have when he compiled his data: in 1911, when, after Gustave's death, his son Robert exercised the right of preemption of a third of the company, he paid 55,336,063 francs for his father's 15,666,666-franc share, or some 350 percent of its nominal value.[3]

Kaufmann found another reason for the decline of Rothschild influence in the firm's withdrawal from active stock trading, a direct consequence of the 1898 law requiring that brokers open their books (something this private bank would not do). Thus orders from regular Rothschild clients were handled by registered brokers, the purchased certificates confided to De Rothschild Frères for safekeeping. But since stock issues were the lifeblood of capitalistic development, Edouard and his cousins were excluding themselves from the mainstream of twentieth-century business—leaving them only a spectator's seat on the riverbank.

But what had changed most in the last decade of the nineteenth century and the first of the twentieth was the Rothschild position on significant foreign bond issues. Whereas in the past the family bank had been in direct contact with countries seeking financial help, by 1910 that role had been abandoned to large deposit banks. Henceforth Rothschild's principal activity was to manage the assets of its own industrial holdings—assets that left its coffers only at the moment of distribution of dividends to shareholders inside or outside the family. At the same time, the firm's private banking function continued to find favor with foreign governments, crowned heads, old aristocratic families, leading capitalists—some of these clients having been with the Rothschild bank for two and even three generations.

The overriding principle at De Rothschild Frères was liquidity; thanks to its ability to lay cash on the counter on demand, it enjoyed a reputation for reliability that no other bank, no matter how big, could match. (The Rothschilds of later generations would learn for themselves that there would always be clients for whom a checkbook marked "Rothschild" proved, quite simply, irresistible.) Then the Paris bank was still the best channel for transactions between the Bank of England and the Banque de France (the British sometimes left their gold in the Rothschild vaults at Rue Laffitte, ready for the next transaction). Assets of such dimensions, concluded the investigator, made Rothschild a solid rock, the best port of call in hard times. Its loss of material power was compensated by having preserved all of its moral power. "One makes sure to invite it to join all major financial transactions."[4]

Nor did the firm's seeming eclipse discourage those who required a bright Rothschild star in order to ground their belief in the existence of a "financial oligarchy." These Rothschilds simply *had* to be among the invisible rulers of the nation: in that very year, 1910, a left-socialist analyst trained his guns on the directors of the Banque de France, the real "rulers" of the country's wealth. The first director on his list was Edouard de Rothschild, one of "the real kings of France," also of course one of "the railroad kings." But it was the bankers who counted. The left-socialist publicist noted that four of the six bankers on the Banque de France governing board had a rather particular origin. One (Edouard de Rothschild) required no further identification; three others were Protestants. All four, the Jew and the Protestants, had maneuvered for control of the Banque de France to keep it from "Catholic royalists."[5]

Truly Edouard didn't see himself as one of the invisible rulers. A presidential election was coming up in 1913, and in a letter to his London cousins, Edouard de Rothschild acclaimed all three of the principal candidates as acceptable because they were strong, capable of facing down a turbulent Parliament. "The country desires order and tranquillity," he explained, "and has had enough of financial adventures and despoiling fiscality." The cabinet headed by Raymond Poincaré had been admirable in its moderation; now Poincaré was one of the candidates for president. "The exchange waits with anxiety for the election of Mr. Poincaré, to be saluted by a rise in government bonds." Poincaré was elected, yet joy did not leap from the pages of Edouard's letter to London the following week. "The best means of arriving at a result is always a policy of prudent economy that all governments seem to ignore at the present time, particularly the democracies. When one borrows, and when one is obliged to borrow ... one must not be surprised at the decline in one's own equities. ..."[6]

Of course Edouard shared the abiding Rothschild craving for peace, and this was a time of heightened tensions. Already a crisis with Germany over African possessions had seen German guns pointed at the Moroccan coast; clearly the next war would engage old enemies. But to prefer peace did not mean to ignore the difference between right and wrong. In a letter to London, Edouard made it clear that the "general feeling" of the country was to stay close to Britain; obviously he himself agreed.[7] When war came, French and British Rothschilds behaved like other Frenchmen and

Britons serving their colors. The Rothschilds of Vienna fought as well as they could with the losers.

The western allies were hardly on a war footing in August 1914, but an intricate web of alliances predetermined their behavior: Germany and Austria-Hungary on one side; France, Britain, and Russia on the other. It has been said that the general staffs were ready before their foot soldiers were. The *casus belli*, the assassination in Sarajevo of Archduke Francis Ferdinand, heir-to-be of the Austria-Hungarian Empire, could have led to regional war, in the context of years of tension in the Balkans; the powers saw it otherwise. France and Germany had both been building up their forces for a new battle over Alsace and Lorraine; now, on August 1, 1914, the French ordered a general call-up of troops, rejecting Germany's invitation to remain out of the conflict. Germany declared war on France two days later.

Before that day was over, the French government was asking De Rothschild Frères—in strict confidence—to borrow upwards of $100 million from the United States, in part for the purchase of American war materiel, in part to build up a gold reserve. Rothschild turned to J. P. Morgan in New York, with a telegram delivered to Morgan's Paris office and coded for transmission:

> We put our services at disposal of American bankers to obtain for the French government that it does a financial operation in United States America [*sic*] although its Treasury is in excellent state STOP[8]

Getting American money for the French war effort was not to be that easy, for the important reason that the United States was not ready to see its gold sail away to Europe. A few days later the French, and the French Rothschilds, were back with a lesser demand: they were only asking for $10 million now, to be spent in the United States—and no gold. It was even too early for that; for the moment all Morgan could do was to arrange a swap: French francs to be turned over to the U.S. consulate in Paris to help it deal with extraordinary expenses for American tourists surprised by the war;

in return the French embassy in Washington would be credited with a corresponding sum in dollars.[9]

That was enough for propaganda purposes. For Morgan was able to announce that it had been appointed as representative of the French government to establish that country's credit, as well as to facilitate trade between the United States and France.[10]

Rothschild files testify to the bank's phenomenal efforts during four years of war in handling government loans and war bonds.[11] There would be help from Morgan after all. For the French sorely needed American support, but couldn't borrow the American way, by depositing shares as collateral. They didn't have acceptable equities, for one thing; and they wished to avoid the implication that the signature of a French government wasn't sufficient without a material guarantee. In June 1915, Finance Minister Alexandre Ribot found the way: the borrower of dollars would be not France at all, but the French Rothschilds. The Morgan bank in New York was to make funds available against American railroad shares (sold on the Paris stock exchange); its loan would nominally be destined to De Rothschild Frères, but in fact the credit would be established in the name of the French treasury, with no commission for the Rothschilds. The funds finally made available were in excess of $40 million.[12]

Let it not be thought that J. P. Morgan was taking the side of the Allies by lending to France and to Britain, so Morgan was to tell fellow bankers—no more than they were pro-German. They were just doing a pro-American deed in behalf of American trade. It wasn't a war loan; they were only giving customers time to pay (and these happened to be the best customers America ever had).[13]

A confusing transaction. Rothschild family legend has it that Morgan demanded that the guarantee come not from the French government but from the Rothschilds.[14] Anti-Semites never quite understood. They'd see the transactions with Morgan not as assistance to the French war effort but as a gift to the Rothschilds from their "man" in power, President Poincaré.[15]

There was no Rothschild letter to London on August 1, the day of the call to the colors, or on the following days, which saw a cascade

of declarations of war, with the perfidious German drive through
neutral Belgium to attain France's industrial north. "Excuse us for
not having engaged in regular correspondence with you and thus to
have failed a tradition which means so much to us," were Edouard's first words to his London cousins when he broke his silence
on August 11. "But events have taken a turn so rapidly tragic that
one could only remain silent, for all comment would be vain." He
noted with satisfaction the absence of recriminations: "Our country
is proving of an admirable composure, a resigned but unshakable
courage. The guns are firing, let's learn to stand by."

Of course all business had ceased, finances were in crisis—but
"for us R." there was sufficient cash on hand. Liquidity remained
sufficient on August 20—fortunately, for the demands were many:
cash withdrawals, industrial activities, requests for loans—and for
charity. (The French Rothschilds were hoping to repatriate funds
held for them in London.) By August 24, French forces were in full
retreat, but the war was hardly over; Edouard preferred to believe
the good news: "Our army is intact."

In early September the Rothschild general staff was in Bordeaux, for the French government—with the Germans now so close
to Paris—had transferred operations there, and wanted the banks,
above all the Banque de France and the Rothschilds, to be close
at hand. "The Rue Laffitte has settled in Bordeaux!!" Edouard
informed his cousins. "And it's the only thing in my entire life I
hadn't foreseen—I was ready for anything, except this!" He had
brought his top managers, as well as the directors of the Compagnie du Nord, and all were kept quite busy, while in Paris the main
office remained open for payment of dividends. He was hoping to
be able to arrange a French treasury bond issue in London—when
asked. Again a letter bubbling with enthusiasm for the French
army, for the British ally. "The whole country is united behind a
single idea, that of driving out the invader. . . ."

Now forty-six, Edouard was unlikely to be called up for military
service. But cousin Robert, Gustave's son, was at general headquarters; Edmond's Jimmy was at the front, and before long second
son Maurice would join him. "God protect them."

They were all back in Paris before Christmas, delighted to be
there, Edouard was pleased to tell London. It had been hoped that

their return would coincide with the total evacuation of French territory by the Germans; that, alas, was not for now.[16]

Far from the war zone, the British Rothschilds were in a position to assist French finances through bond issues, and Rue Laffitte had begun arrangements for such transfers from the outbreak of hostilities. By March 1915 the stakes were raised. For his correspondence on the matter with his London cousins Edouard now had singular assistance: he would turn his letter over to the French Foreign Ministry, which encoded it for transmission to the French ambassador in London, who would have it decoded and delivered to the bank's offices in New Court. (Edouard pointed out in a message of March 15, 1915, that the Paris bank offered nothing but its own signature as guarantee for such war loans, and hoped that this would suffice.)[17]

In August 1915, one year after the outbreak of war, Edouard described for his London family the situation as it was to be until the war's final weeks. The enemy now occupied "the richest part of France, from the industrial, mining, and economic points of view"; for example, the French now had to import millions of tons of coal from Britain, coal that in other times would have come from its own northeast. Edouard did not add—his uncles and cousins knew it full well—that the Nord railroad company was a singular casualty of the German occupation of the industrial north. "The first obligation incurring to us as to every Frenchman," Edouard did say, "is to place at the disposal of our government all resources we command both in France and abroad (and especially abroad)." Subsequent correspondence conveyed the gratitude of the French Rothschilds for help they (and the French Finance Ministry) were getting from London. "United on the battlefields, we are also united in finance!"[18]

While Edouard helped France wage war according to his means, his cousin Robert was distinguishing himself at the front. Mobilized as a lieutenant, he received citations in 1917 and 1918 both for battlefield reconnaissance and services as an interpreter between French and British forces. His family château at Laversine was transformed into a military hospital, his wife (née Nelly Beer) into a nurse.[19] On the eve of the war Edmond had formally designated his son James—Jimmy, then thirty-six years old—as the

man who would carry on his life's work in the Holy Land; before
the war ended Jimmy was in Palestine, helping to form a Jewish
battalion in the British army of Gen. Edmund Allenby that would
wrest Jerusalem and Damascus from Germany's Turkish ally.[20]

Even Henri—portly Henri—saw action. Nearly two decades
earlier, when he already weighed well over two hundred pounds,
he had been assigned to an auxiliary detachment during his regular military service; now, at forty-two, by concealing the fact
that he suffered chronic albuminuria he was taken on as second
lieutenant in the medical corps—but then a vaccination to protect
him against typhus laid him low. Sent to Dinard for convalescence,
he financed a military hospital there. By 1917 he was in charge of
the military hospital at Soissons—as close to the front as one could
get without being in a trench.[21] His wife Mathilde's voluntary
war service would be mocked by an anti-Semite dandy: at the
Compiègne hospital, said he, she wore the uniform of Jewish
nurses, "that is, the outfit of Catholic nuns, with a pearl necklace
added."[22]

Clearly world war offered the family no immunity from polemics.
In the columns of La Libre Parole, then on the floor of the French
Senate, one Sylvain Gaudin de Villaine distinguished himself by
attacking Jews in general, Rothschilds in particular, for selling
strategic raw materials to Germany; such fraudulent shipments, he
argued, were unnecessarily prolonging the war. His principal target was the company Le Nickel, in France's New Caledonia colony,
for allegedly delivering precious metals to German plants (or allowing them to be shipped); to the speaker it hardly mattered that
the allegation was under investigation, or that in fact the Rothschilds had no management responsibilities in Le Nickel.[23]

Business was done, all the same. The bank's archives contain
evidence of daily contact between the French Rothschilds and
their New York agent August Belmont concerning Rothschild
American interests, which included stakes in the New York Central railroad and the companies that made up the New York City
subway system (then private), as well as war loans. During the
weeks leading up to the U.S. entry into the war in 1917, cables
from Belmont read like news bulletins, keeping Paris informed on
the attitudes of President Wilson, political circles, Congress.

Shortly after the Russian Revolution of February 1917, a cable from August Belmont Jr. announced the Wall Street reaction:

> Russian Revolution and German retreat are counterbalancing unfavorable influence of destruction American vessels.

Then America itself joined the war, and the Rothschilds were ready to participate in U.S. Treasury war loans.[24] Family legend has it that Royal Dutch was furious when the new Soviet regime began to expropriate their Caucasian fields—as if the Rothschilds had known what was going to happen, and had gotten rid of their oil fields just in time.[25] In truth, the Rothschilds remained tied to the fate of Royal Dutch because they owned a good piece of it. And like everyone else they had been left with a lot of worthless paper after the Bolshevik takeover, needing help from the French Finance Ministry and the Banque de France in honoring obligations to French bondholders (and they got help).[26]

The war did more than anything had ever done in the years since young James opened his Paris bank to change the way business was carried out in France. The franc, which never budged in value—which was as good as gold and *was* gold—now needed protection (and protectors). It would slip against the pound sterling, against the dollar, only to be propped up again. A currency that had always commanded respect would henceforth be treated as an invalid; one could no longer depend on prices—or wages—that had been stable ever since 1870. Wealth that had a value expressed in paper, when taken out of the safe, proved to be only paper.

One could hardly plan under such conditions; one dared not build. For Edouard de Rothschild, who was fifty years old when trumpets sounded the armistice in November 1918, it was the end of a world.[27] Turbulence in money markets did much to reinforce his unwillingness to take risks, when risk had always been part of capitalism; reluctant to try new things, he could hardly recommend them to his clients. Alongside a shy Edouard, there was that powerhouse Horace Finaly, a virtuoso banker who was to do at Paribas what the Great Baron had done at Rue Laffitte in the heroic past. In the uncertain years following the Great War, Banque de Paris et des Pays-Bas seemed untroubled by doubt as it moved into foreign markets, or launched new industrial investments in France while De Rothschild Frères contented itself with the old.[28]

Then there were the Lazards, that other immigrant family, who with their cousins the Weills would repeat the Rothschild adventure, but with more confidence in the American side of the business; and America was beginning to count now.[29]

It was certainly easier to be free of ties to the family bank; Edmond's maverick son Maurice would discover that. For at present, strengthened by the self-confidence of a war veteran, he was going to do what no member of the banking Rothschilds was supposed to do, and certainly not during Edouard's reign. He was going to get himself talked about, written up, as a candidate for national office.

In family legend, as in truth, Maurice had until then devoted more energy to spending than to earning. He was the elegant young man-about-town, taking summer holidays at Marienbad, winters at Saint-Moritz, raising horses, hunting in India, passing the rest of his time with "the prettiest women of Paris" (the women as expensive as the horses and the hunting parties). In a seemingly dismissive remark, his cousin Henri observed that when Maurice was elected to the Academy of Fine Arts his only credential was his father Edmond's extraordinary art collection. By the end of the 1914–18 war, his wife, Noëmi (née Halphen)—they had married in 1909—joined her voice to the urging of well-meaning friends that Maurice *do* something with his life; the something was to be politics—as it happened, another expensive toy.[30]

It was ever the way in France to run for office in a district far from home; one needn't even possess a vacation residence in the region. Maurice chose to run as member of Parliament from the remote and mountainous Hautes-Pyrénées district, where modest rural voters might well look to a Rothschild as an answer to their prayers. He saw to it that his wall posters featured an outsized portrait of himself accompanied by the unambiguous slogan: "My name is my platform."[31] And why not, for candidates at the time as in our own time were expected to make material promises. Here was a man with the means to fulfill some of them, and without waiting for the legislature to vote the funds.

An unexpected portrait of Maurice as candidate comes from the private diary of Abbot Arthur Mugnier, a confidant of Paris's idle or accomplished rich, an early-twentieth-century Goncourt in his conscientious attempt to paint his contemporaries in words. "Baron Maurice de Rothschild wished to talk to me concerning his candidacy in Lourdes," he notes on August 17, 1919—Lourdes being a premier site of Catholic pilgrimage as well as one of the key towns of the electoral district. "He is seeing a lot of priests down there." Rothschild talked to the churchman about the famous grotto, revered as the site of an apparition of the Virgin. "It's so odd to hear this Jew interest himself in this essentially Catholic pilgrimage site," comments Mugnier with supreme understatement. "The baron asks me to tell the bishop that he is not sectarian, and will help him both to organize special trains for pilgrims and on political and religious matters: freedom of teaching in religious schools, the recall of teaching nuns [expelled from the school system a dozen years earlier]. Governments can do nothing, he says, without his family," Mugnier quotes Maurice. "The Rothschilds are, thanks to their banks, the finance ministry, the real one, the one that we can't do without."[32]

In the euphoria of the immediate postwar days, it made sense for Maurice to run under the colors of the National Bloc, a center-right coalition loosely tied to the coattails of victorious premier Clemenceau, called the "Tiger." And although many ardent Catholics preferred to vote for the Radical Socialists, declared enemies of the Church, rather than for a Rothschild, Maurice was elected, a member of the new majority.[33] After the election, *L'Illustration* devoted a page to portraits of "New Faces of the New Chamber." Among them was one of postwar France's most influential and controversial political leaders, the Socialist Léon Blum; another was the bigot Léon Daudet, director of the reactionary-royalist organ *L'Action Française*. The last photograph, at the bottom of the page, revealed a young playboy, his top hat set back on his head, a carnation in his lapel. "Baron Maurice de Rothschild, breeder," read the caption.[34]

SAVING THE FRANC

*A*ll bankers bank on the firmness of their currency; one doesn't have to be a Rothschild to care. In the nineteenth century the gold franc was a rampart. During the reign of the Great Baron the slippage in its value was barely perceptible to Frenchmen for whom money was not a profession. If in Alphonse's time the franc remained as solid as a rock, in Edouard's first years—the climax of the Belle Epoque—the franc actually gained in value.

In the 1914–18 conflict, France lost 10 percent of its able-bodied men, not to speak of the incalculable shortfall in births. In no other war had there been so much damage or destruction of bridges and roads, mines and factories. Much productive agricultural land was inaccessible during the conflict, unusable thereafter. Shortages of food and essential goods led to higher prices, and that to an angry and increasingly militant workforce. The Russian Revolution served a new generation of labor leaders as a lesson in methodology; it was also a lesson for conservatives.

The franc was to lose three-quarters of its purchasing power in the years from 1914 to 1918, maintaining its place in world markets only thanks to support from the United States and Britain.[1] For a banker there was also the matter of the national debt, money owed not only to the major allies but to individual French men and women who heeded appeals to buy war bonds. The debt could only grow with the demands of postwar reconstruction. German reparation payments might have helped—had Germany been in a position to pay them.

If there were Frenchmen who failed to realize what was happening to their economy, foreigners were there to tell them. The value of francs plunged against American dollars and British sterling.

France had a good shepherd in Raymond Poincaré, once ceremonial President of the Republic, more usefully prime minister beginning in January 1922. Brilliant lawyer, gifted orator, member of Parliament at twenty-seven, he was still young when he served as minister of education, then of finances. His term as president coincided with the buildup to World War I, and then its successful conclusion. Now he had another battle on his hands: it was for him to find and enforce measures to strengthen the franc; help from the allies would come only as France showed it was ready to help itself. In the absence of support from the British and American treasuries in 1924, France again turned to a private source, New York's Morgan, for a dollar reserve to allow France to bid up its own currency. Once again Rothschild was one of the intermediaries. And when the franc did rise, thanks to what the Rothschilds were saying and doing, those who speculated on a stronger franc took a profit. They included both Edouard and his banking family and S. M. Rothschild und Söhne in Vienna, invited by Edouard to join him in sustaining the French currency (not incidentally, they would also be sustaining the Vienna bank weakened by the collapse of the defeated Austrian Empire).[2]

Legislative elections in May 1924 brought in a new majority, the self-styled Left Cartel whose social policies (and readiness to print money) eroded the confidence of investors. Now the franc was to decline to a bare *fifth* of its prewar strength. A meeting has been recorded between Premier Edouard Herriot, president of the Radical Socialists, and a delegation of the board of the Banque de France led by Edouard de Rothschild; the date was January 15, 1925. Herriot promised to defend the franc (and did defend it in words). In further meetings with Herriot's finance minister, Rothschild, as spokesman for the board, warned of threats to the franc at home as from abroad; in France, so Rothschild was quoted, the loss of confidence was due both to "the clerical right and Communist extremists." Rothschild felt that the last elections had given the impression that France was going Communist. "There was a movement of alarm. The reactionaries exacerbated it." He feared that the decision to raise salaries of civil servants went in the wrong direction. "One agrees to raise them, but how does one pay?"

The board's own solution, as voiced by Rothschild, was national unity—of the center-right National Bloc and the Left Cartel—together with a balanced budget (through cuts in expenditures rather than new taxes). Against the prevailing wisdom, Edouard de Rothschild insisted on free movement of capital in and out of France. Viewing these events from a distance of half a century, an analyst suggested that as the franc weakened, and with it the capabilities of the Left Cartel, the power of the conservative board of the Banque de France grew—for what these sages demanded was a climate of "confidence" unobtainable under the present dispensation.[3]

Testimony to the enduring power of the French Rothschilds and of their titular leader, even in a world not of his making.

Edouard in action—Edouard the eternal conservative—can be captured in dialogue at this moment, thanks to a scholar's digging into minutes of a meeting of directors of France's railroad systems, this at a time (in July 1924) when the Radical Socialists were demanding the rehiring of thousands of employees dismissed following a national rail strike. Would the Chamber of Deputies attempt to *impose* reintegration of strikers, by law? The head of the Rothschilds made clear what his position would be. "I want us to insist," he told fellow railroad owners, "that we shall not bow to the law, and that we'll fight it to the end. . . . We'd be anti-patriotic criminals if we did otherwise." It was decided to mount a press campaign to warn of the consequences of a labor force run wild; the strikers did not get their jobs back.[4]

Foreign financial authorities—British as well as American—were as one with their French banking colleagues in their conviction that no amount of support could save a franc that was being eroded by an inflationary government; restoration of the value of the currency required a commitment to conservative fiscal management. In a meeting of influential bankers with officials of the Finance Ministry in May 1926, Rothschild and the governor of the Banque de France were seconded by directors of Banque de Paris et des Pays-Bas and Lazard Frères, and by the independent banker Louis Louis-Dreyfus. All agreed that it was essential to reassure investors as well as small depositors. Failing that, the risk was of a panic whose consequences could not even be foreseen.[5]

The battle for the franc can be followed, virtually hour by hour, in the posthumously published diary of the governor of the Banque de France during those crisis years. Emile Moreau had a first meeting with Edouard de Rothschild and his fellow directors shortly after taking office in June 1926. At once he saw Rothschild as a foe; from what he knew about the banker's views, they clashed with his own. To Moreau, the best one could hope for in desperate times was a stabilization of the franc's current value—in other words, a freeze at the level to which it had fallen against other currencies and gold. On the contrary, Baron de Rothschild and his conservative allies demanded a return to the stronger franc of prewar times—a significant revaluation. The battle lines were drawn.

Moreau's first days in office were stormy, coinciding with a run on state savings banks, the fall of another Herriot government (blamed by that politician on the "wall of money"). In July, returning to office as leader of a government of national unity, Premier Raymond Poincaré was obliged to issue a humiliating appeal to citizens to pay as much of their taxes as they could immediately, even before receiving their bills. His reason for being, he announced to the Chamber of Deputies, was the defense of the franc. In August a new law authorized independent measures by the Banque de France to defend the currency, but did not call for a return to its prewar parity.[6]

It was a struggle between bankers and the Bank—but not all bankers stood with patriarch Edouard now. The moderns—Lazard and Paribas among them—were quite ready to see a freezing of the value of the franc at a realistic level—meaning a lower level than before. They argued that a more expensive currency would price French exports out of the market, aggravating the economic crisis, creating unemployment, augmenting labor strife. The moderns also believed that in order to obtain further foreign support, notably loans from America, some compromise would be necessary (notably on the amount of war reparations it was reasonable to demand from defeated Germany).[7]

Moreau had to wear silk gloves in dealing with his board, above all with Edouard de Rothschild. His diary shows him virtually conspiring with Premier Poincaré to find a way to let the franc seek its own level without provoking the baron's explosive resignation. Against the Rothschild position, both Moreau and Poincaré were convinced that any attempt to raise the value of the franc by artificial means would so restrict the national economy that Frenchmen would feel the pinch and revolt against it.[8]

In his diary Moreau depicts a Rothschild so French in his orientation that until then he had refused to accept the idea of repaying France's debts to its allies; now (in November 1926) Baron Edouard shows himself more conciliatory. "It was not acceptable that France settle the question of interallied debts under a threat," he explained. "Today we have sufficient currency for our needs. . . . Maintaining its dignity, France will pay its debts to the extent it can."[9]

Still, the feud between governor Moreau and his most influential board member continued. In the spring of 1927 Moreau confided to his diary his conviction that rather than understanding the need for stability of the currency at its natural level, Rothschild was speculating on a rising franc; he noted with dismay that the baron had come out publicly for a revaluation upwards (at the general assembly of shareholders of his railway company)—something a board member of the Banque de France oughtn't to do. Moreau was obliged to take countermeasures to curb feverish purchase orders for francs, notably by drying up the supply of pound sterling available for speculation. His portrait of Edouard at fifty-eight is not flattering: a man without his own ideas, who when asked for an opinion on bank tactics says he must think about it—and comes back the following day with somebody else's reply.[10]

The year 1928—the last before the Wall Street crash—was decisive. Despite its volatile currency, France under Poincaré had achieved remarkable stability; its budget was in balance. Elections in April strengthened Poincaré by giving his national unity group the majority it required. What remained to be done was to define the franc—to reward the advocates of raising its value, or to put them in their place. Premier Poincaré himself, Emile Moreau knew, was at heart with those who wished to return to prewar values. . . . In the face of these good people, Moreau also knew, the role of the bank and its technicians seemed heartless. They had to insist on the irreparable damage to the economy that revaluation would cause.

To make his point, at the beginning of June 1928, the governor of the Banque de France simply threatened to resign. Clashes with the conservatives led by Rothschild became more frequent; the baron (and his ally François de Wendel, one of the country's leading manufacturers) would now simply fail to attend regular board meetings. But on June 21 Raymond Poincaré went to the Chamber to argue for stabilization of the franc at its present level, and won parliamentary approval; by vote of June 25 a new franc was born, a franc weighing in at sixty-five milligrams of gold—one-fifth of its prewar value.[11]

In his diary governor Moreau records the atmosphere at the meeting of the board shortly after monetary reform was voted. Wendel and Rothschild make an embarrassed entrance; Moreau shows himself "quite cool" to them; he can afford to be, now.[12] Later this moment would be taken as the beginning of the end of Rothschild hegemony over the national bank.[13]

Edouard's prudence was to manifest itself in other areas. Risks for which earlier Rothschilds were famous were now being taken by Lazard and the other bankers of twentieth-century commerce and industry; they became international bankers à la Rothschild when the present head of the Rothschild dynasty shied away from foreign involvements.[14] "The incentives of the fathers do not spur the descendants," an observer of the Rothschild saga—writing on the eve of Wall Street's collapse in 1929—was to explain. "Inherited wealth, education, refinement, a secure social position, are softening influences. They breed scruples, morbid ideas of responsibility, squeamishness about methods, oversensitiveness toward public opinion. Still more destructive of the will are roots in the soil; and the later Rothschilds let patriotic and party considerations interfere with business interests."[15] No one would say it better.

This didn't signify that the family was closing its door to the

world—hardly a thing one could say about a group whose investments were global. In the early years of the post–World War
decade the Paris Rothschilds began borrowing (through Morgan)
for the Compagnie du Nord, beginning with a bond issue having a
face value of $15 million.[16] In turn, Edouard's bank reached into
the bowels of New York by buying into Interborough Rapid Transit, the subway line that then served most of the city's under-
ground. The investment would later seem less judicious, as New
York's municipal authorities kept a tight lid on fare increases,
squeezing private shareholders. IRT went into receivership, after
which it became a matter of protecting bondholder interests; in the
end the city took over the private subways.[17]

What the Rothschilds were confronted by in the New York
subway system they were already living with in France, where
government policy on salaries—raising them, that is—made it
increasingly difficult to operate the railroads. Here it was the
Rothschilds who were asking for state intervention—a takeover of
the deficit, or authorization of a rise in fares, taxes on competing
means of transport by road and water, a lightening of those paid by
the railroads.[18]

One foreign market was written off. After the ravages of revolution, leaving bondholders with worthless paper, the new Soviet
Union began looking around for guardian angels. In November
1924, following the introduction of state capitalism under Lenin's
New Economic Policy (NEP), the Paris Rothschilds received a telegram from the official Inpravbank in Moscow suggesting a renewal
of relations, offering to deposit up to $1 million with Rothschild.
"Please indicate terms." The Rothschilds replied that owing to
present financial circumstances they couldn't accept the money.[19]

Here is another family portrait, as sketched in the last years of the
Roaring Twenties, a decade that came to be known in France as
the Crazy Years (an expression certainly not inspired by the even-
tempered Rothschilds). Once again the portraitist is Elisabeth de
Gramont, who is received by Edouard at home on Rue Saint-
Florentin (where of course she had dined with Edouard's father).
"Edouard likes to surround himself with his contemporaries when

they are pretty," she says (though the observation still falls short of what might be understood as crazy years). His wife, Germaine, "receives with a lovely smile and seems distracted when paintings are discussed." ("I don't remember if it's a Raphael, I'll ask Edouard," Elisabeth hears her say.)[20] In retrospect, Edouard's daughter was to call him "the last gentleman," although she also remembered his violent temper. He was far from being as frail as his photographs make him out to be, despite the tuberculosis that had clouded his early adulthood and was to come back at the end of his life.

Endowed with a deep sense of justice, he was passionately Jewish.[21] That he was a *French* Jew is clear from something he said at a general assembly of the Paris Consistory just before the war of 1914–18, in reaction to what seemed an alarming wave of immigration from central Europe that was bringing in Jews who *lived* as Jews and didn't simply practice Judaism. "These new arrivals do not understand French customs. . . . They remain among themselves, retain their primitive language, speak and write in jargon."[22] Wasn't that "jargon" the Yiddish of James and his brothers?

Edouard's personality may have been stronger than his physique; he was a celebrity at the stock exchange. A later manager of the bank would also conclude that his prestige far outweighed the significance of his activity of the time.[23] He now shared power with Robert, for by the mid-1920s Gustave's son was an increasingly active junior partner, even as the role of their uncle Edmond declined. But if near blindness kept the old man away from business, it did not see a decrease in his good works in Palestine, where Edmond now had a fully committed deputy in son James, now well into his forties. There were to be more settlements, new centers for research and development, committed like the old ones not to the ideology of colonization but to its practicality.[24]

Simon Schama, historian of the Palestine Rothschilds, lets us follow Edmond on his fifth and final visit to the Holy Land in 1925, an uplifting time, when Jewish immigration was booming, the British rulers making it possible for Jews to become citizens after a two-year waiting period. Hebrew was now one of the three official languages of the country, and now there was a Hebrew University with working scientists and scholars. Even the long-contested agricultural experiments seemed to be healthy. His journey across the land not yet called Israel was triumphal; Edmond was revered, observes Schama, as a resuscitated Herzl might have been. But he kept his head. Although now committed to a Jewish national home, as he declared in his spiritual testament to the congregation of Tel Aviv's Great Synagogue, he insisted that the symbolism of Jerusalem take second place to more urgent matters, such as farming and industry, village development, the consolidation of Tel Aviv itself.[25]

Back in Paris, the oldest French baron endowed a Fondation Edmond de Rothschild pour le Développement de la Recherche Scientifique, equipping it for higher studies in chemistry and physics. By 1927 the foundation had created an Institut de Biologie Physico-Chimique for pure and applied research, assembling physicists, chemists, and biologists (one of the first recruits was Jean Perrin, who had won the Nobel Prize in physics just a year before). On grounds bordering the Rue Pierre-Curie in the Latin Quarter, then the property of the University of Paris, Edmond's foundation proceeded to put up facilities hailed as surpassing anything then existing in Europe or the United States.[26]

Elisabeth de Gramont remembered a sickly Edmond, accompanied everywhere by his personal doctor, and remembered also his baroness of simple tastes (flowers were among them), a daughter, Myriam, who was misanthropic, a son, Jimmy, who was both "misanthropic" and far away in England. And then Maurice, "the best known, the rowdiest, the most ubiquitous of barons de Rothschild."[27]

He certainly must have been, in the 1920s; only Maurice seemed to be truly enjoying the Crazy Years. His status as a member of Parliament added a rich assortment of people to his parties—Aunt Julie's palazzo with its masterpieces, frequented (so cousin Elisabeth de Gramont observed) by politicians from both sides of the Channel, open to "members of the Academy, lovely ladies, and high society." And presiding over them all—Maurice, as sleek as a rajah.[28]

His constituency in the remote Hautes-Pyrénées didn't send him back to Parliament in the May 1924 legislative elections that brought the Left Cartel to power. In that deprived electoral district, too much had been expected of a Rothschild, and during the campaign his adversaries didn't let any of his unfulfilled promises escape unnoticed.[29] Momo returned to Paris somewhat chastened, resolved to give up politics—at least for the time being, since public service hadn't been kind to him.

An unexpected development led him to throw off his funk. In another province of southern France, the Hautes-Alpes—another mountain district with peaks even higher—a newly elected deputy died suddenly; a by-election was called. As he later reconstructed those frantic days, Maurice was approached by a member of Parliament from the opposite side of the political spectrum (a Socialist), and urged to run. The voting took place on July 27 and August 10, under the French system of two ballots. Maurice got the seat.

But the contest set off a storm. For Maurice de Rothschild, son of Edmond, grandson of James, was quite simply accused of fraud; a parliamentary inquiry was ordered, and it rendered a damaging report. This candidate who in 1919 had campaigned on his family name had this time chosen a constituency in which he was totally unknown three weeks before the election; to make himself known, his accusers said, he resorted to generous cash handouts.

A second report, submitted to the Chamber of Deputies on April 1, 1925, based on a fuller investigation, was equally generous with details. In one village Maurice de Rothschild had allegedly offered 5,000 francs—over 20,000 of present-day francs—to buy uniforms for a company of volunteer firemen, 1,000 francs for a railing to be erected around a war monument, 500 francs for a community baking oven. There had been a 500-franc gift for a village festival, 1,000 francs for a railway employees' cooperative (but this was turned down), 500 francs for a bowling club, 1,000 for a school charity. In a single town, noted the report, there had been cash gifts for a hundred people, ranging from 1,000 francs down to 20. Fathers of large families who approached him got 100 francs each, a worker wishing to travel to a large city to vote was handed 100 francs for the trip, each of the three village postmen received 50 francs, and so on.

In his defense the candidate remarked that his defeat for re-election to his previous seat in the Hautes-Pyrénées was proof enough that he hadn't bought his way into office. He denied the specific charge that he had disbursed a total of 1.6 million francs in the Hautes-Alpes. To the allegation that he had sent out 800 letters to voters, each containing 50 francs, he declared that he'd sent out only 200 letters, and the notes were of 20 francs and not 50. "I recognize that my situation as a candidate, in no matter which district I campaign in, is difficult with the name I bear," he confessed to fellow deputies. He didn't deny that he had offered financial help here and there, when asked for it. If he had "relieved some hardships," he was delighted to have done so; which of his colleagues would reproach him for that, or have failed to do the same? "When I visited a village and the mayor showed me an unfortunate woman giving birth on a bed of straw, should I have told him, 'Tell me about it after the elections'?" Could he have rejected little orphans?

He might have been tried on the charges, but they were covered by a presidential amnesty. Maurice declared that he should have preferred a trial, for then he could have seen all the accusations and had the opportunity to refute them. He asked for a chance to prove his case in a formal inquiry; his adversaries demanded a simple annulment of the election.

The plot thickened when the accused candidate himself accused Louis Cluzel, the Socialist deputy and newspaper owner who originally urged him to run, of really wanting a cash gift from a Rothschild so that he could buy a printing plant. For his part, Cluzel remembered that Maurice was happy to hear that only twenty thousand voters were expected to turn out, for that meant he would have to corrupt only that many people. (In fact Rothschild won the election by 10,248 votes, to 9,500 for the candidate of the Left Cartel; only three months earlier the Cartel had *carried* the district by a 2,500-vote majority.)

Socialist deputy Léon Blum summed up the case against Maurice de Rothschild. Both the charges and the counteraccusations called for annulment of the election. "Who in this assembly," asked Blum, "could think that because there is a corrupted party— and I refuse to accept this hypothesis—this is a reason to validate the corrupter?" The Chamber didn't go along with him, voting 180 to 178 for a formal inquiry rather than throwing out the election results at that point—the first time it had done so since 1902.[30]

The investigators took their time, coming back with a report only a year and three months later, at the beginning of July 1926 (all the while a quieter Rothschild, cousin Edouard, was defending his conception of the franc in the corridors of power). Once again the opposition to Maurice had a joyful time citing the testimony of witnesses to that colorful campaign. One deputy repeated the remark a voter made at an anti-Rothschild meeting: "Mr. de Rothschild did more in five minutes than you in an hour, because he gave us a lot of money, and you're only giving us words." There was also the story of a bystander who managed to extract 820 francs from Rothschild's treasury on a variety of pretexts. "That was a good day," the man was quoted, "especially since I risked nothing, not being a voter in the district."

Communist deputies, who led the fight against seating Rothschild, revealed that he had sent baskets of pheasants to members of Parliament. The Communists had refused them, but had anyone else? Yet while evidence of Rothschild largesse was undeniable, parliamentary investigations—by a large majority—favored validation of the by-election. In the words of their spokesman, Maurice de Rothschild hadn't thrown money around; he'd been *asked* for money: "His name was considered the symbol of fabulous wealth." He quoted a witness who had said, "We thought it was a gold mine for our district." A district, indeed, with a tradition of alms-seeking.

The spokesman cited the testimony of another witness who had alleged that a Rothschild aide had offered him 200 francs for his support—and then read out a letter in which the accuser specifically asked Rothschild for money for his young children, sick wife, and aged mother; for a fee, the solicitor wrote, he was ready to renounce his previous political position. Voters had testified that gifts from Maurice de Rothschild hadn't stopped them from voting against him. The inquiry concluded that the election was swung not by money but by local politicians who supported him; the candidate had forced nobody's hand.

A particularly telling piece of evidence was the handwritten text of a poster message signed "A Catholic Father," urging a vote against Rothschild because he was Jewish. The author of the anti-Semitic poster was none other than the Socialist Cluzel. (By then

Cluzel was no longer a member of his party's parliamentary group.)

Maurice spoke in his own defense, fortified by the committee's support. He reminded fellow deputies of his diminished status ever since the inquiry had begun; he hadn't been able to speak out on grave issues then affecting the nation.

The Chamber repudiated its investigators, voting against Maurice de Rothschild by 209 to 86.[31]

So he ran again, in the same Hautes-Alpes, and this time won with 10,539 votes (his closest rival got only 3,151). He ran again in the next general election, in April 1928, and won again.

But even though he had often taken the floor in his early years as a deputy—on matters ranging from schools and hospitals to breeding horses—he was never again to address the Chamber.[32]

BEFORE THE DEPRESSION

*O*n September 30, 1926, that year of rejection and triumph for Maurice de Rothschild, his wife, Noëmi Halphen—one of that race of strong Rothschild women (and she not even born a Rothschild)—gave birth to a son. He'd be called Edmond for his paternal grandfather (until then the youngest son of the Great Baron had no grandchild).[1] By then living apart from unpredictable Maurice, Noëmi set her sights on a sleepy Alpine mountain village, Megève, helping it take its first baby steps into international society; later, with her son's support she'd make it the winter resort par excellence. For—thanks to Maurice's inherited wealth and what he'd add to it when he finally got around to earning and not spending—the second Edmond would grow up to be the richest of all the Rothschilds.

All this while another branch of the family was preparing for fame. It had almost happened to Henri, for by now this doctor/scientist/automobilist/yachtsman was launched on his second (or was it a third?) career as a playwright. The nom de plume "André Pascal" was scant camouflage, as a review of one of his comedies in 1923 tells us: "In these difficult times, can a millionaire make us feel sorry for him because he's too rich? André Pascal seems to have thought so, in presenting his new play at the Antoine Theater. . . ." The poor rich hero, exploited by all his friends, finds happiness by taking a false name and pretending to be poor; a young salesgirl falls for him. "One knows that the pseudonym André Pascal is a cloak for Dr. Henri de Rothschild. . . ." The satire was penetrating, thought the critic, and that would explain the author's decision to withdraw the play after the premiere, for fear that his real-life models would be identified.[2]

It was the first and only time Henri/André took a play off the boards. He wrote for the stage all through the 1920s, and more often than not took the woes of the rich as his theme. When he built his palace in a park, the Château de la Muette on the western rim of Paris, a new street was opened to serve it, called (then and now) Rue André-Pascal.

Even a boating accident—his yacht *Eros* hit a reef while sailing off of the Swedish coast—was worth a page in *L'Illustration* (the action photos taken by Henri's son Philippe).[3] Henri, the critic of his 1923 play noted, had created a "gold-plated" role for pretty Marthe Régnier; soon Marthe was a regular passenger on the *Eros*, introduced simply as Henri's companion.[4] When the writer Colette was invited aboard the yacht, she found herself surrounded by a show-business crowd, a dressing-up crowd, treated to fairy-tale luxury. The yacht had "everything," she confided to a friend, speaking of a newly fitted-out *Eros II*, a thousand-ton craft with a crew of thirty-three, "even cabin-to-cabin telephones, to say good morning while still in bed."[5] And Henri's plays were getting better and better notices. "Le Grand Patron," for example, was the tale of a celebrated but poorly paid surgeon who, in a second marriage, is tied to a frivolous young spendthrift. So the good doctor agrees to serve as chairman of a company; less scrupulous managers lead it to bankruptcy; then he wins the Prix Nobel and all is saved. "Moving and dramatic," a reviewer promised.[6]

Perhaps Henri's best work was a small volume entitled *Tour du monde,* his account of a round-the-world trip that he saw as a tribute to Phileas Fogg, the Jules Verne hero who did the trip in eighty days. Henri's—like Fogg's, accomplished by steamer and railroad but in far more luxurious circumstances—took 150 days and not 80, but included a leisurely visit to Hollywood, with lunches at the big studios among the stars, a tête-à-tête dinner with Charlie Chaplin, then some shopping in New York before the return sail to Le Havre on the *Normandie.* The irony is that the journey, and the book, were quickly forgotten—even by Henri, who overlooks them in the memoir written only a few years later during wartime exile.[7]

But the truly famous man in Nathaniel's "English" line was going to be Henri's son Philippe, who joined his father when he opened the Théâtre Pigalle, later taking over as director, working with writers such as Jules Romains and actors such as Louis Jouvet; after a brief apprenticeship in Hollywood, he also began to make movies.[8]

Once again we hear about it from Colette, who had met Philippe aboard the *Eros* during a cruise through the fjords of Norway. He told the already famous author of his plan to produce a film version of the novel *Ladies' Lake* by Vicki Baum, and wished Colette to adapt it. Then twenty-nine years old, Philippe recruited a young director, Marc Allégret, and young stars Simone Simon and Jean-Pierre Aumont. They had help on the scenario from Allégret's good friend André Gide.

The famous but impecunious Colette was impressed by the Rothschild style. Philippe had leased a whole floor of an elegant hotel on the Bois de Boulogne to keep his team together. In the frantic final days of preparation of a shooting script, Rothschild and Allégret took a suite in the Champs-Elysées hotel where Colette lived year-round in an attic room; they were able to get rooms just a floor below hers.[9]

Emulating his father, Philippe kept a yacht of his own, entered it in the Coupe de France (a prize that happened to have been endowed by Baron Alphonse). The cup had long been out of French hands, but Philippe won it back from a Norwegian defender. He'd have gone on to the gold cup sponsored by the King of Spain, but withdrew in August 1926 on the death of his mother.[10] Then and later, Philippe wrote poetry and short stories, translated Elizabethan poems and the plays of the sixteenth-century dramatist Christopher Marlowe. He adapted no fewer than six plays by a contemporary, Christopher Fry.[11]

And still he hadn't found his life's work. With a doctorate—a son of Henri would have to have one—in physics and mathematics, he did postgraduate work in optics. As early as the 1920s his father had dispatched him to the family vineyard in Bordeaux; this young scientist doubling as a man of the world might know what to do with the venerable Château Mouton-Rothschild. Above all it needed a face-lifting, which in this case meant applying modern techniques to enhance both the quality and the reputation of the famous red.[12] He didn't consider the job done until he had lobbied the authorities into changing the traditional Bordeaux classification of Mouton from second-growth to first-growth status—which it certainly deserved.

By the time Henri's branch of the family was ready to reap the benefits of reborn Mouton, the depression of the 1930s was killing the wine trade. The publicist in Philippe took over. He invented Bordeaux's first "brand," an echo of the elegant Mouton-Rothschild at least in name; in fact his Mouton-Cadet was a blend of lesser wines. But the label had the right sound, and covered a product that almost everyone could afford. At the same time he began acquiring neighboring vineyards, beginning in 1933 with Château d'Armailhacq.

In those years even the best wines were turned over to dealers for marketing; Philippe decided to bottle his own, a practice that later became current for top-of-the-market growths. He'd go on to number his bottles, and to commission well-known artists to design the labels. Before the end of his life Philippe was a celebrity, a role easily assumed by his successor and daughter, an actress at the Comédie Française under the name Philippine Pascal.

And he'd made a celebrity of his wine. In that region, where the rival Rothschild vineyards are neighbors, a wine authority discovered one result of Philippe's lifelong crusade: there the name "Rothschild" is usually understood to refer to Philippe's Mouton, and a letter addressed simply to "The Rothschilds" will automatically go to Mouton (as if those quieter Rothschilds hadn't been cultivating elegant Lafite for well over a century).[13] Another connoisseur who toured the Bordeaux vineyards was struck by the contrast between the marketing wizards of Mouton and the more sober proprietors of Château Lafite, the wine of the Great Baron and his descendents. To visit Château Lafite after Mouton, he said, "was like entering a monastery."

Of course the Rothschild vineyards were competitors, and Philippe wasn't the sort to pretend the contrary. There was a story that he'd pour the rival Château Lafite for dinner guests, making sure to serve it with a curry so its qualities were drowned out.[14]

Only in winemaking could family solidarity be troubled by commercial rivalry. If the Henri-Philippe "English" branch seemed far removed from the banking Rothschilds, as late as the 1920s Philippe de Rothschild's older brother James Nathaniel (whom his father, Henri, preferred to call James-Henri), after serving as a combat pilot over Serbia in the Great War, found a job in the bank on Rue Laffitte. By 1928, when he was thirty-two, this James was an executive of a Rothschild railroad.[15]

The family also continued to maintain cross-channel ties. In Paris in 1924, Edouard got the news that the ancestral home on Frankfurt's Judengasse—that humble ghetto house—was sorely in need of repair. The cost, so the Rothschild agents in Frankfurt had told him, would be some 4,000 gold marks. He relayed the estimate to his "dear cousins" in London, who agreed to share the burden of rehabilitating that material souvenir of their beginnings. The house we see in photographs is the house as restored in 1925. It remained standing until ancient Frankfurt was razed by bombing during the Second World War.

There was also the discovery that employees of the old Frankfurt Rothschild bank, who, on its closing in 1901, had been hired by another bank with a promise of retirement pensions to which the Rothschilds had contributed, were now (in 1925) being treated badly—the successor bank having dismissed them without notice. London and Paris agreed to honor this family debt of honor.[16]

Even an angry Rothschild could serve the public good, as when Adèle, daughter of Mayer Carl and the widow of Salomon James— son of the Great Baron—refused to leave her property to her only child, Hélène, who had married into non-Jewish Dutch nobility. The legacy included an elegant town house on Rue Berryer in a particularly desirable quarter of central Paris; Adèle preferred to see it go to the government's fine arts administration, for use as a cultural center to be called the Fondation Salomon de Rothschild.[17] (An early visitor, President of the Republic Paul Doumer, was assassinated by a madman there in 1932.)

But it was the altruism, and the solidarity, that impressed Elisabeth de Gramont, a part-Rothschild far enough removed from the core to be observant of and touched by family identity and respect for hierarchy, which she explained as "the Jewish sense of patriarchy." She was the daughter of a duke, she'd marry another, and knew what she was saying when she expressed a conviction that the Rothschilds had no peers in their grand style, their taste for opulence, but also in their readiness to use their limitless funds to save a family member who had committed "costly errors."[18]

In Guy, born to Edouard and Germaine on May 21, 1909, we have the first member of the banking family to offer a lucid account of growing up a French Rothschild; it is also through Guy that we come closest to his self-effacing father. However unaggressive Edouard may have seemed, it is clear that he did not intend to let his only surviving son sit back and live on his income. (There had been a first son, named for his grandfather Alphonse, who died following an appendectomy at the age of four and a half; Guy was then eighteen months old.)

He must have seemed, young Guy, so different from other children: he got driven to school by a chauffeur. But *he* knew that he wasn't being spoiled, for his days were organized with quasi-military discipline. It was one's duty to work, first of all in school (and to get through one's exams); one also had a trade. Religion was there to be respected.[19] Still, his earliest childhood was enhanced by the magic of Ferrières, encompassing (for a child) not only its parks and ponds but its labyrinthine basement whose corridors led to servants' quarters and laundry rooms and wine cellars and more. Early childhood also meant the happy disorder of wartime—the Great War broke out when he was five, lasting till he was nine—when cousins Alain, Elie, Diane, and Cécile sometimes shared the refuge of the castle grounds, particularly when the Germans approached Paris with their giant cannon called Big Bertha.

In war and then in peace, there was the fascination of a world of domestic servants that a child (but not his parents) could approach, and there were no fewer than thirty persons to make life easier for the lords and ladies of Ferrières: butlers, laundresses, chambermaids, and cleaning women, those who hauled the wood and lit the fires; another fifty persons tended the gardens and park. Weekend guests brought along their own servants: chauffeurs and valets, aides who loaded the guns for hunting. One employee had as his unique function the preparation of salads; Guy guessed that it was because his father had found one particularly tasty, and promptly decided that its creator should henceforth do nothing else. Another member of the staff, an Englishwoman, had been engaged expressly to bake muffins, scones, and buns—treasured by Edouard, whose mother, Leonora, was of course an English Rothschild. (Thanks to his mother, Germaine, and to his imported nurse, Guy spoke English before he learned French; his father helped by talking to the boy in English as well.)

After 1918, Ferrières returned to its true vocation as the family's autumn residence. In October, however, when racing at Longchamp in Paris was still in progress, Edouard attended all the events in which one of his many horses was entered, and on those days he'd sleep at Rue Saint-Florentin. At the height of the hunting season, Guy's parents would spend only the middle of each week in Paris.

Weekdays at the castle found Edouard at work, studying papers that might concern his responsibilities at the Banque de France or the Compagnie du Nord, papers brought to him regularly from Paris. There would be golf in the afternoon, and Germaine might join her husband on the green. Back in the house Edouard played billiards with his children. Neighbors occasionally joined them for tea. Guy's parents also had their charities and other duties in the village, but, he decided in restrospect, in truth they didn't have very much to do. They probably enjoyed it that way.

A seeming contradiction with the work ethic in which Edouard was inculcating his son, just as Edouard's attire seemed in contradiction with his choice of a pastoral setting. As Guy put it, "dressing for the country," for his father, did not at all signify abandoning wing collars—collars that later were to be strictly reserved for evening dress.

So for Guy in early childhood, then in his first years at school, even Ferrières represented constraint and obligation, codified existence. Before high school it was rule by governess, with set hours for walking, cycling, riding. Life became tolerable only during high school, when (on days off and vacations) he could indulge in some grown-up pleasures, including the legendary hunts (he'd been given a child's gun early). He could also accompany his parents to the golf course (it was his mother who'd teach him to hold his clubs).

Even walks became interesting, when accomplished in the company of adults other than governesses. The castle grounds contained an enclosed deer park, rare birds, and even some monkeys; there were a vegetable garden, an orchard (when the family was in Paris, a carriage—later a motor vehicle—would arrive each day with a load of fresh fruit and vegetables from Ferrières). Then the stables—large enough to hold a hundred horses, some for riding, some for transport (used in the past to draw carriages and carts, later to serve the hunting parties), plain workhorses for the farm.

In the proper season, weekends would be spent in Chantilly, that paradise for horsemen which was also the family's holiday home at Easter and during the months of July and September; there Edouard had built a medieval-style manor. Guy learned what a future stable owner must know about horses. In Chantilly *and* in Deauville too, for the family repaired to that Channel resort each August, Edouard dividing his time between the celebrated racetrack and the family stud farm at nearby Meautry. Guy remembered how their horses followed the Rothschilds from home to home, from Ferrières to Paris, Paris to Chantilly, sometimes to Dieppe or Dinard for a sea change.

In Paris itself, where home was the Rue Saint-Florentin mansion in which Talleyrand had entertained, young Guy's top-floor room faced the Place de la Concorde, with a view of the Eiffel Tower. They still had a "mob" of servants—not so rare at the time, remarked Guy, for housework was then one of the leading outlets for labor. When his parents returned from an evening on the town, there was always a caretaker in livery waiting up for them, and a chambermaid to attend his mother. His sisters—Jacqueline two years his junior, Bethsabée three years younger than she—shared Guy's revolt against their parents' overprotectiveness. Both became allergic to luxury, constructing lives of their own as far as possible from the family orbit.

Rothschild he might be, but Guy was sent to a state high school, for the democratic education his father had also received. This didn't mean that the new boy was going to be like all the other boys, for this one was accompanied to school each day, and not only by the chauffeur who drove him there, but by a personal valet (who would pick him up at noon for a healthy walk home). Strict surveillance was his mother's idea; later Guy would ask her what had she been afraid of. "Doubtless," Germaine replied, "I was afraid you'd be raped!" (He also remembered her concern when he went off to a skating rink at the age of ten or twelve. "Well," she asked on his return, "you didn't meet any ladies there? For you know, they might not realize that you're still a little boy!") As soon as he could, Guy persuaded his chauffeur to stop the automobile at a distance from school.

Surveillance also created insecurity, convincing the boy that at bottom he couldn't fend for himself—to the point that on a day when no one came to fetch him, he asked a teacher to walk him home. Once when he was allowed to visit friends on the Breton coast near Dinard, they took him to the movies, then to a party. He made the mistake of telling his mother, and was never allowed to see his hosts again.

He'd have the best of tutors to try to improve his very average grades; one of them was later a high official in the ministry of the economy, another (René Fillon) became a director of the Roth-schild companies, a distinguished economist and government ad-viser. Guy easily won his high school degree, the all-important *baccalauréat*, but he hardly felt integrated into school life; part of the blame, he knew, belonged to his own withdrawn nature. But another part belonged to all the little humiliations that had con-tinued for so long—the obligation, for example, to wear short pants when fellow students were already dressing as men.

He celebrated his eighteenth birthday on the day Charles Lind-bergh touched down at Le Bourget airport after his solo flight across the Atlantic. Guy was at his window to watch the victory parade, the American hero in an open car, applauded by a delir-ious crowd. Henceforth Guy was allowed to attend his parents' social evenings (the first was a dinner for Raymond Poincaré, who had already been a president of the republic and was then engaged in saving the franc with Guy's father).

Dinners of the sort seemed interminable (with two soup dishes, one a bouillon and the other thick, then eggs or fish, game, roast meat, then cold meat and salads, two desserts, cheese, fruit, wines white and red, champagne, sweet wine with desert, digestive liqueurs). "I would like to be elsewhere," Guy remembers his mother whispering to him, in English, as she was about to enter the dining room on the arm of Monsieur le Président Poincaré.

In those days there was no proper school to prepare one for a career in business; Guy enrolled at the Sorbonne and at the Paris law faculty, did well at both. Henceforth the only restrictions on his freedom were those made necessary by his workload. When it was time for the military service that every young Frenchman was expected to perform, there was choice, and Guy chose the cavalry, which took him to the celebrated riding school at Saumur on the Loire. He ended up as a second lieutenant; later his cavalry unit converted to motor vehicles, and he got a taste of motorized warfare during two training periods before the outbreak of war in 1939.

He rather enjoyed being treated like everybody else (treated roughly, in other words), during long months of strict drill, of early rising to a trumpet call, cold water in the lavatories. But then he won the right to rent a hotel room in town, with some time at the end of each day for a hot bath and dinner alone or with friends—before returning to the barracks. And every weekend a Rothschild chauffeur would turn up for a fast drive to Ferrières, for the hunt; Guy would be back in Saumur Sundays before midnight.[20]

GUY'S APPRENTICESHIP

*I*t was a wicked time to be joining the bank, as Guy de Rothschild had a right to feel when, in the autumn of 1931, he walked through the massive street gate at 19 Rue Laffitte, for the first time as an adult on adult business. Only the day before (it happened to be the holiest of Jewish holy days, Yom Kippur), the United Kingdom had announced the devaluation of the pound. Having completed his compulsory military service, Guy was there to learn, and certainly trained to lead—as son of the bank's principal director, Edouard (who then shared ownership with Edouard's old uncle Edmond and his cousin Robert). Guy also knew that what others might take for a career in a bank, a Rothschild saw as a priesthood.[1]

Actually it was *not* the worst of times, for the Rothschilds—in France and nearly everywhere else—had come through the first postwar decade unscarred. The judgment of a historian of the family, first published in Germany in 1928, was still valid when it appeared in French translation in 1930 (Guy would have read it then). "Today, and after a century and a half of existence of their bank, the Rothschilds remain solidly implanted," wrote Count Egon Cesar Corti. "Their name and their wealth are famous the world over. It is vain to try to evaluate their fortune, for the total sum changes constantly and cannot be estimated. . . ."[2]

Guy enjoyed an orderly, well-thought-out apprenticeship. The bank officer to whom he was entrusted, his father's first assistant, was a most patient man. He read the morning papers aloud, commenting on events that might affect the business of the bank. On the practical side, this deputy taught the twenty-two-year-old crown prince how to interpret stock-market quotations, how to decipher the books. Guy was assigned letters to write (one of his correspondents was a Cardinal Pacelli, future Pope Pius XII, then in charge of Holy Office finances, and who kept a small account—as did other greats of the world—at MM. de Rothschild Frères).

He found reminders of past glory at every hand, some of them unfortunate (in that they were no-longer-relevant practices or functions). His elders still occupied the fine old buildings acquired or built by Great Baron James, occupying numbers 19, 21, and 23 on Rue Laffitte. The core of the bank remained the "grand bureau," an outsized room with five windows on the street, between each of which a tall desk served one of the partners. Curiously, the desks were placed perpendicularly to the window wall, so that the partners sat one behind the other. Each of them, when necessary, could retire to a private office, but the bank's quotidian business got done in this very public space. On each desk lay a row of buttons, each button wired to summon a senior employee; there were telephones too, but Guy's father used his principally to call in one of his managers—not to communicate with the world beyond Rue Laffitte.

Beyond the grand bureau the bank resembled any other twentieth-century institution. And yet the rites continued to be respected. Attendants then and later (right up to nationalization in 1981) wore full-dress coats. There was an end-of-year ceremony at which employees waited their turn to receive a handshake from each of the partners and a suitable bonus, in an envelope that also contained an indication of what next year's salary would be. Of course, Guy knew that elsewhere in this austere institution the private offices were carpeted, their walls covered in velvet, and there were leather sofas; the privileged had access to a private dining room. (That area of the bank dated from the era of Queen Hortense, the mother of Napoleon III, and had served the Great Baron as living quarters.)[3]

The archives let us intrude on a touching family affair: Edouard's announcement to his Austrian and English cousins in the autumn of 1932 (just a year after Guy entered the bank) that he was giving his son a power of attorney. (This allowed him to sign correspondence, but didn't mean that he was a partner, not yet.) One can also read the reply of Louis von Rothschild, head of the Austrian bank. "I do hope that when he [Guy] is given responsibility for business, the times will have become more tranquil and agreeable than they are now for the Vienna house."[4]

Indeed, Vienna's problems were among the first of the century to trouble the placidity of Rue Laffitte. Incredible as it may appear in hindsight, given the seemingly hopeless economic, social, and demographic position of France in the first decade following World War I, the world crisis had largely spared the country's financial activity. Wall Street had been devastated, and had ruined most of its practitioners, panic had spread to most other business centers. . . . Was it because of France's decreasing significance in world markets? For the fact is that a full year after New York's tremors shook the world the French were still enjoying relative prosperity, a budget surplus, a growing gold reserve in the Banque de France, satisfactory employment, and a reasonably healthy manufacturing sector whose competitiveness had predictably been augmented by the 1928 devaluation.

France *was* being affected by the universal slump, but didn't know it yet. Frenchmen would have to wait a while longer to perceive the decline in foreign trade, the payments deficit, the fall in production, the bank crisis. One of the evident causes of French distress was the inability of Germany to pay agreed-upon war reparations, and the realization of France's allies that to insist would be to kill the goose.[5]

Yet even the crash of a bank in a far-off country could affect western Europe's economic health, confirming the collapse of credit, thus of the possibility of trade; alas, the bank was Louis's. Of the members of the Vienna family, only one was at the helm of the banking business and industrial holdings (while his brothers played). That was Louis, "the silkiest, most stoic, most smoothly and untouchably finished grand seigneur yet sired by The Family": so wrote a Viennese of the next generation, Rothschild biographer

Frederic Morton.[6] That was going to be the problem—getting Louis, the great lord, to listen to somebody else.

While the essence of Rothschild activity in Austria was concentrated in the family bank, S. M. Rothschild und Söhne, the Vienna Rothschilds also controlled the country's leading financial institution, Oesterreichische Credit-Anstalt für Handel und Gewerbe, virtually a national treasure. So much so that in early October 1929—three weeks before Wall Street's Black Friday—the Austrian government informed Louis that the country's principal real-estate lending facility, Bodenkreditanstalt, was failing; its collapse would be "catastrophic." So the Rothschilds were asked quite simply to take it over, to merge it with Credit-Anstalt. Louis saw no way to say no to his country, and indeed had to say yes without having time to examine the sick bank's books.

From Paris, Edouard told him he'd been right to do what he did. "Thanks to your decisiveness and courageous attitude," he wrote to Louis (on October 18), "you saved Vienna's finances and avoided events that could have been extremely serious for your country and that would certainly have had repercussions in other financial capitals and markets." He still expected that Louis could save Austria's leading land bank from collapse.[7]

But it was not only the land bank, it was postimperial, diminished Austria itself that was in trouble, its credibility and its credit. And the Austrian disaster was the signal for continent-wide panic, dragging down banks all over central Europe. Meanwhile, Louis was further compromised by the failure of an asset in far-off northern Europe, the Amstel Bank in the Netherlands.

By May 1931 it was clear that nothing could be done to stave off the collapse of the Credit-Anstalt; the point now was to save the Viennese Rothschild bank, the Rothschild name, and Louis, for soon public opinion and the press were demanding that the Austrian government identify those at fault and prosecute them. For his part, Louis was prepared to dispose of personal properties, even to pledge the family's crown jewel, the Vitkovice (Witkowitz) steel mills in Czechoslovakia that had been Rothschild property for nearly a century.[8] Before the dust could settle he was indicted, forced to liquidate personal equities to keep out of jail. By then Austria was living in the shadow of its turbulent neighbor, with the

coming to power of the Nazis in Berlin; "Red Vienna" became
their target. But Louis ignored the new political context just as he
had ignored the economic one.

It was time for an appeal to family solidarity, since formal ties
no longer bound the French Rothschilds (or the British Rothschilds for that matter) to their Austrian cousins. Help would come
in the form of cash: low-interest loans from both Paris and London,
in the total amount of $8 million. Cash, yes, but not an underwrit-
ing of Louis or an endorsement of his ways.[9]

We can capture the emotions of the Paris Rothschilds thanks to
a revealing bank memorandum that has survived that troubled time.
It is now the beginning of spring 1933, and Edouard has joined his
family on a winter holiday at their villa in Cannes. Still he must deal
with this crisis that won't blow away. He has turned to the family
sage, Uncle Edmond, now eighty-seven years old, for advice; Edmond has scribbled a reply, and it is read to Edouard on the telephone by one of his Paris deputies (the time is noted: 7:00 P.M. on
the evening of March 28). Edmond does *not* advise his nephew Edouard to invite Baron Louis to Paris, although if he decided to come
he obviously couldn't be prevented from doing so. Nor should the
French Rothschilds—even if, thanks to their loan, they now have a
financial interest in Louis's salvation—send people from Paris to
audit the Vienna bank's accounts. "That is very dangerous because
it suggests involvement or support from the Paris house," insists
Edmond. "What is happening in the Vienna bank does not concern
us. We advanced funds, it's a question of honor for Vienna to reimburse them. . . . This matter of honor in our families has always
been the overriding point of view. One need only recall the sale of
the silverware." Here Edmond referred to the legendary sale of the
family silver by his father, Baron James, when threatened by bankruptcy during the financial crisis that accompanied the 1848 revolution. "The Vienna house is not our business," so Edmond
summed up his advice—one almost hears the thunder in his voice—
"and in sum, as one of the heads of the Paris house, I do not wish
to give them any money, not a penny more."

That said a good deal about the respect with which the fast-
spending, imprudent Louis was regarded. In a telephone call from
Cannes early next morning, Edouard expressed his own fears.

Clearly the Vienna Rothschilds were on the road to disaster; Louis was stubborn, refusing advice on reducing expenses—or on selling stock to meet current obligations. Soon Edouard and his associates would be hearing from their own sources that Louis had spent too much on trying to save the Credit-Anstalt; he'd have been better off getting out of Vienna. The legal action against him had been dropped, but with the rise of the Nazis in neighboring Germany, his problems were only beginning. If Louis did not reduce expenses he would have to begin selling property, but even that would mean asking London and Paris for more money in another couple of years.

The French cousins could take comfort from a report published in the *Frankfurter Allgemeine Zeitung* on September 23, 1933—published in Germany, after all, and six months after Adolf Hitler assumed dictatorial powers. The paper told of the donation of Vienna Rothschild properties to the Austrian government, in return for which Louis had been absolved of responsibility for the difficulties of the Credit-Anstalt as well as Dutch Amstel, problems surmounted (said this surprisingly sympathetic account) by Louis's voluntary reduction of both his fortune and his expenses. Funds for the rescue operation, which included reimbursement of depositors and dealing with the cascade of company failures in the wake of the collapse of the bank, had been obtained by loan. To date, the Vienna Rothschilds had met all of their commitments, with debts outstanding only to affiliated foreign banks (the French and British Rothschilds were surely among them). As a consequence the credit of the Vienna bank, declared the Frankfurt daily, was now totally reestablished.

But the French Rothschilds were hearing something else from their own sources in the Austrian capital. In December 1933 an informant warned that if the Nazis came to power in Austria they would surely exploit the Credit-Anstalt affair. He advised getting Louis out of Austria (the excuse could be a health problem, and Louis could spend the winter at Edouard's residence in Cannes).[10] Yet Louis stayed on, saving his banks and his reputation, even reimbursing Paris and London with part of his central European holdings, including the Vitkovice works.[11] He was still there when the Nazis came.

*   *   *

Whatever reassurance Guy de Rothschild acquired by reading
Count Corti, the French bank as it revealed itself to him during his
apprenticeship dispelled illusions. He found De Rothschild Frères
to be more of a family "secretariat" than an active bank. It managed—unprofitably—a number of private accounts; it was always
ready to subscribe, loyally, to new government bond issues. But
that was all.

In a word, pure immobility—Guy's word. Yet this immobility
had not affected the bank's reputation for honesty, for reliability.
Even in the family's industrial investments—for Edouard's generation had continued the heavy involvement in railroads, mining,
and electrical production and distribution, as in oil—the bank in
the time of Guy's father no longer took the initiative, simply managing what it already possessed. Royal Dutch, for example, whose
fate in the 1930s was shared by the Rothschilds. As the world's
economic activity declined, so did oil profits. So the senior executives of Royal Dutch were to tell a Rothschild emissary in March
1932: "Prices are bad everywhere, and except for a few rare places,
money is not being made."[12]

Yet there was now a new face on Rue Laffitte, the first of a line
of highly competent, well-paid senior managers to whom would be
given some of the authority, if not the power, of the owners. The
new recruits could offer organizational skills and varieties of experience that the family could not have found within its own ranks.
And when the new managers were good, they could be very good.

The first of the new breed, René Mayer, would later be a finance
minister, then a prime minister, still later head of the groundbreaking European Coal and Steel Authority (precursor of the European
Community). He was hired by Edouard. In post–World War II
France, Edouard's son Guy was to take on another nonfamily manager, Georges Pompidou, who left only to become Charles de
Gaulle's prime minister, then president of the French Republic.

Son of a businessman, with a formation in letters and law similar
to Guy's—even a distant cousin of the Rothschilds through his
mother—René Mayer was a senior civil servant in France's supreme administrative body, the Conseil d'Etat, before joining the

Rothschilds at the age of thirty-three; no novice he. He became an officer of the family's Northern Railway, a director of a number of Rothschild industrial companies, and when the time came for negotiations with the antibusiness Popular Front government in 1936, Mayer would be up to it; he'd have the rank as well as the experience. Meanwhile Guy was appointed secretary of the board of the Compagnie du Nord, a job with limited duties but a window to the wider world of business and capital markets. He was given a small firm of his own to run, a maker of electrical accumulators. He couldn't earn very much for the family, but he could learn useful things about industrial management. In 1936 Edouard turned over a one-fifteenth share of his stake in the family business to his son and junior partner.

As for De Rothschild Frères, it was still not doing very much, to Guy's keen disappointment. Edouard and Robert and their associates went through the motions of being bankers, but the great adventures were all behind them. The bank seemed the mirror of a dormant France. But Guy de Rothschild was young.[13]

Part of the problem was Edouard's precious franc. In the first years of depression the government's attempts to preserve the value of the Poincaré franc resulted in deflationary policies that gave preference to prudence over expansion, promoting budget reduction and low prices at a time when industrial dynamism was needed. Soon French production had fallen behind not only that of its allies but of the nation it had defeated, Germany.[14] What a New Deal could do—devaluing the dollar to promote consumption—old dealers in France could not. The economy grew stale, unemployment soared. France was ripe for a shake-up.

Darryl Zanuck, who was soon to unite his Twentieth Century studio with Fox, put the Rothschilds on film in 1934. "The House of Rothschild," in which George Arliss played both Mayer Amschel and his son Nathan (and Boris Karloff an evil Prussian), offered a somewhat fanciful account of the family's role in Napoleon's defeat and the battle against anti-Semitism. The final scene, in which the king of England makes Nathan a baron, was filmed in primitive Technicolor, and the movie was nominated for the Academy Award for Best Picture. It played nearly everywhere in the world, but not in France; Edouard and his family saw to that. They continued to see to it that as little as possible was said about the Rothschilds (and French privacy law supported their efforts).[15]

Yet their very existence seemed to call for ostentatious manifestations; just being a Rothschild won a headline. Marlene Dietrich came to Paris in 1933; in *The New Yorker* magazine, correspondent Janet Flanner described the famous actress as "the belle of the Baron de Rothschild's ball—or [she] would have been had she consented to dance with any husband but her own."[16] Which Baron de Rothschild? Edouard? Robert? Henri? Philippe? No matter, presumably, to a public more often than not obliged to content itself with a "Baron de."

Nor could one be secretive about the racetrack. Withdrawn Edouard—the baron most often referred to under the unhelpful "Baron de"—was a celebrity if only because of his passion for horses, his wise choice of jockeys and their mounts. This was the golden age of Edouard's stable, whose star was Brantôme, winner of the French Triple Crown, the three most important events for two-year-olds. Soon Brantôme would take the coveted Arch of Triumph prize and cinemas were showing a short film called "Brantôme, Invincible Horse"; years later, reporting its death, a daily headlined: BRANTOME DE ROTHSCHILD IS DEAD.

Guy grew up in the aura of this respected stable, one of the oldest in France. Withdrawn Edouard owned some eighty brood mares and another ninety horses trained for racing, most of them two or three years old; he won the important Prix de Diane five times, the Arch of Triumph twice. Edouard's son might have preferred to grow up on a golf course, but he made it a duty to follow his father to the stables. Often now the Rothschild whose picture appeared on the sports page would be Guy.[17]

He found it easier to adapt to the life of the socialite in Paris, especially the café and night life, with elegant Fouquet's for drinks after the races, the Café de Paris or Pré Catalan for a proper meal. There were the obligatory formal affairs given by the upper classes for one another, requiring white ties even for the youngest heirs.

But it was through his mother that he was to hear that "charming Alix" had lost her husband. Alix Schey de Koromla was already

twenty-six, but then Guy was now twenty-eight—and still waiting
for the ideal bride. Descending from an old Hungarian family, born
Goldsmith-Rothschild on her mother's side, she was then living in
Germany when her first husband died; she had a five-year-old
daughter, Lili. Guy had found a woman he could live with, and the
summer after their first meeting, at her family estate near Brati-
slava, they were formally engaged. They married in Paris at the
end of December 1937, and for their honeymoon sailed to New
York on the *Queen Mary*.[18]

Edmond, the family sage, grandfather to all the banking Rothschilds, died on November 2, 1934; he was eighty-nine. His seniority led many to assume that he had been in charge at the
bank.[19] Indeed, his opinion had counted, but he had long since
relinquished quotidian activity. Then in his final decade he had
been all but blind, accompanied everywhere by a woman who read
to him—for he continued to care about the world.[20]

Living, he hadn't weighed heavily on the banking Rothschilds;
his death created a problem. Long years before, Edmond's son
James Armand, British subject and resident, had ceded his equity
in the Paris company to his father, whose sole banking heir was
now Maurice (there was also daughter Miriam, who by Rothschild
tradition and statute had no stake in the business). Now, with
Edmond's death, the rebellious, turbulent Maurice controlled a full
third of the capital of De Rothschild Frères, an equal partner with
Edouard and Robert. There was a similar division of shares at
Château Lafite, except that there Edmond's one-third share continued to be divided between his sons Maurice and James Armand
("Jimmy" to everyone).[21]

Clearly Maurice—whether in his private life as a ladies' man or
in his unconventional public one—lacked the requisite profile of a
Rothschild partner (he would have frightened away clients attracted by the bank's reputation for discretion).[22] It became necessary to buy him out, a decision even Maurice could accept as
reasonable, although the ways and means of cutting ties created
bitterness that would last a lifetime. There was a cash settlement,
retroactive to the date of Edmond's death—underscoring the truth

that not for a day had Maurice been involved in the administration of the firm.

But the compromise had not been won easily. The question, of course, was how to divide assets equitably (for Maurice was to be given his share partly in cash and partly in shares of Rothschild-controlled equities). One bone of contention was the Compagnie Agricole de Lukus in Morocco—an activity, Maurice conceded (in a letter dated August 10, 1936, to his "dear cousins"), that had been developed by Edouard and Robert "after my poor father, worn out by illness and age, had been obliged to leave the sole management of the Rue Laffitte to you, while still contributing, against his will, to an expense of over 80 million francs invested in recent years in this Moroccan agricultural enterprise." His dear cousins had put a price tag on Lukus that he found questionable. "You are certainly of good faith, but your evaluations err on the side of excessive modesty." Rejecting an estimate that would signify "still another advantage, equally unjustified, to your profit," and after eighteen months of trying to reconcile their differences, he took the momentous step of calling in the lawyers. A Rothschild was suing other Rothschilds.

The plaintiff's writ in this virtually secret suit evoked history, recalling Great Baron James's wish "that the three branches descended from him always be represented" in the family business. And so, until his death, Edmond, the last surviving son of James, had been an associate of the bank, despite his great age and his poor health, "solely with the idea of assuring the entry of the only one of his children in a position to represent his line, Maurice de Rothschild." Maurice's complaint alleged that until his father Edmond's death, neither Edouard nor Robert had ever objected to an eventual partnership with him, and thus they profited up to the last minute from capital provided by old Edmond—including the investment in Morocco. Only after Edmond's passing, in November 1934, had the cousins refused to consider cousin Maurice a partner; in a spirit of family conciliation (said Maurice's lawyer), he had agreed to the liquidation of his share of the company. But the agreement concluded in July 1935 had not settled the matter of that expensive Moroccan venture, most of the stock of which belonged to the bank.

The proceedings dragged on; they were even leaked to a scandal sheet. (It took sides, describing Maurice as "a mix of real intelligence, alert and adapting easily, with total bad faith and above all unequaled boorishness." It quoted his alleged remark about cousin Henri de Rothschild: "He's a lucky man, having lost his parents early!")[23] The parties accepted arbitration, with a cash settlement paid to Maurice by Edouard and Robert; the agreement was signed on September 26, 1939, three weeks after the outbreak of European and world war. All three cousins—Edouard, Robert, and Maurice—declared their satisfaction, acknowledging "their common desire to maintain family traditions among themselves."[24]

THE TWO HUNDRED FAMILIES

On the sixth of February, 1934, Guy de Rothschild stood at his window on Place de la Concorde to watch history being made. In fact the riot that bloodied the square that day was only the final event, the culmination of a series of attacks of growing gravity against republican government symbolized by the lower house of Parliament just across the Seine. In a climate of social unrest, the right and not the left had seized the initiative. The good reason was the explosive Stavisky scandal, named for Alexandre Stavisky, naturalized Frenchman, Jew, and bank swindler, who appeared to benefit from well-placed accomplices and tolerant friends. A cluster of extremists—members of Action Française, right-wing war veterans, and proto-fascist youth groups—had answered the call for a march on what they considered a corrupt Parliament.

It was not intended to be a nonviolent manifestation; the protestors came armed. Shots were fired as the police defended the bridge leading to the Chamber, there were shouts and screams from the crowd moving in waves back and forth over the vast square—Guy watching all this from his perch. Mounted police charged into the demonstrators, who threw tiny metal balls under the horses' hooves to make them fall, and they did. Other rioters sought to cut the horses' hocks with razors.[1] In the end the mob was stopped on the Concorde side of the river. But before the square became quiet again there were seventeen dead (one a policeman) and 2,329 wounded (1,664 of them on the side of the law).[2] If the Chamber of Deputies remained inviolate, something happened inside all the same, as the hasty resignation of Radical Socialist premier Edouard Daladier made way for a conservative government no more likely to be able to come to grips with what was ailing France.

A curious time. For if the Rothschilds opposed the right-wing extremists, they found common cause with another right-wing movement that happened to share their anticommunism, their devotion to God and country. The paradox was that the Croix de Feu (Cross of Fire), a quasi-mystical assembly of war veterans, was both the extreme and its contrary. Under the charismatic leadership of Lt. Col. François de La Rocque, wounded and decorated in the Great War, the Croix de Feu had been one of the groups that had summoned its troops onto the streets of Paris that day. Unlike the others, La Rocque refused to attack the seat of legitimate government, and actually withdrew as disorder spread. For that he was to become a pariah to the extreme right (as he already was to Communists).[3]

Much of France's business community saw the Croix de Feu as a force for good, at worst as a counterfire to right-wing extremist agitation. Colonel de La Rocque had long been employed by a leading industrialist, Ernest Mercier (connected to the Rothschilds through their investments in electrical power). While the Communists were tarring La Rocque and truly fascist extremists with the same brush, the Croix de Feu was being welcomed as a participant in memorial services for Jewish war veterans, under the aegis of the Central Consistory and the Consistory of Paris, beginning in that pivotal year 1934—to the violent objection of left-wing Jews.[4]

This paradoxical situation was fodder for the Communists, whose daily organ *L'Humanité* came up with the headline COLONEL DE LA ROCQUE AT THE ORDERS OF BANKERS ROTHSCHILD AND FINALY. The reference was to Horace Finaly, the fiery Jewish financier who had made the Banque de Paris et des Pays-Bas the aggressive institution it was in the between-the-war years.

French Communists found it easy to connect La Rocque to Ernest Mercier, Ernest Mercier to the Rothschilds. But the party organ also alleged that high finance was behind the attempted coup of the sixth of February. The Rothschilds and the Finalys favored deflationary policies, noted *L'Humanité*, with a reduction of salaries and pensions. And La Rocque led their assault troops.[5]

It was a time when French fascists, emulating their German model, were frightening their flocks with tales of a Jewish alliance with the feared Bolsheviks of the Soviet Union; surely it was as awkward for these right-wing extremists as it was for French Communists to find that one particularly conspicuous anticommunist, Colonel de La Rocque, saw fit to share the podium with leading Jews. But the effective protest against La Rocque's presence came from the Jewish side, for some local chapters of the Croix de Feu were more extreme than others, a few were openly anti-Semitic, and La Rocque had failed to disavow them publicly. When he appeared at the Rue de la Victoire synagogue on June 14, 1936, to participate in a commemorative ceremony for war veterans, a crowd on the street protested his presence noisily. Inside, La Rocque stood alongside Rabbi Jacob Kaplan and the president of the Consistory of Paris, Robert de Rothschild. It would be the last ceremony of its kind.[6] Three days later Léon Blum's Popular Front cabinet included La Rocque's movement among private militias banned by decree.

The ideological attack on a hypothetical "two hundred families" who dominated France suffered from similar ambiguity. To militant Socialists, to the more moderate Radical Socialists concerned by the predominance of big business and high finance, to denounce oligarchy seemed a matter of social justice. The first significant formulation of the battle cry of the 1930s was presented to a Radical Socialist congress by Edouard Daladier on October 28, 1934 (nine months after he had resigned the premiership in the face of the extremist assault on Parliament):

> Two hundred families are masters of the French economy and therefore of French policy. These are forces that a democratic state should not tolerate. . . . The influence of the two hundred families weighs on the fiscal system, on transportation, on

credit. The two hundred families place their own people at the head of state. They influence public opinion through control of the press.[7]

"The two hundred families" soon became a rallying cry, easily assimilated by the Communists and their trade-union allies. It was quickly adopted by the extreme right, including militant anti-Semites, for it could be shown that many of the families targeted were Jewish (or—nearly as bad—Protestants). And then extreme left and extreme right shared a target: the Rothschilds.

There was a simple explanation for the "two hundred." Under the bylaws of the Banque de France, an institution established by the first Napoleon, France's national bank was directed by government appointees but controlled by its private shareholders. The fifteen-member board—twelve of them chosen from among the principal shareholders—answered to a general assembly composed of the two hundred most important shareholders. The seed of myth.[8]

Myth that often played with numbers. Some social reformers found it easier to envisage one (and not two) hundred oligarchs. The Communist organ *L'Humanité* found that twenty-five industrial groups were responsible for the country's misery. Logorrheic Louis-Ferdinand Céline, whose anti-Semitic vituperations were unique in their violence in prewar France, wrote in 1937: "They talk of two hundred families; they should talk of the 500,000 Jewish families that occupy France." (That in his polemical essay *Bagatelles pour un massacre.*) A year later (in *L'ecole des cadavres*) he found that there was really only one all-powerful international family: "the Jewish family, the great international feudal power that ransoms us, drugs us, robs us, lords it over us."[9]

In a slightly more rational exposition of the anarcho-rightist case, a periodical in the spring that brought the Popular Front to power devoted an issue to "The 200 Families," actually identifying 203 persons representing 57 families who held 1,312 seats on the boards of leading corporations. Some three hundred names were regularly found in business directories, and these were the people who controlled the nation's intellectual life, the media, charity, even the churches. "When the archbishop of Paris, the Great Rabbi, and the president of the Consistory of Reformed [Protestant] Churches participate together in meetings for sacred union, the two hundred [families] rub their hands; they think of elections going the right way, of obligatory conformity."

Myth that recalled the nineteenth-century polemics of Toussenel and Drumont, myth that was to nourish the gullible, as well as the incurable paranoids who formed the shock troops of extremism during the Depression years, then later during the German occupation of France. In another product of 1936, an exposé of "financial feudalism" published by the Communist party, the author insisted that despite appearances the Rothschilds were as strong as ever in France; they only tried to appear less powerful as a cover-up, for they still "held the controls of the whole French economy."[10]

Then suddenly the myth became a winning political slogan, as conservative politicians helpless in the maelstrom of global depression were swept from office in the elections of spring 1936, bringing to power a Socialist-Radical coalition endorsed by the Communists, a French cabinet headed by the Popular Front's ideologist Léon Blum, and a platform calling for, among other things, "the liberation of the State from the grips of financial feudalism by establishing the nation's sovereignty over the Banque de France through the dismissal of its board of directors."[11]

"You will have seen today the results of the French elections," Edouard's cousin and partner Robert wrote their London cousins on May 4, 1936. "I am sorry to say that they are most unsatisfactory." He foresaw "difficult days, weeks, and months, as all skies— internal, financial, and external—are terribly black."[12]

REFORM OF THE BANQUE DE FRANCE
IS VOTED 430 TO 111

So read the headline in *L'Humanité* on July 17, referring to the Popular Front majority action of the previous day. The initial instinct of the lower house of Parliament had been simply to nationalize the bank—taking over privately held shares against compensation, but this could not have gotten through the more conservative Senate. As finally voted, the law abolished the board of advisers, in which Edouard de Rothschild had been first among equals, replacing it with a council in which shareholders were vastly outnumbered by experts from government and quasi-governmental institutions. The general assembly of the Banque de France, previously limited to "the two hundred," was now opened to all 40,000 shareholders.[13]

The Senate approved the reform by a vote of 190 to 74. One of the senators who voted with the Popular Front was Maurice de Rothschild.[14]

The left coalition suffered its first major setback a year later, when the Senate refused to accord Léon Blum the power to legislate by decree in order to reorganize the country's finances. A new cabinet headed by Radical Socialist Camille Chautemps (with Blum as his vice-premier) pursued Popular Front objectives, though with less conviction. Still, reorganization of the privately run railroads was high on the agenda.

Nationalization was effected by decree, under the plenary powers denied to Léon Blum but granted his successor on June 30, 1937. Chautemps was authorized to "reduce the deficit of the railroads through higher fares and coordination of lines."[15] The measure was signed on August 31, just before Chautemps's writ expired. The point was to improve the efficiency of the railroads by eliminating waste of material and duplication of service, and to bring about economies in management. Henceforth the seven existing railroads—the Rothschilds' Nord among them—were subordinate to a public corporation, the Société Nationale des Chemins de Fer (SNCF).

The reform could hardly hurt the private owners more than the post–World War I slump already had. They had been piling up deficits for years, deficits caused in large part by the obligation to operate under ground rules set by government, aggravated by Popular Front labor and social reforms, among them obligatory wage increases, a forty-hour workweek, expanded annual vacations with pay. (The combined annual deficit of the seven railroad companies, with their 55,000 miles of track and half a million employees, had amounted to nearly four billion francs in 1936; it would be nearly six billion in 1937.) So if the Rothschilds and fellow owners

were now obliged to transfer their assets to the newly created
SNCF, they were able to rid themselves of their liabilities too. They
gained more than they lost.[16]

Indeed. In payment for its material and real estate, the Compagnie du Nord received a hefty packet of shares of the SNCF, while
a trusted Rothschild manager sat on the board of the new company.
The old Rothschild railroad company thus became a formidable investment group, and a profitable one. "The bankers had easily
passed the cumbersome and costly railroad sector on to the state,"
a Rothschild admirer and critic observed with a note of irony. "That
didn't mean the old owners didn't resent nationalization as a form
of plundering. After all, they felt in a way as if they had been thrown
out of their own house. But it is probable that with time they were
able to see the advantages in some nationalizations."[17]

"The reign of the rail magnates is over," proclaimed the Socialist party organ *Le Populaire* in an editorial accompanying the
announcement of the creation of the SNCF.[18]

Divestiture could not always and everywhere be negotiated in the
turbulent 1930s; there would not always be a soft landing for the
divested. In Austria, where pressures from neighboring Nazi Germany now amounted to bullying, Louis von Rothschild worked
incessantly to save what could be saved of family assets, in anticipation of the country's total surrender to Hitler. The rescued
property included the Vitkovice plants in still-free Czechoslovakia, transferred with the help of friendly and disinterested third
parties into British hands. Meanwhile, Austrian lawyers were fighting off legal and fiscal threats to vulnerable Rothschild und Söhne,
in the wake of the Credit-Anstalt disaster. The imbroglio was
aggravated when a lawyer hired by Louis declared that he had
bribed Austrian officials and committed other illegal acts in the
service of the Rothschilds. So another lawyer was hired to block
further prosecutions, and he succeeded in getting the case against
the first lawyer dismissed (and even managed to head off blackmail
efforts by the first lawyer and by a former Credit-Anstalt official).

It looked as if Louis would come out of it all unscathed. Then,
in March 1938, reassured by the patent indifference of the western

democracies, Adolf Hitler found a pretext for sending his troops across the border; he decreed the little nation a province of the Reich. Louis de Rothschild was arrested. He'd be released in a year's time, thanks to the efforts of his Paris cousins; he'd even get to Paris, leaving everything—including the family silver—in Nazi hands.[19]

ROTHSCHILDS AT WAR

he rising menace of Hitler, making it increasingly evident to the worldly-wise (and the Rothschilds were certainly in that category) that Nazism would spill over German borders, would spill over or be consciously exported, aroused contradictory feelings in the French family. They were anti-Hitler from the first hour, of course. But they also found it tempting to shut Germany out of their minds, as if nothing the Nazis did could affect Frenchmen, even Jewish Frenchmen.

The Rothschilds shared both reactions with other conservative Jews, like themselves members of the affluent class dominant in the Association Consistoriale des Israélites de Paris (ACIP), the official organ of the Jewish community. Yet the massive influx of refugees from eastern Europe had engendered a newer generation of more militant groups, whose leaders were quite prepared to raise their voices against the Nazi threat. In this they received little support from the ACIP, whose leaders (the Rothschilds among them) felt public protest would be counterproductive.[1]

French Jews often suspected that it was the refugees newly arrived from the east who were responsible for anti-Semitism; they irritated French sensitivities with their uncivilized look and behavior. This point was made by Baron Robert de Rothschild, Edouard's cousin and president of the Consistory of Paris, speaking to the general assembly of that organization in May 1935: "The crisis raging in France has engendered a xenophobia which too often degenerates into anti-Semitism." Jewish leaders responsible for defending the interests of the community, he added, had to warn fellow Jews who had only recently immigrated and were therefore not yet thoroughly familiar with French customs and mentality. "It is essential that foreign elements assimilate as quickly as possible. . . ."

Baron Robert apparently interjected a further remark—not published in the official minutes of the assembly but carried in the Yiddish press: "Immigrants, like guests, must learn how to behave and not criticize too much . . . and if they aren't happy here, they'd do better to leave."[2] The speech provoked vehement protests; it would be held against the family.[3]

Six decades later, given what we now know about Nazism, Robert de Rothschild's admonition seems insensitive. In the context of the 1930s, when the immediate danger seemed to come from within and not without, the priority of community leaders was integration. Then fifty-three years old, Robert became president of the Consistory of Paris, succeeding his uncle Edmond, in 1933, the year Hitler came to power. (Cousin Edouard, who by then was sixty-five, remained at the head of the Central Consistory, following Consistory—and Rothschild—tradition.)

Indeed, far from turning his back on the rising Hitler menace, as early as June of that same year Robert encouraged the founding of a relief agency for German victims of anti-Semitism. (By statute, the Consistory itself was limited to religious and cultural activity.) Insisting on ideological neutrality, Baron Robert steered the new group away from partisan groups and activity; the emphasis was on material aid to the escapees from Nazi territory: emergency shelter, medical aid, food, proper documents, permanent quarters for those with jobs, vocational training for those without. In its first year of existence the committee registered some eleven thousand refugees, assisted 1,894 of them. Most of the financial support came from within France's Jewish community, with further assistance from its American and British counterparts.

The operation was not to go smoothly, for the newcomers, who arrived despoiled of their possessions, were entering a France

sinking deeper every day into economic stagnation. One of the
tasks of the relief agency was to convince public opinion, and the
authorities, that refugees could be an asset to France rather than
a liability. It was also necessary to preserve the group from infiltration by Communists who would use it for propaganda purposes,
thereby compromising its effectiveness.

By 1934 public opinion had grown even more hostile to refugees, making it difficult for the government to offer them permanent residence. It was now that Robert let his frustration appear—
for it would have helped had the refugees taken more pains to show
that they could look and act like everybody else. (As the family
recalled it, Robert pushed so hard to obtain immigration certificates for Palestine that even Chaim Weizmann, the Zionist incarnate, feared he was moving too fast.) In 1936 the aid group was
replaced by CAR, the Committee of Assistance to Refugees, again
under Baron Robert's presidency. He also took charge of a new
Center of Documentation and Vigilance (CDV), which became the
action arm of the Jewish community, sharing offices (and personnel) with the Consistory—this at a time when more militant anti-
fascist groups, Jewish and nonsectarian, were making themselves
heard. Unlike the more combative movements CDV let it be known
that its action "to be useful, must remain discreet." It gathered
information on anti-Semitic movements and individuals in France,
published reports, encouraged counterpropaganda by other groups.

But of course the greater danger came from abroad, threatening
the existence of Jews throughout Europe, not only those in Germany. Following the explosion of anti-Semitic violence in Germany
on November 9, 1938—the infamous Kristallnacht—the Night of
Broken Glass—during which Nazi hoodlums burned down syna-
gogues and assaulted Jews (ostensibly in reaction to the murder of
a German embassy officer in Paris by a Jewish refugee), the Consistory hastened to organize a coordination group for "aid and
protection." Inhibitions against open opposition to fascism and
anti-Semitism were abandoned; the Consistory began to engage in
more conspicuous activities, actively lobbying the government.
(One result was an April 1939 ban on incitations to race hatred.)
By now the established Jewish community, for all its conservatism,
was actually involved in surveillance of anti-Semitic movements,

training Jewish boy scouts in combat sports, sending them out on the streets to rip up anti-Jewish posters or to harass vendors of anti-Jewish periodicals. The war had begun before the war.[4]

In hindsight it may all seem clear; in fact Palestine did not appear to be a viable alternative for the bulk of European Jews in the Nazi years. For one thing, the British kept a tight lid on immigration in the face of Arab hostility. Rothschild archives indicate just how far afield those who assumed responsibility for the plight of Hitler's victims might be ready to go. One finds a letter from Robert de Rothschild in January 1939, forwarding a proposal to his London cousins concerning the purchase of 100,000 acres of land in Brazil's still-wild Mato Grosso "for colonization purposes." Later that year, Paris transmitted a recommendation that the London Rothschilds look into a plan to settle Jews on a plain in the Sudan's Upper Nile valley between Malakhal and Bor—in deepest Africa. "Naturally it is a thing which involves very high capital, but if what [the advocate of the project] says is true, it would be a huge territory for the moment, with no population and where Jews might organize between themselves an important colony."

There was also time for individual cases. Paris to London (the letter is either from Edouard or Robert), the same month: "I enclose a note on a little German refugee girl who is in London and sick. She is a sister and daughter of an old family of very good musicians and we have been looking after the brother here who is leaving for America in a day or two. . . . I cannot remember the name of your tall gentleman who is looking after your refugee business, but would you be so kind as to hand him that affair with my best recommendation?"[5]

In March 1939, just six months before Hitler's attack on Poland, Edouard's wife, Germaine, opened an old house at the edge of the Ferrières domain, the medieval-style Château de la Guette, as a hostel for refugee children. The insane violence of the Nazis' Night of Broken Glass had occurred just four months earlier; the parents and the elder brothers and sisters of these children were now in concentration camps. Later, on the eve of the German march into Paris in June 1940, the children (about 130 by then) were evacuated to La Bourboule (also to be the refuge of the Paris bank); there Baroness Germaine had taken over a hotel for her wards. The youngest of the children were sent to the local primary school, the older ones to professional schools in nearby towns, or placed with families. Some of the older boys were moved to an ostensibly safer southeastern region, where they were found by French gendarmes in the national roundup of Jews in August 1942, interned, then saved from deportation by their teachers.

Long after the departure of Edouard and Germaine for the United States, the work in La Bourboule was pursued by others; more than thirty adults died in its service. As the German occupation was prolonged, the children were dispersed, hidden under their own or false identities. Some were taken under the protection of Quakers of the American Friends Service Committee and brought to the United States. Others found their way to Palestine. As far as is known, ten children, all of them fifteen years of age or older, were sent to camps, and one survived. But the whereabouts of twenty other young boarders of the Château de la Guette group remain a mystery to our day.[6]

The best evidence is that the Rothschilds were as unready for what was in store for France as most French men and women (as well as a high proportion of their leaders). *New Yorker* correspondent Janet Flanner recorded a vignette of Senator Maurice de Rothschild, who could be assumed to be following European affairs closely. On the eve of the war, this reporter found him at what she called "the great costume ball of the summer" given by Count Etienne de Beaumont. Guests wore costumes inspired by Racine (whose tercentenary was then being celebrated), and Maurice was "garbed as the Ottoman Bajazet," displaying his mother's famous diamonds on his turban, on his sash "the rare Renaissance jewels which are a part of his family's Cellini collection."[7]

It must have been frustrating for professional agitators to find the Rothschilds so docile, so unready to give up their peaceful ways. To the extremists, the Rothschilds simply had to be war-mongers. Thus, on the front page of the always astonishing daily *L'Action Française,* its chief propagandist, Charles Maurras, denounced French personalities he found to be lusting for war; one of his targets bore a name "thrice famous in our history . . . famous as a Jew, famous as moneyman, famous for incarnating a certain kind of Jewry and bank, more or less identified with France."

As Maurras saw it, the Rothschilds had become rabid about fellow Jews "molested"—his word—in Germany. While Robert de Rothschild presided over relief committees, his cousin Edouard "doesn't stop vomiting curses against traitors, liars, incompetent persons," i.e., those in government who refused to follow the war party.

Next day Maurras pursued his campaign against the Rothschilds and "the Jewish war," noting that his opening salvo had stirred up the Rue Laffitte. In a subsequent issue the editorialist seemed to be contradicting his thesis when he described the Rothschilds as pro-Franco and anti-Republican in Spain because of mining interests there; they were switching sides, he explained, only because of Hitler's persecution of the Jews. Until six months ago, said Maurras, Edouard and Robert had shown themselves to be reasonable, while cousin Maurice was cooperating with the Popular Front and the Communists.[8]

Guy de Rothschild describes that summer; yes, he expected war. Getting ready in July of 1939 for a long vacation far from Paris, he spent a morning at the bank to sort his papers, making separate piles for documents "to evacuate" and "to discard"; he hated the idea of exposing either his professional or his private life to enemy eyes. His wife, Alix, was convalescing after a miscarriage, and they had decided on a Mediterranean cruise.

It was while sailing off the coast of Corsica that he heard a radio report of the rapprochement of Stalin and Hitler by means of the Ribbentrop-Molotov treaty of nonaggression; when he tried to telephone Paris from the harbor, he found that only official calls were getting through. That night they crossed to the mainland, docking at Saint-Tropez. The couple found an obliging Rothschild (Robert's daughter Cécile) to drive them back to Paris; the very next day, as he remembered it, he discovered his number on a poster listing officers summoned to duty in the general call-up that came in anticipation of war.[9]

At the beginning, the older Rothschilds could only sit out the war—that "phony war" which involved little or no combat from the Allied declaration of war on September 3, 1939, until the late spring of 1940. Only then did Edouard and Germaine take leave of French soil, with their second daughter, Bethsabée; their destination was the United States, as it was for Robert (who in that earlier war had received three citations for bravery), accompanied by his wife, Gabrielle, and their daughters Diane and Cécile.

Edouard's son Guy was sent to the front. Robert's Alain, who only the previous January, after his twenty-ninth birthday, had been given signatory power at the bank,[10] was called up as an officer on August 20 to join a reconnaissance group of an army corps garrisoned just north of Paris, at Compiègne. When the Germans invaded France in 1940 he won a combat citation during the hopeless attempt to contain the surprise German offensive through the Ardennes. Badly wounded in Belgium three days later, he was taken prisoner, and spent the next four years in a German POW camp.[11] As for his brother Elie, a junior officer in the mounted cavalry, he too was captured by the Germans on the northeastern front. Alain and Elie were to meet in captivity in October 1944, at a POW camp near Lübeck—a camp designed to punish the rebellious.[12]

The war caught old Henri de Rothschild in Switzerland, where he had been living ever since contracting a mysterious illness on a cruise to China in 1935; his doctors changed their minds and sent him to Portugal, where he was treated for depression, and he stayed on in Lisbon. Restless Henri, sixty-eight years old when the Germans occupied France, obviously couldn't sit still in exile, nor could he conduct medical experiments or write frivolous plays. So he took up pen and paper to compose a history of the French Rothschild family, and when a granddaughter, James-Henri's daughter Nicole, turned up for a visit, she typed it for him.

The very public man Henri was would certainly have been surprised at the fate of his book, which he had printed at his expense in Portugal: no Rothschild archive has a copy today, nor is it in the French National Library or any other known repository in Paris or London.[13]

Henri's ebullient second son, Philippe, was found by the call to arms on his yacht, sailing off Arcachon with his wife, Lili, and daughter Philippine. He made a hasty return to Paris to take up duty in the air force, but was confined to a hospital bed with a broken leg (acquired not in an airplane but on skis) when the Germans overran France.[14]

Only Guy, through recollections written in retirement, lets us see the daily duties of a Rothschild at war. In the months before the fighting broke out, his regiment was attached to a light armored division, which included some heavy tanks as well as a brigade of armored vehicles, some artillery, and two regiments of cavalry troops. The division consisted entirely of reservists, meaning it was the last to be equipped, and the equipment, when it finally arrived, was inadequate, the machine guns ancient models, and there were no antitank guns at all. He was attached to a motorcycle platoon, and weeks passed before he got the regulation vehicle with sidecar, and its engine was unpredictable. When an aging lieutenant, a veteran of the First World War, fell sick, Guy took over his squadron of dragoons (two hundred men in all, including a machine-gun crew and an office staff).

Eight months of phony war ended precipitously, in the night of May 9–10, 1940, as Hitler's troops crashed through the frontiers of neutral Belgium and the Netherlands, in a drive toward France's northeast industrial and mining heartland. Days later a second breakthrough occurred, farther south, in a forest region deemed impenetrable, across a river deemed uncrossable; soon the best French troops—rushed north into Belgium with their British allies according to a plan that seemed logical to the Allied high command—were bottled up. The battle of France was all but over a month after it began.

The French—even French soldiers, above all their officers— were slow to comprehend the extent of the disaster. Guy's division had been sent to the exposed northeast; on the morning of May 10 it was billeted at a small village near Cambrai. The wake-up call was brutal. Orders were to march into Belgium; crossing a bombed-out village along the way, the men saw the war's first victims.

They were given an impossible mission: to hold, with the small forces and inadequate arms at their disposal, lines under attack by vastly superior forces, beneath skies dominated by the enemy's screaming Stuka dive-bombers. There were incomprehensible orders—incomprehensible until Guy realized that he was being moved from one position of retreat to the next, often after no engagement with the enemy. Communications were rudimentary; in the whole northern campaign he never saw a radio. If there was any logic in what they were being ordered to do, it was to organize a retreat in such a way as to delay the enemy advance.

There were moments of close and intense combat all the same, as on May 26, when Guy was ordered to attack in the face of enemy cannon; he began with 135 men and ended with no more than 40. Two of his noncommissioned officers were killed as they conferred with him. Even the retreat was accomplished under fire. Guy received a citation to the Order of the Army, acknowledging his command of a counterattack on May 26 "under violent enemy fire."

This phase of the war ended for him, as for so many others, at the beach of Dunkirk. Ordered to assemble his men there, he drove and then walked for twenty-four hours. On the night of June 1–2 the survivors of his group crossed to Dover on a British destroyer. Uninjured troops were quickly shuttled back to France to continue the combat, Guy and his men via the Brittany port of Brest, then overland to Evreux in Normandy, where he found his wife still at their country house (and could show her the Croix de Guerre he earned on the Dunkirk dunes). And then back to action—an action of successive withdrawals south of Paris, sometimes to find that his men had been overtaken by German troops moving faster. The war was over.[15]

Browsers in the archives, turning the pages of the always revealing correspondence between the Paris Rothschilds and their "dear cousins" in London, find few signs of tension, or indications that precautions were being taken in the months preceding Hitler's surprise attack. Here is patriarch Edouard, preparing to send a money gift to Hebrew University in Jerusalem (on January 18, 1940); here young Alain renews his membership in the British Automobile Association. Or Edouard—still in January—is getting replacements for plants from the Royal Seed Establishment in Reading, England:

> As I told you, my gardener assures me that only ten to fifteen out of the plants can be saved and I hope that in saying so, he is being pessimistic.

Where it all started:
Mayer Amschel's
house in the Frankfurt
ghetto. *PHOTO COURTESY
OF ROTHSCHILD COLLECTION*

James de Rothschild.
*PHOTO COURTESY OF
BIBLIOTHÈQUE NATIONALE*

Portrait of Baroness Betty, the wife of the great Baron James de Rothschild, painted by Ingres. *PHOTO COURTESY OF ROTHSCHILD COLLECTION*

Portrait of James de Rothschild, by an unidentified painter of l'Ecole Anglaise. *PHOTO COURTESY OF ROTHSCHILD COLLECTION*

Three sons of James: Alphonse, Gustave, and Edmond. *PHOTO COURTESY OF ROTHSCHILD COLLECTION*

VISITE DE FERRIÈRES. — L'Empereur plantant l'arbre commémoratif de sa visite au château.

Napoleon III plants a tree on his visit to the Rothschild estate at Ferrières. *PHOTO COURTESY OF ROTHSCHILD COLLECTION*

The Great Hall at Ferrières. *PHOTO COURTESY OF COLLECTION OF GUY DE ROTHSCHILD*

Photomontage postcard of Baron Edmond de Rothschild (1845–1934) at the Zikhron Ya'akov Vineyards. *PHOTO COURTESY OF MUNICIPAL MUSEUM, RISHON LEZION, ISRAEL*

Baron Edmond de
Rothschild. *Photo*
courtesy of Rothschild
Collection

Alphonse de Rothschild on
a magazine cover. *Photo*
courtesy of Bibliothèque
Nationale

Alphonse de Rothschild bows to King Leopold II of Belgium as Baroness Leonora looks on. *PHOTO COURTESY OF BIBLIOTHÈQUE NATIONALE*

Baron Edouard de Rothschild. *Photo courtesy of Rothschild Collection*

An anti-Semitic caricature of Baron James. *Photo courtesy of Bibliothèque Nationale*

Caricature of Maurice de Rothschild as a candidate for parliament in 1924. *Photo courtesy of Bibliothèque Nationale*

Caricature of Henri de Rothschild in uniform (World War I) on the beach at Deauville. *Photo courtesy of J. Chennebenoist*

Edmond de Rothschild, grandson
of the first Edmond. *PHOTO COURTESY
OF SAVOUR CLUB*

Edouard de
Rothschild on his
arrival in New York
(wife, Germaine, at
center; daughter,
Bethsabée, at left.)
*PHOTO COURTESY OF THE
AUTHOR*

Henri de Rothschild. *PHOTO COURTESY OF BIBLIOTHÈQUE NATIONALE*

Robert de Rothschild. *Photo courtesy of Rothschild Collection*

Elie, Guy, and Alain de Rothschild at the bank in the 1970s.
Photo courtesy of Rothschild Collection

Elie de Rothschild. *PHOTO COURTESY OF BIBLIOTHÈQUE NATIONALE*

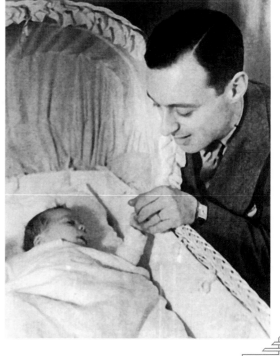

Guy de Rothschild with infant David (1942). *PHOTO COURTESY OF ROTHSCHILD COLLECTION*

Guy and Marie-Helène de Rothschild at Chantilly (Prix de Diane, June 1957). *PHOTO COURTESY OF BIBLIOTHÈQUE NATIONALE*

Marriage of Philippine. Left to right: groom Jacques Sereys, Philippine de Rothschild, Philippe de Rothschild, choreographer Serge Lifar, actor-director Maurice Escande. *PHOTO COURTESY OF BIBLIOTHÈQUE NATIONALE*

Château Lafite Rothschild today. *PHOTO COURTESY OF DOMAINES
BARONS DE ROTHSCHILD*

The famous label. *COURTESY OF THE AUTHOR*

Batsheva de Rothschild in Tel Aviv. *PHOTO COURTESY OF THE AUTHOR*

Eric de Rothschild at
Lafite. *PHOTO COURTESY OF*
DOMAINES BARONS DE
ROTHSCHILD; PHOTO BY MICHEL
GUILLARD

David de Rothschild. *Photo courtesy of Rothschild Collection*

Castle of Ferrières as it appears today. *Photo courtesy of the author*

The only indication that there is a war going on appears in correspondence in which a lieutenant Guy renews a subscription to a British periodical, and a second lieutenant Elie to *Punch, Rire,* and *Esquire.*[16]

Before the end, of course, Edouard and his associates did what had to be done. Some family assets were transferred abroad, to be held in accounts not specifically identified as Rothschild (for one never knew). To protect nonfamily clients of the bank, their holdings were placed in banks in seemingly safer regions of France; not, re-membered Guy, for fear of the German invaders—for the banking Rothschilds refused to believe that the capital would fall—but to protect against eventual damage by bombing or shelling.[17]

A record of one of these transfers shows up in a roundabout way, thanks to a postwar legal affair. As early as 1939 Edouard dis-patched one of the family's most portable treasures, the precious shares of Royal Dutch oil stock, to a Montreal bank. After the fall of France in June 1940, Canadian bank officers who knew how to read the letter of the law blocked the account—France was occu-pied, after all, and were these not enemy assets? By then Edouard and his wife and youngest daughter, Bethsabée, were refugees in New York, literally living on the family jewels.

After the war, when it was finally ready to return to Rothschild what Rothschild had deposited, the bank in Montreal billed Edou-ard $22,000 as a custodial fee. He refused to pay, sued, and won.[18]

There was certainly nothing discreet about the family jewels; they made a headline in *The New York Times* nearly a month after the fall of Paris:

*Rothschilds Bring
$1,000,000 in Gems*

———

*Member of Noted Banking
Family Arrives on Clipper
With Wife and Daughter*

An accompanying photograph showed Edouard at New York's LaGuardia Airport with Germaine and Bethsabée, he "carrying a bag containing gems valued at $1,000,000." The story described the baron as "a slight and tired-looking man of 70 years," who "shied from reporters and refused to discuss politics, finance, economics or any other subject." He did say that he was pleased to be back on American soil, recalling his first visit in 1890, just half a century earlier.

When they got a look at what the Rothschilds were carrying, customs inspectors took Edouard and Germaine into a private room; someone let it be known that the gems were "museum pieces." But reporters did note that the baron was still carrying the bag when they left the airport.[19]

VICHY

The banks got to the Vichy zone before Marshal Pétain did. Anticipating a German invasion of Paris, the capital's principal financial institutions (on the advice of the Banque de France) had already transferred their management, and as much of their assets as they could, to what seemed the safer Auvergne province of France's south-central mountain redoubt, a region well equipped to take in transients thanks to the profusion of hotels built in happier times for visitors to its spas. On June 14—the day Paris fell—the headquarters of De Rothschild Frères was formally transferred to La Bourboule, a town of 2,700 inhabitants until then better known for its thermal baths than for banking. The Rothschild billet turned out to be the Grand Hotel (rated "good average comfort" in the *Guide Michelin*—call it second class; only two of its sixty-seven rooms had baths).

By then Philippe Pétain had taken charge of the last French government of the Third Republic in its Bordeaux retreat. An armistice was signed in the Compiègne forest on June 22, leaving the Germans in control of Paris and northern France and the Atlantic and Channel coasts, with an ostensibly independent French government (under Pétain) in charge of what remained. That government chose Vichy as its capital—for it too was a watering place amply endowed with hotels.[1]

The Vichy regime—proclaimed the French State to distance itself from the former Republic—was quickly infested by extremist ideologists who could not have prevailed in a France free to choose its leaders; one of the doctrines they held in common was anti-Semitism. As early as July 23, 1940, Pétain decreed that "All Frenchmen who left mainland France between May 10 and June 30 . . . will be considered to have sought to remove themselves from the responsibilities and duties of members of the national community": by leaving they had renounced their French citizenship. The property of such persons would be confiscated, to be sold after six months, the proceeds going to the Vichy state's welfare agency.[2] Characterizing those who had left France, the pro-German French press used a word the decree had not: desertion.[3]

Of course most of those who had emigrated were Jews aware of the fate in store for them in a German-dominated France. The Vichy government radio made that evident in identifying persons whose property would be seized, and the collaborationist press in Paris made it clearer still:

A FIRST LIST OF JEWISH
FUGITIVES PUBLISHED IN VICHY

Obviously the Rothschilds were conspicuous on the list—Edouard and Robert notably—although the front-page story mentioned not these discreet bankers but the very public personage of Maurice, the intrepid senator from the Hautes-Alpes who had actually sat in Parliament in Vichy on the date Pétain was given full powers—and had voted no.[4] Later, in September, a decree issued in Paris identified the Rothschilds whose property was to be seized: Edouard, Robert, Henri, Philippe, Maurice.[5] An old list of Rothschild real estate in Paris—nearly one hundred buildings—was leaked to the collaborationist press.[6] And the hunt was on.

A document that has survived—thanks to the postwar Nuremberg war crimes trials—is the travel pass of one Dr. Karl Rasche, agent of the Nazi occupiers of Czechoslovakia, who was en route to Paris to take over Rothschild files concerning their foreign investments in order to determine ownership of the Vitkovice steelworks in Czechoslovakia, now part of Hitler's Reich.[7] In La Bourboule, meanwhile, Guy de Rothschild was quietly arranging to shift what could be saved of the bank's remaining assets to a friendly fellow bank.[8]

Guy was not listed among the "deserters." Even the most fanatical of collaborationists might respect a decorated French officer—at least at that early stage of the Nazi occupation. So he could live freely, at least in Vichy-controlled France. He got there as soon as he was released from uniform, improvising an itinerary from one town to the next, changing trains five or six times, arriving to find a makeshift bank, loyal employees who had come down from Paris, and even a few family members.[9] One of them was Henri's son James, who had also been rescued from the beach at Dunkirk, and had since been discharged from his obligations as a major in the air force.[10] James's daughter Nicole was also there, and stayed in what she considered a dreary if decent and even healthy place as long as the family did; leisure hours were devoted to parlor games.[11]

Guy found the village charming enough, sited as it was on a stream surrounded by benign mountains.[12] His wife, Alix, after sailing to Argentina with her daughter by her first marriage (on one of the last ships available to the Rothschilds before escape by sea was denied to them), eventually made her way to New York. Now, in autumn 1940, she flew back on Pan American Airways' *Yankee Clipper* for Lisbon; Guy met her as she crossed the Spanish border and accompanied her to their Auvergne retreat.[13]

In La Bourboule, a comforting sixty miles over hilly roads from Pétain's Vichy, Guy began to organize the remnants of the family empire. But since the bank had done little of significance in recent years, there was obviously not very much for it to do in La Bourboule.[14] In Paris, the offices on Rue Laffitte had been taken over by the Pétain government for use by its national relief agency. A skeleton staff had been able to stay on, in the charge of a trusted Rothschild bank officer who did what he could to keep La Bourboule informed. When necessary, they used professional smugglers to move messages across the line separating German-controlled territory and the Vichy zone—messages that were succinct and often discreet (referring to the Germans, for example, as "our new friends").

One of the things Guy was able to do was to utilize funds from

the bank's remaining assets to pay indemnities to retired personnel (at a time when such benefits were still voluntary and not
mandatory).[15]

In retrospect, those early weeks of Nazi occupation and Vichy
doctrine appear idyllic. On September 27, 1940, the first German
decree concerning Jewish business ordered that signs be placed on
Jewish-owned companies to identify them as such. Then on October 18 the Nazis were ready with a second decree, calling for the
appointment of administrators to take charge of Jewish-owned
firms. Pétain's government, which had been nullifying the citizenship of Jewish Frenchmen under the July decree, now (on October
3) published its notorious Statut des Juifs, signed by France's
World War I hero Philippe Pétain, together with Pierre Laval,
Adm. François Darlan, and seven other cabinet officers. After
defining Jews as anyone with three Jewish grandparents, or two if
the subject's spouse was Jewish, it banned them from government,
teaching, the armed forces, state-supported enterprises, the press,
and the cinema, while providing for limits on the number of Jews
exercising other professions. A later decree, on June 2, 1941,
banned Jews from banking, the stock exchange, real estate, advertising, and other activities considered sensitive.

By then Vichy had set up that iniquitous agency called the
General Commissariat for Jewish Questions, whose purpose was to
coordinate anti-Jewish operations, notably by identifying Jews and
Jewish enterprises and property. Indeed, under a clever scheme to
let industries and professions purge themselves, banks and other
institutions were required to set up "committees of organization";
the bank committee, in November 1940, had no difficulty recognizing Rothschild as Jewish.[16]

All this to the acclaim of that reborn species, the French Nazi,
now totally in charge of the press in Paris (a press controlled, and
when necessary subsidized, by German occupation authorities).
Paris-Soir, for example, was now only an ersatz newspaper created
by the Germans, a clone of the real daily *Paris-Soir*, which had
retreated to central France, where it was still being published by
prewar management. Rothschilds deprived of citizenship? At the

top of the front-page masthead of the counterfeit *Paris-Soir,* a box offered this comment:

> So the Rothschilds
> cease to be French!
> But were they ever?[17]

One Paris collaborationist paper, whose title was its program—*Au Pilori* ("To the Pillory")—specialized in denouncing Jews and other Frenchmen unlikely to be sympathetic to the Nazis. An article on the Rothschilds began as follows:

> The Jew being a nauseating and smelly being in the true sense of the word, he likes to dirty, to tarnish everyone superior or who doesn't kneel before him.[18]

In October of that first year of German rule, in an article bearing the subtitle "Judeo-Masonic English Infiltration of Chantilly," *Au Pilori* identified Rothschild relatives and friends who continued to live in the Paris region, notably in and around Chantilly, where (said the writer) even town halls were still subject to their influence, as well as that of British intelligence and of the Freemasons. (One can guess that local officials and other persons identified in the article were subjected to particular scrutiny by German and French authorities after that.)[19] A few weeks later the same paper—fearing that the Rothschilds stripped of French nationality might get it back—devoted a page to "frightening revelations" purportedly proving that the family had pushed for war against Hitler for personal gain.[20]

It never got as bad as it could have been. One reason was the very fanaticism of many of those responsible for carrying out Nazification, which made it difficult for them to be convincing to decent Frenchmen. Another—a serious factor from the start—was the conflict between German occupation authorities anxious to spirit away Jewish-owned property, and the Vichy French who wished to separate Jews from their possessions while keeping the property in

France. The result was a crossfire of decrees, a tug-of-war for the juiciest morsels.

There was a third, unexpected, factor. Many Frenchmen in official positions were not Vichyist or pro-German at all. Holdovers from the Republic, they continued to care about their country, and did what they could to thwart or retard arbitrary, antidemocratic, racist measures whether ordered by Vichy or Paris. Guy de Rothschild sat out these early months of occupation as the decrees exploded one after the other—depriving his father of his citizenship, then thanks to the successive decrees restricting their rights, creating what was virtually second-class citizenship for all Jews. Having decided to ride out the storm, he soon discovered that nobody within sight or hearing shared the new ideology; he was *not* a pariah.

When he met his wife at the Spanish border on her return from the United States he learned that she didn't share what she considered his illusions; for her the French themselves were now the enemy. Yet she must have been impressed when a French gendarme at a roadblock, after examining her husband's papers, told him, "It's a great honor for me to meet a member of a family so well known and respected." During lunch at an inn along the way they discovered personnel and guests intently listening to a Free French news broadcast from London.

He'd later say that he never met anyone who admitted being pro-German, and this despite occasional trips to Vichy. Reflecting on those dark years, he could feel that nothing had been saved—while everything was saved. And if "everything was saved" it was thanks in part to middle-level civil servants who showed no enthusiasm for executing Vichy's Hitler-inspired decrees; most were anti-German, some actually partisans of the Free French leader Charles de Gaulle.

The Vichy official responsible for enforcing the new decrees at the Rothschild bank in La Bourboule dictated a long document that Guy was able to read, since the secretary obligingly changed the carbon paper after each sheet was typed and passed the carbons on to him. He discovered a bland report written by someone who obviously wished to make no waves. This official actually facilitated the sale of bank assets to friendly buyers who would hold on to them until the family could buy them back.[21]

*   *   *

In Paris, where the Germans sought to convey the impression that life continued as before, in theaters and cinemas, restaurants and cabarets (there was no better way to exploit French industry and agriculture for the Nazi war than to keep the nation on an even keel), the plan to reopen a racetrack was complicated by the evidence that most good horses belonged to the Rothschilds and others whose property had been confiscated. It was suggested that the stables be registered in the name of the administrator who had been assigned to manage the seized property.[22]

Not even wines that were a pride of the French as much as of the Rothschilds were spared, for of course the Lafite and Mouton vineyards were tangible assets; worse, the strategic port of Bordeaux and its hinterland were territories the Germans kept under direct control in the armistice agreement. At Lafite, for example, some fifty German officers and men were billeted in the family castle, whose loyal staff kept the best wines safe. (The bookkeeper rigged the ledgers to transfer ownership of most of the wines from Rothschilds deprived of citizenship and property to the younger Rothschilds who had fought under French colors, and were now French prisoners in German custody.)

There were legends—like the legends surrounding the occupation of Ferrières by Bismarck and his Kaiser in 1870. One story had it that a senior German officer who in civilian life had been a wine dealer protected the best wines from pillage by warning German officers at Lafite and Mouton that Germany's supreme hedonist, Hermann Goering, would certainly want them. Then when the Germans were ready to annex Lafite because an owner of record, Edmond's son Jimmy, was a British subject, Vichy argued that it was French state property because the principal owners had left the country, forsaking their citizenship, and so their property had been legally confiscated by the French state.[23]

In their zeal, when they began rounding up Jews for mass deportations to the death camps, the Nazis hovered about Rothschild charitable institutions, seizing patients from the Rothschild Hospital by categories—lawyers, shopkeepers. . . . At first they left tubercular patients alone, if only to protect themselves; later they came back to deport even those.[24]

Today we can let ourselves be astonished by the evidence of this gang war between Vichy and the Nazis for plundered Jewish assets. There is the directive dated September 17, 1940, addressed to the head of German occupation forces in France and signed by Field Marshal Wilhelm Keitel, commander-in-chief of the Wehrmacht, referring to Hitler's order that valuable enemy property (to the Germans, Jews who left France were considered enemies) was to be seized and placed at the disposal of the Gestapo. It declared inoperative and illegal all transfers of property to the French state or private persons, specifically including property found in the home of Edouard de Rothschild on Rue Saint-Florentin.[25] Vichy's salvo was a decree signed by Pétain on October 5, empowering the Public Property Office, a department of the Finance Ministry, with responsibility for looking after seized assets.[26]

There were times when Nazi pillagers stumbled over one another to get at booty. Thus a report of the Feldpolizei on October 13, 1940, describes a raid on the Rothschild bank, where agents discovered that an officer of a German department called the Devisenschutz-kommando was already holding the fort. They nevertheless proceed to place seals on all the files and accounting ledgers in sight.[27]

The archives of the horrendous General Commissariat for Jewish Questions are filled with enigmas. Jewish property is discovered, administrators are appointed . . . then nothing happens. The property—be it town house or country manor—is not dismantled, sold, or otherwise transferred, and this despite the fanatical energies concentrated in this twentieth-century equivalent of the office of the Grand Inquisitor. The property belongs—belonged—to a Rothschild; it should now be someone else's, but nothing happens.

That nothing happens often seems due to an administrative slowdown. The inquirer may wonder whether the slowdown is deliberate; after a while he suspects that it is. He guesses that the man dragging his feet is the director of the Public Property Office; Rothschilds who survived the Vichy years confirm the guess.

Maurice Janicot was not the only decent official still serving in government during the war years, but he was a particularly decent one. Such civil servants did what they could (for example) to identify Rothschild managers who were not Jewish and who could be appointed administrators of seized property; they'd be sure to treat it gently, not to sell it off too quickly. Château Lafite got that kind of protection; so did the bank complex on Rue Laffitte.[28] Born on the third of September 1889, fifty years to the day before France's declaration of war on Hitler Germany, Janicot acquired a law degree before joining the Finance Ministry at the tender age of twenty, worked his way up to the directorship of the Property Office for the Paris region, an appointment he obtained in November 1937. He began his career in that department and retired in the job—getting no postwar promotion or particular thanks for his behavior under enemy eyes. He never broke the law, simply used it to protect and not to punish. He and Guy de Rothschild both understood that; when they met after the war, Janicot threw his arms around Guy, who acknowledged him as a true Gaullist.[29]

GOERING

For people who were supposedly omniscient—who, in the imagination of their enemies, were among the secret rulers of the world—the Rothschilds had been naive about the Nazis. Because these stubborn patriots— Edouard and Robert—simply did not believe that the Germans could overrun France (even after Hitler's attack on May 10, 1940), they hadn't done much about hiding their most precious possessions—their unrivaled collections of art. Only the fear of bombs moved Edouard to have priceless art treasures crated for storage at the family estate at Reux, outside Pont l'Evêque in Normandy. And that was where the Germans found them, conveniently wrapped for the return journey. Since Ferrières was considered safe from Luftwaffe raids, all the art displayed there was left on the walls, on pedestals, on chests and tables, where the Germans could inspect it at will. (Luckily, in the tapestry salon, precious works designed by François Boucher had been covered with canvas to protect them from sunlight, and all through the occupation the Germans imagined that they had been removed.)[1]

Looking at surviving evidence—and that includes messages exchanged between Hitler and his chief lieutenants—one is tempted to say that the Nazis invaded France mainly for its masterpieces. Certainly art was a priority target, and by then the Germans had acquired some experience in looting occupied countries. Hitler's diplomatic representative in Paris, Otto Abetz, who knew his way around, thanks to a prewar career as a friend of French culture, was specially designated by his Führer to track down the masterpieces that could be branded enemy property for looting purposes.

In a directive to the German military commander of Paris on July 1, 1940, Abetz ordered the transfer of the most valuable works to the German embassy, the spacious town house at 78 Rue de Lille originally acquired for his own comfort by a king of Prussia. By mid-August, Hitler's ambassador had a team of art experts in place to inspect and appraise "public and private objects of art, and especially Jewish ones"; the Führer himself, with Foreign Minister Joachim von Ribbentrop, would personally decide which works were to remain in France and which would be transferred to Germany.[2] Art owned by the French government would be used as bargaining chips in the war reparations agreement. Art owned by French Jews would become German, period.

It was now that the paper war began with Vichy over who had the right to plunder Jewish homes—but the Germans *had* the goods. In their boots, with guns in their belts, they marched through Edouard de Rothschild's home on Rue Saint-Florentin, they motored out to Ferrières; in those first months of occupation the victors took what they pleased from the houses of the Rothschilds and other prominent Jews, who included some of Paris's leading art dealers.[3] Only when the property was located deep inside the Vichy zone could the Pétain government get to it before the Germans did:

> *Tarbes, September 26*—Police have discovered in a house on an estate belonging to Baron Maurice de Rothschild ... a large number of ancient tapestries, art objects, and gold coins, with an estimated value of 350 million francs, that the former member of Parliament ... had removed by truck from [his home in] Maisons-Laffitte at the beginning of June. This property has been confiscated.[4]

To make room inside the German embassy for other business, plundered paintings and sculpture were taken to the Louvre (an

arrangement welcomed by the museum's directors, for they hoped
it would give them an opportunity to make an inventory of the
booty). But by the last week of October 1940 the rooms available
at the Louvre couldn't hold any more of the art that was being
hauled in by the looting raids. There happened to be an empty
building nearby, the Jeu de Paume museum at the corner of the
Tuileries gardens and the Place de la Concorde (just opposite the
Rothschild house on Rue Saint-Florentin). And so the two-story
pavilion built as an indoor tennis court, later transformed into a
Louvre annex to exhibit contemporary foreign artists, was henceforth a tomb for stolen art, as well as a workplace for specialists
who seized and sorted it, and who prepared to take it away.[5]

By now a curious personage had entered the picture. Alfred
Rosenberg was Hitler's pet intellectual, the mad theoretician of his
anti-Jewish, anti-Bolshevik crusade. At the age of forty-seven this
somewhat erratic man held the title—cumbersome even in Nazi
Germany—of Beauftragte des Führers für die gesamte geistliche
und weltanschauliche Erziehung der N.S.D.A.P.—Delegate of the
Führer for the Inspection of Intellectual and Doctrinal Education
of the National Socialist Party. He had volunteered to probe the
occupied territories for documents of historical value, but by specific order of Hitler on September 17, 1940, his authority was
extended to art and libraries. Out of this mission came the Einsatzstab, Rosenberg's special commando responsible for ferreting
out Jewish-owned art.[6]

Armed with his Führer's confidence, Alfred Rosenberg was not
the kind of person to let a desired object escape his reach. In a
note for his own files, recording his conversation with Hitler on
September 16, he raises the question whether Vichy's decision that
seized Rothschild art was now French government property should
prevail. Rosenberg felt that Rothschild art was Jewish property—
and therefore now belonged to Germany: "The Rothschilds are an
enemy Jewish family, and all their machinations to save their
possessions should leave us cold." Hitler agreed entirely; nothing
must stop them from taking everything, and as soon as possible.[7]
Next day came Wehrmacht commander-in-chief Keitel's order confirming German proprietary rights; Reichsleiter Rosenberg, it concluded, "is authorized to transfer to Germany objects that seem of

value to him, and to place them under guard. The Führer will eventually decide what will happen to them."[8]

There was a temporary lull in the battlefield war; now the combat continued in the drawing rooms of Paris, as successive raiders from the Einsatzstab Rosenberg, assisted by the German security service (the Sicherheitsdienst), and when necessary by the French police, hauled their truckloads of booty to the Jeu de Paume. Before they had finished, some seventy-nine major Jewish collections had been pillaged; in all, 203 collections were seized, for a total of 21,903 works, among them masterpieces by Rembrandt and Rubens, Vermeer, Frans Hals, Goya, and Velasquez, not to mention Germany's own Cranach, England's Gainsborough and Reynolds.[9]

Imagine the astonishment of a man from Vichy, an officer of the Commissariat for Jewish Questions, confronted with evidence of the scope of the looting of art objects his own organization had hoped to get its hands on; as it happens, a copy of one official's report has survived. He speaks of the mass of objects taken from the Rothschild vineyard estates at Lafite and Mouton, of the art found on Rue Saint-Florentin, in a Rothschild depository in the Banque de France in Nevers, also of the discovery of the crates stashed away at Reux in Normandy.

And of course there weren't only Edouard and his immediate family; there was Henri, whose Château de la Muette had been emptied by the Germans; there was his cousin Maurice, plundered at 41 Rue du Faubourg Saint-Honoré and at the Château d'Armainvilliers in the Seine-et-Marne district, not to speak of the works of art and the stock certificates found at his vault in the Paribas bank. There was cousin Robert, looted at 23 Avenue de Marigny, the "English" Philippe (Henri's son), and Eugene (brother of Louis of Vienna).

Indignantly the Commissariat official reported how the Germans carried out their looting without permitting Vichy-appointed administrators to keep a record of what was taken, and often (as at the Bordeaux vineyards) in the face of protests by finance inspectors and even the district governor.

As a consequence the Jeu de Paume now served as a repository of property that in Vichy's opinion belonged to Vichy, since it had been seized from denationalized Jews, yet there was no way Vichy could find out what was happening to it. The writer of the report concluded that the French must ask for an inventory of the seized properties—and restitution.[10]

Fat chance. Because of the fat man. Once a lithe and handsome war hero, a combat ace, later (and perhaps still) a drug addict, a bemedaled *Reichsmarschall* whose corpulence made him an ideal subject for cartoonists, Hermann Goering was nevertheless close to Hitler, and wielded some of his authority. Accustomed to easy living, he had a tendency to confuse his personal property and interests with those of the Third Reich. His grand entrance into the Jeu de Paume museum, now bursting to the seams with looted masterpieces, seems more appropriate to the vaudeville stage than to history.

There is a reliable witness to this scene: a young woman who had been employed at the Jeu de Paume when it served as a museum, a key figure in packing and shipping the museum's art to safety in an earlier stage of the war. Despite German orders that French personnel make themselves scarce, Rose Valland decided to stay on, to look and to listen. Henceforth she worked in an environment of helmeted, booted soldiers, policemen wearing brown uniforms and swastikas. The Germans began bringing in their booty on October 31, 1940; by November 3 the abandoned Jeu de Paume had become one of the world's great museums—its walls covered with masterpieces, its floors with priceless rugs. The choice of paintings seemed disparate, but everything was good. The best came from Edouard de Rothschild.

Rose Valland watched as Goering entered, dressed (to her astonishment) in civilian clothes—a long overcoat and a fedora. He was accompanied by his personal expert, officers of Rosenberg's Einsatzstab and of the Luftwaffe, all of them superbly uniformed. Goering looked at everything. Later Valland realized that this visit, by whetting Goering's appetite, changed the history and the direction of Nazi art policy in France.

The Marshal of the Great German Reich—to translate the title he accorded himself—spent the whole day at the Jeu de Paume, but he hadn't seen everything; there wasn't enough wall space for proper display of all the paintings that had been seized. So he stayed on in Paris and was back at the museum two days later to inspect the rest. He was clearly delighted by what he was seeing, commented on his favorite works, consulted authorities. He particularly liked Van Gogh's *Langlois Bridge in Arles,* a portrait of the infanta Margareta-Teresa from Velasquez's studio, Fragonard's *Child with Buddha,* Bonnard's *Work Table* (we know this because the paintings were soon crated and shipped to him).[11] It was settled; henceforth Alfred Rosenberg and his action commando had a priority customer in Reichsmarschall Goering.[12]

Before leaving Paris, Goering dictated and signed an order confirming the new dispensation. Art seized from Jews and now at the Jeu de Paume would be sorted according to destination: the very best to be placed at the disposal of Hitler, after which came those "that could serve to complete the collections of the Reichsmarschall." Other works—rare books as well as art—were to be earmarked for donation to German universities (at Rosenberg's discretion), still others would go into German museums. The confiscation of Jewish property would continue under the responsibility of Rosenberg, in liaison with German occupation forces.[13]

Hitler had specifically asked about one legendary painting: Vermeer's *Astronomer,* which showed a scholar contemplating the globe, believed by some to be a self-portrait. On November 13, Alfred Rosenberg sent a secret and personal message to Hitler's deputy, Martin Bormann, to tell him they'd found the painting in the Rothschild collection. *Heil Hitler!*[14] (The priceless Vermeer had been in the family as far back as Alphonse.)[15]

If the rapacity of the Nazis enraged French authorities helpless to prevent it—enraged both Vichy ideologists who wished to carry out their own spoliation of French Jews *and* French patriots who sought in vain to slow down the looting—it also excited jealousies among the Germans themselves. A surviving document reveals the dimensions this rivalry assumed in the early months of German occupation. On November 21, in a personal letter to Rosenberg, who in principle was now responsible for all confiscations of art, Goering let him know that others claimed to have the same right— notably Foreign Minister von Ribbentrop. If Goering was now exercising a priority, he wanted Rosenberg to realize that it was thanks to him, the Reichsmarschall, that so much Jewish art had been discovered despite well-camouflaged hiding places. He had used funds to bribe informants, and detectives of the French criminal police. Goering reminded Rosenberg that he himself possessed the most important private art collection in Germany if not in Europe, a collection featuring German, Dutch, and Flemish primitives, seventeenth-century Dutch masters and eighteenth-century French, with some Italian works; one day it would be willed to the state, he said, and the Führer approved his intentions.

Now Goering planned to buy some of the seized Jewish paintings—particularly by artists not yet represented in his collection; the price would be set by a French expert. Only a few works were involved, he assured his party comrade—fifteen in all. *Heil Hitler!*[16]

New York had become a rallying point for dispossessed Rothschilds. Doubly dispossessed, for many assets they had managed to hold outside of France were now frozen to keep the Germans from getting at them (even Vichy had a lien on such properties, for the seizure of Rothschild possessions was now law in Pétain's state, and the United States continued to maintain an ambassador in Vichy). The Rothschilds were fish out of water in the New World, in part owing to their long-standing reluctance to carry out significant business operations there. Finally they decided to recruit a young Dutch national, Peter Fleck, to help them organize a secretariat to coordinate attempts to get at their blocked funds. Among other things, they owned a small bank in occupied Amsterdam that had a gold reserve in the United States; Fleck was able to get at the money.[17]

On their arrival in New York—with the now famous bag containing $1 million in jewelry—Edouard and his wife and second daughter, Bethsabée, proceeded directly to upstate New York where their elder daughter, Jacqueline, had settled only a year earlier with her husband, Gregor Piatigorsky. When Edouard and Germaine moved from there to an apartment in Manhattan, Bethsabée, now twenty-six, moved into a flat of her own for the first time. Bethsabée found her father reserved in his attitude toward New York, although of course he was grateful for having found asylum there. There was little work he could do, but he could use his position as head of the Consistory to speak up for French Jews.

Bethsabée took courses at Columbia University, and worked for a time at a New Jersey chemical factory before joining the Free French in London.[18]

Robert de Rothschild didn't fly the Atlantic; he embarked on a small, 180-passenger ship packed with ten times that number of refugees, reaching the British coast on June 20, less than a week after the fall of Paris. His fellow passengers included the popular French playwright Henry Bernstein and his companion, Eve Curie (daughter of Pierre and Marie Curie). From Britain they boarded a proper ship for Montreal, docking there at the beginning of August. Later, when they were all in New York and Robert was lamenting the loss of his citizenship, Bernstein reassured him: "What's the difference? It's as if you'd been asked to give up your entrance card to the Vichy casino." The remark reached German Paris, where it appeared in the anti-Jewish paper *Je Suis Partout* (except that the paper perfidiously omitted "Vichy" and thereby distorted its meaning).[19]

The turbulent Maurice seemed to have had an equally turbulent journey to freedom. A report in *The New York Times* on his arrival in a Scottish port on July 8 described him as haggard; he seemed to be suffering from a head injury.[20] He sailed to Montreal on the same ship as his cousin Robert; this time the *Times* described him as "nervous and shaken," but neglected to mention the appearance or condition of other passengers.[21] He had left behind his divorced wife, Noëmi, and thirteen-year-old Edmond—but they couldn't have been safer anywhere in France than in Noëmi Halphen's mountain resort, Megève. They could be even safer *outside* France, in Maurice's splendid domain of Pregny in Switzerland, to which they traveled by bus before the end of June. There they were to spend the war years, drawing on the meager funds Maurice had left behind to maintain the estate. In his first years of exile, Maurice wasn't living much more comfortably, dependent at first on what brother Jimmy could send him from London.[22]

Robert's sons Alain and Elie remained in German captivity, but their line was sure to survive them, for on October 3, 1940, a son was born to Alain—on the other side of the Atlantic Ocean where his wife (née Mary Chauvin du Treuil, converted to Judaism for her marriage) had taken refuge. (When Alain got news of the birth of his son he attempted—unsuccessfully—to escape.) The male child was given the name Eric, inspired by Alain's first letter from the POW camp to his wife, in which he explained that a pair of binoculars given him by his friend Eric Warburg had stopped a German bullet aimed at his chest; it entered an arm instead. (Eric Warburg would be his benefactor a second time, in May 1945, when, as a U.S. Air Force officer, he participated in the liberation of the Lübeck camp where both Alain and brother Elie were then detained.)[23]

Caught when planning an escape from his POW camp, ebullient Elie had been transferred to the formidable high-security prison in Colditz castle, designed for difficult prisoners, but also for eminent ones. The fortress turned out to be more restrictive than even a soldier caught by the enemy might expect, for one day a hotheaded French officer, spouting Action Française clichés, physically attacked a fellow prisoner who happened to be Jewish (and who happened to be Robert Blum, son of the Popular Front leader). Other officers intervened, so to stop the free-for-all it was decided that the two antagonists should be confined in separate sections of the castle. The Germans leaped at the opportunity to segregate Jewish officers. (Elie heard none of his fellow captives object to that.)[24]

Henri's son James-Henri had helped preserve what could be preserved at the family bank in La Bourboule. Following the Vichy ban on Jews in banking, he moved his family to the relative safety of Cannes, then in the care of Italian occupation forces that were not following Nazi and Vichy policy on Jews to the letter. It was there that daughter Nicole, an irrepressible sixteen, seized the opportunity to slip out of family life to visit grandfather Henri in Lisbon (in time to type the manuscript containing his version of the Rothschild saga).

But her parents wanted Nicole home, and never mind that home was Vichy France; Guy de Rothschild informed her of that when he arrived in Lisbon to board the Pan American Clipper flying boat that was to take him to New York in November 1941. Dutifully she returned to Cannes. Not too long after that, her father slipped out of the house to begin a journey along the coast to Spain. By prearrangement his wife, Claude (née Dupont), followed the same route a week later with daughters Nicole and Monique. James got across the Pyrenees safely, and waited for his family at their agreed meeting point in Barcelona.

The women weren't so lucky. On the French side of the mountain border they checked into a hotel at Font-Romeu—using the family name of Henri's companion Marthe Régnier—while waiting for a guide to smuggle them over the Pyrenees. (Once Nicole left their room to find Monique downstairs, playing Ping-Pong with a German officer; she happened to be junior table tennis champion of France.) They spent the better part of a week on arduous mountain paths on which others had died of cold (or were apprehended by frontier guards), at last reaching the Spanish side, to be arrested when they tried to pursue their journey to Barcelona without permission. James-Henri caught up with them during their forty-eight-hour detention in a Barcelona jail. Then to Britain and de Gaulle.

James-Henri had his work cut out for him in the Free French forces. His wife, Claude, one of the first women to reach Bayeux after the Normandy landing, as a liaison officer with British and American forces, accompanied the liberation troops into Paris and beyond, ending the war a captain with 355 women in her command. Nicole, who was just eighteen, was taken into the British army, and transferred eventually to the Free French air force. She landed on Utah Beach shortly after the first waves of American troops on D-Day, ending the war as a lieutenant. (Once, after the liberation of Paris, she discovered that one of the soldiers she was drilling was Bethsabée, Guy's sister, ten years older than she.)[25]

The pretext for Vichy's arrest of Henri's other son, Philippe, had been shaky from the start; after breaking his leg he had been granted convalescent leave, and was spending it in the Vichy-French protectorate of Morocco when he was taken into custody. A fellow air force officer, Pierre Mendès-France, was in the same prison on the same charge; they'd both be transferred back to France for trial. There the case against Baron Philippe was dismissed after long months (but he was able to add a suite of prison poems to his collected works). He even got his French nationality back. Mendès-France wasn't so lucky. Although he himself had gained Morocco in hopes of continuing the war there, he was tried in May 1941 for desertion, and given a six-year jail sentence. Six weeks later he escaped and made his way to Britain, to continue the air war all the same, but in the RAF.

Determined to get to Britain, there to be ready for battle when battle there was, thirty-nine-year-old Philippe begged his wife to accompany him (the time was November 1942, the place the Château de Marzac in the Dordogne, where resistance friends had put them up). Lili wouldn't think of leaving France. "Why play the hero and take unnecessary risks?" she asked him. "You won't come back alive." She herself, born Countess Elisabeth Pelletier de Chambure, had never become Jewish; she believed she was safe enough.

So he left without her. When she was arrested at Chalon-sur-Saône on the charge that she was using a forged pass to cross the demarcation line separating Vichy France from German-controlled territory, Lili's fate was sealed—for she was a Rothschild. The Nazis sent her to the notorious Ravensbruck concentration camp, from which she was not to return. This non-Jewish Rothschild was the only member of the French family bearing that name to die in deportation.[26]

FRANCE
WITHOUT ROTHSCHILDS

*I*n a memorandum from Yves Regelsperger, who held the exalted rank of Director of Economic Aryanization, to one of his colleagues at the inglorious Commissariat for Jewish Questions, he asked whether other property besides that of the Rothschilds was owned jointly by denationalized Jews (such as Edouard de Rothschild) and those still accepted as French citizens (like his son Guy).

> It is important to have an early response so that I can reassure the Occupation Authorities concerning the condition under which Rothschild family property is being liquidated, and be in a position to deal with ill-advised insinuations that the family is receiving preferential treatment with respect to the law concerning Jews.[1]

The document suggests that even a civil servant conscientiously devoted to anti-Semitism had to worry about opinion—not so much *public* opinion as the taunts of pamphleteers who were delivering their denunciations under the benevolent eye of the occupation authorities. For even in the absence of Rothschilds, the Rothschilds were targets; even their horses remained Rothschilds. The Paris newspaper *Au Pilori* certainly thought so; in demanding that

"Jewish stables" be liquidated in March 1941, the paper noted with indignation that the Rothschild stable had reappeared "barely camouflaged," its trainer listed as owner. But now, when one of the horses of the group comes in first, the crowd cheers as always, "Rothschild won!"

A month later *Au Pilori* was able to announce that its complaint had been heeded. Four of the forty-four Rothschild horses would be auctioned; but why only four, and "the least good"?[2]

In our own time, looking at the persistence of prejudice in his own country, which had lost most of its Jews in Nazi death camps, a Polish author was mesmerized by the phenomenon of anti-Semitism in the absence of Jews. German-controlled France was also like that. Because of the blossoming of a native fascism that could not otherwise have prevailed, anti-Jewish discourse was at least as violent in the German years as in prewar days. A remarkable column in *Au Pilori*, targeting specific personalities to be "nailed to the stake," focused on Edouard de Rothschild—even though it found nothing evil to say of him, for he had been "the elegant and social one, the benefactor of the gang." His benign behavior, added the paper, had been designed to fool the gullible. Even his horse races had been honest—for that was good publicity; a lesser owner might manipulate the races to win 50,000 francs, but what was 50,000 francs to a Rothschild? So people would say, "Rothschild saved me from ruin; he's not a Jew like the others."

The Rothschilds had fled, concluded *Au Pilori*, and so avoided a pogrom. But they were thinking of returning, and since they were still rich, the lawyers at the Commissariat for Jewish Questions were "ready to be helpful."[3] (Like many collaborationist papers of German Paris, *Au Pilori* found Vichy institutions too soft on Jews and democrats; the Gestapo did it better.)

One of the stars of this anti-Semitic Never-Never Land was Louis-Ferdinand Céline, armed with his formidable prewar reputation as a novelist. Now, in the columns of *Au Pilori*, he accused Pétain himself of being a Rothschild lackey. Céline worried that the French were pro-Jewish—how could one fight that?[4]

But *Au Pilori* reached its depths, and there proved its influence, in an attack on Baroness Philippe de Rothschild (Elisabeth de Chambure, known in the family as Lili), for she was showing herself everywhere in Paris. "When does she go to a concentration camp . . . ?" The editorialist noted that she had married in a Jewish ceremony and therefore must be considered Jewish under French and German law. (The marriage, *Au Pilori* added helpfully, had taken place at Henri de Rothschild's Château de la Muette on January 22, 1935, at 11:00 A.M.)[5]

We've seen that the editors of *Au Pilori* got what they asked for.[6] Lili was sent to a camp, and never came back.

Rothschilds could no longer be found in France? The campaign could be directed at their place of refuge. A tract published in that first full year of occupation worried that now that the "Rothschild tribe" had gone to the United States (and it was a good thing to see the end of these "Jewish sharks" who had done so much harm to France), one needed to be concerned at the installation in the United States of the "chief" of the tribe (Edouard), recognized by Jews as Prince of Israel, leader of Jews everywhere.[7]

Meanwhile, cooler heads went about their plundering. On the fourth of February, 1941, Reichsmarschall Goering was back in Paris, carrying photographs of paintings he wanted; his personal choices and works destined for the Führer were put aboard a special train, after being appraised—and undervalued—by a terrified French expert. Many were shipped in the large black chests the Rothschilds had used to pack their precious collections.

In March, Goering was back for more. Henceforth the operation was routine, selection and packing taking place behind the guarded doors of the Jeu de Paume. By then Philippe de Rothschild's paintings had been discovered in the vaults of a bank at a beach resort southwest of Bordeaux, unearthed by a German financial task force that also got its hands on Rothschild family jewels hidden at Banque de France regional offices, as well as at Banque de Paris et des Pays-Bas. It almost wasn't worth the trouble, since Goering barely looked at the amassed precious stones, taking just six items of the three hundred spread out for his examination.[8]

So Alfred Rosenberg was proud of himself when he drew up a report to his Führer on March 20, 1941, announcing the successful completion of the looting mission he had begun the previous October. A twenty-five-car train had been loaded with the most valuable paintings, furniture, tapestries, and other art objects and jewelry, representing the best of the collections of the Rothschilds and other wealthy Jewish families (including the art-dealing Wildensteins and the David-Weills of Lazard Frères). This precious cargo was delivered to Neuschwanstein—a pinnacled fairy-tale castle set on a mountain top in Bavaria, a stage set more than a reality, built by mad king Ludwig II to evoke lost and legendary worlds. Rosenberg also let his Führer know that still more precious paintings—these in the main belonging to the Rothschilds and hand-picked for Hitler by Goering, had been sent in two special freight cars to Munich, and there placed in an air-raid shelter under the Führer's own official residence.[9]

The long-secret, now accessible files of the Commissariat for Jewish Questions allow us to see how difficult it could be to carry out one's task conscientiously in the despoiling profession. Here was the Neuilly stable of Elie de Rothschild—a junior officer still in a POW camp. The Commissariat had duly put the horses up for sale, but there were no buyers. It tried an auction, but nothing happened there either; Elie was to get his stable back without fuss in May 1945.[10] Elie's older brother Alain, also still a war prisoner, was the subject of a stack of memoranda concerning his house on Rue du Cirque in Paris; eventually it was put up for sale—but found no takers. Alain simply moved back after the liberation of Paris, with the right to sue Vichy's temporary administrator for damages; but of course the administrator had vanished, as most of these individuals seem to have done.[11]

There was the matter of Maurice's son Edmond, then fifteen years old but owner of record of considerable property, the use of which was at the disposal of his father during the latter's lifetime. If, under Vichy law, Maurice's property now belonged to the national welfare agency, how to sell Maurice's right to use a minor's property when the property itself couldn't be sold? (Young Edmond was listed as a resident of Megève, although he was certainly now across the Swiss border at Pregny.) The Vichy-appointed administrator thought he could find his way around that, if he were also appointed administrator of Maurice's right of usage and then sold *that*. In fact none of young Edmond's properties, which included a town house on Avenue Foch, ever got sold.[12]

And that wasn't the most difficult case. What about Maurice's sister Miriam, fifty-seven years old in 1941, owner of the Château de Bailgu, facing the Bois de Boulogne? The Commissariat had an administrator on the spot, a man subsequently dismissed as not quite reputable; before he left he had placed a high estimate on the value of the house, and decided that only the government could afford to buy it. The city came through with an offer—considerably lower than what the administrator (whose fee depended on the value) said it was worth. Time passed. By September 1943 the governor of Paris stepped in, with a surprising comment that the sale of the estate to a public authority like the city of Paris "is of all possible solutions the one that creates fewest difficulties for the future." It seemed a way of saying that the Nazis and Vichy were not going to be around forever. The house was never disposed of; the future was indeed protected.

Yet in the unreal world of the Commissariat for Jewish Questions, it was possible to pursue fantasies until the very end. Miriam's town house on Avenue Foch was put up for sale on June 20, 1944, two weeks after the Allied landing in Normandy, which was obviously going to affect such property transfers in the capital of France mighty soon. A widow purchased the house, but the sale had to wait for the customary legal approval of the sale. The administrator panicked, for his fee would be paid only after the property changed hands, and he knew the procedure took months. His last desperate memorandum is dated July 20, the day German officers tried to kill Hitler, and a little over a month before Paris was liberated. Another house owned by Miriam was actually disposed of, but at the liberation the unforeseeing purchaser readily agreed to return it.[13]

And the tug-of-war continued. In a memorandum at the end of February 1941, Vichy once again protested the German preemption of Rothschild works of art and stock certificates, as well as some recent pillaging of silver and clocks on Rue Saint-Florentin.[14] Moving ever faster, the Rosenberg commando, on Berlin's orders, sent a secret police unit to Rue Laffitte to remove Rothschild family archives; it took 760 crates to hold them.[15]

Vichy sent protest after protest; the Germans would have none of it. Reichsleiter Rosenberg himself saw it necessary to justify what the Nazis were doing, after a formal plea from the Commissariat for Jewish Questions. The only property confiscated was Jewish property, declared Rosenberg. The Jews and the Freemasons had caused the war; by conquering France the German army had liberated the French people from the influence of international Jewry. There was an armistice, he agreed, but the Germans didn't include Jews in it.[16]

The continued existence of a Rothschild bank without Rothschilds, even without assets, remained a bone of contention. On the last day of May 1941 the good Maurice Janicot, who, in addition to being director of the Paris Public Property Office, had been appointed temporary administrator of De Rothschild Frères, attempted to clear up ambiguities (or perhaps to confuse everybody) in a report to the Commissariat. He pointed out that the bank, now officially transferred to La Bourboule, belonged to three partners: Edouard, with fourteen-thirtieths, Guy with one-thirtieth, and Robert with one-half. Although the shares of Edouard and Robert had been seized, the bank continued to have a Jewish managing director in the person of Monsieur Guy de Rothschild, who handled day-to-day activities under the control of a representative of the government. With the bank now located in the Vichy zone, the administrator—Janicot himself—could not proceed with its liquidation; De Rothschild Frères didn't even possess a building in German-occupied territory, since Rue Laffitte was now occupied by the national welfare agency, its original furnishings having been divided between that Vichy institution and the occupation authorities. The bank did still hold some stocks and bonds, but its only activity was to make possible the withdrawal of funds by old clients. "None of its employees is Jewish," Janicot added.[17]

But Monsieur Guy was. And within forty-eight hours of the signing of Janicot's memorandum, the revised Statut des Juifs, banning Jews from the banking profession, was issued by Darlan's government, with the signature of "Ph. Pétain" at the top of the page. Soon the Germans had a Rothschild specialist in Paris to probe further, for it did look as if the bank might vanish before their very eyes, and somehow that was not what the Nazis desired (it was as if the symbol of their enemy were slipping through their fingers). Almost playfully, Maurice Janicot announced that he was giving up his no-longer-meaningful role as Rothschild administrator; the Germans replied that he couldn't do that. Yes he could, said Janicot, for under Pétain's new decree, Guy de Rothschild couldn't exercise his functions as managing director, thus there was no management and the company ceased to exist. So how could Janicot serve it as administrator? There could be a liquidator, however, and Janicot accepted that role.

The Germans would have none of that. They had appointed Janicot, and only they could divest him of his function. So Yves Regelsperger of the compliant Commissariat reinstated Janicot, who was to report to him, notably on Guy's assets. But since De Rothschild Frères had disappeared in the absence of a legal managing director, and since the Domaines already controlled the shares of Edouard and Robert amounting to twenty-nine-thirtieths of the totality, they were obliged to liquidate the company. And because no Jew was now connected with the bank, the Aryanization procedure couldn't apply.[18]

One imagines the wringing of hands. . . . Replying to a citizen worried about the alleged impunity of the Rothschilds—as the collaborationist press was complaining—the Commissariat noted that "to its great regret" it had not handled Rothschild family properties: "this family having lost French nationality, the Public Property Office was responsible for the liquidation."[19]

Now for certain there was no longer a role in France for the last survivor, Guy de Rothschild. He had stayed on in La Bourboule after the ban on Jews in banking, and during much of the give-and-take between the Germans and Vichy, between the French scoundrels of the Commissariat for Jewish Questions and the good Frenchmen of the Public Property Office. His senior aides wished him to stay, convinced that the worst was behind them, but Guy felt that there was little more he could accomplish in the Vichy zone, and a lot somewhere else.

He and his wife were able to obtain American visas thanks to his parents' friendship with Eleanor Roosevelt (and at the time the United States still recognized Vichy). But Frenchmen of military age were not allowed to leave France. Certainly the rule should have been waived for a Jew, but Admiral Darlan (who by then had replaced Pierre Laval as chief of Pétain's government) feared that the Rothschild name was too much of a symbol, and that softness on his part would be remarked.

The problem was resolved step-by-step. Guy and Alix crossed over to Vichy-controlled Morocco, where the family still maintained interests. There Guy learned that Pierre Pucheu, whom he had known in the business world, was now Vichy's Minister of the Interior. Granting the visas, Pucheu added a verbal message to the intermediary: "Jews caused a lot of harm to my country but Guy has always been a good citizen; if he can begin life over again elsewhere, I am happy to let him go." The Guy de Rothschilds crossed the frontier into Spain in October 1941, and crossed another border to Portugal for the Pan American Clipper flight to New York.[20]

The press was waiting as the plane carrying Guy and Alix docked at LaGuardia Airport on October 27. A reporter listened as Guy attempted to explain Pétain's continued popularity. "He has a thorough understanding of the French people and a glorious past. Understand," he added hastily, "I mean that the Marshal himself is popular, not particularly his government."[21] Later he would complain that the press had distorted his comments about the France he had left behind—a result of the political schism of the French exile community.[22]

For the first time in a century and a quarter, there were no Rothschilds in France—certainly no active ones. It didn't seem to matter; they were such rich material for the crackpots. . . . One of those, Jean Peron, contributed another volume to the shelf of invective, concluding (unexpectedly) with the suggestion that the family wasn't as influential as it used to be. "One thing is certain: The Rothschilds deserted France at the moment of its difficulties, and that is sufficient proof that they were not attached to our country by deep roots, that only the question of money kept them here."[23]

The very rich archives of the Commissariat for Jewish Questions confirm that one could make a career of Rothschild-baiting without Rothschilds. For the struggle for these missing souls continued between the combative Commissariat and the prudent Property Office.[24] At one point the Germans thought they were on to something. After America's entry into the war, it occurred to them that since Edouard and Robert, whose shares represented twenty-nine-thirtieths of the Rothschild bank, were now in the United States, their possessions represented enemy property; *now* it all belonged to Germany.[25]

Surely the staff of the Commissariat had uncomfortable moments. How to deal with charity hospitals run by Rothschild foundations? Maurice Janicot's Property Office thought it had a simple answer: Since the Rothschild family held no property rights either in the convalescence home of the Fondation Alphonse de Rothschild in Chantilly or in the Fondation Rothschild hospital on Rue de Picpus, leave them alone! The Commissariat wasn't so sure. Perhaps the Rue de Picpus installation, whose patients were in the main Jewish, could be turned over to a Vichy-sponsored Jewish agency. And since the Chantilly facilities treated patients irrespective of religion, it could simply be Aryanized. The dilemma continued to preoccupy the Commissariat's legal staff and financial experts. (Some of their reports were typed on the back of letterheads of France's official Mickey Mouse magazine, *Le Journal de Mickey,* which was published by a Jewish-owned company that had been disposed of earlier.)

There was a tentative decision to dissolve the Fondation Alphonse de Rothschild while putting its Chantilly convalescence home under the authority of the public hospital system. At that point the minister of health, obviously not wishing to get involved, found excuses. Finally it was decided to leave things as they were. But in July 1944—one month before the liberation of Paris—the Commissariat was still anxious to get its hands on the substantial property holdings of the Fondation Rothschild, which they believed was in the care of a man who had once worked for "the Jew Rothschild" (the new and nasty way that victims of the Commissariat were being referred to in official communications).[26]

But the occupation hadn't yet reached the depths of absurdity. That would take the arrival on the scene of a singular individual, Dr. Alexis Carrel. Born French in 1873, he had gone to the United States, where he had won a Nobel Prize in medicine for pioneering work on blood vessels and organ transplants. In the pre–World War II decade he had shocked the sensitive with his book *Man, the Unknown,* which suggested that scientists might accelerate natural selection. But since one could not eliminate the weak (even if one could cease to protect them), one could very well strengthen the strong. Thus would a nation obtain "a nonhereditary aristocracy." His solution was selective breeding—eugenics.[27] Charles A. Lindbergh, hero of an earlier time, was Carrel's disciple and collaborator.

So it was no surprise that Dr. Carrel thought he had found a home in the new Europe. With German blessings and Vichy endorsement he was at last going to be able to give institutional form to his theories. His French Foundation for the Study of Human Problems was proclaimed a public institution by Marshal Pétain by decree of November 17, 1941. The kind of work he intended to do was explained by him in the foundation's journal: "Many immigrants, as one knows, have been allowed into France. Some are desirable, others are not. The presence of groups of foreigners undesirable from the biological point of view is a certain danger for the French population." The good doctor expected to be able to come up with ways to deal with these foreigners.[28]

He also thought that he had found the way to get himself a laboratory. There was a fine building with excellent facilities in the heart of Paris's university quarter. It just happened to be the headquarters of the Institut de Biologie Physico-Chimique, endowed by Edmond de Rothschild, and either the German occupation authorities Carrel was dealing with or his friends in Vichy would have told him that this institution was presently the subject of intense scrutiny.[29]

Naturally the Commissariat for Jewish Questions backed Carrel, although the files show that its best detectives failed to find evidence of "Jewish influence" at the institute.[30] Indeed, Jewish scientists had long since disappeared from its laboratories, as had a number of non-Jews who had joined the anti-Nazi resistance. (At least one of the Jewish scientists was apprehended and sent to a camp.) But until the arrival of Alexis Carrel there had been a modus vivendi: the Rothschild name was removed from the façade and from the institute seal and letterheads, while its personnel respected German injunctions not to carry out hostile activities. A German scientist who had joined the Rothschild institute before the war, ostensibly as a refugee from Hitler, suddenly showed his colors; he became the official representative of the occupation authority inside the ex-Rothschild laboratories.

But a takeover would be attempted all the same. On June 12, 1942, the governor of the district signed a requisition order "for the needs of the Nation"—in fact for Carrel's needs. There was an outcry among scientists against the closing of a significant scientific institution (whose current activities included development of an antityphus vaccine with the Pasteur Institute, and research on the manufacture of insulin). Carrel rushed off to Vichy to consult Pétain, and returned with a proposal to give up the laboratories if the Academy of Sciences so requested; he was hoping to become a member of the Academy—a wish quickly granted. The next round was the evil Commissariat's, blocking funds that the ex-Rothschild institute received from the Eastern Railway on the grounds (still) that the institute was Jewish.

In the spring of 1944—the spring of D-Day—the Commissariat was still looking for ways to close down the Institut de Biologie Physico-Chimique, intending to hand it over to the University of Paris. The institute's board met to decide to appeal the decision (the date of their meeting was June 6, 1944, as news began arriving of the Allied beachhead).

Whatever the Commissariat would have done next is a matter of speculation.[31] Later apologists for Carrel took comfort in the fact that he was not prosecuted for collaboration with the enemy after the war. He *was* suspended from his functions, his institute converted to the pursuit of more pragmatic activities. But then he died on November 5, 1944, less than three months after the liberation of Paris, before the purge trials got under way.[32]

LIQUIDATING THE LIQUIDATORS

*A*s Guy remembered his wartime year in New York, it was fruitful in contacts, also in friendships, both with Americans and fellow exiles. All the same he was restless, and looked to engagement in the Free French forces opposing Vichy for release. Rothschild prudence should have led him toward General Henri Giraud, one of the authentic heroes of the lost war. But he thought with his heart and not with his head, and so opted for Giraud's rival as supreme leader of the resistance, that very junior general Charles de Gaulle.

His parents lived comfortably, if one managed to forget prewar Rothschild lifestyles. And indeed Edouard had never become used to exile. Once when an object placed too close to the edge of a table fell to the floor, Guy heard him say, "You see, Germaine, it wouldn't have fallen in France." For a time Guy and Alix shared his parents' apartment; later they moved to a flat of their own on 102nd Street and Fifth Avenue.

One bit of brightness in a grim time: A son was born to Alix on December 15, 1942; they'd call him David. By then the Allies had landed on the coasts of French North Africa, the French consulate in New York had become the consulate of Free France, and there the birth of the infant destined to be the head of the next generation of French Rothschilds became the very first entry in a new registry of children born to citizens of the republic.

After a long wait in New York, which he attributed to traditional French bureaucracy, in March 1943 Guy was suddenly called in, told to be ready at an hour's notice. He sailed to Britain on a small freighter carrying arms and food; when it was torpedoed in mid-Atlantic he was one of the last off the burning ship, among the survivors picked up by a corvette. His travel orders, when he presented them to the Gaullists in London, were stained with fuel oil.

He had the impression that no one quite knew what to do with the officers and men sent to Camberley, a training camp an hour's train ride from London. As an experienced combat officer, Guy was appointed instructor, later deputy chief of the camp. The day came when, like all officers rallying to de Gaulle, he was summoned to Carlton Gardens, London headquarters of the Free French, to be introduced to their chief. Charles de Gaulle, he couldn't help noticing, remained stone-faced when the name Rothschild was pronounced, melting only when he asked what the new recruit wanted to do; he was there only to follow orders, replied Guy. De Gaulle seemed surprised; apparently that was not what he was used to hearing from his volunteers. To Guy the meeting was a disappointment. He attributed de Gaulle's coolness to news he had just received of the accidental death of a prestigious officer who only recently had joined the Free French.

There was to be no war for a while. But in London, where Guy was sent after three months at Camberley, he endured the punishing air raids. When at last he won an assignment, it was to join a liaison group designed to guarantee an immediate Gaullist presence in liberated territories, once the Allied forces had established their beachhead in Normandy, for de Gaulle feared more than he feared the Germans that his Anglo-American benefactors intended to set up a military government to "occupy" France. (From de Gaulle's point of view, it was for the Gaullists to do that; they already represented the legitimate government of France.) Guy was given responsibility for assigning French recruits to appropriate British operational units; but that did not put him on the invasion beaches.

He thought he was being talked about for an intelligence assignment, in liaison with French resistance movements; nothing happened. Later he learned that it was his name that had been the obstacle. It was the kind of anti-Semitism with which he was all too familiar: the Gaullists had been happy to find Jewish recruits when they needed manpower; now, with victory in sight, they feared a negative reaction if the Free French movement seemed to contain too many Jews. Guy would get to France at last, attached to Gen. Pierre Koenig at SHAEF (Supreme Headquarters Allied Expeditionary Forces).

In a matter of days he was in Paris, a post-liberation Paris of partisans sporting armbands, brandishing guns; the city lacked electricity, public transport, even food. On Rue Laffitte he found a faithful senior manager, René Fillon, who had stayed close to the bank, preserving family interests as best he could. Fillon had been working with a skeleton staff; other employees could still be found in La Bourboule, in the ex-Vichy zone.[1]

All the way back in 1870, as minister of justice in the government that took charge after the capture of Napoleon III in the Franco-Prussian War, Adolphe Crémieux (himself a French-born Jew) was able to push through a decree granting French citizenship to the Jews of Algeria; he would be a bugbear of anti-Semites ever after. Vichy lost no time in abolishing the Crémieux decree. Then in November 1942 the Allies swept over Algeria and soon the Free French were nominally in charge, in the person of that other leader, General Giraud. It was his decision, announced in a speech on March 14, 1943, not to reverse Vichy: the Crémieux decree would not be revived. (His reasoning was that it had created a distinction between Jews and Muslims.) Giraud followed up his ill-timed declaration with a formal decree that appeared even less generous than Vichy's (which had at least made an exception for Algerian Jews who had fought for France).

Old General Giraud was a good Frenchman and a brave one. He had escaped from a Nazi prison camp, then he had escaped from Vichy, but he obviously hadn't understood much about the nature of this war. From his New York base, old Edouard de Rothschild, speaking in his capacity as president of the Central Consistory of the

Jews of France (and "of Algeria," he made sure to add), expressed regret at a decision that "gives rise to a feeling of anxiety among all those who have been victims of the racial laws and among the miserable human beings tortured by the Nazis." Abrogation of the Crémieux decree, he pointed out, "arbitrarily and illegally deprives of their citizenship French citizens, born on French soil, whose ancestors were citizens of France." It "proves the desire of some of the leading personalities in Algeria to attempt to maintain anti-Semitism in North Africa. . . ." And this, he warned, "will have a detrimental effect on the prosecution of the war."

Giraud had his American supporters, old French hands in the State Department like Sumner Welles, Under-Secretary of State, who felt that Baron de Rothschild was presenting an erroneous picture, for General Giraud had abolished Vichy's anti-Jewish racial laws; further, the abrogation of the 1870 decree would not affect the citizenship of Jews born in France or descendents of French-born Jews. So Baron Edouard had to take up his pen again. Clearly Mr. Welles and his advisers were as unfamiliar with what was going on as the seasoned military hero had been. For Rothschild hadn't been talking about Jews born in France; Giraud had called into question the status of Jews born in French Algeria. "The Crémieux decree is as much a part of the statutory fabric of France as any other law," he explained. "The reenactment of its cancellation, which was a part of the odious and retroactive Vichy decrees, is a vicious discrimination made between men of European civilization, based uniquely upon their religious affiliation, and constitutes a grave and permanent danger for the present and the future."[2]

Charles de Gaulle understood that. But he was to arrive in Algeria from London only in May 1943, and he had other priorities, principally to gain control of the Free French movement whose leadership he was then obliged to share with Giraud. He heard the grievances of the Jewish community, and by October 20 had changed Free French policy: at last Vichy had been overruled. Shortly thereafter, General Giraud stepped down as co-chairman of the French Committee of National Liberation, and from public life.[3]

*   *   *

The restoration of the Rothschilds would be a long and slow process, for the law was the law (even in our day, much Vichy law is still on the books). Read about it in *The New York Times:* on the ninth of November 1944, two months and a fortnight after the liberation of the French capital, the Council of State restored the citizenship and civil rights of Henri de Rothschild, making it possible for him to reclaim property confiscated by Vichy. The decision confirmed an earlier order of de Gaulle's provisional government, now established in Paris, to abrogate the Pétain state's discriminatory legislation; it applied not only to Henri but to all Frenchmen who had been denationalized by Vichy.[4]

That kind of restoration was probably the easiest kind. But what to do about the intricate and often self-serving confiscations by the Germans on one hand and the Vichy French on the other (complicated by the collaboration of many Frenchmen with the Germans and against Vichy)? And what about the tacit collaboration of otherwise well-meaning people in the despoliation of their fellow citizens? The exclusion of Jews from banking under the June 1941 Vichy decree? In fact nothing at all would be done to redress that grievance, or to indemnify Jewish bank officers dismissed without pay under the Pétain rule. To punish "institutional collaboration" would have been to punish nearly everybody; that, in the opinion of the liberators, would have impeded economic recovery. Business and businessmen weren't to suffer for what they did or what they let happen during the German years.[5]

Moreover, so Guy de Rothschild discovered, everybody had been a Gaullist all the time! But he remembered one episode at a dinner party only days after the liberation of Paris at the end of August 1944: a Free French officer spotted a Gestapo collaborator among the diners. The Gestapist and his wife were invited to leave, obliged to walk between two rows solemnly formed by the other dinner guests. (As a liaison officer attached to the Allied forces, Guy himself had to deal with the case of a man accused of collaboration; he invited the suspect to disappear, and after a moment of astonishment the man did.)

There were less noble affairs, as when a leading horse owner was slapped in public at the smart Longchamp track, and by someone who couldn't have been very proud of his own wartime record.

Another time Guy had to serve in a jury of honor hearing the case of a Jew accused by a Jewish survivor of having saved his own life at the expense of someone else.[6]

Soon this Rothschild heir assumed a public role—a natural one for a Rothschild—as spokesman for the Jewish community. In December 1944 he was in the United States for the annual meeting of the American Jewish Joint Distribution Committee, the lifeline for the devastated communities of Hitler Europe. Speaking as Captain Guy de Rothschild, attached to General Koenig (now military governor of Paris), he described the distress of the Paris Jewish community, while thanking the committee for relief and rescue programs responsible for saving the lives of thousands of French Jews.[7]

Philippe, the Rothschild who had suffered a death in the family, was to discover the more subtle damage that the occupation caused to his heritage. As a Free French liaison officer with the British Second Army, he had followed Allied forces to the beaches of Normandy. In liberated Paris he learned that the family's Château Mouton was now serving as headquarters of the French Forces of the Interior, the FFI, while a division of German troops were holding a pocket on the estuary above Bordeaux. Still in beret and combat uniform, he made his way to the Médoc to find ruined fields and empty houses, filthy walls and floors inside. But he was soon surrounded by his faithful staff, and the vines had been preserved.

To begin the job of rehabilitation, he'd have to settle in with daughter Philippine (an only child, and now motherless). Philippe had a flash of inspiration when he stared out at the temporary huts erected in the park, containing German prisoners under FFI guard; soon, with official approval, he had them tearing down the temporary shelters, removing wires, repairing roads, hauling away the old guns; later he put them to work building over half a mile of road between Mouton Rothschild and the Armailhacq vineyard acquired just before the war. (Nearby, at Lafite, the competing Rothschild clan had a similar thought. There war prisoners were employed in the vineyards.)

It was then, with the debris cleared away, the vineyard operating again, that Philippe made his decision. In the past he had dis-

persed his energies; now he would concentrate them. "The Mouton
fields are worth a life," he decided.[8] The real battle between
elegant Lafite and brash but getting-better-every-day Mouton was
under way.

Now the arduous task of tracking down and recovering Nazi plunder could begin. Confiscated funds, liquidated stocks and bonds,
might in the end be traced (it would simply take an army of
accountants and a country-wide, or even a Europe-wide, search).
Faithful Rothschild employees had no trouble recovering equities
that had been placed with friendly buyers committed to returning
them. A member of the staff embarked on a legendary tour of
remote provincial caches to recover odd lots of stock that had been
stashed here or there.[9]

Old masters were another story. The leaders of the Great Reich
had taken special pains to store their booty; the hiding places were
the same mountains that the Nazis had chosen for their last stand.
Finding the ravished art would call for a precise record of what was
missing; returning it to their owners required that the owners be
found. And all this had to wait upon the successful outcome of the
war. For if the Normandy landings of June 1944 were followed by
the liberation of most major French cities and towns in August and
September, it would take another winter and the first weeks of
spring 1945 to reach Berlin and victory.

A corps of American art experts had been assigned to Allied
forces crossing Normandy, and followed them into Paris. Among
the specialists, the first among equals was James J. Rorimer, then
thirty-nine, in civilian life curator of the Department of Medieval
Art at the Metropolitan Museum in New York (and of its annex, the
Cloisters, atop a ridge overlooking the Hudson River). Henceforth
Rorimer was a Monuments, Fine Arts and Archives officer, attached to advancing Allied forces. In Paris he made immediate
contact with his French museum counterparts, among them pertinacious Rose Valland, who appreciated this American who didn't
keep his French colleagues at a distance.

First, she and her museum colleagues had an urgent request:
that Rorimer find a way to get American and French tanks out of

the vicinity of the Louvre museum where they had been parked, so as not to draw Luftwaffe bombs. That Rorimer was able to do.

Meanwhile, on their side the French were setting up an art recovery committee with Rose Valland as its secretary, setting it up in the very Jeu de Paume that had served the Nazis as a way station; it was a manner of exorcising the memory of Herr Rosenberg. The commission began with a modest dowry: some hundreds of minor paintings that Rosenberg hadn't deemed worthy of plunder. It started by recording the claims of victims of the looting—an inventory that soon added up to 100,000 stolen works. Museum director Jacques Jaujard was able to give Rorimer a list of Einsatzstab Rosenberg offices and depots in Paris itself.[10]

The immediate problem was to make sure that advancing troops—both French and Anglo-American—gave priority to the protection of stolen art as they fought their way across Germany. In April 1945, Lieutenant Rorimer was assigned to the U.S. Seventh Army, which was about to invade a region certain to be overflowing with hidden treasures. So he had the privilege of penetrating the secrets of awesome Neuschwanstein castle. "From the lower court, where American guards were on duty, we climbed a long flight of steps to a second court surrounded on three sides by the wings of the complicated structure," he was to recall of that extraordinary moment. "The verticality of the surrounding mountains was repeated in the structure of the castle, so that in going from one series of rooms to another one had the feeling of climbing up the mountainside."

A compliant watchman produced a large cluster of keys, unlocked a door to still another stairway. There they found a room with thick walls and the narrowest of apertures, stacked to the ceiling with crates, each with the telltale mark of the Rosenberg Einsatzstab stenciled on it. Then another winding stairway, another strongroom, more booty.

Rorimer discovered that every room in the immense castle except for the throne room and other ceremonial halls was packed with plundered art. Behind a heavy steel door, well camouflaged, the visitors came upon two large chests containing Rothschild jewel collections, rare manuscripts, and over a thousand pieces of silver from the Banque Lazard's David-Weill family. The American officer walked through the rooms "as in a trance," he remembered later, "hoping that the Germans would live up to their reputation for being methodical," for without inventories it would take twenty years to identify all the booty.

Indeed. For now the chief custodian—who had been at the castle longer than Hitler had been in power—showed them a wing of the castle with its own entrance. This was the Rosenberg commando's workstation, with its photographic laboratory and file rooms—containing those essential inventories seized from the collectors themselves (sometimes it had been their only record of what they owned). Rorimer had the rooms closed off with wax and cord, using an ancient Rothschild seal reading SEMPER FIDELIS. He learned that some of the looters were still in the village adjacent to the castle; among them was one of Rosenberg's henchmen, Bruno Lohse, who had also served as Goering's personal agent. Lohse and other Rosenberg men were taken into custody by men from the Office of Strategic Services (OSS), the American intelligence agency, whose legal staff knew the files and catalogs would be perfect evidence for future war crimes trials.

But this was only the Rosenberg booty; now it was time to track down the most fabulous prize of all—the Goering collection, whose contents could only be guessed at from the reports of the Reichsmarschall's twenty visits to the Jeu de Paume. Rorimer—by now Captain Rorimer—had a hunch that Hitler's "Eagle's Nest" at Berchtesgaden might hold the answer to the riddle, if only because of the importance that Alpine site held in Nazi lore. He began his search there with no clue at all as to possible hiding places. Then, when news came in of Goering's capture, he was able to interrogate him through the good offices of the French officer who was keeping the prisoner happy with drugs and alcohol. In this way he learned of Goering's final train journey to Berchtesgaden, accompanying carloads of art from his precious and stolen collection; all Goering knew was that the railway cars had been parked in tunnels.

The main group of paintings was found; in succeeding days still more were located in a cement cave in nearby woods. "After all, I'm a Renaissance type," was the way Goering explained his behavior to the French officer interrogating him on Captain Rorimer's behalf.

Soon Rose Valland, who by then had gotten herself appointed to the staff of Gen. Jean de Lattre de Tassigny's First Army, with responsibility for recovery of art in the liberated sector assigned to the French, obtained American approval to inspect Einsatzstab depots so as to identify art stolen from France, then to get it shipped home without red tape. Over 1,400 crates were thus returned unopened, to be unpacked and sorted once again—poetic justice—in the Jeu de Paume. When the Einsatzstab Rosenberg files were scrutinized, it was found that the most important single source of plunder had been the Rothschild family, with 3,978 items taken from nine locations.[11]

And, miraculously, although it took some years, most of it was returned. Indeed, it was back on the walls and atop pedestals and in display cases before the death of Edouard (but that was in 1949).[12] Much of the credit belonged to a Parisian expert, Pierre André, his wife, Marie-Noëlle, and their staff; the Maison André had been founded in 1859, and Pierre André's grandfather had helped the Great Baron James begin *his* collection. Since the Rothschilds had already sold their prewar home on Rue Saint-Florentin, which became an annex of the American embassy, Edouard and Germaine moved into temporary quarters on Rue Georges-Berger off the Parc Monceau, which is where their art caught up with them; Pierre André opened the cases and compiled the catalog. Much of the furniture and other art objects required repair (furniture happened to be André's specialty).

The Andrés did discover that some paintings were never returned, among them a Watteau and a Rosa Bonheur. To her expression of regret for their loss, Baron Edouard said to Marie-Noëlle: "Oh, you know, one always leaves feathers." When the Rothschilds moved from the Parc Monceau into a fine house at 19 Avenue Foch, inherited from Edouard's deceased sister Béatrix, Marie-Noëlle remarked that Edouard had mounted a photograph for all to see: an American GI holding up Vermeer's *Astronomer*.[13]

Not the Jeu de Paume, but its twin pavilion on the Seine side of the Place de la Concorde, was the setting for the final episode in the looting story, a public exhibition of "Masterpieces of Private French Collections Recovered from Germany," held in the summer of 1946. "This is the final act of a frightful and admirable adventure," the prefacer began. "It was from this lovely Tuileries that these works of art were taken, and they return to the same tranquil . . . garden today."

Visitors to the exhibition were not to learn the names of the proprietors of the works on display, but when a painting had been selected for Hitler or Goering, that fact was noted. There was no indication of interest by either Hitler or Goering in the *Portrait de la Baronne Betty de Rothschild* by Ingres, but it was among the paintings stolen by the Einstazstab and recovered.[14]

REVIVAL

*W*hen the crowd gathered about the paddock became aware of who was walking toward them, there was momentary confusion—and then a cheer. It was Edouard de Rothschild! Perhaps he was the devil incarnate to practitioners of conspiracy theory, to radicals of right and left; to ordinary human beings at the racetrack he had been an honest man and a dependable breeder; need one say more?[1]

There were other scenes: Edouard in his last years, as imperious—as "Rothschildian"—as ever he had been, although now confined to a wheelchair. Irascible with the nurses who took turns at his side at home on Avenue Foch, Baron Edouard wouldn't let anyone put him to bed. He insisted on going hunting, so there he would be at Ferrières in a wheelchair, surrounded, as if miraculously, by bevies of pheasants.[2]

But the Rue Laffitte was another matter; even a man accustomed to being first among equals could understand that. In December of that first year of peace, seventy-seven-year-old Edouard called in the notaries, and signed over sufficient additional shares—technically he was selling them—to make Guy his equal partner. The following month cousin Robert, then sixty-six years old, transferred half of *his* equity in De Rothschild Frères to sons Alain and Elie in equal shares. As it happened, Edouard survived his younger cousin, for after the death of his wife early in 1945, Robert retired to Switzerland, and died there at the end of 1946 (having willed the balance of his shares to his sons).[3]

There would be further changes in the immediate postwar years—in the law, first of all, which, under the reform-minded Fourth Republic, required that financial institutions define themselves either as merchant or deposit banks, with different rules for each. It may have been the wrong move—but the partners saw no other—so they opted for merchant banking. Their choice, and the evidence that they weren't actually engaged in many of the financial activities associated with such banks, reinforced the conviction of outsiders that De Rothschild Frères was merely a holding company for the family's own equities, not to be taken seriously in the business world.[4]

The new man at the helm was determined to change that image. Yet Guy de Rothschild, who celebrated his thirty-sixth birthday in the first month of peace (May 1945), was fully aware of his shortcomings. He had received no professional training, nothing like a Harvard Business School diploma, and certainly his apprenticeship in the dormant old bank of the 1930s was hardly the equivalent of an MBA. Lacking the experience that would tell him precisely how to go about what he wished to do, he adopted a pragmatic, trial-and-error approach as he set about developing the family business into real business.

Only later, much later, did he acquire the conviction that dimension counted in today's business world; only then would he and his cousins put together existing assets to create such a critical mass.[5] In June 1946, in conformity with the legal requirement that assets be revalued to take account of the depreciation of French currency, the bank's nominal capital was raised from 50 to 250 million francs (some 96 million francs at this writing).[6]

That Guy already understood a great deal in his first year as head of the bank is clear from a memorandum he circulated among his associates in January 1946. He began by taking note of France's postwar mood—shared with the rest of liberated Europe—an "anticapitalist" climate that, in France, manifested itself in the nationalization of large enterprises and the establishment of increasingly restrictive corporate law. France was in still deeper trouble because of a chronically weak franc, which in 1946 was worth only one-fortieth of its 1941 value. He feared that the country's "endemic incapability" was bound to lead to the abolition of private banking.

But right now, said Guy, the family must choose. Either they'd accept their new diminished status—and then the children of the present generation would simply have to learn a trade, choosing chemistry or even farming—"Or else let's hold on to this immense asset represented by our name." His proposal: Let some Rothschilds stay in France so as not to abdicate; let others establish themselves in the United States to build up a proper House of Rothschild there. "Creating a Rothschild Bank in America is an effort worthy of the best of the Five Gentlemen of Frankfurt. . . ."

In the end, inertia won. He would stay in France, as would cousins Alain and Elie. They'd build or rebuild their homes and their business—for the greater glory of Rothschild. These first postwar years were necessarily devoted to assessing damage, dealing with quotidian problems. Later Guy reflected that in this early phase of his captainhood he could have made good use of an experienced deputy to guide his hand in developing the bank; even his best and most reliable executives lacked the qualifications. In the first days of liberated Paris the firm had to make do with a basement for the half-dozen or so staff members who had survived the occupation, for Vichy's relief agency still occupied the main rooms above. De Rothschild Frères then served a handful of clients, but its assets hardly made it a merchant bank.[7]

Edouard de Rothschild died on June 30, 1949. His passing inspired a rite that had accompanied other family deaths. The rite required that the death remain secret in the first hours, while the family discreetly unloaded large bundles of stock on the exchanges—Royal Dutch, for example, and De Beers. This dumping had the immediate effect of sending prices sliding, so that at the end of that day the value of the deceased's holdings was diminished, thereby reducing estate taxes (they'd be paid, notably, on 720 million francs' worth of Royal Dutch—a little over 100 million francs now).

The unloading was a regular and an accepted practice, as Edouard's son and chief heir well knew; not enough money was involved to cause a scandal, or call for investigation.[8]

There had been another death in the immediate postwar months: that of Henri in October 1946. He left money—and James-Henri would appreciate that; he also left the fabulous Mouton vine-yards—to Philippe, the son who had known better than his father how to make them blossom.[9] But he willed his father's equally legendary collection of books and manuscripts (to which Henri himself had contributed significantly) to France's National Library, where it became one of that institution's treasures.[10]

In Philippe, certainly, Henri had created a showman in his own image. When a Paris newspaper had the temerity to write about yachting cups without speaking of his, Philippe's letter to the editor deserved a prize of its own:

> It seems to me impossible that you are unaware of my sig-nificant participation at the helm . . . in prewar regattas. . . . During a fifteen-year period my *Cupidon* yachts participated in a thousand races and won well over half of them.[11]

Guy had inherited something else: the leadership of France's Jewish community. But in modern France that antique institution still called the Consistory no longer held the same significance. A relief organization modeled on the American Joint Distribution Committee was bound to be more relevant in the post-Hitler de-cade. It took the form of the Fonds Social Juif Unifié (FSJU), which assembled Jews, religious or not, and regardless of political affil-iation. Not long after its founding, Guy assumed the presidency and kept it over the years, as charitable resources were redirected from victims of Hitler to the massive migration of Jews from trou-bled North Africa. In his double role as president of the Consistory and of the FSJU, Guy carried on the senior Rothschild's traditional role as spokesman of French Jewry and defender of imperiled Israel, without becoming a Zionist for all that (another Rothschild tradition). Israel's pioneer prime minister, David Ben-Gurion, asked him point-blank, after Guy hesitated to call himself a Zion-ist, would he raise his son in Israel? And Guy had had to reply, frankly, no.[12]

Surely his wife, Alix, a Hungarian born in Czechoslovakia, was more of a true believer; among her philanthropies—which included aid to creative talents and the founding of Paris's Musée de l'Homme—there was the Youth Aliyah, a movement supporting young settlers in Israel. In the Rothschild universe—whose frontiers roughly coincided with those of Normandy—she and not Guy had become mayor of the tiny village of Reux outside Pont-l'Evêque, near the Rothschild estate. The manor and its dependencies were severely damaged after the Allied landing in Normandy; Guy and Alix set about the long labor of restoring granges, stud farm, paddocks, apple press, and cellars. They left the main house till last, and when they attacked that, they made it look better than it had before the war, by removing ugly turn-of-the-century modifications.

Guy had inherited his father's passion for horses, raising and racing them; in taking over from Edouard, he also assumed the role of the country's premier breeder. He made his debut in autumn 1949, just months after his father's death. (The show had to go on; horses were kept at the top of their form or they were nothing.) But he admitted to feeling intimidated when he entered the paddock at Longchamp as the new headman. Two of his horses were in the running for a prize; the one he wasn't counting on came in first, and his confidence returned. In the season that followed he won some and lost some (lost more than he won). Finally, again with a horse he wasn't counting on, he took the prestigious Grand Prix de Paris, then another and another prize. The Rothschild colors, which had seemingly been eradicated by the Nazis and their French acolytes, finished the season in first place, with more victories in classic races than had been gained by any other single owner in recent memory.[13]

In 1952 a muckraking journal, in an exposé of French plutocrats, ran a "who's who" of the Rothschild dynasty; seven of the sixteen lines on Guy concerned his stables, with the names of his star horses. The anonymous author added, perhaps meanly, "Guy de Rothschild is, at least nominally, the present head of the Banque Rothschild."[14] And it was true that one saw Rothschild names and faces more often in the society and sports columns than in the fine print of the financial pages.[15] The all-time star of his Meautry stables would be Exbury; a month after Exbury won the esteemed Arch of Triumph Prize, Guy made the cover of *Time* magazine.[16]

In the persons of his cousin's sons Alain and Elie, Guy had associates who, if they were not more skilled in finance than he, possessed (each in his way) a strong personality. Robert's older son, Alain, was thirty-seven when he joined the bank in 1947, after spending a year in New York; in the Rothschild manner he'd get his own niche in the family business, representing the bank as board chairman of corporations it controlled. By all accounts Alain was a reluctant banker, at least as absorbed by Jewish community affairs as by the business day.[17]

Seven years his junior, Elie—considered by everybody who knew him the most strong-willed of banking Rothschilds—was assigned an old family albatross, PLM (the Paris-Lyon-Marseille line), which he proceeded to transform into a lively travel organization operating a worldwide chain of hotels and restaurants. He'd also get responsibility for Château Lafite, and the credit for its restoration after wartime desecration, its move into the black after having long been a money-losing indulgence.[18] He was perhaps too ambitious about his wine, for rival Rothschild grower Philippe later complained that the neighborly relations maintained in earlier generations between Mouton and Lafite disappeared with Elie, who was as much a crusader for one vineyard as Philippe was for the other.[19]

So the transformation of the old bank of the Great Baron James, which bank in recent times had been handled as a bundle of good bonds tied with a ribbon and kept in a drawer, became possible now. Later Guy confessed that he couldn't have done what had to be done during Edouard's lifetime, not wishing to shock the old man in his last years. One of his first tasks was to assess the stock certificates that had been hidden in friendly banks during the occupation.

The exercise taught Guy something: if the bank itself had been a negligible business in the years between the wars, the family still held shares in a number of significant outside companies, and sometimes it was the principal shareholder. The company of companies, of course, was the Compagnie du Nord, Baron James's great railroad adventure, and even if the Popular Front had nationalized railroads, Nord still controlled considerable assets— notably in mining and oil. It was a public company, quoted on the stock exchange, and a potentially powerful one.

Guy learned something else: even in firms in which the Rothschilds were the controlling stockholders, they had remained silent (again a result of Edouard's shyness about business, for if anything went wrong, he worried, the Rothschilds would be blamed). When young Jacques Getten, whose father was a director of the Compagnie du Nord, got a job with parental help at a shipping concern called Saga, he didn't even know that it was a Rothschild company, since its chairman wasn't a member of that family; as far as he was concerned, the Compagnie du Nord had a financial interest in Saga, and that was that. Half a dozen years later, when a Rothschild man came in to ask Saga to open an account at De Rothschild Frères, Getten's reaction was "What business is it of yours?"[20]

On the same principle, the bank didn't manage its clients' stock portfolios, on Edouard's conviction that "if the customer makes money he'll find that normal, but if he loses he'll say 'Rothschild ruined me.' "

With tact—for the new policy was put into effect before Edouard's death—companies owned by the bank transferred their liquidities to De Rothschild Frères, while family members brought in their own holdings. Now they had working capital. That made it possible to guarantee credit; more, by setting up a brokerage, the bank could earn commissions from its clients' stock transactions instead of watching them go elsewhere. Soon Guy and the reborn bank were involved in a number of new activities, some of them deriving from postwar restrictions (as by assisting clients in foreign investments without the necessity of exporting francs, this at a time of strict control of currency transfers). He'd make Rothschild one of the first banks to enter the computer age (sending a top manager to study at IBM).

The truly major change came when Guy took over the chairmanship of the Compagnie du Nord on his father's death, although even that was hardly a shoo-in. There was a corporate crisis at the very start, with hints that a minority stockholder was ready to mount a challenge for control. It made the new chairman realize that with so much stock in private hands, he wasn't at all sure that the Rothschilds could win a corporate battle. The dispute was resolved, but from that time on, Guy knew that the market was lying in wait for him; he'd have to demonstrate authority. Full control would come about in 1953, when new legislation made it possible to set up an investment fund into which were placed family interests in leading corporations such as Royal Dutch, Le Nickel, and Peñarroya. As the principal shareholders the family could use the fund for other investments, while Nord in turn fed the bank with fees and commissions.[21]

Henceforth Guy and his cousins had their choice of strategies. As in the past, the bank could act as promoter of a new venture (or individual Rothschilds, engaging their own capital, could assume the risk); when desirable, the Rothschilds and outside partners could join forces in the investment. And now with that seemingly magic instrument, the investment fund, the family could go to the market for major financing—for the greater good of public and Rothschilds alike.

The fund began with a dowry of four billion francs, representing the bank's industrial investments, plus shares held individually by Guy, Alain, and Elie in major groups such as De Beers, the Compagnie Française de Pétroles, and Le Nickel, with more than twenty international investors in the portfolio of the Compagnie du Chemin de Fer du Nord (including Belgian railroads, mining in the Belgian Congo, part ownership of the Banque Ottomane, Royal Dutch Shell, and even of a Société Française de Pénicilline). "How not to remember that England's fortune was built on coal?" Guy de Rothschild asked a meeting of shareholders in March 1957. "It is not outlandish to imagine that the exploitation of recent discoveries could, over a period of twenty years, give our industry a new stimulus, raising it to first place in Europe."[22] By 1964, a little over a decade after its founding, the assets of the Nord fund—spread over 116 different enterprises, of which fifteen large corporations represented 40 percent of the total—were valued at 19.6 billion francs.[23]

Looking back, Guy de Rothschild saw 1955 as the year of the opening of Africa—the beginning of intensive French investment in exploiting that continent's oil and raw materials on the eve of decolonization. He was particularly proud of a venture he handled personally, developing iron mining in Mauritania, a program that required building a railroad—an old Rothschild habit—connecting the mine to an ocean port 375 miles distant. There were some good years, and then a series of disasters, with a precipitous fall in iron prices, then nationalization by a newly independent African government. Developing the Saharan oil wells of French Algeria was a venture encouraged by the French government, and one to which the Rothschilds heartily subscribed. But the assets of their company, called Francarep ("rep" for research/exploitation/petrol), were nationalized when Algeria won independence, the corporate logo henceforth to cover investments in oil exploration in other parts of Africa, the North Sea, and Italy, as well as phosphates in Florida.

Between 1955 and 1962 the partners created seven investment funds in oil and other raw materials—nearly all succumbing to nationalization by newly independent states. Finally these funds were merged with the Compagnie du Nord's own investment group, which, by the end of the 1970s, was estimated to be worth about half of Banque de Paris et des Pays-Bas or 60 percent of Compagnie de Suez—two French giants of our time.[24]

In those years no one among the banking Rothschilds would have accorded more than a passing thought to their absent cousin Maurice, the playboy senator, the man their fathers had bought out, and then had fought in the courts; he had been out of sight and out of mind since the war. But something important had occurred during Maurice's involuntary exile in the United States. In 1942, when he was sixty-one years old, living less well than he liked, but having a clear idea of what he was missing, he began to frequent the markets, and notably the commodities exchange. He developed a flair, borrowing to buy raw materials at their low, selling quickly when they went up. Surely it was more than a game, and vestigial memories of family investments (his own father Edmond's fondness for raw materials in remote places must have helped him bet right). The point, as he'd later tell it to his son Edmond, was that whether high or low in the short run, strategic raw materials such as copper and tin, highly prized ones such as coffee and sugar, were blue-chip investments (just as diamond mines were, and he placed his chips there as well). It was wartime, not depression time.

In a decade this Rothschild formerly rich through inheritance became a self-made Rothschild billionaire. On his return from the United States he elected domicile not in ruined France but in buoyant little Switzerland; Pregny, after all, was one of his homes. Family legend has him dealing from this elegant lakeside house—another folly designed by Joseph Paxton—surrounded by priceless art treasures; he'd work lying on his bed, surrounded by five telephones (his secretaries relegated to a small pavilion elsewhere on the spacious grounds).

The rich get richer; with inherited wealth and his American fortune, Maurice couldn't go wrong; he'd bequeath both his riches and his method—not to speak of Pregny—to a son who was to be heard from.[25]

Something else happened at Guy's bank in the 1950s decade: Georges Pompidou. He'd become the nonfamily wizard the postwar Rothschilds knew they needed, although at the beginning he was far from being the experienced banker Guy also thought he needed. Born in 1911 in the remote Cantal district, his father a schoolteacher, he was raised to teach—and to teach literature (while working for the Rothschilds, he put his name to a fine anthology of French poetry). Pompidou had slipped away from his high school job to work for Charles de Gaulle at the liberation, leading to a brief though distinguished civil service career.[26]

But he wanted something more, and Rothschild executive René Fillon knew that, and told Guy de Rothschild; all that lacked was the proper niche. When Fillon insisted, Guy invited him in, finding Pompidou "sympathetic . . . and determined." Later, when he was summoned from relative obscurity to become de Gaulle's prime minister, still later when he was elected the nation's president in his own right, studies proliferated on the character of this Auvergne country lad whose qualities had been sufficient to help him over all the barriers erected by the establishment against young men of his station.

At the beginning Guy de Rothschild couldn't have known that he had found the right man, as Guy's father had found René Mayer a generation earlier (the difference—but it was also a difference in generations—was that Mayer was Jewish and remotely related to the family, while Pompidou was neither). But he'd give him a try. There was a problem company in the group, Société Transocéan, created after the war to set up barter trade arrangements not requiring the export of French francs—then strictly regulated. By the time Pompidou joined the group (at the beginning of 1954) the kind of business Transocéan was doing had become less profitable; Pompidou was to look into that. Guy's new recruit accompanied him on a business trip to Africa involving Saga, the ocean transport company of which Transocéan happened to be an affiliate. In no time at all Pompidou had come up with a plan for the ailing affiliate; Guy put him in charge.

If Pompidou had little to do with business and finance before he met Guy, he assimilated fast. His chance came when René Fillon withdrew from the firm to enter politics, and a replacement hired to run day-to-day affairs at the bank resigned; there was an opening now, and in those days before management became a science, it seemed sound practice to trust men of good general culture to learn while doing. Pompidou became director of De Rothschild Frères, invested with the authority of a full partner; from then on, he and Guy together made the law.

Their relationship extended beyond office hours—practically a first for the Rothschilds, who by tradition had erected high walls around their castles. Later the scandal sheets would attribute the very public friendship between the Guy de Rothschilds and the Georges Pompidous to social-climbing on the part of the ambitious provincial and his showy wife. The same yellow press attributed sly motives to the Rothschilds, who through Pompidou became closer to de Gaulle.[27]

In fact, Guy avowed, a change in his own status had something to do with it. Guy had a new wife, and she had quickly recognized Georges's qualities in the course of a hunting weekend at Ferrières; henceforth there would be a weekly rendezvous of the couples at Ferrières, a Deauville holiday together, winter sports.

Nor did Guy's remarriage pass unobserved; in fact it was the Rothschild scandal of its time. The divorce, first of all, from the well-loved and much-admired Alix. Then the infatuation of this forty-six-year-old man for impetuous, stunning twenty-five-year-old Marie-Hélène de Zuylen de Nyevelt van de Haar, herself divorced from a Count François de Nicolay—and she a Catholic, and not about to convert; *this* was a first in the history of the banking Rothschilds (although in fact the paternal grandfather of Marie-Hélène had married a Rothschild, the daughter of Guy's great-uncle Salomon).

A marriage of fire and water they'd call it—but Guy could point out, in retrospect, that it lasted. This man of routine whose life seemed bounded by office and golf course married, he'd say, "fantasy, disorder, the unpredictable."[28]

For Wallis, the Prince of Wales had given up an empire. This Rothschild bowed to the inevitable, becoming the first of the first sons to resign from the presidency of the Consistory (while continuing to preside over the relief agency FSJU). Although he had grown up in the Jewish rite, he was not a believer, but his memoirs betray his preoccupation with the loss of Jewish identity in the children of mixed marriages.[29]

Marie-Hélène had come to the marriage with a child, Philippe de Nicolay; he would be raised as a Catholic. After her marriage with Guy she had a second son, Edouard Etienne Alphonse, born on December 27, 1957, to be raised in the faith of *his* fathers.[30]

T W E N T Y - E I G H T

THE BANKS ROTHSCHILD

The days were long past when under German protection the ill-intentioned could indulge in facile anti-Semitism. Times were hard for the pamphleteers. In the post-Hitler era, as the truth became known about the dimensions of Nazi terror, it was impolitic (and soon illegal in France) to indulge in blatant racism. But fanaticism hadn't died; most of the fanatics had escaped the clumsy efforts of the postwar purgers.

And so a French magazine, once the darling of anarchists and iconoclasts, now (in 1952) a mouthpiece for the radical right, published still another simplification of Rothschild history. It cited the anti-Semitic ravings of Alphonse Toussenel a century earlier in *Jews: Kings of Our Time* (but didn't dare repeat them), denounced Rothschild arrogance but not Rothschild Jewishness, although it found a way to define the Dreyfus affair as a strategy devised by French Jews to combat anti-Semitism. (The writer also shows the Rothschilds fleeing France in 1940—but doesn't say why.) "More than ever they have a hand in a variety of activities," announces this writer, as if surprised that the family had pursued the family business. "They have even created or gotten their hands on a certain number of new ones."[1] Encouraging news for the early efforts of the postwar Rothschilds, then engaged in salvaging what they could.

In an exposé seemingly modeled on those of Edouard Drumont, veteran polemist Henry Coston, although patently handicapped by postwar inhibitions, was nevertheless prepared to say that "the entire French economy is dominated by the Rothschild bank."[2] That was in 1955. Three years later Coston was back with another revelation: "Should we remind you that if our republic has a president, it also has . . . a king, Mr. de Rothschild, and that it is easier to find a pamphleteer ready to insult the occupant of the Elysée palace than to denounce the dealings of the magnate of Rue Laffitte?"[3]

Guy de Rothschild was not quite king of France, his bank didn't quite dominate the economy, but the partners were making a living now. There were successive augmentations of capital—like squirrels carrying their harvest to the tree trunk, Guy, Alain, and Elie were pouring their profits back in. The young Rothschild executive Jacques Getten (son and grandson of veteran Rothschild managers Pierre and Maxime Getten) was summoned to the Rue Laffitte soon after the arrival of Georges Pompidou. He was then managing director of the bank's Saga shipping affiliate, but Pompidou wanted him to take over financial management of the bank itself. Pompidou outlined the strategy for the new investment bank he was constructing, a bank that would do everything except lend capital. France was entering a new industrial age based on the transformation of the raw materials of its far-flung possessions, and the Rothschild bank intended to participate fully in the new adventure.

Later Getten remembered being pleasantly surprised by the suave newcomer, captivated by his charm. Pompidou grasped things quickly, including Guy's dreams for the bank. Baron Guy, Getten decided, was Pompidou's contrary: extremely cool—a coolness probably due to a supreme shyness. Paradoxically he appeared more interested in mining than banking; Getten guessed it was because he was born a banker and didn't have to do anything to become one.[4] Pompidou and the Rothschilds presided over a meeting each morning at 10:20, and there everything was decided. Later on, when this very private bank finally established a credit department, every loan was granted or denied at the 10:20 meeting.

The smooth operations of Rue Laffitte—and indeed of the world outside—were disrupted in May 1958, as France felt the shock of the global decolonization movement on what it had considered until now its own soil, that Algerian territory conquered and settled a century and a quarter earlier, and where over a million Frenchmen now lived and worked alongside an indigenous Muslim population. France was soon split in two by a colonial war that shouldn't have happened, while senior officers let it be known that they would not give up French Algeria no matter what Paris said. Only one intrepid officer could face them down; to avoid civil war the republic called on Charles de Gaulle, and by doing so accepted his conditions. Such were the "events of May" which brought the Free French chieftain back from retirement to head a government of public safety, and then to preside over the rewriting of a French constitution in his own image. Before the year was over Premier de Gaulle was president of a Fifth Republic.

A brief but necessary introduction to what was to follow: the departure from Rue Laffitte of Georges Pompidou, who on the first of June was put in charge of de Gaulle's staff. During a meeting with Guy de Rothschild to announce his departure, Pompidou assured him that he had no intention of going into politics. Once the grand lines of the Gaullist Fifth Republic had been hammered out, he'd return to the private sector—he was, he insisted, as stubborn as de Gaulle.

And he was true to his word. Back at the Rue Laffitte after six months during which he served as midwife to the birth of the new republic, Pompidou slipped easily into the banker's life, becoming—thanks to Rothschild wherewithal and connections—almost as visible a social creature as Guy himself. This didn't prevent him, Guy knew, from seeing de Gaulle regularly, serving as an occasional and informal and confidential adviser (often advising the impetuous general just to calm down, so Pompidou confided to Rothschild). But from then until April 1962, when Pompidou became President de Gaulle's prime minister, Pompidou devoted all his energy to the bank; Guy was sure of that, and even resigned from the chairmanship of the family plum, the Nord investment fund, to give the job to Pompidou.[5]

The Pompidou connection provided rich material for students of the relationship between government and private capital—a subject about which the Rothschilds had often served as a prime example. Thus the Marxist historian Jean Bouvier and his followers made much of how the newly created Fifth Republic, with Pompidou at de Gaulle's side, came to the rescue of Le Nickel, that major Rothschild mining investment in French New Caledonia then headed by an old Rothschild warhorse, René Mayer. Despite its monopoly on French markets, Le Nickel was in trouble, a result of a decline in demand leading to the collapse of world prices. The company had made new investments in the hopes of surmounting the difficulties, but before they could bear fruit help was needed. Le Nickel got the subsidy necessary to allow it to unload its production at the new, lower market levels. De Gaulle's regime changed French currency (chopping two zeros off old francs to get new ones), and the decision to manufacture one-franc coins in pure nickel could not have hurt New Caledonia. . . .[6] Later, when the United States banned the importation of French nickel and its derivatives because some of it was being acquired from Fidel Castro's Cuba (whose mines were exploited with Soviet assistance), the American action was seen in France as retaliation against de Gaulle and his anti-NATO foreign policy.[7]

Both of Baron Edmond's sons died in 1957. First, that May, James Armand—Jimmy, the French Rothschild-turned-English, member of Parliament, celebrated turfist.[8] In September it was his brother Maurice's turn; he was seventy-six when he died. By making proper use of what he inherited, including the bulk of the fortune of Edmond, youngest son of the Great Baron (a "nineteenth-century fortune" it would be called)—Maurice had become the richest Rothschild of them all; and *his* son Edmond, who was about to celebrate his thirty-first birthday, was his sole heir. (Maurice died in Switzerland, his son was a Swiss resident, so there'd be no inheritance tax to pay.) Edmond II grew up in Paris, where his paternal grandparents had made sure that he and his divorced mother lacked for nothing—a villa on the park, a platoon of domestic servants.[9] Later he attended the University of Geneva, going on to Paris for a bachelor's degree in law.

The younger Edmond had not been part of his father's wheeler-dealing; indeed, his biographer (wife Nadine) describes his growing up in a household where money was not supposed to exist. During stays in Megève he had simply assumed that the luxury Hôtel d'Arbois and its ski lift belonged to the hotel manager, for his mother never said she owned them. At twenty-three, with no formal training in business, he had gone to work for his cousin Guy, serving his apprenticeship in import-export at Transocéan (that difficult postwar enterprise Guy would later assign to Georges Pompidou), traveling for the company to Latin America.[10] His second wife remembered that he had left his father's art collections in the crates in which they had been kept since World War II, and then when he opened them found himself at the head of one of the world's great private collections, the legacy of grandfather Edmond and father Maurice, of aunts Julie and Miriam; sufficient incentive to want to add to it.

The second Edmond was ready to go into business for himself at twenty-four, in Buenos Aires; later in Paris he tried his hand at foreign trade, making use of what he had learned at Transocéan. At twenty-seven he opened a bank of his own, La Compagnie Financière. By then he had decided that he would not go the way of the family's main branch, whose investments had made them manufacturers and miners and shippers. Instead he would finance other people's businesses, encouraging start-ups, providing fresh capital for existing ventures. The point was to provide seed money to medium-sized enterprises, reducing the stake as soon as they could stand on their own feet.

It worked with the Club Méditerranée, one of his great early coups (for a time he held 42 percent of its capital); it flopped with Inno-France, in its debut as a new kind of discount department store.[11] Compagnie Financière enterprises didn't have to be oil wells; usually they were not. There were some classic blue-chip participations (like De Beers and diamonds). But one venture became France's leading television weekly, another the country's leading toy manufacturer; another sold wine by mail and still another ice cream. And then there was that almost sentimental, extraordinarily lucrative family affair: the pursuit and extension of his mother's resort hotel business. Even the family love affair with Israel, in the time of this second Edmond, often took the form of hard-nosed business; one of his ventures was the Israel General Bank.[12]

A family love affair—skipping a generation. Edmond's biographer-wife Nadine points out that this second Edmond made the pilgrimage to Israel that his father, Maurice, never did. There Prime Minister David Ben-Gurion told him that the best thing he could do for Israel was to create jobs.[13]

His second marriage, to Nadine (after an unsuccessful first one), proved that he could be as much of a nonconformist as ever his father was, even more so in his choice of brides. Nadine was born in France's industrial north, her mother a worker in a cotton mill, her father unknown; she'd grow up in poverty, work on an assembly line, live in maid's rooms and do maid's work to round out her wages. A pretty face and body saved her: successively she was a painter's model, a chorus girl, a starlet (occasionally an unclad one).

When Nadine Lhopitalier—stage name Tallier—met Edmond, she was twenty-eight years old, he thirty-three and married. She admitted in her memoirs that she was seven and a half months pregnant with his child, and confined to bed, when the wedding ceremony was performed by the city hall officer who arrived at their apartment all fitted out in his ceremonial sash.

"I'll have to marry a young lady of good Jewish society," Edmond had once told her. She couldn't change her social class, but she could her religion; after learning what she had to learn, she got the Great Rabbi's blessing for that. Their son Benjamin, born on July 30, 1963, was raised as a Jew. Home life was Pregny on Lake Geneva, one of the great confidential museums, but also Maurice's Armainvilliers estate east of Paris, plus a proper town house on Rue de l'Elysée opposite the presidential palace, built to measure behind a Second Empire façade.[14]

Just as his grandfather had upset Rothschild tradition—upset his brothers too, by the depth of his commitment to Palestine—outsider Edmond II became an unofficial spokesman for the Jewish state, not fearing to go further than conservative Jews concerned to show themselves French first; on her side, Nadine became president of French WIZO (the Women's International Zionist Organization). Faced with Arab hostility on all its borders, guerrilla attacks and a buildup of enemy forces, in June 1967 Israel launched its preemptive strike driving Egypt out of the Sinai desert, the Syrians from the Golan heights, the Jordanians from the river Jordan's west bank and Jerusalem, creating secure and defensible frontiers for Israel while weakening its international support, earning it a condemnation as "aggressor" by President de Gaulle.

Before the Six-Day War was over, both Edmond and cousin Alain (then president of the Consistory) were in Israel. Edmond was one of the first civilians to reach the Second Temple wall after it became accessible to Jews for the first time since the founding of their state.

Back in France, and never mind de Gaulle, as chairman of the fund-raising arm of the Coordinating Committee of Jewish Organizations of France, Edmond issued an appeal to fellow Jews expressing his "immense pride" in Israel's military victory, adding, "The military victory was the victory of the Jewish people isolated in a hostile or indifferent world." That was not to everyone's liking. "No, I don't belong to the Jewish 'people,'" one reader protested in a letter to the press. "Like most French Jews, I belong to the French people...."[15]

During the Six-Day War, when President Charles de Gaulle publicly attacked what he defined as Israeli aggression, his prime minister was Georges Pompidou. Pompidou had been called out of the bank (de Gaulle had literally summoned him from his office there) in April 1962, and he would keep the job almost as long as de Gaulle kept his. The Pompidous dined at the Rothschilds' on the day after the nomination, Guy's wife declaring, "I don't know why, but I have the feeling we'll never again be together as we are now." And indeed, after serving as prime minister for six long years, Pompidou was to become the second president of the Fifth Republic, and die in office.

His departure was a severe blow to the bank, for Pompidou had taken on increasingly important responsibilities, and was about to get more. No one around could fill his shoes, and Guy didn't even bother to look for anyone, certain that he now had the experience, and the staff, to go ahead with the long-planned development of Rothschild interests.[16]

But the return of the Rothschilds to the inner sanctum of government, via Pompidou, wasn't lost on critics. The Parisian satirical weekly Le Canard Enchaîné said it in two small boxes placed at either side of its front-page masthead:

R.F.   R.F.

République française   Rothschild Frères[17]

The Communist party's *L'Humanité* headlined: "The director of the Rothschild Bank has formed his government." A reactionary royalist organ, *Aspects de la France*, accused de Gaulle of delivering the nation to "foreign finance."[18] In 1969, when Pompidou was elected president, a *Humanité* editorialist proclaimed, "With a former Rothschild aide at the Elysée Palace, the Bank remains in power."[19] The Bank perhaps, but not the Rothschilds, who would have occasion to regret the frequent hostility to Israel shown by the Pompidou regime.

Following Pompidou's death in office in 1974, Guy de Rothschild attempted to explain his friend's attitude. He had indeed been a friend of Jews, even of Israel, and when de Gaulle had decreed an embargo on that country during the Six-Day War, Pompidou had done what he could to delay its application. But he hadn't understood the passionate side of Israel, expecting from that country "the behavior of an old power."

During his years as premier they'd remain friends, Georges and Guy, lunching once a month at Guy's office (not at the bank, but at the more discreet Peñarroya headquarters on Place Vendôme), or at the prime minister's residence. On occasion the Pompidous joined the Rothschilds for a traditional weekend at Ferrières. It became more complicated when Pompidou attained the lofty position the Fifth Republic had created for its president; intimate meetings became rare, and Ferrières was out. They'd be more likely to meet at a presidential hunt or an Elysée reception.[20]

But the postwar bank was well launched now, the development of its industrial side proceeding according to plan. One achievement was the joining of all Rothschild mining activities into a single unit, a true French multinational, on the way to becoming one of the country's largest; they'd call it Le Nickel for its best-known component. The companies included Rio-Tinto, which, after the Second World War, had gone beyond copper mining to uranium, lead, zinc, even emeralds, operating in North and South America, Australia, and Africa (while in fact Rio-Tinto's original core activity was being liquidated in an increasingly nationalist Franco Spain). Peñarroya had also begun in Spain (with coal), expanding to lead and zinc in France, Italy, North Africa, and Brazil, to copper in Chile. The Rothschilds had been investors in New Caledonian nickel since 1884, becoming involved in operations starting in the 1920s; now Le Nickel was to be the cornerstone of the new emphasis on mining.

It was when Peñarroya needed restructuring and Georges Pompidou, tapped for the job, was abducted by de Gaulle in 1962 that Guy became a hands-on chief executive. A first for him, running day-to-day operations of a public company with a management packed with engineers, and thousands of employees around the world.[21]

The 1960s also saw the embryonic development of American activities, with a proper bank created from existing stateside assets. The novelty was that this was a fifty-fifty association with N. M. Rothschild in London. It was the beginning of a beautiful friendship, the origins of a New York investment bank later to be rechristened Rothschild, Inc., of a second bank in Zurich, and field offices wherever in the world they seemed to make sense.[22]

Even an expert could be confused by the proliferation of Rothschild investments. At the end of 1965, and for the first time, the French banking commission published the balance sheet of the Rothschild bank, and economists all but pounced on it. What surprised, in the column listing assets (totaling 421.5 million francs—some 2.6 billion present-day francs) was the proportion of negotiable instruments, the near absence of stock certificates. "Here is a merchant bank that seems to be behaving like an old-fashioned deposit bank," noted a specialist. Its assets placed it among the smaller French banks (Crédit Lyonnais reported assets of some 20 billion francs at that time—or 125 billion now). Then the economist seemed to be having second thoughts. One does understand that the Rothschild *bank* is only an element of Rothschild *group* holdings.[23] Indeed.

Actually they didn't have to be all that big; after a century and a half of just being Rothschilds, they could have gone bankrupt and still have fed myth. The evil Henry Coston was back, with a book on the "return" of the two hundred families, arguing that there were no longer two hundred but a single family, for they were now all tied together thanks to intermarriage.[24]

When the novelist Roger Peyrefitte, whose successive books were so many succès de scandale, decided to focus on Jews he invented a Rothschild cousin who escorts the chief actors of his tale through the worlds of high society and politics, commenting on who is and who is not Jewish. This piece of documented fantasy suggested that famous Christians (including infamous anti-Semites) were actually Jewish, while some who appeared to be Jewish were not. We learn that Georges Pompidou has a nose that would make a Jew jealous, and "grasping claws" just as Jews do—which (says one of Peyrefitte's characters) is what attracted the Rothschilds to him. The book's hero, Georges Sarre (the novelist's stand-in), has decided to make a study of Jews, focusing on the Rothschilds and their wealth, which has allowed them to buy everything and everybody (all said in the guise of admiration).

By repeating a century and a half of slanders about the Rothschilds, often to deny their veracity, the book serves as a virtual anthology of anti-Rothschildiana. These Rothschilds, thinks Peyrefitte's hero, are "the only permanent power we have in France." And they always manage to ingratiate themselves with those they pauperize.[25]

THE BIG CHANGE

*I*t seemed a good idea at the time; in retrospect, not so good. Still obsessed by the conviction that significant size would be the determining factor in the postwar business world, Guy de Rothschild turned his attention to the family bank. For if the industrial and mining activities of the Compagnie du Nord continued to expand in the 1960s, the bank itself seemed to be marking time—yet banking is what counted most for the family. The legendary Rothschild financial tool was being underemployed.

But there might be a way to faster growth, and without sacrificing the family's reason for being: it would be consumer banking of sorts, inviting a select clientele to deposit funds at Rothschild (and then making profitable use of these funds). It would mean opening branch banks not only in Paris but in France's most promising regional business centers.

The conversion of the bank went hand in hand with the transformation of its traditional headquarters, for those fine old houses on Rue Laffitte, as grand as they were, contained only some 43,000 square feet of office space, on grounds large enough for a functional building containing four times that area. The cousins proudly commissioned a leading American architectural firm, Harrison & Abramowitz, to come up with a contemporary structure to replace the landmark houses of the old bank. France was growing, and the Rothschilds were respecting tradition (thought Guy) in remaining abreast of their times.

They made the announcement a solemn occasion; the year 1967 lent itself to it, proclaimed the 150th anniversary of the founding of the French Rothschild bank. At the end of April the press was invited into the grand bureau (one paper called it "the grand salon with its somber wood paneling"); only when everybody was seated did Guy appear ("like an actor after the curtain goes up," he'd remember). He was flanked by his partner-cousins Alain and Elie; even the loner Edmond was present, to underscore family solidarity and the importance of the event.

Henceforth—beginning on the first of January, 1968—De Rothschild Frères was a limited-liability company. It got a new name— Banque Rothschild—as well as a significant increase in capital from the Compagnie du Nord, which holding company—with some twenty thousand shareholders—now owned close to 70 percent of the bank, becoming the pivot of the group. Banque Rothschild would function as a deposit bank, explained Baron Guy, for "today more than ever we all know that banks can only develop and perform services by collecting more and more liquidities from the broadest possible clientele in the widest possible area."

If they were turning their backs on merchant banking, he added, the truth was that Rothschild had never been such an institution, strictly speaking. Nor did he believe that merchant banking was the right business for the Rothschilds, or for the times. (Only Banque de Paris et des Pays-Bas was properly structured to handle industrial enterprises: "It does so with a talent that one admires but that one cannot usefully imitate.")

To the inevitable question from the floor, Baron Guy—chairman of the board of the transformed bank—assured the world that the cousins would retain a significant minority of shares, as well as sufficient stock to block adverse decisions in Nord, which would henceforth be the parent company.[1]

When the bylaws were rewritten to conform to the new corporate structure, Guy inserted a proviso that the bank could bear the Rothschild name only as long as a Rothschild played a key role in it. Clairvoyance?[2]

*   *   *

It was a brave new world; Guy got the critical mass he wanted. Later he would see the flaws. Enamored of the notion of savings as the key to capital accumulation, he had (so he later realized) misread the true future of banking: corporate finance, mergers and acquisitions.[3] The positive side was stressed at the general assembly of Compagnie du Nord shareholders after its first full year of activity following the decision to make Nord the pivot of all Rothschild financial and industrial activities: first, the capital, which had risen from 52.8 million francs at the beginning of 1967 to 335 million at the end of 1968; then the balance sheet, which showed activity multiplied by ten (to nearly five billion of today's francs). This kind of expansion made Nord a leader in its field, and would now permit "balanced diversification," as well as still greater public participation.

But not without guarantees, and of the best kind. "The Rothschilds are the single biggest investors, and also bring to bear their credit, their name, and whenever possible their knowledge of national and international finance," the stockholders report concluded reassuringly.

Affiliates of the Compagnie du Nord were organized into sectors. Among financial institutions, for example, Nord now controlled both the Banque Rothschild, with revenues of some 37 million francs (about 205 million now), and Amsterdam Overseas Corporation in New York, a financial institution with assets of $80 million. In mining and metallurgy, there were minority shares in Peñarroya and Le Nickel (which remained the umbrella for the group's global mining operations). An oil company, Socantar, was the single biggest earner of the group, with nearly 17 billion present-day francs in annual sales. And more, much more, including a rump Compagnie Auxiliaire du Nord which continued to exploit railroad cars, a holdover from the Great Baron's Compagnie du Chemin de Fer du Nord.[4]

On paper the new group was off to a good start. At the beginning of 1968 the Compagnie du Nord was ready to float a stock issue to finance acquisitions. At least that was the plan. But in Paris the month of May was the setting for one of those peculiar because unpredictable historical upsets, when rank-and-file workers, frustrated by what they felt to be their meager share of the general prosperity, joined a flash revolt by the rapidly expanding student population seeking to open windows to fresh air both in school and in the world they would meet outside. The spring 1968 revolution, if that is what it was, saw the shutting down of factories and public administrations, the paralysis of transport and the banking system—yet by statute the Compagnie du Nord was obliged to spread its results before the shareholders at the end of June. "All the calculations that I have just summed up for you were made, I remind you, in an apparently stable world, with well-established values," Guy declared to the general assembly; it could have been his great-grandfather James talking, in the spring of 1848, except that the Great Baron hadn't had to report to shareholders.[5]

That autumn, interviewed by a business weekly, Baron Guy confessed that the spring events had traumatized him, as it had every business leader; they all had felt as if Judgment Day had arrived. He realized that both junior management and personnel felt frustrated when they were not consulted or even informed about the problems of the companies for which they worked. He was all for making room for the younger generations—as long as it was understood that it still took time to acquire experience, which is why there was a need for the "less young" as well. Nor should it be forgotten that corporate power was now largely in the hands of managers—those without invested capital; the Rothschild companies, for instance, were no longer exclusively Rothschild. The family's power now derived "from a moral heritage, a credit one might call incorporeal, and why not say it—tradition."

He was a poor prophet, in any case, when he told the interviewer, "I have to say that I'd be astonished if the Rothschilds were dispossessed in the name of justice and equality."[6]

But for the time being the economic consequences of the May tremor seemed to have been surmounted. In 1969 the Banque Rothschild enjoyed a profitable year, returning 20 percent on capital. Under the new lineup Guy was chairman, Alain and Elie vice-chairmen; among the board members there was a British Rothschild, Evelyn, whose mother was French, and whose association with his Parisian cousins was to endure, even to expand with time. Although the new deposit bank opened only a handful of branch offices, they were in carefully selected locations, and deposits were flowing in. The bank was also satisfactorily involved in the stock market and in foreign exchange. A new mutual fund had been introduced under the unbeatable name Rothschild-Expansion.[7]

So at the beginning of the 1970s everything was in place for a smooth flight—everything except the economic climate. Even before the ballooning of Middle Eastern oil prices in 1973 sent the global economy into shock, leading industrial nations had begun to feel the effects of a rare combination of currency inflation and market depression—the phenomenon that became known as stagflation.[8] Yet the renovated bank survived, even prospered, with a new mutual fund launched alongside Rothschild-Expansion.[9]

Still, no one thought of the reborn bank as a challenger of the giants. "You can't compare the power of the Rothschild bank of 1850 with that of 1972," Elie de Rothschild cautioned an interviewer. "At that time there were no Paribas, Crédit Lyonnais, and [Banque Nationale de Paris]. We were the first. Today we're not so stupid as to think we're something other than what we really are, the fifteenth."[10]

And if prudent and clever planning *could* make something out of nothing in money manipulation, there was little one could do with commodities on world markets—with, for instance, the fall in demand for nickel. Henceforth Rothschild industrial and mining interests followed the downward slide of the economy in France and nearly everywhere else.

Everybody wanted out, including an American investor Guy had picked up in the more upward-looking 1960s, when nickel production was being expanded in New Caledonia. Henry Kaiser, son of the industrial wizard who had churned out the ubiquitous Liberty ships of World War II, had joined forces with the Rothschilds in building a major plant in the New Caledonian capital of Nouméa. Now, in the sober seventies, the directors of Kaiser Aluminum, alarmed at Le Nickel's continuous calls for new capital at a time when markets were falling, were asking to be let out, and bought out.

To raise the capital for that, Guy de Rothschild was obliged to divest himself of some family jewels—family minerals actually—by selling 50 percent of Le Nickel to a government corporation. At the same time a new mining group called Imétal was created to serve as an umbrella for Rothschild mineral interests, its principal owner (with 20 percent) to be the Compagnie du Nord. In the vision of Guy de Rothschild, Imétal was not simply a holding operation or a way of cutting losses, but an instrument of expansion.

Cash-rich thanks to the sale of half of Le Nickel, Imétal could go fishing for new investments, not so much in raw materials as in processing, and why not in that terra incognita for the Rothschilds, the United States of America? For now they did have the expertise of the New York Rothschild affiliate, New Court Securities, which, with investment bankers Kuhn Loeb, soon came up with a few suitable candidates. The result was a hostile takeover bid for a Pittsburgh manufacturer of steel and alloy tubing called Copperweld, one of the first such won by a foreign firm. For after some ugliness in the courts and even on the streets—with trade union protests against the "baron" and cries of "Frenchies go home!"— the baron emerged victorious. It was an $80-million purchase, a choice item to stuff into the Imétal stocking. Soon Baron Guy could toss in a 25-percent slice of the U.K.'s Lead Industries Group, followed by majority control of France's leading private producer of uranium. But the 1970s, with reduced levels of economic activity owing to successive rises in oil prices, a chronically weak American dollar, and universal pessimism, were not going to permit full realization of anybody's potential.[11]

There were further divestitures, notably of a stake in La Générale Alimentaire (sold to a longtime Rothschild ally, James— known as Jimmy—Goldsmith), in the oil group Antar, and in the construction industry.[12] But the public face was a broad smile. On the fifth anniversary of the reorganized company it was made clear that, deposit bank though it might be, Rothschild had every intention of developing its activities in merchant banking.[13]

Yet the question of size—inadequate size—continued to haunt the firm (and the business world lying in wait outside). Technically Rothschild was still a deposit bank, and a small one of its kind. (There were rumors of possible mergers with other private banks, even with the growing Compagnie Financière of cousin Edmond.)[14]

In 1975 the Banque Rothschild acquired over two-thirds of Discount Bank France, part of Jimmy Goldsmith's Générale Occidentale group—a modest addition, since Discount was only a quarter of Rothschild's size. This was followed by the absorption of the Banque Stern, the Société Continentale de Banque, the American-owned Compagnie Européenne de Banque. . . .[15]

It was patchwork, all the same. The changes that should have been decisive came about in 1978, first with the coming to the front of the stage of Guy's thirty-five-year-old son David, "the dauphin" as he'd be called, to serve as general manager of the Banque Rothschild, with Elie's son Nathaniel, then thirty-two, as his deputy. David's first public assignment was a thankless one: to explain the disappointing results the bank had to show for 1977, with profits plunging (from 20 million francs in the previous business year to 8.5 million). "You don't come out of an economic crisis unscathed," he said simply enough. There had been a rapid swelling of the payroll, augmenting expenses. By now the bank operated twenty-one branches, and it had been calculated that it took between four and five years for a new branch to move into the profit column. The government had clamped down on credit, and business clients were reducing deposits in the face of persistent slump.[16]

So the Rothschilds undertook some essential reorganizing in the autumn of 1978, when a decision as momentous as the 1967 transformation was unveiled. Now the Banque Rothschild was to swallow its parent, the Compagnie du Nord—a consequence not only of the bank's present weakness but of severe and unacceptable losses in Nord's own operations owing to the quasi-universal slowdown. As David explained it, the merger of Nord and the family bank gave the latter a stronger capital base (raising the capital in fact from $60 million to $200 million in 1978 dollars). Skeptics were heard to say that the reorganization merely transferred questionable investments from the Compagnie du Nord to Banque Rothschild, at the risk of impairing the bank's own credit rating. In *The New York Times* a correspondent noted rumors "that the French Rothschilds are in trouble," repeating the comment of one French banker that almost every major business decision they had made in the last ten years had been bad.[17]

Yet from the family's point of view, merging the bank with the Compagnie du Nord was the *only* solution—concentrating strengths, allowing new synergies, it also made fiscal sense (because Nord's general costs came out of dividends, while in the bank they would be considered expenditures before taxes). And it put the name Rothschild on the big board of the stock market.[18]

What they needed was time to exploit the new state of affairs, to take a hard look at costs, replacing management as that proved necessary, for they had the critical mass they required now. They only needed time, and they weren't going to get it.

Looking at this cascade of events shortly after they occurred, a business writer, Jean Baumier, could only think of the word *decline*, decline not only for the family business but for the family. "The personal fortune of [the Rothschilds], about which there is great mystery, is critically affected." In the face of mystery, one looked for surface events, such as the very public abandonment of the grand Ferrières castle by Guy, the selling of part of the castle's art and antique furnishings. Or the sale of Alain's large town house opposite the Elysée Palace (it became a residence for guests of the President of the Republic). Then after the death of Guy's mother, the sale of that grand house on the Avenue Foch (to serve as the embassy of Angola).[19]

These liquidations were a sign of something, surely, just as the divestitures of their castles and yachts by other millionaires of the Western world were signs (in these years they found ready buyers in the oil-producing nations). It was also true that a generation was passing, and the successor generation saw other ways to spend its money.

In 1979 Guy was seventy, retirement age; so he retired from the chairmanship of the bank, succeeded by Robert's son Elie, at sixty-two the youngest of their generation (Guy had also been chairman of his beloved Imétal, but there his successor was chosen from outside the family).[20] Elie's older brother, Alain, celebrated his seventieth birthday in January 1980, and soon after that abandoned the few responsibilities he had retained (notably the chair at the affiliated Discount Bank). He was then president not only of the Central Consistory but of the Conseil Représentatif des Institutions Juives de France (CRIF), a more recently created organization that was speaking out in ways the tradition-bound Consistory could not. He'd give up the chairmanship of the Consistory in June 1982, but remain at the head of CRIF until felled by a heart attack during a visit to New York that autumn.[21]

But the forsaking of Ferrières had to be seen in its context. After the war and his second marriage, Guy (with Marie-Hélène) had indeed restored the castle's grand salons, making the house more livable than ever it had been, thanks to the installation of modern conveniences. They threw the kind of grand balls there that Baron James would have appreciated and for which Guy's Marie-Hélène was becoming famous—and not only in France. But the 1970s were what they were, bad business decisions or no, and even a Rothschild could feel that in this day and age possessing a Ferrières was no longer reasonable; the status of their tenant farmers—tenant farmers!—had long been an anachronism. And how pass on a Paxton's folly to the next generation? Who'd pay the inheritance tax? Who'd want to?

So the great house itself, and a substantial sweep of grounds, was given to the University of Paris. That nonprofit institution would use it as a study and conference center under the name Fondation Marie-Hélène and Guy de Rothschild (today a salon or suite of salons can be rented for wedding parties or even to make a costume film). Baron Guy and his baroness kept enough of the grounds to protect a smaller house built to their specifications. (Another parcel of Baron James's original terrain belonged to James's great-grandson Edmond.)[22]

And they still had the Château de Meautry, a fifteenth-century manor with its working stud farm, so close to Deauville and its beach, nearer still to the racetrack, to the golf course, populated by house guests in summer and young horses year-round. (Guy's divorced wife, Alix, had kept Reux, a short drive away, until her death; it became the country domain of David and his family).[23] Then in 1975, not too long after Guy had at last convinced Marie-Hélène that they didn't need that dinosaur of a castle at Ferrières, she discovered that the landmark Lambert mansion at the prow of ship-shaped Ile Saint-Louis was available for purchase. It was another monument, built by the architects of Versailles alongside the Seine in the very heart of Paris; Voltaire, who had lived in it, called it a palace for a philosopher-king. In more practical terms, it had room for the whole family and then some, room also for the great art collection that Alphonse had begun, and that Guy's mother had tended on Avenue Foch until her death; the paintings retrieved from Germany such as Vermeer's *Astronomer* and Ingres's *Baroness Betty* were among them. In every way the Lambert mansion could become another great house of the Rothschild dynasty; a year would be needed to restore and redecorate it, making it ready for Marie-Hélène's soirées.[24]

Nor were the Edmond de Rothschilds idle during the 1970s, as they shuttled between their Paris town house on Rue de l'Elysée and their castle on the lake outside Geneva. One of Nadine's Pregny parties, she'd recall with pride, drew guests from as far away as the United States—Senator Edward Kennedy, Audrey Hepburn, Gloria Swanson, Yul Brynner, Gregory Peck—and more princes from vanished monarchies than one could imagine.[25]

They were all making wine now. In postwar France, recession or no, making food and the wines to accompany often assumed industrial proportions, tempting to investors; for a Rothschild it was also tradition, of course, and a sport of sorts. So in 1972 Edmond— already part-owner of the family marvel Château Lafite, and a Midas who seemed able to produce gold even in hard times— decided to buy and build up a vineyard. He set his sights on a modest field in a promising area of production, Listrac in the Médoc region, and went about it as he did with start-up businesses in every other field: patience, expertise, and pump-priming (with a continuous outlay of cash in the mid-1970s when there was little optimism to spare—some of the cash coming from his share of Château Lafite).

He began with 187 acres of fallow land, and by 1979 had added another 138. Out of his efforts came Château Clarke, whose owner promised he wasn't seeking to attain the status of a grand or even a second growth. He would simply make honest wine for the middle classes, and pay considerable attention to its marketing. Almost at once it was earning the lion's share of its sales abroad. "Nobody in France had ever reconstituted a vineyard," he would tell an interviewer. He confessed he had been struck by the way California wines were being created thanks to technology and investment; he wanted to do the same.

If at first Edmond had gone for quantity, he changed course at the end of the decade; henceforth his best wine would go out with Château Clarke labels, the rest as a more ordinary Haut-Médoc. But the ambition showed through. A reporter noted the initials *CR* over the entrance gate to Edmond's domain at Listrac; it seemed to prepare the stage for the future introduction of a Château Clarke-Rothschild.[26]

While cousin Edmond was beginning from scratch, the irrepressible Baron Philippe was achieving a lifelong goal: in 1973 his Château Mouton-Rothschild benefited from a revision of the mid-nineteenth-century classification of Bordeaux wines, from "second growth" joining Château Lafite among the firsts.[27] Before the end of the decade he had surpassed even his own reputation for public relations, in crossing the Atlantic to find the nearest equivalent of his beloved Médoc, the vineyards of California's Napa Valley. An agreement two years in the making brought together a well-known Napa Valley grower, Robert Mondavi, and Baron Philippe; their partnership was to result in a superior red marrying "classic Bordeaux techniques and current California technology." The first vintage of this new wine, to be christened Opus One, was prepared for bottling in 1979. Labels reproduced the silhouetted profiles of Robert Mondavi and Baron Philippe.[28]

In comparison to the thunder produced by old Philippe, the intensive plowing by young Edmond, movement at that other Rothschild vineyard, the Great Baron's Château Lafite, was barely perceptible as a new generation took over, Baron Elie ceding his place as the family's delegate to his nephew Eric, Alain's son. That too would change.

THIRTY

MITTERRAND'S FOLLY

ationalization has ever been the fruit of anger and revenge, expressed through outright seizure of private property and means of production, often enough without compensating the owners. It happened that way in Russia after the October Revolution and in the nations of Eastern Europe that fell into Stalin's hands following the defeat of Nazi Germany. In a republic such as France, nationalization involves negotiation and just compensation (except when it implies punishment, as happened after the Second World War to the Renault automobile works, a notorious auxiliary of German military authorities).

Ideally, in the minds of Socialist theorists, the targets of nationalization are capitalist exploiters who have grown rich at the expense of the working class; the working class through the state will take over this wealth, represented in part by tangible assets such as factories and mines. The timid efforts of the Popular Front in the 1930s were overshadowed by the achievements of the postwar liberation government, which, under Charles de Gaulle, carried out the systematic takeover of large banks and insurance companies, also of the production and distribution of energy; most of the companies and groups nationalized in the late 1940s could still be found in the public sector at the beginning of the 1990s.

The Gaullists were idealists but not necessarily Socialists; now, in 1981, France would get its first Socialist president, and with a

Parliament he could count on. All during the previous decade the economy had been marked by sluggishness. French president Valéry Giscard d'Estaing, elected for a seven-year term in 1974, failed in his bid for reelection at least in part because of inability to cope with economic distress. And although new president François Mitterrand won an absolute majority for his Socialist party in the legislative elections that followed, he respected a pre-election alliance with the Communist party. Their alliance was inspired by a Common Platform hammered out in the gloom of the 1970s between Mitterrand and Georges Marchais, representing the Communist party; it contained a ringing promise for the 1973 parliamentary elections that nationalizations would be at the top of their legislative agenda, with banks and industrial groups the first targets.[1]

The left coalition failed to win in 1973, but the themes that had inspired the Common Platform were not forgotten. In 1980 Mitterrand repeated his promise to nationalize "key sectors of the economy," among them "the totality of the bank and financial community, notably merchant banking and financial holding companies. . . ."[2] The pledge was confirmed in Mitterrand's platform the following year—the crucial year.[3]

Impeccable ideology; admirably consistent. In practice the implementation of such a program would call for a veritable army of skilled government managers capable of taking over and running nationalized firms; in a time of economic slowdown (and the early 1980s were such a time), it would require incalculable funds to get the economy moving again, guaranteeing, if not expansion, then at least sufficient stability to maintain existing employment levels. And if the Socialists were to nationalize and attempt to revive companies whose results were regularly in the red, it might mean diverting government money from urgent goals and promising economic investments—into a black hole. Nationalization made the least sense in the worst of times.

In retrospect, Guy de Rothschild attributed the 1981 nationalizations to the country's "left-wing malady." Certainly from the strictly economic point of view, attacking the Rothschilds made little sense ("the bank was so small, it mattered so little").[4] Concretely, the Banque Rothschild's annual report for 1980—the year preceding the Socialist victory—spelled out just how bad things were. The international context was unfavorable, and although

France was outperforming much of the industrialized world, there were ominous signs: a growing trade deficit, a declining national product per capita. The bank showed little growth, hampered as it was by severe restrictions on credit. The group's gross turnover nevertheless rose from 925 million francs in 1979 to 1.3 billion (equivalent to about 2.6 billion francs now), two-thirds of it coming from the bank proper, exercised through the Banque Rothschild and its affiliates Compagnie Européenne de Banque, Discount Bank, and Nord Financier. The flagship bank reported deposits in excess of 3.4 billion francs (some 6.8 billion now), placing it in the number-ten position among deposit banks in France. And still, Guy de Rothschild would observe later, so much more needed to be done, if only to overcome the effects of France's worst economic crisis in forty years.[5]

The bank's industrial portfolio then included a 20-percent stake in Imétal (which, despite continued losses at Le Nickel, was showing a profit), some 35 percent of Francarep (oil), 63 percent of Saga (shipping), 37 percent of PLM (hotels and restaurants).

The assembly at which bank president David de Rothschild was to present the annual report to shareholders had been scheduled for May 27, 1981. That would turn out to be just seventeen days after the election of the president whose program called for nationalization of credit. "Today," David remarked, "I deplore with you that the simple announcement of the threat of nationalization has in just a few days led to a fall of 40 percent in the value of your shares."[6]

It was clear that the decision to nationalize or not would be based at least in part on size. The Rothschilds might be caught in the net only because of their decision three years earlier to merge the family bank with the industrial holdings of the Compagnie du Nord; could that decision be reversed, separating bank and industrial holdings, as in the past?[7] Not if the Communists had their say. The party daily L'Humanité was soon ready with a headline bearing its own interpetation of events:

THE ROTHSCHILDS MANEUVER

They plan to combine assets of their bank and a subsidiary to receive a fat indemnity and keep the group's fortune hidden.[8]

The reference was to a meeting of bank personnel at which David de Rothschild outlined a plan that would have created two companies, one for the Banque Rothschild and other financial affiliates such as the Discount Bank, the other for industrial holdings that since 1978 had been owned by the bank. In the view of the Communists—who clearly had not been reading the gloomy annual reports—the family would then protect from nationalization "the intrinsic wealth" of its industrial holdings, letting the government nationalize "a banking network all but dismantled." Thus they would "distort the letter and the spirit" of the nationalization vote.[9]

There would be no time for restructuring, whatever the motive. And when the nationalization law was placed before Parliament it became clear that the criterion for takeover would be assets (for banks the sum eventually fixed was one billion francs in deposits). When the cut-off figure was announced, Rothschild was found to be eligible for nationalization, while Lazard Frères (generally believed to be close to the Socialists) was not.[10]

The parliamentary battle was spectacular. Though they didn't have the votes to stop this new nationalization program, the conservative opposition had ingenuity, tabling a record number of amendments (one thousand) to parry the proposed law; even the Socialists were said to be split between minimalists and maximalists, with Premier Pierre Mauroy standing firm in his intention to nationalize seven major groups, two financial institutions (Paribas and Suez), and thirty-six banks (in the end there would be thirty-nine).

There were those in the cabinet who thought that the government was being too generous. "All those billions [of public funds]," an unnamed cabinet secretary was quoted, "should have gone to the unemployed!"[11] As the national assembly began considering the bill providing for state control on October 13 an opinion poll was published showing that 50 percent of the French favored the measure (to 29 percent opposed).[12] "A symbolic event" was how the Communist party organ announced the nationalization of the Banque Rothschild—although it had hardly been one of the biggest among candidates for takeover.[13] "The private banks represent only about a quarter of the French banking sector since the big institutions were nationalized by General de Gaulle's Government in 1945," a correspondent of the austere *Times* of London reported. "But, despite their limited importance, they hold a sinister place in Socialist and Communist political mythology. . . ."[14]

The bill was approved on October 26, 1981, by a vote of 332 to 154. But in January 1982 a constitutional tribunal called for a revision of the provision concerning compensation; the sum would be pegged to share value at the end of 1980, and dividends distributed for that business year, adjusted upward by 14 percent for monetary depreciation. Parliament quickly convened to amend its text, signed into law on February 11.[15]

The reaction of the family had been summed up by Guy in his front-page testament headed "Adieu Rothschild," only a few days after the first parliamentary vote.[16] The resentment could only increase when the government appointed as its representative in the bank a longtime Rothschild executive with Socialist sympathies, Michel de Boissieu.[17] Later, when the younger Rothschilds engaged in new business activities, the most ardent of the doctrinaires wanted to prevent them from doing so, as if one could nationalize people.[18]

Since Rothschild profitability was by then next to nil, and stocks were depressed across the board, the indemnification (paid in public debentures easy to cash in) was less than it could have been, but that was hardly the fault of the government.[19] All told, the owners received close to 450 million francs (some 700 million of today's francs), which David de Rothschild felt was a fair settlement, although not necessarily a "good deal." The family itself was to receive only 35 percent of the total, representing its equity in the Banque Rothschild.[20]

Cynics would say that many of the victims of the Common Platform had done very well indeed; Rothschild and some others had been "in virtual bankruptcy," so a banker was quoted. "The government was in such a hurry to pass a law that it didn't even ask for an audit of the companies."[21]

For their part, since their stock was down, the Rothschilds would not have chosen to sell their property just then, if given the choice. Being obliged by law to sell represented singular injustice.[22]

*   *   *

All those years back, Guy de Rothschild had written his safeguard clause into the bylaws: without a Rothschild at its head, the bank couldn't use the Rothschild name. In fact the government might have ignored that stricture—the nation's law standing above corporate law. But the public powers went along with the suggestion of the Rothschilds that the new bank on old Rue Laffitte be called Compagnie Européenne de Banque (the formerly American-owned company specializing in the financing of industrial equipment and commercial real estate, originally acquired by Guy and his cousins in the euphoria following their transformations of 1967).[23]

One of the assets Guy most regretted losing was control of his own baby, Imétal, built up over the years from the family's far-flung mining interests, and certain to grow again when conditions allowed for growth. Of course the government walked away with the bank's equity in Imétal and other industrial activity that had been merged into the bank only a few years earlier. But Imétal itself was not nationalized, and family members owned a minority interest in this group in their own names; *that* couldn't be taken from them.[24]

Years later, when Imétal needed the kind of know-how the Rothschilds might provide, its private owners invited the family to join the board. David de Rothschild saw that as a "true comeback." (It is the only one of their pre-1981 holdings with which the family remains connected.)[25]

There are moments in the Rothschild saga when the outsider wants to stop the clock and start asking questions. There is an obvious one to ask concerning the drama of their dispossession. Why hadn't the family anticipated seizure, say by splitting up the group into smaller units? Not necessarily in 1981, under the gun and under the eyes of their enemies, but a decade earlier, when the Socialists and Communists had made their ambitions known? Others had taken anticipatory steps, not always successfully, but would it not have been worth trying?

Guy was the fatalist. Having lived through the earlier nationalization of the Popular Front years when the Compagnie du Nord was the prime target, he was convinced that nationalization was like an act of God, and one doesn't try to protect oneself from an act of God. Moreover, François Mitterrand hadn't been the favorite to win the vote in May 1981; smart money had been placed on President Giscard d'Estaing (and indeed Mitterrand hadn't won as much as the incumbent had lost). After the election it was too late to separate bank and bank assets (Guy and his family wouldn't have had the cash to try—and had they done so, the government most certainly would have retaliated).[26]

Indeed, if the family bank *hadn't* been merged with the Nord holdings in 1978, the government still would have taken over the Rothschild bank and with it their traditions and reason for being— leaving the family its industrial interests fated to follow the decline of world markets. "In sum," he'd reflect, "we should have lost the essential to hold on to the accessory."[27]

Guy's son David, heir to the director's chair of the bank, had done his own thinking about the inevitable takeover. He too felt that there was no time to do anything, while the financial situation of the group hardly allowed for aggressive countermeasures. In any case, when so momentous an event occurs, one is paralyzed psychologically; certainly one is tempted to wait and see.[28]

At the time of Mitterrand's election, the Banque Rothschild was run from day to day by a three-man directorate consisting of David, cousin Nathaniel (Elie's son), and longtime Rothschild executive Jacques Getten. (Soon after the victory of the Socialists, Getten, who was not the first in his family to work for the Rothschilds and would not be the last, had begun to draft a curriculum vitae—for the first time in his life. But he was not going to leave the Rothschilds if they would have him and needed him; they would and they did.) As the distant menace seemed more and more likely to become a real one, the three men decided to act as if it would indeed become real.

Looking at available assets, they focused attention on an existing holding company called Paris-Orléans (or P.O.), one of the channels through which the family controlled the bank. Then, when nationalization seemed ineluctable, they used P.O. to set up a financial operation called P.O. Gestion—not a bank but a structure with some of the attributes of banking. They had six to eight months ahead of them; they worked discreetly. After nationalization, P.O., one of the owners of record of the Rothschild bank, received its share (some 7–8 percent) of the indemnity. So there was some money now—and a core activity that would be the nucleus of future development.[29]

The directors dismissed the idea of setting up a commercial bank, for that would demand considerable capital investment. But merchant banking was within their range; it needn't extend credit or open branches, or offer windows for walk-in customers. Little infrastructure would be required to serve as financial counselor to major corporations, or to engage in money management (starting with the capital of family and friends, then of faithful clients who insisted on following the Rothschilds wherever they went). The model, in David's vision, was the Banque Lazard.[30]

They didn't steal managers away from the old bank on Rue Laffitte, or even customers; there were to be new faces on both sides.

And Guy de Rothschild once again packed a valise, gathered up his papers, and flew to New York: another American exile while preparing for better days. If in France the family bore the taint of "losers," the United States was virgin territory; everything was possible there. One of the possibilities was to take the small but not unsuccessful American investment company the French Rothschilds ran in partnership with their British cousins and make a proper bank of it.[31]

With Evelyn, head of N. M. Rothschild in London, Guy transformed New Court Securities into Rothschild Incorporated. They recruited a Wall Street high flyer, Robert Pirie, then forty-seven, described in *The New York Times* as "a truculent New York takeover lawyer." And Rothschild, Inc., was on its way. Small at first, certainly in capital, but with larger-than-life Pirie as president, and some larger-than-life clients including the "voracious" investor Sir James (Jimmy) Goldsmith and the undefinable Robert Maxwell. From the start Pirie was left to his own devices, for his principals were certain that they had chosen the right person. David de Rothschild saw him as "a man with green fingers. . . ."[32]

For their part, Pirie and his directors well understood how much of the new bank's "capital" really derived from the family name. "When we were still New Court, people would frequently ask for our balance sheet and ask what our capitalization was," Wilbur Ross, Jr., in charge of corporate finance, was quoted. "I can't remember the last time anyone asked. With the Rothschild name, people take a lot for granted."[33]

Guy attributed the fighting spirit of the younger Rothschilds to a desire to take up a challenge: other family banks had survived, why shouldn't theirs? Why should they have to become voluntary exiles to exercise their trade? When the nationalization law went into effect in 1982, Guy's son David had not yet celebrated his fortieth birthday; Alain's son Eric was two years David's senior. Henceforth they were equal partners, with David in charge because he had the experience.

Although born in wartime New York, David had begun school life in liberated Paris. He'd remember that even in a private elementary school, mention of his name elicited sarcastic remarks and ironic smiles from other children. It was easier to deal with adults, he'd tell an interviewer. "For they know that even if your name is Rothschild you aren't different from anyone else. We each have two hands, two eyes, two legs."[34] He was sent to regular state secondary schools (for a time, while living with his mother at Reux in Normandy, the high school was in Deauville), graduating from the Paris Lycée Carnot. From there to a good college, the Institut d'Etudes Politiques, where he studied economics. (Later he was to describe his university studies as "modest.") His military obligation under the French draft law was satisfied by his participation in a technical assistance program for French-speaking Africa, after which he entered the family business. Eventually he became a director of Le Nickel, then general manager of the Compagnie du Nord.[35]

Cousin Eric lived in New York until the age of seven, at which time his father, Alain, decided that France was where he wanted to be. But this child was to be international all the same, attending prep school in England, then a Paris high school (Janson de Sailly), going on to study engineering at the Zurich Polytechnical School. It was taken for granted that he would eventually join the family bank or one of its affiliated companies. He began at the shipping concern Saga, working there for several years before transferring to the bank. He dealt with corporate finance back in the 1970s, when old-timers at the bank didn't see the utility of engineering mergers and acquisitions; later he returned to Saga as chairman (Guy credited him with having turned the company around). After nationalization the government-appointed managers actually asked Eric to stay on until Saga and other industrial operations were sold off. Saga was sold to the Compagnie Financière de Suez, a powerful investment bank that survived (and thrived) after Egypt's takeover of the canal.

By then the new family bank was ready for business, and Eric was happy to be part of the adventure. (He received a little less than 50 percent of the stock, since a minority participation was reserved for David's half-brother, Edouard, son of Guy's second marriage.[36]

There could have been a third partner. Nathaniel, Elie's son, was thirty-six years old when the guillotine fell on the Banque Rothschild. He had drawn up plans for the new company with Eric and David, sharing their resentment at what had been done to their heritage. But like his father, Natty was strong-willed and outspoken; a graduate of the Harvard Business School, he would be quite American in what the business press characterized as his ambitious, entrepreneurial style. After moving to the United States to oversee Rothschild, Inc., the fifty-fifty New York bank partnership between the French and British Rothschilds (as co-chairman), Natty fell out with his Paris cousins in 1984. And suddenly he was allied with another maverick Rothschild, Jacob (nemesis of *his* cousin Evelyn), who ran his own financial empire separate from the traditional family bank in London.

Natty's break with the family, the alliance with Jacob, was "tantamount to divorce rather than just a job change," a former Rothschild Inc. executive confided to the press.[37] He soon tore himself free again, to become sole owner and operator of Nathaniel Rothschild Holdings, which manages companies on its own and its clients' behalf from a New York base.[38]

T H I R T Y - O N E

EDMOND AND THE OTHERS

A,Jew to the Pétain regime, a pariah under Mitterrand, that's enough for me." Guy de Rothschild's
reaction to the government's seizure of the fam-
ily bank, forceful and blunt, would not be quickly forgotten, nor
was his decision to leave France. In turning the spotlight to another
Rothschild, the nonconformist son of the breakaway Maurice, a
business fortnightly headlined

A ROTHSCHILD

IN SOCIALIST FRANCE

Not all Rothschilds Emigrate
Among Those Remaining, Edmond Tells Us Why

The *why* was evident: Edmond was both a French citizen and a
Swiss resident, but his Paris investment bank was only one component of an empire controlled from the safe haven of Switzerland
through the Compagnie Financière Benjamin et Edmond de Rothschild S.A. (The son of Edmond and Nadine, and only nineteen
years old at the time, Benjamin was then in school in the United
States.) French activities were actually directed through two holding companies, the Compagnie Financière in Paris, and a Société

Française des Hôtels de Montagne, this last encompassing mountain resort hotels and restaurants—but also dairy farming in the
Seine-et-Marne district (where his Château d'Armainvilliers, with
its 6,400 acres of woodland and fields, was the region's number-
one *propriété agricole*).

He had been careful, Edmond told an interviewer, to focus on
activities not requiring heavy initial investment. Traditional banking wasn't feasible in France because of governmental limitations
on credit; hence the stress on advisory services, and on his international network. Indeed, after what happened to his cousins in
1981, he was considering further expansion to the Western Hemi-
sphere and the Far East rather than Europe, where—his own
childhood memories told him—a Jew was always suspect, and one
would never feel sorry for a Rothschild. And yet the family name
would have to appear on a street-front plaque in Paris again; it
might be his (although only if the other branch—David and
Eric's—agreed).[1]

An art restorer who knew all the Rothschilds and made frequent
visits to Edmond at Pregny—Edmond came to art appreciation
late, but when he did, he learned quickly, and quickly turned his
castle into an Ali Baba's cave—discovered him to be the least
"Rothschildian," least regal that is, of the clan.[2] Surely he was the
most outspoken, and not only about Israel and his Jewish identity.
Although he declared his solidarity with the dispossessed banking
Rothschilds, he often appeared friendly to the Socialists. One of
his directors, Henri Emmanuelli, was active in that party, later
becoming a minister in the cabinet of Mitterrand's militant premier
Pierre Mauroy (the nationalizer).

So there seemed to be a Rothschild leaning ever so slightly
leftward, and he the richest of them all by far. In 1985 the business
magazine *L'Expansion*'s list of the fifty wealthiest Frenchmen
placed Edmond in the number-four position, with a fortune estimated between 2 and 2.5 billion francs; Guy de Rothschild was
number forty-one, with 600 to 650 million.[3] In their public face the
Rothschilds were interdependent, in private not always. Edmond
was ever the outsider. "I'm the junior of the junior branch," he'd
say.[4] It was more complicated than that. Since his grandfather
Edmond had been the youngest of Baron James's sons, a genera-

tion had been skipped along the way: Edmond II was the Great Baron's great-grandson, as was Guy, but Guy was already retired; Guy's son David and Alain's son Eric were *great*-great-grandsons. On the family tree, Edmond was the senior.

Edmond's Paris company remained small, as investment institutions go. "We're a tiny bank with assets of four billion francs," Bernard Esambert had let it be known at the end of 1984. Yet its clientele was drawn from the elite, for it offered "high tech" services, thanks to which it had been growing each year by 20 to 50 percent.[5] In 1989 a business directory listed Edmond as honorary chairman of the Banca Tiburtina de Credito e Servizi, president of the Banca Privata in Lugano, of the Caesarea Development Corporation (a vast beachside project on the Mediterranean coast north of Tel Aviv), the Israel General Bank, and Israel European Company. Companies of which he was a board member included De Beers Consolidated Mines Ltd., Club Méditerranée, Compagnie Luxembourgeoise de Télédiffusion, Ferruzzi Agricola Finanzaria, Hachette, Publications Filipacchi, Société Financière de Banque. The Compagnie Financière in Paris had ties with over fifty banks, investment companies, and funds.[6]

Nor should Edmond's Nadine be overlooked. Stimulated by daily confrontation with her dynamo of a husband, she took to writing for money, directing her message to women readers who were also homemakers—a sure road to success. Advertising her "recipes for becoming an indispensable woman," a French book club told its members: "Nadine de Rothschild has considerable experience in this subject. . . ."[7] She also created her own perfumes packaged in candles, sprays, and dried flowers, as well as a line of jewelry. And her husband's growing wine interests inspired her to invent a special blend of liqueurs for ladies.[8]

David, Guy's son, married in 1974—married (as his father had) outside the faith. The couple would have daughters who would be raised as Catholics, and a son—Alexandre, born on December 3, 1980, to be confirmed as a Jew on his thirteenth birthday. This seeming apostasy created no visible stir, for the Rothschilds had long since ceased to exercise strategic functions on the religious side of the Jewish community. This did not mean that David wasn't going to do what the community expected the reigning Rothschild to do: good works. He replaced his father as chairman of the Fonds Social Juif Unifié, one of the three leading institutions of the French Jewish community (with the Consistory for religious matters, the newer Conseil Représentatif des Institutions Juives for political affairs). He became chairman of the United Jewish Appeal of France, a joint project of the FSJU and the Israeli fundraising organization Karen Hayesod, as well as chairman of the Foundation for French Judaism, which solicits donations and legacies for preserving Jewish heritage.[9]

In February 1983, *Paris-Match* devoted a double page to the kind of news its readers hungered for. It featured a family photograph of David de Rothschild with his wife, Olimpia, the daughter of Italian prince Aldobrandini, and their three children: Lavinia, then seven years old, Stéphanie, five, and Alexandre, two. The occasion was the election of David to the Jockey Club, "the most aristocratic and closed circle in France," following in the footsteps of Baron James and of James's son Edmond. David told the interviewer that he saw the event as "perfectly compatible with my financial activities and my responsibilities in the French Jewish community." Did he feel himself Jewish, Rothschild, or French? "For me, being a Jew and French is the same thing," he was quoted. "The name Rothschild bears a certain number of constraints and privileges I try to honor." He could be both loyal to his family and a good patriot. And if some members of that family had chosen to leave France, he himself was attached to tradition and continuity, for which reason he had taken up the challenge of rebuilding a house of Rothschild in France. Moreover, he had been mayor of Pont-l'Evêque for the past six years (succeeding his mother), and intended to run again.[10]

Soon there was other promising news. Having set up their pocket-sized financial venture, P.O. Gestion, in a second-floor office of the small Time-Life Building on Avenue Matignon, not far from the Champs-Elysées, the new partnership of David and Eric applied for the status of merchant bank. Although the French banking association raised no objection, the partners still required governmental approval, not to speak of permission to put the family name on the door.[11]

Another year would go by before they received the right to set up a true and proper private bank, the ownership divided between family members (44 percent), the Paris-Orléans holding company (21 percent), Britain's N. M. Rothschild (12.5 percent), the Compagnie Financière Edmond de Rothschild (10 percent), Rothschild Zurich AG (7.5 percent), and a group of longtime banking colleagues, Martin Maurel (5 percent). "We don't seek to remake a Rothschild bank, but simply to try something new," David explained. It would be a company offering financial services to business groups and institutions, but also to individuals; banking as such would remain a marginal activity.

They were now ready to roll—as "P.O. Banque." For the government proved unbending: there was not to be another bank called Rothschild. "We couldn't get a charter and revive the name at the same time," David de Rothschild told a financial reporter in March 1986.[12] The pretext for the government's refusal was the confusion that might develop between a new Rothschild bank and the old one, that ravished bank now officially called the Européenne de Banque but all too often referred to as "the ex-Banque Rothschild." Already David de Rothschild had been asked to promise that he would not compete in any shape or manner with the Européenne (which, ever since nationalization, had been in the red).[13]

It was known that the Socialist-Communist coalition considered the return of the family to banking "politically unacceptable."[14] "There is still no question of calling the newborn bank Rothschild," declared the Communist party's official daily—clearly worried that the family wouldn't stop trying. "Will employment in France benefit from the newcomer? The Rothschild family hasn't changed since nationalization. Its objective remains more than ever the desire for maximal profit. . . ."[15] In a timid attempt at brand identification, the new bank of David and Eric was already featuring the five Rothschild arrows on its stationery; beneath "P.O. Banque" one could also read "Groupe Rothschild."[16]

But no government is eternal; elections for the renewal of Parliament were scheduled for March 1986. The betting was on the center-right and against the majority the Socialists had enjoyed until then, and victims of the 1981 nationalizations made no secret of their hope for a return to conservative rule. Moreover, in interviews David de Rothschild let it be known that he fully intended to purchase shares of banks and industrial companies that would be sold back to the private sector by the new government. They did not wish to re-create an industrial conglomerate resembling the old Compagnie du Nord, but to be "active investors in a few businesses that will complement our banking activities." By now—March 1986—P.O. Banque was managing some $400 million of its clients' funds, with capital assets of $6 million; its 1985 earnings before taxes amounted to 25 percent of net worth. "We're still small," Rothschild told *The New York Times*, "but the goal is to double the rate of return to 50 percent by 1988," this to be accomplished by greater involvement in corporate finance, mergers and acquisitions, trading in bonds.[17]

The center-right did win; privatization was very much in the cards. Under surviving president Mitterrand there was now a conservative premier, Jacques Chirac, whose minister of economy and finances Edouard Balladur was given responsibility for undoing the effects of the 1981–82 nationalization. For their part, the Rothschild cousins—David and Eric on one side, Edmond on the other—decided to pool their resources in order to bid for stock of the large corporations soon to be returned to the private sector. They called their new investment company Saint-Honoré-Matignon, a reference to the respective addresses of their banks.[18] By October 1986 the cousins on Avenue Matignon were able to announce that they had won the right to use the family name again, as Rothschild & Associés Banque. (And of course on Rue Saint-Honoré, cousin Edmond could call his establishment Compagnie Financière *Edmond de Rothschild*.)

They also obtained symbolic reparation of sorts. Both Rothschild companies were selected (from a list of seventy candidates) to advise the Chirac-Balladur government on one of the most important of the privatizations, that of Paribas, France's and perhaps Europe's largest merchant bank; its sale to the public—some 19 billion francs of stock—would be the Bourse's biggest transaction ever. The cousins had submitted their proposals to an official selection committee, known in the profession as a "beauty parade." Had some members of the committee wished to make amends? Possibly, although in retrospect David de Rothschild didn't think decisions of that importance were made for sentimental reasons.

Whatever moved the committee, their choice justified the headline in a morning daily:

LE COME BACK

DES

ROTHSCHILD[19]

There were to be more such headlines. "The Return of the Rothschilds" was one, introducing a profile of the family at the end of that momentous year 1986. It was a somewhat different family now, with Guy having returned from New York but no longer active, his cousin Elie having chosen London for his retirement (or semiretirement, for there was always a directorship or two available for a living Rothschild).

The partners in the reborn family bank were at least as reassuring as their predecessors, and eminently photogenic. "David and Olimpia—an Italian admirably pretty and well born—give a classy image of the new generation," gushed the news weekly *Le Point*, "although quite *low key*, to use that peculiar language halfway between French and English favored by the Rothschilds."[20]

That other suave gentleman, Eric, was visited at his home away from home—Château Lafite—by the wine expert Cyril Ray, for by then Eric had replaced his uncle Elie as the man in charge of the family vineyards. He had remained a bachelor until he was nearly forty-four, then married Donna Maria-Beatrice Caracciolo di Forini; of a Neapolitan ducal family, she converted to Judaism as Eric's own mother had done.[21] But not without smoke and thunder, for nearly a decade had gone by since David's marriage to an Italian Catholic, and the French Jewish community, increasingly dominated by less worldly, more orthodox elements (including groups that had migrated en masse from the newly independent states of North Africa), was neither as tolerant toward Rothschilds nor as liberal about the ways of assimilated Jews in republican France as community leaders of earlier times. Now the Consistory board itself was to come under attack. "We shall see, once the cards are dealt out again, whether there is still a place for us," a journalist quoted Baron Eric.[22] Henceforth his principal role in the Jewish community would be to preside over the Committee of

Jewish Social Action of Paris: another Rothschild, another philanthropist.

Unperturbed, Eric and Marie-Béatrice (as the French would call her) made a home for themselves and their children to come in the house his father had built at the back of the large garden on Avenue Marigny (after Alain disposed of the great house on the street).[23] David became the only banking Rothschild to break with tradition by taking up residence on the Left Bank (just steps away from the Luxembourg palace and park).

It was the shock of nationalization that determined Eric (acting for the family) to take a keener look at Château Lafite and its commercial possibilities.[24] Out of that examination came a reorganized winemaking group, operating as Domaines (plural) Barons (plural) de Rothschild. The flagship vineyard Lafite had long been sponsoring a lesser wine, sold under the label Moulin des Carruades; it came from the same grapes, the same terrains, but from vines under twelve years of age (Lafite's growers didn't think a truly superior wine could be obtained that way).

As early as 1964 the family had acquired another vineyard, Château Duhart-Milon, originally classed as a fourth growth. It needed upgrading, and the Rothschilds knew how to upgrade. Such growths would go out to the world under the colors of Domaines Barons de Rothschild: each, if not a classic, represented what Cyril Ray called "the best of its own kind." By 1984 a first-growth Sauternes was added to the stable, with the acquisition of a majority share of Château Rieussec.[25]

Before the end of the 1980s, Eric and his cousins had followed their competitor Baron Philippe to California, with a stock-swap between Domaines Barons de Rothschild and Chalone Inc., owners of admired growths in the neighborhood of Salinas, California.[26]

But of course the first creator of a Rothschild wine group had been Philippe, who in his final years—he died in 1988, at the age of eighty-six—was still selling his personality as much as his wine (both of them via Baron Philippe de Rothschild S.A.). His pride remained the flagship Château Mouton-Rothschild, but there was also the more modest Mouton Cadet, and now a Château Mouton

Baronne Philippe (which Philippe's daughter would package under its original name, Château d'Armailhac). In our day, although the vineyards are now in the care of the wine baron's daughter Philippine, Baron Philippe de Rothschild S.A. still harbors nearly a dozen different wines, among them a highly regarded Clerc-Milon.[27]

Following the death of his mother and the liquidation of the estate of Baron Edouard and Baronne Germaine, Guy had not only given away Ferrières. He made more news with his donation of the precious Vermeer, *The Astronomer,* to the Louvre, where it became one of that already great museum's greatest treasures. Obviously inheritance tax was involved, and there had been complex negotiations with the government, which included an authorization for Rothschilds to export and sell two Goyas and a Frans Hals.[28] At the time of the Vermeer gift, an art magazine let it be known that in a century the family had given as many as fifty thousand works to public institutions (the accompanying illustrations showed a few of them, including a sketch by Rembrandt and a superb illuminated manuscript, *Très belles heures de Notre-Dame,* that had been created for the Duc de Berry—a gift to France by Maurice).[29] A decade earlier Guy's sister Bethsabée had given the Louvre a Hans Memling, *The Flight to Egypt,* while sister Jacqueline had given Pieter de Hoogh's *The Drinker.*[30]

Nearly every branch of the family was a prominent donor to charity, often a builder or a creator of good works. In 1986 the press reported that some 40 million francs had been spent since 1982 through the Fondation de Rothschild presided over by Eric, in addition to three million francs provided each year for low-cost housing projects through a separate Fondation de Rothschild chaired by David. The latter activity manages some two thousand low-rent apartments, the income going to maintenance and investment, the surplus to the upkeep of Jewish community property (including religious schools). Meanwhile Baron Edmond was disbursing 15 million francs annually for such works as the Fondation Ophtalmologique Adolphe de Rothschild, one of Paris's three leading private hospitals (with 230 beds, including 18 in neurosurgery, and over 1,000 outpatient consultations per day). There was also his grandfather's Institut de Biologie on Rue Curie, the one almost appropriated by Vichy's protégé Alexis Carrel, an internationally respected laboratory.[31]

Of course progress had redirected traditional philanthropy. With medical advances the need for sanatoriums had disappeared; orphanages became children's homes, patients formerly cared for in private charity hospitals were covered by national health insurance or public welfare. As early as 1954 the Rothschild hospital on Rue Santerre had been donated to the public welfare agency, although the Fondation de Rothschild continued to support religious circumcision in the maternity ward, and deliveries of kosher food to observant Jews throughout the public welfare hospital system.

Robert's sons, Elie and Alain, had turned over the family's Château de Laversine to serve as a training center for youth. Later Alain was to provide funds for a psychiatric clinic for preventive medicine, to which a unit that would do home visits for children under four was subsequently added. Through the main Rothschild Foundation the banking family had expanded facilities at their retirement homes and geriatric center (making use of the Château de la Guette, near Ferrières, which had been Baroness Edouard's hostel for refugee children). On his side, in addition to his scientific and medical philanthropies, Edmond set up a network of clubs for problem adolescents.[32]

If Edmond was often in Israel on business—and his son Benjamin would follow him there—only one Rothschild of the banking dynasty ever settled in the Promised Land. Bethsabée, Guy's sister, had begun visiting Israel periodically in the first postwar decade. And one day Bethsabée became Batsheva—taking the Hebrew form of her name. While in New York as a friend and supporter of Martha Graham, she had created the Batsheva de Rothschild Foundation for Art and Sciences to promote concerts by contemporary composers, and not incidentally to finance the productions of Martha Graham and other dance companies, as well as to record Graham's choreography on film. Once, in 1956, Batsheva had brought the famous dancer to Israel.

So it seemed perfectly natural for this culturally industrious Rothschild to continue along the same lines in Israel, both as benefactor of music (baroque and modern) and dance; hence a new

Batsheva de Rothschild Foundation for Art and Learning. There was also a Batsheva Crafts Corporation in the same spirit, and before she was done she had set up two science foundations (she wouldn't have been a Rothschild if she hadn't, and her own Sorbonne degree was in biology).

But dance became attached to her name, as banks and wines had made the names of other Rothschilds. The Batsheva Dance Company was launched in 1964, with Martha Graham as artistic adviser; three years later Batsheva opened a dance studio in Tel Aviv, one of the rare schools teaching both classic and modern ballet. That and her dance troupe were given the name Bat-Dor (acknowledging the contribution of her teaching partner Jeannette Ordman). It became a full-time activity for Batsheva, with such sidelines as the Israel Center for Dance Medicine, opened in 1985.[33] A recent visitor to the vast if dingy studios in downtown Tel Aviv found this energetic woman, bowed by age, rushing in and out of rooms occupied by slender young ladies bending and kicking.

MODERN TIMES

he young Rothschilds were certainly not the Lazards, who, during most of this century, reigned in
the chosen hunting grounds of the latter-day Rothschilds, although the Lazards—kings of the new merchant bank,
the bank of financial engineering—were models one could emu-
late. The gentlemen from Lazard Frères (who were now mainly the
David-Weills) had demonstrated that a banking dynasty could take
in nonfamily associates without losing its identity, let alone ownership or control.[1] The Lazard system allowed an established institution to recruit experts from promising new areas of finance and
industry; again, on the Lazard model, one could conduct transactions on both sides of the Atlantic and on either side of the Channel; modern business worked that way, modern banking had to
follow. If a Jimmy Goldsmith—Sir James Goldsmith for the
record—was equally at home on the markets of London, New York,
and Paris, so must be his banking adviser and friend David de
Rothschild. David's great-great-grandfather James could have told
him something about that.

At the end of the 1980s, when Lazard was earning more money
than both the Paris and London Rothschilds together, Lazard's
Michel David-Weill was quoted, "The historical error of the Rothschilds was that they never really had an American base, of the

kind we at Lazard have built up over forty years. . . . If you want to be a champion or even a semi-champion, New York is the arena." And David de Rothschild allowed himself to say, "In future it will be more difficult for Lazard to improve its profitability than for us to catch up!"[2]

He didn't really believe that Rothschild in France would overtake the pacesetter of the profession. But David de Rothschild has let it be known that he is working for the moment when, after his own retirement, he will overhear a conversation in which an American businessman looking for a European connection will say, "Naturally Lazard is the biggest, but there is *also* Rothschild."

In an economy that was moving again, the path to even quicker riches for banker and client alike was "M&A"—mergers and acquisitions—and not necessarily friendly ones; in such things Rothschild ally Jimmy Goldsmith was a past master. He made headlines in October 1986 with his successful takeover fight—against a powerful Italian financial rival—for France's number-two book publishing group, Presses de la Cité; in this he was assisted by the new Rothschilds. Modestly, David would admit that he had been selected by Goldsmith out of friendship; the machinery available to a bank was necessary to the engineering of a takeover, and Rothschild had simply provided the machinery. But Goldsmith had called the shots.[3]

There would be an even more spectacular takeover in New York two years later, again involving an attention-getting medium, the large educational and general book publisher Harcourt Brace Jovanovich, a company whose directors (as minority shareholders) definitely did not want to be forced from their shaky perch. And certainly not by the potential buyer, one of the most flamboyant operators of his time, rags-to-riches Robert Maxwell. Operating from his London base, through Robert Pirie of Rothschild in New York, Maxwell offered an astounding $1.7 billion for Harcourt, a sum higher than any previous takeover bid for such a property. One of the fiercest firefights in financial history ensued, not excluding the exchange of public insults.

More tellingly, Harcourt's William Jovanovich concocted what had become known in the market as a "poison pill"—a means to discourage even the hardiest of financial pirates by making a hostile acquisition more expensive. This particular pill contained a $3-billion recapitalization (a deliberate indebtedness that discouraged Maxwell, but that would later prove the undoing of Harcourt Brace Jovanovich itself).

Maxwell soon returned to the front pages, dragging Pirie and Rothschild Inc. with him, thanks to another hostile takeover bid for a publishing giant, Macmillan Inc., in heated competition with other buyers (one of them a "white knight" favored by Macmillan's own management). Bidding was intense, defense tactics adroit (under the counseling of that other merchant banking wizard, Lazard Frères). Macmillan produced its own version of a "poison pill" through a promise to sell the buyer it preferred four of its most profitable affiliates, should the white knight's takeover bid fail. (The point was to deprive the victor—Maxwell—of the company's "crown jewels.") Maxwell sued for unfair advantage and won, walking away with the Macmillan empire for a total outlay of $2.6 billion—a considerable sum even for him. His Rothschild helpers came out of it with $12 million in fees—their biggest prize until then.

Rothschild Inc.—a Franco-British partnership, but with so much more at stake both financially and symbolically for the recovering Rothschilds of Paris—was now very much on the American map. And Maxwell wasn't the only "foreign predator" on its client list, thanks to the unstoppable Pirie, whose tactic was to convince overseas traders—mainly British—that quite a number of undervalued American companies were ripe for takeover. He helped Jimmy Goldsmith in the acquisition of Crown Zellerbach, the timber giant, in another headlined and hostile takeover. He mapped out the strategy for the assault by London's Hanson Trust against SCM (formerly the Smith-Corona typewriter firm).

In the four years ending with the Maxwell takeover of Macmillan at the end of 1988, Rothschild Inc. advised on M&A deals worth $19.4 billion; it was nevertheless still considered a minor player in Wall Street. Sir Jimmy explained to *The New York Times* that the "weakness" of the New York Rothschild bank was its lack of capital: it could only offer advice, after which its clients had to turn to other sources to finance their bidding.[4]

As early as 1945 Lazard—then led by Pierre David-Weill—had

promoted three of its top managers as managing partners (in earlier times it had been hard even for a younger brother or a distant cousin to attain that inner circle).[5] It was a tack worth trying, and David de Rothschild volunteered the information that in scouting for senior staff who could be co-opted as partners he was following the Lazard model. (David's father, Guy, felt that this was also the "American" way of doing business, and in fact it was the way things were done in the United States by Goldman Sachs as well as Lazard, although not in London by N. M. Rothschild.) A first for the Rothschilds, who in 170 years of existence had never yet accepted a partner lacking the family name.

Anointing a top manager or specialist with partnership offered a stimulation—and identification with the firm—that no cash incentive could equal. It also gave the new managing partner a professional and even a social rank he might not otherwise enjoy. Adopting the legal structure of a limited partnership, the Paris Rothschilds didn't go as far as the Lazards in sharing ownership with nonfamily associates. New Rothschild managing partners— none of whom brought capital into the firm—received a minority financial interest, with a claim to profits before the family was remunerated. Control remains firmly in the family, even if nonfamily partners may take away a larger slice of profits than their nominal percentage of capital would have allowed under a corporate structure. Nonfamily partners can block decisions—can commit the firm—but cannot wrest control from the family.[6]

The first to be chosen as a non-Rothschild Rothschild partner could not surprise: Jacques Getten, who had literally grown up in the company his father and grandfather had served so loyally, and whose specialty was industrial finance. The second was a true outsider, and more of a surprise. For Jean-Charles Naouri was nobody's man—and indeed, he'd be a Rothschild managing partner even as he set himself to building an investment company in his own name, operating in separate quarters and in total independence of Rothschild.

By then thirty-eight years old, Naouri had come out of school a winner (both Harvard and France's elite Ecole Nationale d'Administration). He first came to public notice as private secretary of Socialist cabinet minister Pierre Bérégovoy—which did not perturb the Rothschilds (nor apparently did Naouri's indictment for alleged insider trading in a bid for the newly privatized bank Société Générale). And far from minding Naouri's moonlighting with his own investment company, called Euris, an ingeniously structured holding instrument that allowed it with a relatively small initial placement to control significant shares of blue-chip companies such as L'Oréal, Canal Plus, and Carrefour, David de Rothschild actually helped him to set it up. The novel position of Naouri in the Rothschild bank and as head of his own investment company signifies that Naouri turns first to Rothschild when he needs a bank, while Euris is quickly informed when the Rothschild partners identify a good investment—a relationship said to be privileged, but not exclusive.[7]

Another new Rothschild managing partner, Jean-Claude Meyer, who was forty-three when he joined the firm at the beginning of 1989, had been over that ground before. He came in from Lazard Frères, where he had occupied a similar position. A resident managing partner of Rothschild (which Naouri was not), Meyer took charge of international activity, becoming a vice-chairman of Rothschild Europe (his opposite number was Russell Edey, managing director—but not a partner—of N. M. Rothschild in London). Meyer's firm conviction is that the true vocation of his bank today is M&A—mergers and acquisitions—and he intends to keep Rothschild & Cie. in the top rank. Indeed, in 1993 it was the number-two bank in France in this field (following Lazard Frères).

And then the arrival of another financial wizard, in the summer of 1994, created something of a sensation in banking circles. Christian de Labriffe, forty-seven, had been a full partner at Lazard, the first of his rank to have resigned from that prestigious institution before retirement age. Was Lazard losing ground—or was it Rothschild that was gaining? "We're not going to try to make Rothschild & Cie. another Lazard," Labriffe was quoted, "but to build a house just as professional with its own personality."[8]

Up to the end of 1992 it could be said that David was the only Rothschild among the bank's half-dozen full partners (even if he happened to be the senior and controlling partner). It was then that his half-brother Edouard appeared on the scene. He was born on December 27, 1957, issue of Guy's marriage to Marie-Hélène, and *his* American formation included an MBA at New York University's Graduate School of Business Administration. He worked for a while at the Wertheim investment bank in New York, then went on to London to join his British cousin Jacob's firm, moving into the family bank in 1987 at the age of thirty.

Rothschild to the core, Edouard took to horse breeding in the United States and Ireland as well as France (he keeps a stable at his father's stud farm, Meautry, in Normandy), breeds *and* races his horses just as grandfather Edouard did, as Guy (but not David) does. He struck gold the first time out in 1988, with a top-rated filly named Ochi Chornya, which that year won races both in France and in the United States (in Arlington, Illinois). He likes to think that there are similarities between racing and investment banking: in corporate finance, one deal in five or ten pays off, just as one has to enter five or six horses to win with one. In both fields one should learn to be a good loser. As managing partner number seven of the family firm, he would be given many opportunities to test his character—for his chosen field, or the field chosen for him, is mergers and acquisitions, at a recessionary phase of the business cycle that hasn't been kind to such transactions.[9]

In one way young Edouard is different from all the other managing partners save David: he owns a piece of the firm. The family controls the bank and its other interests in part through P.O. (Paris-Orléans S.A.), whose chairman is David's cousin Eric. Rothschild & Cie. Banque is 40 percent P.O.-owned; another 49 percent is in family hands (David, 15 percent; Edouard, 13 percent; Eric and his family, 21 percent), with minority participation by cousin Edmond's Compagnie Financière (8 percent) and the family's longtime friend, the Compagnie Financière's Martin Maurel (3 percent).[10]

Rothschild Continuation Holding is the instrument for family control of Rothschild banks and branches in twenty countries. Through the investment group S.H.M./Francarep ("S.H.M." standing for Saint-Honoré Matignon) the family manages a broad gamut of investments in oil, real estate, minerals, and construction materials—this through old faithful Imétal—as well as in other investment and venture capital groups ranging from Club Med and magazines (cousin Edmond's specialties) to insurance and Hermès luxury goods.[11]

It makes for an impressive list of directorships. Both David and Eric, for example, are on the board of London's N. M. Rothschild; David has responsibilities at Jean-Charles Naouri's Euris, as well as in luxury manufacturers Louis Vuitton and Veuve Clicquot Ponsardin, Eric in Fédération Continental insurance and Warburg Brinckmann Wirtz.[12]

They struck gold early on. In 1990 Rothschild in Paris got a prize customer in Philip Morris, engineering the $4.2-billion takeover of the Swiss candy and coffee maker Jacobs Suchard, an acquisition adding Suchard's $3.9 billion in revenue to the $44.8 billion the American tobacco and food company had posted for the previous year. It was the largest such acquisition ever recorded in Switzerland, and Europe's biggest of the year (although dismissed by a Rothschild competitor as "a brilliant accident"). And of course it put the Rothschilds back on the map and near the top again in M&A, very precisely in second place after Lazard among French merchant banks.[13]

The Rothschild partner who handled the sale, as it happened, was that former Lazard specialist in cross-border transactions Jean-Claude Meyer, who the same year carried off some other brilliant accidents, notably in assisting the French Pinault group in the sale of its Chapelle Darblay paper mills to the Finnish pulp and paper producer Kymmene Oy; in his early years at Rothschild he also arranged the acquisition of Switzerland's Mövenpick hotel and restaurant chain by a German investor, and the purchase by the British hotel-restaurant group Forte of the Wagons-Lits highway restaurant chain.

David and his partners, of course, wouldn't have described the sale of Suchard to Philip Morris as an accident—even a brilliant one. Advising British Airways on its purchase of the largest independent French airline, TAT, and assisting the Marone-Cinzano family in the sale of its controlling stake in Cinzano to the U.K.'s Grand Metropolitan were equally lucrative assignments at the beginning of the 1990s, when Western European economies had begun to slow down again.[14] When all returns were in, Rothschild could report record profits for 1990 in the amount of 57 million francs (the following year was a quite satisfactory one, but profits were a more "normal" 47.3 million).[15]

They became newsmakers again, the French Rothschilds, as minority partners in Germany's first all-news television channel, sharing ownership with such giants as Time Warner, the world's number-one media group.[16] Through New York affiliate Rothschild Inc. they even seemed ready to manage countries again, through an agreement signed with the former Soviet republic of Kazakhstan to assist the leadership of this newly independent nation, five times the size of France, in the privatization of its industries and free-market exploitation of its oil and mineral wealth.

And if the role of the Rothschilds in the privatization of Paribas seemed a confirmation of their resurgence in 1986, what to say of the disclosure (during the summer of 1994) that the French government had selected David de Rothschild's bank as special adviser in the process of privatizing the company that had been the symbol of all the major nationalizations: the Renault automobile works.[17]

New York remains a key to many doors for the French Roth-schilds. Through its diverse activities in investment banking, cor-porate finance, asset management, real estate, investment management, and venture capital services, Rothschild Inc. is an asset that both French and British Rothschilds can offer as an enticement to clients with equally broad horizons. Historically the Paris family has always been closest to American operations, how-ever modest; today its members are convinced that New York is vital to them. One can't be engaged in investment banking and *not* be there.[18]

Yet times change, and not always for the better. If, in the roaring eighties, New York's Rothschild Inc. stood tall thanks to the am-bitions of acquisitions-minded corporate boards in an overheated economy, a great deal changed at the beginning of the nineties, when the industrial nations entered a recessionary phase, accom-panied by a rash of failures. Need a merchant banker worry? Almost at once a new opportunity emerged, and it was one pre-cisely geared to hard times.

Restructuring it was called, the polite name of a rescue operation to save shareholders from the errors of the recent past, notably by dealing with the consequences of bankruptcy. A new brand of ex-pertise was needed. And so a takeover specialist like Robert Pirie was less on call than his senior managing director Wilbur L. Ross, Jr., whose expertise was in negotiating recapitalization of companies that had been enticed by high-interest debt in the late and unlamented junk bond era (when corporate managers used such devices to raise quick money, with scarcely a look over their shoulders at what the future might cost them because of their hasty financing).

Early on, Ross put Rothschild on the new map by coming to the rescue of New York promoter Donald Trump, who had often filled the business pages—sometimes the front pages—with his cascading deals. The problem concerned one of Trump's most conspicuous creations, a Never-Never Land resort complex called the Taj Mahal; by rescheduling debt, Ross was able to save the promoter from total loss of his property (he came out of it with 50 percent control).

By 1991 the best guess was that Rothschild Inc. was earning $1.5 million monthly in restructuring fees; Ross personally was receiving a gratifying one-third of that. Sometimes Ross and Rothschild worked for the original and indebted owners, at other times for creditors hoping to recoup at least part of the investment into which they had plunged in the earlier euphoric era.[19] Thus Ross, who was being called "the king of restructurings,"[20] represented unsecured creditors of Drexel Burnham Lambert (the junk bond experts); the case came to notice when a bankruptcy judge objected to the fee Rothschild Inc. was charging (and reduced it from $261,000 to $100,000).[21]

These new directions seemed to call for a new director, so in mid-1992 pioneer Pirie was replaced as president and chief operating officer both of Rothschild North America and its subsidiary Rothschild Inc. His successor was Gerald Goldsmith (no relationship to Jimmy), then forty-nine years old and a ten-year veteran of Rothschild Inc., most recently as executive managing director (his earlier career had been at the Wall Street brokerage house E. F. Hutton).[22] The point was to place another strong personality in a position to do what he knew how to do well.[23] A year later Pirie retired from active functions at the bank, becoming a nonexecutive director.[24]

With 140 employees in a recent count, New York's Rothschild Inc. remains a small fish in a big pond. For a long time New York pulled more than its own weight in M&A; today it is a minor player in every area in which it is active except restructurings, but there it is a major one.[25] On joining Rothschild Inc. at the beginning of 1993 to deal with cross-border transactions, Yves-André Istel made it clear that expansion was in the cards. "Any firm that has been around in the late eighties has plenty of capacity," he was quoted.[26] In a reviving economy M&A has come back with a vengeance, and one can expect the Rothschilds to move up front again.

But for the moment it was bankruptcies, and more bankruptcies—O tempora! O mores! One of the biggest of the busts was the real estate dynasty Olympia & York, whose unraveling created anguish in London and Toronto as well as New York (its parent company in Canada declared bankruptcy in May 1992). With O&Y's global debt estimated at $12 billion, everything at stake seemed oversized. Here Rothschild Inc. represented Olympia & York creditors threatened with loss of their investment. The solution negotiated by Wilbur Ross for American noteholders was payment in kind: they were to receive a large office tower in lower Manhattan (at 55 Water Street) owned by O&Y; in return they would cancel the $548.3-million debt owed on the building. (Alternatively, they could accept a cash buyout offer representing twenty-seven cents on the dollar.)[27]

There was more drama in the failure of National Gypsum Company, a manufacturer of wallboard, whose utilization of asbestos, alleged to be a major health hazard, set off an avalanche of legal actions for injury; here Wilbur Ross for Rothschild represented a minority group of creditors who monitored plans for rescuing at least part of the company through reorganization, while making provision for settlement of medical claims.[28] In the same year (1993), on another front, Ross was standing up for bondholders of the giant natural gas company Mesa Inc., owned by venture capitalist T. Boone Pickens. In the face of heavy short-term losses and over $1 billion in long-term debt at high interest, Pickens's only hope was in negotiating a restructuring of Mesa's liabilities, while Ross's job was to see that his clients weren't forgotten.[29]

Humdrum activities, depressing in their implications, but banks don't have to close in hard times.

ROTHSCHILD LEGENDS

*I*n these days, when banking is so often humdrum bookkeeping, when so much decision-making is subject to prior scrutiny by legal agencies and post-mortem investigation by legislators, it is harder than ever for an entrepreneur (however plucky) to furnish material for legend, unless he is ready and willing to volunteer his services as a media celebrity à la George Soros, Jimmy Goldsmith—or the late Robert Maxwell (whose abrupt death by drowning—voluntary or otherwise—led to the unraveling of a financial empire built on deceit and likely fraud). Edmond, grandson of Edmond, manages that tour de force. Less transparent than the Great Baron in his heyday, he is an even more familiar face to his contemporaries. Surely the ways and means of the media in our time have something to do with that.

Thus in 1992, when *Fortune* magazine placed Edmond on its list of billionaires (although in a modest rank: he was far down, at number 202 on a list of 223), his wealth was estimated at $1.1 billion. The magazine added with some humor: "Baron Ed [*sic*] estimates his personal fortune to be around $50 million. This figure might be accurate if he were referring only to the nest egg that his ancestor Mayer Amschel had in 1780."[1] Clearly, "Ed" had chosen a low profile.

Or had he? Stories leak out, or are spread, notably by Edmond's author-wife, Nadine. In a book about life with her baron, she describes their Rue de l'Elysée quarters in Paris—in a sense the last surviving Rothschild extravagance, with its "tropical lake enhanced by a ten-foot-high waterfall surrounded by a forest of fig and banana trees," and this revelation is duly reprinted in a popular account of the "new two hundred families." (The same book tells us that when the Edmonds invited high society to a party in Megève, they found they had no suitable place to put up their Rockefeller guests, so Edmond simply purchased a neighboring chalet; among his other properties, we learn, are residences on the southern Brittany coast, at Ischl in Austria, on Corsica, and in Caesarea on Israel's Mediterranean shore.)[2]

"A Rothschild who isn't rich, Jewish, a philanthropist, a banker, a hard worker, and who doesn't practice a certain way of life just isn't a Rothschild!" a writer for a Paris daily heard Edmond say, as if the baron were offering his own resolution of the problem of being at once discreet and legendary. "Rich he is," the reporter added, "ten times, perhaps a hundred times more so than his cousins." He was thought of as the richest man in France (but was this Swiss resident really in France?), able if necessary to live on the income of his income.

Baron Edmond denied that he was as rich as all that, although he allowed that his wealth exceeded $500 million (which is ten times more than the figure *Fortune* got from him). The problem was that his equity was so widely dispersed, and how evaluate all the real estate, all the art—for example the Rubens hanging in the manor at Pregny, that inestimable property covering over forty inestimable acres high above Lake Geneva? There were the fabulous Paris soirées, the succession of yachts that raced (and won) in the Mediterranean. . . .

This man could give away millions of dollars at a time, say for Israel caught in a war. He was one of that country's leading foreign investors, his Israel General Bank (portfolio management and merchant banking) the country's most solvent. In addition to an industrial zone at Caesarea sprawling over 1,200 acres, he was planning a 740-acre shopping center there (he stressed that his grandfather Edmond had acquired this coastal land not from native Palestinian Arabs but from Orthodox Christians and the Ottoman

Empire). He offered some figures to the press, such as the five billion French francs in assets of his Banque Privée in Geneva, which reported profits of 90 million francs. He had sold his interest in the Bank of California profitably in 1984; he had also made good money in the development of Club Méditerranée, while admitting to negative results in the Belgian Inno chain, as well as the Compagnie Générale du Jouet (and its U.S. affiliate, Heller), which declared bankruptcy in 1985 with losses of one billion francs (he paid them off, and managed to find new jobs for most of the firm's thousand employees).[3]

While it is not one of the giants, Edmond's Paris bank exploits lucrative niches, and offers some attractive mutual funds on the market. It can claim to be a world leader in privatizations (rated fourth after three British banks), a leader also in corporate advisory services and M&A. Small though it is, under the management of Bernard Esambert it seized opportunities to grow in every direction (in 1990, for example, it absorbed the activities—and the offices—of Chase Manhattan Bank in Monte Carlo).[4] With total assets of nearly 11.3 billion francs in 1992, it reported net income of 3.9 million francs, earned in activities ranging from corporate finance and M&A to exchange markets, export credits, and mutual funds.[5] It extended its counseling in privatization to the newly liberated nations of eastern and central Europe, notably Hungary and Czechoslovakia. Among its subsidiaries are the Banque de l'Eurafrique, specializing in real estate financing, the Compagnie AEP (international trade), Knox Partners (a New York–based specialist in M&A, financial engineering, and private investment), Financière Boréale (investment funds), Saint-Honoré Finance et Conseil (which earned the group a rank among the ten leading merchant banks in the French M&A market).

Of course it maintained privileged links to the other banks of the Edmond de Rothschild group, among them La Compagnie Financière Benjamin et Edmond de Rothschild in London, the Banque Privée Edmond de Rothschild in Geneva and Fribourg, the Banca Privata Solari e Blum in Lugano, the Compagnie de Trésorerie Benjamin de Rothschild (also in Geneva), the Banque Privée Edmond de Rothschild in Berlin, the Banque Privée Edmond de Rothschild (Océan Indien) on Mauritius.[6]

And then of course there is the association with his French and British cousins, Rothschild et Compagnie Banque in Paris, N. M. Rothschild & Sons in London. When David and Eric resuscitated their bank after nationalization, they wanted to call it Rothschild Frères as in times past, but Edmond hadn't liked that; to his mind the traditional name belonged to a bank with which all the brothers including himself would be associated. So they called themselves Rothschild & Associés, a little later Rothschild & Cie. Yet today Edmond's 8-percent share of David and Eric's bank is intended as a message: that if there are separate and distinct Rothschild banks in France, they are friends. (Rothschild España is a joint venture of Edmond's Compagnie Financière, N. M. Rothschild, and Rothschild & Cie. Banque, each partner holding a third.) David sits on Edmond's board of directors. The two Paris banks are competitors in many areas (although Edmond's and not David's makes loans to industry, is more involved in money management, less in counseling). Each tries, earnestly, to avoid trampling the other's flower beds. So when David and Eric were ready to open a Swiss bank, they made sure to place it in Zurich and not Geneva.[7]

Quite naturally there are jealousies, even maneuvers for strategic advantage—which family is free of that, and would it be a normal family? "Edmond and David: each man for himself," reads a headline in the financial press. The writer concedes Edmond's position in privatization, but adds that David's bank and London's N. M. Rothschild together represent a strong challenger (NMR being the world's number one in this very specialized area, according to a 1992 classification).

It doesn't escape notice that Edmond has tightened his bank's structure to facilitate passing it on to his only son, Benjamin (who studied computer science and communication at a California university—and thought he'd really wanted to become a film and TV producer, at least for a time). Since Benjamin was only thirty years old in 1993, Edmond was reluctant to see an alliance between his son and David, which could only work to the latter's advantage because of his seniority. If an alliance between the Edmond and David branches isn't possible, there seems more likelihood of a meeting of minds between Edmond and Jacob (Edmond called his lone-wolf London cousin "the most talented man in the family on financial matters").[8]

*   *   *

Each successive Rothschild vintner has had to be more pertinacious than his forebears in bringing the produce to market. With his means, and the late-twentieth-century facilities for promotion that his means can buy, Baron Edmond has created an industrial revolution of sorts with the extensive vineyards of Château Clarke and the adjacent estates of Peyre-Lebade and Malmaison, the ensemble representing the second largest domain in the Médoc, producing some 800,000 bottles a year. Edmond himself has said that Philippe de Rothschild had been obliged to succeed, since the Mouton estate had been his only inheritance. As for Edmond, he had expected that a moderately priced wine—his Château Clarke—would help open up the American market. "We thought the Americans would start to be wine drinkers," he explained to an interviewer for a wine magazine. Instead, the world became American—meaning that it lost the habit of sharing a bottle over dinner. "Neither in the U.S.A. nor in France do people drink as much wine at midday. My son would not think of drinking wine at lunch." He was concerned especially for Bordeaux wines, he said, because they must be consumed with food—and require aging. "Now the wines are ready to drink sooner, but this seems inevitable because the restaurants, hotels, and companies need the cash flow." Most new homes, even in France, are built without wine cellars. "Marketing problems are going to be more and more important for selling wine."

Hence the baron's mail-order Savour Club (which he controls, but without day-to-day operating responsibilities). He can use it to launch new brands, such as Les Granges des Domaines Edmond de Rothschild, consisting of a blend of Haut-Médoc vines he acquired in the 1970s; there is even a Château Clarke rosé wine, bottled early, reasonably priced. Through Savour Club, making liberal use of his name and his image, Baron Edmond can also sell brandies (e.g., a Bas-Armagnac called "Réserve Edmond de Rothschild").[9]

Could it be otherwise? Baron Philippe's Philippine obviously doesn't think so, for the marketing of the products of Baron Philippe de Rothschild S.A. remains vigorous: see the advertisement in a London literary magazine for a wine-tasting contest whose winners were promised exclusive tours of the vineyards of Baron

Philippe (runners-up to receive cases of that wine which the baron invented from scratch, Mouton Cadet).[10]

Whether it be quality or good promotion, Philippe's and Philippine's Mouton often draws higher prices at auction than Lafite.[11] Connoisseur Cyril Ray—who happened to be writing a book about Lafite, acknowledged Mouton to be "a bigger, fuller, harder wine"; he quoted Alexis Lichine's *Encyclopedia of Wines and Spirits:* "The high percentages of Cabernet-sauvignon grapes used make it very slow to mature and very full-bodied." Whereas the dominance of Merlot grapes in Lafite gives it what Lichine calls "great finesse and particular softness"; it is "firm yet delicate and supple, with an eventual lightness developed in age." Ray finds Bordeaux-lovers who prefer Mouton, others who swear by Lafite. (He heard a Lafite admirer say, "I don't like Mouton, because I don't like burgundy.") The authority's conclusion is that either of the rival wines can be consumed with pleasure, "though I cannot imagine anyone liking them equally when each is at its most typical."[12]

Aristocratic Lafite is also "marketed" nowadays. The Domaines Barons de Rothschild produces its own full-color brochures bearing the distinctive and insistent five arrows of the family seal; the castle itself is floodlit on summer weekends (it is pictured more sedately in the reproduction of an old etching affixed to each bottle of Lafite-Rothschild). Like the wines of the rival family branches, Domaines is a properly structured business enterprise. Lafite itself remains a partnership, with one-sixth shares now held respectively by David, Edouard, Eric and his family, Elie and his, Edmond and son Benjamin, and a charitable trust (in the care of Jacob in London) for the shares left by Jimmy. And Lafite in turn controls Les Domaines Barons de Rothschild (with nonfamily minority partners).[13]

Domaines does its own marketing and distribution, both the making and the selling under the control of this Rothschild generation's wine man, Baron Eric (who gives 40 percent of his time to the wine business, not more than 30 percent to the bank, the remainder to philanthropic activities).[14] It owns Château Duhart-Milon in Pauillac, the superb Pomerol of Château l'Evangile, the Sauternes Rieussec. It has management responsibility for prestigious Lafite (and also runs Château La Cardonne in Médoc for non-Rothschild owners); abroad, it now holds some 30 percent of the Chalone wine group, with four vineyards in California, and 50-percent stakes in Los Vasos, a first-class Chilean vineyard held by the same family since 1750, and Portugal's Quinta do Carmo.[15]

So the wines are a business; but perhaps they always were business more than sport, even in the days of the first Nathaniel, the Anglo-French Rothschild who acquired the Mouton vineyard, and of his uncle and competitor James, the Great Baron. James's biographer Anka Muhlstein cites a letter Nathaniel sent to his brothers back in London in October 1868, which portrays the Great Baron already speculating on his first vintage, two months after acquiring Lafite: "I sold my wine the other day," writes Nathaniel, "at the wonderfully high price of 5,000 francs the barrel. Our worthy uncle [James] hasn't yet disposed of his Lafite; he thinks the price will rise still higher."[16]

They *do* seem to be playing less. The ones who knew how to play have grown older, more serene; fun seems inappropriate to our times. Baron Guy's second wife, Marie-Hélène, for long years described as the queen of Paris society—"more Rothschild than me," her husband called her—famous for costume balls bringing princes and princesses together with the uncrowned heads of republican Europe, admitted as much to a society reporter. "It will never happen again—it's a different time," she was quoted in 1992. In any case, people no longer know how to "dress," have lost their taste for perfumes; when she gave a party now, it was a charity benefit. She didn't think she'd have a successor when she ceased to organize her evenings, although Parisians were saying that Eric's wife, Marie-Béatrice, could be that successor. (Baroness Guy told the interviewer that her own children would not become party-givers, "not as long as I am there," although they would "afterwards.")[17] In any case they attend all the proper functions. When a daily newspaper described a gala evening at the Opera for Rudolf Nureyev, the reporter noted among the invited guests "all the Rothschilds of Paris."[18]

To see the banking dynasty at its best, it may now be necessary to travel up to Normandy (or to read the small-town press). And of course there is still Ferrières, where Guy spends weekends playing golf, when he isn't busy at his working stud farm at Meautry. Even the house on Ile Saint-Louis is described as "a place of peaceful retirement." The Guys may dine with friends (who include Premier Edouard Balladur), or tête-à-tête in their own kitchen; Wednesdays, the school holiday, Guy takes lunch with David's Alexandre.[19]

David's house on the Left Bank is only rented; home for him is Reux, whose sprawling 320 acres include a stud farm that doesn't interest him much, plus a great old house put together over the centuries. He takes his work for the local township seriously. At one time he was mayor of Pont-l'Evêque while his late mother was still mayor of the smaller commune of Reux, and Guy of Ferrières; it made him think of a British friend's joke about "one Mexican, one general; two Mexicans, two generals; three Mexicans, three generals. . . ." (It was "one Rothschild, one mayor. . . .") Guy and Marie-Hélène might be photographed at the races, David at an agricultural fair.[20] David admits that he isn't quite as active in his role as mayor as he was before the bank became big business again, although he still tries to put in a weekly appearance at the town hall, consulting with the deputy who now does most of the job. And he misses the earlier years when he was able to spend more time with his fellow villagers.[21]

It's too soon to talk about still younger Rothschilds. Elie's son Nathaniel will surely make it in New York, but when he does, it isn't certain that he'll be talked about in *Vanity Fair*. His sister Nelly is a working artist and restorer of art. When the French business magazine *Expansion* notes of Edouard, Guy's son of his second marriage, that he is "sometimes controversial," it is largely because he is "all business"—an attribute of youthful energies. "If you close the door he comes in through the window," his cousin and colleague Eric explains with gentle humor.[22] (One doesn't expect to see Edouard and his wife, née Arielle Malard, at a fashion show or the races on a weekday; they *both* work in banks.)[23]

The most talked-about Rothschild houses now are the ones that are empty. The great old manor on the Seine at the southwestern corner of the Bois de Boulogne, fought over by Vichy and the Nazis during the German occupation, when it belonged to the first Baron

Edmond's daughter Miriam, became the property of a Saudi prince
in the oil-drenched 1970s; he turned to other distractions, but the
all-but-abandoned estate made the papers again when the Chinese
government considered buying it for use as an embassy. (The
castle's 110-acre park now belongs to the town of Boulogne-
Billancourt.)[24]

Ferrières isn't the only Rothschild manor that can be visited.
The dreamlike Villa Ephrussi, in the luxuriant Riviera setting of
the Saint-Jean-Cap-Ferrat peninsula, willed by Alphonse de
Rothschild's daughter Charlotte Béatrix to the Fine Arts Academy
in Paris, has been a tourist attraction for decades; its seven theme
gardens (devoted to art and the sea) have recently been restored.
Indeed, Baroness Ephrussi de Rothschild's original furniture and
priceless collection of art and art objects can be admired up close;
try to do that with a Rothschild in person.[25]

KING DAVID

The bank—by which is meant the mainline family bank, the one that a brash young immigrant with an impossible accent founded so brazenly in the teeth of that closed society of merchant bankers, and which survived down the years with only two detours, one to let the Nazis pass, another to assuage the nationalizers—still owns an asset its competitors will never match: its name. Guy de Rothschild tells the story of a trade fair in the magnificent turn-of-the-century Grand Palais exhibition hall in Paris at which the Banque Rothschild was one of the exhibitors. A woman who came to the stand explained, "I don't want a foreign bank, nor a nationalized bank, and I don't want a Jewish bank—so I come to you."[1] If in the past the Rothschild name was enough to frighten a populist, now it simply stands for banking with safety.

Duration, in the view of present senior partner David, direct descendent of the intrepid little Frankfurter who outwitted Napoleon in Napoleon's capital, is one of his best cards. See how the business world changes and changes—yet here, seated before you at the polished conference table, is a fifth generation of financial counselors, with a sixth growing up at home and surely destined for the succession. Its perdurability makes it easier for the bank to sell itself, and clients enjoy associating with tradition (they can pick up a

Rothschild pencil, decorated with five arrows, at the conference table). To deal with Rothschilds, it has been said, is to go to a tailor, rather than buying a suit off the rack. "Thanks to our name, we can always meet the people we need to see," explains David de Rothschild, pausing before he adds, "But then we have to deliver."[2]

Jacques Getten, that third-generation senior officer (and *his* son Eric works at Domaines Barons de Rothschild, his son-in-law Georges Babinet at Francarep), finds other assets besides endurance to explain the attraction of the latter-day Rothschilds. He is struck, and believes that potential clients are struck, by the extraordinary ethical image the family projects—in part because it *is* a family. When Getten, now senior financial adviser, whose work consists essentially of counseling younger executives in decision-making and developing new projects, receives a newly hired employee, his briefing includes the admonishment: You are joining a club called Rothschild. No matter what your rank is, you must always recognize "the Rothschild element," that is, the philosophy inspiring each decision, which may mean that you won't always agree with that decision. Getten could add to his briefing (but perhaps he does not): At one time or another, nearly every president and managing director of a company in the group has been obliged to leave, precisely because he didn't understand a Rothschild decision, couldn't accept "the Rothschild element." (It has nothing to do with differences of politics or of religion, notes Getten, himself a devout Catholic.)[3]

The present generation of Rothschilds is without illusions about its position in the lineup of financial giants (they almost don't belong in it). Obviously, if the present bank is compared to its nineteenth-century antetype, it has less influence, fewer assets to bring to bear. Yet all in all, considering the trauma and the devastations of the Hitler era (to consider only those), they've been "lucky." Taken together, with cousin Edmond and his global reach, above all thanks to the Paris bank's growing alliance with N. M. Rothschild in London, the family still represents considerable—and increasing—might.[4]

An advertisement in a British business daily is eloquent in this regard. "Benefit from Rothschilds' Global Investment Skills," announces Rothschild Asset Management, whose address is Five

Arrows House, St. Swithin's Lane, London, with offices listed for Paris, Zurich, New York, Hong Kong, Tokyo, and Sydney. "Rothschild Asset Management is a major investment management organisation with an international network of associated companies," the advertisement promises. "The Rothschild Group manages in excess of £15 billion around the world."[5] "Today," reads an N. M. Rothschild prospectus, "the Rothschild Group ranks among the world's leading independent merchant banking organisations. As business has become increasingly international, so the Group has expanded beyond Europe to meet the ever more diverse needs of its clients. It now has subsidiaries and affiliates in twenty countries employing over two thousand people."[6]

David and Eric and their partners also speak of their "group," referring to the banks in France, the United Kingdom, and Switzerland connected through cross ownership, and to the branches they run collectively in Germany, Italy, Spain, and Portugal. They now operate as far away from home as Denver, Colorado, western Canada, and Australia (where the Rothschilds have made a historic breakthrough by establishing a proper merchant bank with a payroll of some two hundred persons, offering regular business banking services such as corporate financing and asset management), not to speak of Mexico City, Rio de Janeiro, Tokyo, Hong Kong, and Singapore ("playing the Asian card," as David de Rothschild puts it).[7] In fact the Paris and London Rothschilds are partners in Europe and North America. London alone controls the subsidiaries in Asia, the Pacific region, and Latin America.

Meanwhile, in Paris, Rothschild & Cie. Banque continues to focus on asset management and corporate finance (in the latter category fall mergers and acquisitions, and that very French and European activity called privatization). British partner N. M. Rothschild has been playing a considerable role in Britain's privatization under the Conservatives, advising the government, notably, in its sale of its equity in British Petroleum, helping British Telecommunications and regional electrical companies make their way into the private sector. In Zurich, Rothschild Bank AG focuses on private banking and managing funds and trusts, while Rothschild representative offices in Spain, Italy, Portugal, and Germany—this last located in Frankfurt, the cradle of all Rothschild banking— serve clients of all three associated banks (Paris, London, Zurich). And so of course does Rothschild North America. As for the Frank- furt location, it is symbolic, but it is also far more than that. Germany's banking capital is considered "strategic" for the group; the Rothschild affiliate there will be expanded, but already it has been involved in significant transnational activity in capital mar- kets and corporate management (such as the takeover of an Italian company by a German one).

It is significant that in describing their activities the Rothschild cousins on either side of the Channel mention indifferently what Paris may have accomplished, or London: true brotherhood. But not quite equality, for the London bank *is* still quite a bit larger, and engages in a range of activities unknown to Paris, such as bullion banking. The world price of gold is fixed twice daily in its offices, while it is a major dealer in other precious metals, a significant actor in foreign exchange and money markets. Together the Paris and London Rothschilds own a substantial share of Smith New Court PLC, London's largest independent market maker and one of the leading world dealers in equities. And of course N. M. Rothschild remains the world leader in privatizations (even if its joint prospec- tuses magnanimously give credit to the Rothschild "Group").[8]

The French Rothschilds follow in the footsteps of their London cousins; while most of their activity is French and European, they are becoming increasingly transatlantic, where the competition comes from the likes of Morgan Stanley, Goldman Sachs, and First Boston. In Paris their chief rivals for a place in the sun are Paribas, Suez, Lazard, and Crédit Lyonnais, all competing in a market smaller than London's.[9]

The market's attitude, in any case, is as favorable as it could possibly be. "I don't know anyone else in finance who can boast of having no enemies," financier Vincent Bolloré has been quoted.[10]

In January 1992 David de Rothschild was appointed deputy chair- man of N. M. Rothschild & Sons in London, placing him in a position to succeed Sir Evelyn de Rothschild as chairman of the

British Rothschild bank. An extraordinary event—of a significance without parallel among Rothschilds of the present century. When, as it is assumed, David does move to the head of the table at N. M. Rothschild—while keeping his place as first among equals in the Paris bank—it will be the first time that a member of the French family controls all the banking activities of the dynasty's main line. It would combine—or move even closer than they presently are— one of Britain's leading merchant banks, and perhaps its most international, and the aggressively international Rothschild & Cie. Banque—one-tenth its size, but having a reservoir of talent and a stock of goodwill considerably bigger than its balance sheet.

Obviously the appointment of David detonated an explosion of speculation in financial circles.[11] To interpret the news required perspective; David would not automatically succeed to the chairmanship in London on the retirement of Evelyn (who turned sixty-two in August 1993). There are other possible candidates for the British succession; while Evelyn's own sons are still in their teens (aged fifteen and sixteen in 1993), his young cousin Amschel (now thirty-six), Jacob's brother, is making his way up in the bank. Perhaps a joint chairmanship—David and someone else—is in the cards.

But there could be a gap of up to a decade in the normal family succession, and that seems to call for David's presence at the top, as Evelyn himself indicated to the London business world (this would not preclude the appointment of a resident British executive responsible for day-to-day operations at New Court). "If something happens to me," Evelyn told an interviewer, "there is David. If something happens to him, there is Amschel. . . . Working as a family has always been our trademark." He made it clear that being Rothschilds, and therefore supremely European, was an advantage no other firm enjoyed.[12] The new unity between London and Paris would represent an alliance "similar in some ways to that created in the last century"—when of course the Rothschild sons formed a single entity.[13]

Meanwhile there has been "progressive integration" of the two houses; jointly owned by London and Paris, Rothschild Europe is more than symbolic in its activities in corporate finance throughout the European Community and in Switzerland.[14] No one imagines that David's bank will ever take over the Goliath in London; on the contrary, as chairman of N. M. Rothschild & Sons, David would be a low-profile arbitrator.[15] The plot thickens when one hears that Edmond de Rothschild is skeptical about the significance of the London-Paris rapprochement. "I doubt that it would be to the taste of the other British Rothschilds," he was quoted, in what is surely a reference to Evelyn's nemesis, Jacob.

The meeting of minds between the mainline London and Paris houses may have compromised the timid efforts at cooperation between Edmond and his son Benjamin on one hand, and David, Eric, and Edouard on the other; indeed, Edmond gave one reporter the impression that he felt the London-Paris axis was directed against him, although he considered himself to be "as legitimate a Rothschild as the others."[16]

Trade insiders have suggested that the London firm's weakness is in its senior management. "Can you succeed in today's competitive financial services market," an anonymous observer asked, "using a structure of family ownership?"[17] (For a time an American general manager was presumed to be Sir Evelyn's successor; after the announcement of David's appointment, he reportedly left in a huff.)[18]

Ironically, it is the smaller bank—David's—that has tackled that problem by co-opting managing partners whose competence and experience—and often their discretionary powers—equal those of the blood family.

Nobody has been heard to call David de Rothschild King David (or Rothschild V, counting from James as Rothschild I). But the legend persists. Each new study of the power elite, of the "two hundred families," necessarily includes this banking family par excellence; indeed, one magazine writer's roundup of the rich noted that "David de Rothschild illustrates . . . the permanence of the two hundred [families] in the French economy."[19] It is certain that the great old banking dynasties have endured, many of them of Protestant or Jewish origin (in France they include Schlumberger and Hottinguer in addition to Stern, Worms, Lazard, and Rothschild).[20] But although Jewish-owned businesses are a minor factor in the total French picture, the nasty myths dear to anti-Semites haven't died; they have only been translated into modern political terminology.

Nowadays demagogues whose stock in trade is the fears and prejudices of simple people have brought the European Community into the equation—Europe becoming, in their confused demonology, a plot of the Freemasons. In this updated version of the old myths, the Rothschilds are working for Europe and against France. The extreme-right French politician Jean-Marie Le Pen announced in 1992 that a pro-Europe and anti-France personality—unidentified—was heard to say, "There's only one more door to break down, that of the nation." A publication close to Le Pen added helpfully that the remark was made by "Baron de Rothschild" in 1970—no particular baron being specified. But of course none of them ever said such a thing.[21]

Just how international the word *international* now means is suggested by reports from far-off Japan, where one mass-circulation magazine attributes Japan's stock market difficulties to a Jewish conspiracy led by the Rothschilds.[22] A small publisher of business books in Tokyo thought that he had found the way to attract readers by denouncing Jewish industrial and financial groups "centered around the Rothschilds," who, so he alleges, are seeking to injure Japan. This publisher also alleges that the sketch of Mount Fuji reproduced on 5,000-yen banknotes actually shows Mount Sinai, which to his mind demonstrates that the Japanese Finance Ministry and the Bank of Japan are already under Jewish control.[23]

Late in February 1994 a Rothschild delegation assembled in Frankfurt, Germany, to celebrate the 250th birthday of the founder of their dynasty, Mayer Amschel. A ceremony was held in the Jewish Museum, a former Rothschild mansion on Untermainkai into which the family was able to move in 1846 when no longer required to live in the ghetto. One of the speakers was Chancellor Helmut Kohl, who declared, "We remember Mayer Amschel Rothschild not only as a great son of the city of Frankfurt am Main but also as an outstanding representative of European Jewry."

Family members, led by Lord Jacob of London and Baron Eric of Paris, visited the old Jewish graveyard adjacent to the vestiges of the ghetto to honor Mayer Amschel's tomb.[24]

Happily, most of the legends about the Rothschilds are pleasant ones; at worst, they are bittersweet, charged with the admiration mixed with envy of those without for those within. Shalom Aleichem told the story of a poor Eastern European Jew who made his way to Paris in an attempt to see Baron de Rothschild, insisting (to the reticent porter) that he had an interesting deal to propose to him. In the end the baron appears. "I'm listening," he says.

"Monsieur de Rothschild, I have found the way to immortality," the traveler from the distant shtetl explains. "Well, go ahead," Rothschild encourages him, "tell me."

"It's simple. To be immortal you have to come to my village, Kasrilenke."

"But—just why is that?"

"Because in Kasrilenke, we never saw a rich man die."[25]

ACKNOWLEDGMENTS

*O*ne who would explore the Rothschild legend must ponder the caveat of economic historian Jean Bouvier, who discovered that no Rothschild—certainly none in a responsible position—had written his memoirs (that ceased to be true when Baron Guy published his). For the early years of the banking dynasty we can rely on well-documented studies by Count Egon Corti and Bertrand Gille, and Gille had access to the bank's archives (which we can all examine now that he has put them in order). More recently, Anka Muhlstein gave us, with her biography of James, the most readable book ever written about a chieftain of this family.

But the Great Baron died in 1868; the works of Gille and Corti are chiefly concerned with his times. As a consequence the present writer has had to come to terms with a further century and a quarter of history, shifting between ancient and modern, from tattered documents yellowed with age to crisp new balance sheets emanating from the financial community. I have interrogated the Rothschilds through handwritten correspondence a century old—and while seated opposite them at home or across a conference table. Deep thanks to those who received me so readily, the barons Guy, David, and Edouard, Elie and Eric, the baroness (although I have never heard her called that) Batsheva de Rothschild; and Rothschild daughters Nicole Stéphane and Anka Begley (née Muhlstein).

I had crucial help from Mrs. Simone Mace of the Rothschild Archive in London; thanks also to Jean-Claude Meyer and Jacques Getten of Rothschild & Cie., to Christophe Salin and Monique Bodin of Les Domaines Barons de Rothschild, Mireille Munch of the Château de Ferrières, Robert Pirie, and Gerald Goldsmith, at Rothschild Inc. in New York.

I am grateful to Chantal Tourtier-Bonazzi and Jean Pouëssel of the Archives de France, to Nicole Richard of the Fondation Nationale des Sciences Politiques; Madeleine Dangu of INSEE; the archivists of the Centre de Documentation Juive Contemporaine; Archives de la Préfecture de Police, Paris; Bibliothèque du Louvre; Instituto da Biblioteca Nacional, Lisbon. And to the librarians of the Bibliothèque Nationale and the Institut d'Etudes Politiques who made my work easier.

Also to Marie-Noëlle André, Judith Cooper-Weill, Prof. Eliyahu Feldman of Tel Aviv University, Michel Hourst, Andrei Makine, Jacqueline Raoul-Duval, and Nicolas Véron.

NOTES

CHAPTER 1. AN END AND A BEGINNING

1. In the manuscript of *Lucien Leuwen* (1835).

2. Nicole du Roy and Francine Rivaud, *Les Français les plus riches* (Paris: Calmann-Lévy, 1987), 31.

3. Talk with Guy de Rothschild.

4. *Le Monde* (Paris), 28 October 1981.

5. Guy de Rothschild, *Contre bonne fortune* ... (Paris: Belfond, 1983), 368.

6. *Le Matin* (Paris), 18 November 1981.

7. Talk with Nicole Stéphane (née Rothschild).

8. *The Guardian* (Manchester), 17 November 1981.

9. Guy de Rothschild, *Contre bonne fortune* ... , 372.

10. Talks with David and Edouard de Rothschild.

11. Guy de Rothschild, *Contre bonne fortune* ... , 369.

CHAPTER 2. FIGHTING NAPOLEON

1. The most complete history of the early Rothschilds, benefiting from archives available in pre-Hitler Europe, is certainly *The Rise of the House of Rothschild*, followed by *The Reign of the House of Rothschild*, both by Count

Egon Caesar Corti (New York: Cosmopolitan Book Corp., 1928). Although the book originally appeared in German, the French translation is used in the present book: *La Maison Rothschild* (Paris: Payot, 1929–30). Corti makes use of previous materials since lost, but available to Christian W. Berghoeffer when he wrote *Mayer Amschel Rothschild* (Frankfurt: Englert & Schlosser, 1922).

2. Bertrand Gille, *Histoire de la Maison Rothschild,* vol. 1 (Geneva: Droz, 1965), 36, who follows Corti *(Maison Rothschild,* vol. 1, 14–16).

3. Jean Bouvier, *Les Rothschild* (Paris: Fayard, 1967), 19.

4. Corti, op. cit., 1:24–25, 31–32.

5. Henri de Rothschild, *La lignée française de la famille de Rothschild (1792–1942)* (Pôrto, Portugal: Costa Carregal, 1943), 21–22.

6. Ibid., 26–28.

7. Gille, *Histoire,* 1:37–42.

8. Corti, op. cit., 1:30–34.

9. Bouvier, *Les Rothschild,* 27.

10. Anka Muhlstein, *James de Rothschild* (Paris: Gallimard, 1981), 30–31.

11. Corti, op. cit., 1:59–60.

12. Muhlstein, op. cit., 34–37.

13. Corti, op. cit., 1:81–82.

14. Gille, *Histoire,* 1:43–44; Corti, op. cit., 91–92.

15. Gille, *Histoire,* 1:46, from French police archives; Muhlstein, op. cit., 42. Corti is best on German and Austrian sources, Muhlstein on Rothschild archives held in London, while Bertrand Gille (e.g., Gille, *Histoire,* 1:45–48) makes optimum use of Rothschild archives now in the Archives Nationales in Paris.

16. Philippe Bourdrel, *Histoire des Juifs de France* (Paris: Albin Michel, 144–160; Bernard Blumenkranz, ed., *Histoire des Juifs en France* (Toulouse: Privat, 1972), 286–301; Michael R. Marrus, *Les Juifs de France à l'époque de l'affaire Dreyfus* (Paris: Calmann-Lévy, 1972), 88–89; Muhlstein, op. cit., 45–51.

17. Corti, op. cit., 1:112.

18. Gille, *Histoire*, 1:49–51.

19. Muhlstein, op. cit., 55–56, based on her examination of James's letters to Nathan in London, preserved in the archives of N. M. Rothschild.

20. In calculating the value of francs in the nineteenth and early twentieth centuries, the author has used tables made available by Madeleine Dangu of INSEE, the French national statistics agency.

21. Gille, *Histoire*, 1:52–53, 56.

22. Corti, op. cit., 1:162–63; Gille, *Histoire*, 1:56.

CHAPTER 3. KING OF THE JEWS

1. Bertrand Gille, *La banque et le crédit en France de 1815 à 1848* (Paris: Presses Universitaires de France, 1959), 370–73; Gille, *Histoire*, 1:57–58.

2. Gille, *Histoire*, 1:448–51.

3. Ibid., 62–66.

4. Corti, op. cit., 1:180–84, 367.

5. Muhlstein, op. cit., 62–67, 69–71, 74–76.

6. Bouvier, *Les Rothschild*, 70.

7. Gille, *Histoire*, 1:61.

8. Corti, op. cit., 1:288–90.

9. Comte Joseph de Villèle, *Mémoires et correspondance*, vol. 3 (Paris: Perrin, 1889), 192–93.

10. Gille, *Histoire*, 1:187–88; Corti, op. cit., 1:222–23.

11. Gille, *Histoire*, 1:82–83.

12. Corti, op. cit., 1:367.

13. Muhlstein, op. cit., 86–88.

14. Quoted ibid., 83.

15. Quoted in Constance Battersea, *Reminiscences* (London: Macmillan, 1923), 73. Lady Battersea was Betty de Rothschild's niece.

16. Gille, *Histoire*, 1:470.

17. Muhlstein, op. cit., 72, 79.

18. Gille, *Histoire*, 1:163–65. Gille gives the division of capital of the brothers' firms in 1828, with Nathan still holding the lion's share (expressed in francs: 28,500,000, Amschel and Salomon each worth 19,693,750, Carl and James each 19,393,750, Salomon's son Anselm 2,083,332).

19. Corti, op. cit., 1:389.

20. Ibid., 393–94, as relayed to Metternich by his Austrian ambassador to Paris, Count Antal Rudolf Apponyi.

21. Ibid., 397–99.

22. John Reeves, *The Rothschilds* (London: Sampson Lowe, 1887), 342–43.

23. Gille, *Histoire*, 1:233.

24. Honoré de Balzac, *Lettres à Madame Hanska*, vol. 1 (Paris: Laffont, 1990), 80. As noted in this edition by the editor, Roger Pierrot, Balzac had met Baron James and Baroness Betty at Aix-les-Bains a year earlier. Now, in 1833, Balzac writes his wife-to-be: "Can you see me, my love, in conference with the prince of money, when I couldn't raise a penny of my own?"

25. Charles Fourier, *La fausse industrie*, vol. 1 (1835), in *Oeuvres complètes*, vol. 8 (Paris: Anthropos, 1967), 224, 659–660.

26. Bouvier, *Les Rothschild*, 109.

27. Corti, op. cit., 2:118–122.

28. Gille, *Histoire*, 1:181–86.

29. Irving Katz, *August Belmont* (New York: Columbia University Press, 1968), 3–6; Sigmund Diamond, *A Casual View of America: The Home Letters of Salomon de Rothschild* (Stanford, Calif.: Stanford University Press, 1961), 6; Rudolf Glanz, "The Rothschild Legend in America," *Jewish Social Studies* 19 (January–April 1957), 19–20.

30. Gille, *Histoire*, 1:377–82; Muhlstein, op. cit., 126–27; see also Bouvier, *Les Rothschild*, 158–61. Saint-Simonianism called for association rather than competition of capital, and indeed the development of railroads, says Robert B. Carlisle, did benefit from the idealism of Saint-Simon's followers, while the government reduced the risk by creating small segments of a national rail network. Robert B. Carlisle, "Les chemins de fer, les Roth-

schild et les saint-simoniens," *Economies et Sociétés* 5 (Geneva: Droz, July 1971), 647–76.

31. Gille, *Histoire*, 1:261–64, 268–71, 276–77; Bouvier, *Les Rothschild*, 121; Corti, op. cit., 2:115–16.

CHAPTER 4. THE GREAT BARON

1. Corti, op. cit., 2:147.

2. Muhlstein, op. cit., 91–92.

3. Ibid., 216–18.

4. Battersea, op. cit., 73–74.

5. Muhlstein, op. cit., 168–69.

6. Ibid., 90–95, 116–17.

7. Ibid., 163.

8. Balzac, op. cit., 1:394.

9. Ibid., 507.

10. Gille, *Histoire*, 1:453.

11. Comte de Nesselrode, *Lettres et papiers,* vol. 8 (Paris: Lahure, 1908–12), 95.

12. Amédée Boudin, *Notice sur la Maison Rothschild* (Paris: self-published, 1844).

13. Corti, op. cit., 2:242.

14. Gille, *Histoire*, 1:283, 292–95.

15. Katz, op. cit., 19; Glanz, op. cit., 9, 15–16.

16. Gille, *Histoire*, 1:299.

17. Henrich Heine, *Lutèce* (Paris: Michel Lévy, 1863), 64–67. (Article dated 27 May 1840, in Heine's regular column in the *Augsburger Zeitung*.)

18. Léon Poliakov, *Histoire de l'antisémitisme,* vol. 3 (Paris: Calmann-Lévy, 1968), 358–63; cf. Muhlstein, op. cit., 136–40; Bourdrel, op. cit., 164.

19. Corti, op. cit., 2:191–95, 202–4.

20. Heine, op. cit., 181. (Article dated 31 March 1841.)

21. Corti, op. cit., 2:118–63.

22. Heine, op. cit., 326–34, from an article dated 5 May 1843.

23. Balzac, op. cit., 2:54; see also 640, 783.

24. Gille, *Histoire*, 1:362–67; cf. Bouvier, *Les Rothschild*, 132–36.

25. Robert F. Byrnes, *Antisemitism in Modern France*, vol. 1 (New Brunswick, N.J.: Rutgers University Press, 1950), 114–18, 121–24; Poliakov, op. cit., 3:382–91.

26. Alphonse Toussenel, *Les Juifs, rois de l'époque: Histoire de la féodalité financière* (Paris: Librairie de l'Ecole Sociétaire, 1845), 4–5. In fact, Toussenel's disclaimer seems to be a response to his publishers, who, in a notice, disassociate themselves from his "aggressions" against "a great people." Ibid., vii.

27. Ibid., 7–8, 22; cf. Byrnes, op. cit., 1:119–21.

28. Muhlstein, op. cit., 151, gives the figure of fifty-five dead.

29. Satan [Georges Dairnvaell], *Histoire édifiante et curieuse de Rothschild Ier, Roi des Juifs* [Paris, 1846], in Archives Nationales 132 AQ 21; cf. Corti, op. cit., 2:243–44. Corti reproduces a letter from Anselm, son of James's brother Salomon, indicating that pamphleteer Dairnvaell had earlier sought to borrow money from the Paris Rothschild bank and had been turned down. Ibid., 245.

30. *Réponse de Rothschild Ier, Roi des Juifs, à Satan Dernier, Roi des Imposteurs* (Paris: Bellay, 1846), Archives Nationales 132 AQ 21.

31. Georges Dairnvaell, *Rothschild, ses valets et son peuple* (Bruxelles: self-published, 1846), Archives Nationales 132 AQ 22.

CHAPTER 5. HARD TIMES

1. Heine, op. cit., 182–83.

2. Balzac, op. cit., 2:54, 76, 81, 92.

3. Henri de Rothschild, *La lignée*, 27, 49, 53.

4. Muhlstein, op. cit., 173.

5. Gille, *Histoire*, 1:473–74; Muhlstein, op. cit., 174.

6. Charles-M. Widor, "Edmond de Rothschild," *Revue des Deux Mondes* (Paris), 15 January 1935, 443; cf. André Pascal [Henri de Rothschild], *Croisière autour de mes souvenirs* (Paris: Emile-Paul, 1932), 20.

7. Muhlstein, op. cit., 172.

8. Gille, *Histoire*, 1:474–75.

9. George D. Painter, *Marcel Proust*, vol. 1 (New York: Random House, 1989), 89–90.

10. Balzac, op. cit., 2:179–80.

11. Gille, *Histoire*, 1:409–10.

12. Reeves, op. cit., 349.

13. Gille, *Histoire*, 2:30–33, 155.

14. Battersea, op. cit., 75.

15. Corti, op. cit., 2:255–56.

16. Ernest Feydeau, *Mémoires d'un coulissier* (Paris: Librairie Nouvelle, 1873), 160–61.

17. Balzac, op. cit., 2:721; Muhlstein, op. cit., 193.

18. Marc Caussidière, *Mémoires*, vol. 1 (Paris: Michel Lévy, 1849), 210–12.

19. The letter from James offering 50,000 francs to the provisional government actually read, "Use it as you judge best to succor the wounded and workers in need." Guy de Rothschild, *Mon ombre siamoise* (Paris: Grasset, 1993), 31.

20. Gille, *Histoire*, 2:35–36.

21. Muhlstein, op. cit., 200.

22. Gille, *Histoire*, 2:36–41.

23. Balzac, op. cit., 2:744–91.

24. Muhlstein, op. cit., 204–5.

25. Balzac, op. cit., 2:929, 996.

26. Emile Barrault, quoted in Edouard Drumont, "Alphonse de Rothschild," *La Libre Parole* (Paris), 27 May 1905.

27. Gille, *Histoire*, 1:581–85.

Chapter 6. Another Emperor

1. Gille, *Histoire*, 2:52; Muhlstein, op. cit., 219.

2. Gille, *Histoire*, 2:52–59.

3. Corti, op. cit., 2:277–78.

4. Jean Bouvier, *Un siècle de banque française* (Paris: Hachette, 1973), 207–8.

5. Gille, *Histoire*, 2:93–99, 110–14; Louis Girard, *La politique des travaux publics du Second Empire* (Paris: A. Colin, 1952), 108–9; cf. Philippe Séguin, *Louis Napoléon le Grand* (Paris: Grasset, 1990), 290–91.

6. Rondo E. Cameron, "The Crédit Mobilier and the Economic Development of Europe," *Journal of Political Economy* 61, no. 6 (December 1953), 463–64.

7. Jean Autin, *Les frères Pereire* (Paris: Perrin, 1984), 304.

8. David S. Landes, "Vieille banque et banque nouvelle: La révolution financière du dix-neuvième siècle," *Revue d'Histoire Moderne et Contemporaine* 3 (July–September 1956), 213–22. At this time the Rothschild banks in Paris, Frankfurt, London, Naples, and Vienna continued to be owned jointly by the brothers (with the four sons of deceased brother Nathan of London), although to conform to the laws of the countries in which they were domiciled, each was incorporated locally. In 1853 the owners of the Paris firm were James, Amschel of Frankfurt, Salomon of Vienna, and Carl of Naples, while James's sons Alphonse and Gustave had powers of attorney. Gille, *Histoire*, 2:565–67.

9. Feydeau, op. cit., 112–23.

10. Gille, *Histoire*, 2:118–19, 169, 183–94, 243, 271, 301–4.

11. Cameron, op. cit., 469–71.

12. Corti, op. cit., 2:304–6.

13. Gille, *Histoire*, 2:183–85, 236–37.

14. Cameron, op. cit., 468.

15. Rondo Cameron and Jean Bouvier, "Une lettre inédite de Persigny à Napoléon III," *Revue Historique* 230 (July–September 1963), 91–96.

16. Edmond de Goncourt and Jules de Goncourt, *Journal*, vol. 5 (Monaco: Imprimerie Nationale, 1956), 192.

17. Corti, op. cit., 2:343–46.

18. Gille, *Histoire*, 2:600–1.

19. Goncourt and Goncourt, op. cit., 6:50.

20. Feydeau, op. cit., 110–48.

21. Ron Chernow, *The House of Morgan* (New York: Atlantic Monthly Press, 1990), 25.

22. Eugène de Mirecourt, *Rothschild* (Paris: Havard, 1855), 35, 41, 50–51, 90–91, 95.

CHAPTER 7. THE NEXT GENERATION

1. Gille, *Histoire*, 1:472–73; Guy de Rothschild, *Contre bonne fortune* . . . , 12–13.

2. Guy de Rothschild, *Contre bonne fortune* . . . , 15–16.

3. Goncourt and Goncourt, op. cit., 3:104–5.

4. Muhlstein, op. cit., 222.

5. Gille, *Histoire*, 2:598; Bouvier, *Les Rothschild*, 279.

6. Muhlstein, op. cit., 226–30; Marrus, op. cit., 84–87.

7. Patrick Girard, *Les Juifs de France de 1789 à 1860* (Paris: Calmann-Lévy, 1976), 131.

8. Quoted in Muhlstein, op. cit., 229.

9. Reeves, op. cit., 351–52.

10. Patrick Girard, op. cit., 204.

11. Maxime Du Camp, *Paris, Ses organes, ses fonctions et sa vie dans la seconde moitié du XIXe siècle*, vol. 4 (Paris: Hachette, 1875), 240–42; cf. Maxime Du Camp, *Paris bienfaisant* (Paris: Hachette, 1888), 316.

12. Daniela Felisini, *Le finanze pontificie e i Rothschild (1830–1870)* (Naples: Edizioni Scientifiche Italiane, 1990), 202–5.

13. Corti, op. cit., 2:289–92; Gille, *Histoire*, 2:68–74.

14. Gille, *Histoire*, 2:596–97.

15. Muhlstein, op. cit., 226.

16. Goncourt and Goncourt, op. cit., 5:118.

17. Diamond, op. cit., 5–11; cf. Katz, op. cit., 144–46.

18. Goncourt and Goncourt, op. cit., 6:208.

19. Corti, op. cit., 2:279.

20. Gille, *Histoire*, 2:262–65.

21. Battersea, op. cit., 76.

22. *Le Monde illustré*, quoted in Guy de Rothschild, op. cit., 18.

23. Quoted in Fritz Stern, *Gold and Iron* (New York: Knopf, 1977), 173n.

24. Battersea, op. cit., 72.

25. Stern, op. cit., 173n.

26. Guy de Rothschild, *Contre bonne fortune . . .* , 19.

27. Louis Girard, op. cit., 273–74; cf. Hubert Bonin, *L'argent en France depuis 1880* (Paris: Masson, 1989), 252.

28. Rothschild Archive, London RFam C/21. Letters of 28 September and November 1863, 16 November 1864.

29. Goncourt and Goncourt, op. cit., 7:175.

30. Ibid., 6:12. The surprise is that later in life Edmond de Goncourt admired James's daughter Charlotte, wife of Nathaniel. Ibid., 14:8, 11. Indeed, Rothschild women are more kindly treated than one would expect from a Goncourt. In January 1888, when Edmond de Goncourt dined at Princess Mathilde's, the Alphonse de Rothschilds were fellow guests with their daughter Charlotte Béatrix, then twenty-four; the diarist describes "a young bride who has all the graces, all the kindness, all the freshness of a child. . . ." Ibid., 15:71.

31. *Enquête sur les principes et les faits généreux qui régissent la circulation monétaire et fiduciaire*, vol. 1 (Paris: Imprimerie Impériale, 1867), 457–80. On the new Fould-Rothschild entente (against the Péreires) see Louis Girard, op. cit., 278–80.

32. Gille, *Histoire*, 2:393–94.

33. Ibid., 503–4, 537, 539–50.

34. Stern, op. cit., 30–31, 40–41.

35. Ibid., 66–67, 73–75.

36. Quoted in Muhlstein, op. cit., 81.

37. Corti, op. cit., 2:396–97. In a polemical work of 1869, *L'empire industriel*, by Georges Duchêne, the author asserted that the Pereires held forty-four

positions as members of the board against thirty-two for the Rothschilds. See René Sedillot, *Les deux cents familles* (Paris: Perrin, 1988).

38. Louis Girard, op. cit., 366–69.

39. Cyril Ray, *Lafite* (London: Christie's Wine Publications, 1988), 36–43.

40. Muhlstein, op. cit., 236–38.

41. Corti, op. cit., 2:398–400; Muhlstein, op. cit., 239–40.

42. Quoted in Bouvier, *Les Rothschild,* 152.

43. Quoted in Guy de Rothschild, *Contre bonne fortune* . . . , 79n.

44. Nestor Roqueplan, *Le Baron James de Rothschild* (Paris: Dentu, 1868), in Papiers Rothschild, Archives Nationales 132 AQ 22.

Chapter 8. French Barons

1. Corti, op. cit., 2:398.

2. Guy de Rothschild, *Contre bonne fortune* . . . , 75.

3. Talk with Elie de Rothschild.

4. Calculations made on the basis of coefficients supplied by Mme. Madeleine Dangu of INSEE.

5. Gille, *Histoire,* 2:569–71.

6. Bouvier, *Les Rothschild,* 205–7.

7. Corti, op. cit., 2:400–5.

8. Quoted in Stern, op. cit., 129–30.

9. Ibid., 135; Corti, op. cit., 2:405.

10. Lucy Cohen, *Lady Louisa de Rothschild and Her Daughters* (London, 1935), quoted in Virginia Cowles, *The Rothschilds* (New York: Knopf, 1973), 151.

11. *Le Temps* (Paris), 15 August 1870.

12. Princesse Pauline de Metternich, *Souvenirs (1859–1871)* (Paris: Plon, 1931), 192.

13. Feydeau, op. cit., 183.

14. Corti, op. cit., 2:406, from Hermann Salingré, *Im grossen Hauptquartier, 1870–71,* 91.

15. Otto von Bismarck, *Lettres de Bismarck à sa femme pendant la guerre de 1870* (Paris: Tallandier, 1903), 89–99.

16. Otto von Bismarck, *Les mémoires de Bismarck recueillis par Maurice Busch*, vol. 1 (Paris: Charpentier & Fasquelle, 1898), 123–29, from Busch, *Tagebuchblätter*, 1:213.

17. Corti, op. cit., 2:408.

18. *Le Soir* (Paris), 7 February 1871, in Archives de la Préfecture de Police (Paris) Ba 1256.

19. Stern, op. cit., 137, 152–54.

20. Corti, op. cit., 2:408–14.

21. Jean Baumier, *La galaxie Paribas* (Paris: Plon, 1988), 19; Stern, op. cit., 326–27.

22. Corti, op. cit., 2:415.

23. Reeves, op. cit., 358.

24. Edouard Drumont, *La fin d'un monde* (Paris: Savine, 1889), 133.

25. Battersea, op. cit., 75.

26. Bouvier, *Les Rothschild*, 208–9, 215–20.

27. Chemin de fer de l'Est, *Assemblée générale*, reports for 1871, 1872, and 1873, in Archives Nationales 132 AQ 77.

28. Corti, op. cit., 2:427.

CHAPTER 9. THE BROTHERS ROTHSCHILD

1. Bouvier, *Les Rothschild*, 221.

2. Ibid., 255–56, 260–62. Bouvier (p. 228) also places Alphonse in a coalition of bankers seeking a world copper monopoly, although he soon withdrew from it.

3. Ibid., 254, 256–59, 262–63. Peñarroya, which began in Spain with lead, zinc, sulfuric acid, superphosphates, coal, and electricity, later extended its activities to Italy, Greece, Yugoslavia, Tunisia, and Argentina. The Rothschilds hadn't been among the founders of Le Nickel, but its president was close to Alphonse, and the Rothschilds were that company's bankers; later they would be significant shareholders. Cf. Jean-Yves Mollier, *Le scandale de Panama* (Paris: Fayard, 1991), 296–99.

4. Talk with Guy de Rothschild.

5. Charles Lesage, *L'achat des actions de Suez* (Paris: Plon, 1906), 34–76.

6. André Maurois, *Disraeli* (New York: Appleton, 1928), 296.

7. Lord [Victor] Rothschild, *You Have It, Madam* (London: self-published, 1980), 22–27.

8. Rothschild Archive, London 000/43 (no. 43, undated); cf. [Victor] Rothschild, op. cit., 27.

9. Chernow, op. cit., 25, 40.

10. Archives of the Préfecture de Police Ba 1256.

11. Marrus, op. cit., 86; Paula Hyman, *From Dreyfus to Vichy: The Remaking of French Jewry (1906–1939)* (New York: Columbia University Press, 1979), 26.

12. Du Camp, *Paris bienfaisant,* 335, 439.

13. Ibid., 316, 323, 329.

14. Goncourt and Goncourt, op. cit., 10:177.

15. A number of catalogs have been published on Edmond's collections donated to the Louvre museum in Paris, e.g., Musée National du Louvre, *L'oeuvre gravé de François Boucher dans la Collection Edmond de Rothschild* (Paris: Editions des Musées Nationaux, 1978).

16. Ludovic Halévy, *Trois dîners avec Gambetta* (Paris: Grasset, 1929), 47–50.

17. Bouvier, *Les Rothschild* 241–43.

18. Rothschild Archive, London XI-101-10 (11 February 1882).

19. Bouvier, *Les Rothschild* 272–73.

20. Rothschild Archive, London XI-101-9 (17 September 1881).

21. Rothschild Archive, London XI-101-10; cf. Stern, op. cit., 346–47.

22. Rothschild Archive, London XI-101-10 (letter of 27 June 1882).

23. Ibid.

24. Paul-Henri Gain, *La question du tunnel sous la Manche* (Paris: Rousseau, 1932), 13–24; cf. Rothschild Archive, London XI-101-9 (1881) and XI-101-10 (1882).

25. Bernard Sasso and Lyne Cohen-Solal, *Le tunnel sous la Manche* (Paris: La Manufacture, 1987), 107–9, 122.

26. Gain, op. cit., 25–32. After the Second World War, the Rothschilds were again involved in planning the "Chunnel," but withdrew before the project took its definitive form. Guy de Rothschild, press conference (1967), in Maurice Druon, *Ces Messieurs les Rothschild* (Paris: Tisné, 1967); talk with David de Rothschild.

CHAPTER 10. "JEWISH FRANCE"

1. Jean Bouvier, *Le krach de l'Union Générale (1878–1885)* (Paris: Presses Universitaires de France, 1960), 8–11; Jeannine Verdès-Leroux, *Scandale financier et antisémitisme catholique: le krach de l'Union Générale* (Paris: Centurion, 1969), 24–25.

2. Bouvier, *Le krach*, 140–53, 164–70, 178–86; Verdès-Leroux, op. cit., 29–30.

3. Eugène Bontoux, *L'Union Générale: Sa vie, sa mort, son programme* (Paris: Savine, 1888), 137–40.

4. Byrnes, op. cit., 1:130–35.

5. Bouvier, *Les Rothschild*, 267.

6. Rothschild Archive, London XI-101-10 (7 March 1882).

7. Léon Poliakov, *Histoire de l'antisémitisme*, vol. 4 (Paris: Calmann-Lévy, 1977), 46.

8. Verdès-Leroux, op. cit., 69–70. For a resumé of the conflict between the little people and the "masters": Pierre Birnbaum, *Le peuple et les "gros"* (Paris: Grasset, 1979), 15–26.

9. Quoted in Bouvier, *Les Rothschild*, 285.

10. Ibid., 284–89; Poliakov, op. cit., 4:59–63.

11. Archives of the Préfecture de Police Ba 1256. Reports dated 1883–84.

12. Goncourt and Goncourt, op. cit., 13:62, 182.

13. Archives Nationales 132 AQ 22.

14. Edouard Drumont, *La France juive: Essai d'histoire contemporaine*, vol. 1 (Paris: Marpon & Flammarion, 1886), vi–vii. For background on Drumont, see Byrnes, op cit., 137–44.

15. Drumont, *La France juive*, 1:328.

16. Ibid., 2:92–95, 104, 106, 108–18.

17. Elizabeth Parinet, *La Librairie Flammarion (1875–1914)* (Paris: IMEC Editions, 1992), 252–56.

18. Goncourt and Goncourt, op. cit., 14:114.

19. Byrnes, op. cit., 155.

20. Poliakov, op. cit., 4:58.

21. Parinet, op. cit., 258.

22. Edouard Drumont, *La France juive devant l'opinion* (Paris: Marpon & Flammarion, 1886), 140–47, 160–63.

23. Archives Nationales 132 AQ 22; cf. Jules Guesde, *Etat, politique et morale de classe* (Paris: Giard & Brière, 1901), 439, 444–47; cf. Adolphe Compère-Morel, *Jules Guesde* (Paris: Quillet, 1937), 297–300.

24. Stern, op. cit., 372–73, 524–25.

25. Simon Schama, *Two Rothschilds and the Land of Israel* (New York: Knopf, 1978), 343 (from a study by Zosa Szajkowski in *Jewish Social Studies*, vol. 4 [1942], 291–92).

26. Henri de Rothschild, *La lignée*, 44–45.

27. Israel Margalith, *Le Baron Edmond de Rothschild et la colonisation juive en Palestine* (Paris: Marcel Rivière, 1957), 5–6.

28. Ibid., 64–65; cf. David Druck, *L'oeuvre du Baron Edmond de Rothschild* (Paris: Editions R.L.J., 1928), 19–29.

29. Schama, op. cit., 25–27.

30. Margalith, op. cit., 63.

31. From David Druck, *Baron Edmond de Rothschild*, quoted in Schama, op. cit., 54.

32. Schama, op. cit., 56.

33. Ibid., 21–23.

34. Talk with Guy de Rothschild.

Chapter 11. Russia and Palestine

1. Goncourt and Goncourt, op. cit., 15:60. The first meeting was in June 1874.

2. Ibid., 18:155.

3. Henri de Rothschild, *La lignée*, 47.

4. Schama, op. cit., 88–95, 103–4.

5. Quoted, ibid., 143.

6. Bouvier, *Les Rothschild*, 280.

7. Goncourt and Goncourt, op. cit., 16:24 (13 February 1889).

8. Ibid., 83–84 (4 June 1889).

9. Stern, op. cit., 446–47.

10. Archives Nationales 132 AQ 67; cf. Eliyahu Feldman, "The French Roth- schilds and the Russian Loan of April 1891" (in Hebrew), *Zion* 56, no. 2 (1991), 162–64.

11. Feldman, op. cit., xii–xiii, 164–71; correspondence with Prof. Feldman.

12. Rothschild Archive, London XI-101-22 (12 May 1891).

13. William L. Langer, "The Franco-Russian Alliance (1890–1914)," *The Sla- vonic Review* 3, no. 9 (March 1925), 566; cf. Herbert Feis, *Europe: The World's Banker (1870–1914)* (New Haven: Yale University Press, 1930), 216.

14. Langer, op. cit., 569–70; Feis, op. cit., 217.

15. Ernest Daudet, *Histoire diplomatique de l'Alliance Franco-Russe (1873– 1893)* (Paris: Ollendorff, 1894), 268–71.

16. *Le Temps* (Paris), 12 November 1891, 4.

17. Daniel Yergin, *The Prize: The Epic Quest for Oil, Money and Power* (Lon- don: Pocket Books, 1993), 58–61.

18. Corti, op. cit., 2:431.

19. Marrus, op. cit., 182–83.

20. *La Libre Parole* (Paris), 13 November 1894.

21. Archives Nationales 132 AQ 67.

22. Rothschild Archive, London XI-101-32 (14 September 1896).

23. Rothschild Archive, London XI-101-33 (8 October 1896).

24. Stern, op. cit., 432–33.

25. Mollier, op. cit., 283–87.

26. Ibid., 300–3.

27. Rothschild Archive, London XI-101-21 (13 December 1890).

28. *L'Eclair* (Paris), 3 June 1890.

29. Archives de la Préfecture de Police Ba 1256.

30. Elisabeth de Clermont-Tonnerre, *Mémoires*, vol. 2, *Au temps des équipages* (Paris: Grasset, 1928), 210–11.

31. Henri de Rothschild, *La lignée*, 37–39.

32. Archives de la Préfecture de Police Ba 1256.

33. Ibid.

34. *Le Figaro* (Paris), 14 September 1892; cf. Jules Huret, *Enquête sur la question sociale en Europe* (Paris: Perrin, 1897), 61–70.

35. *Le Temps* (Paris), 17 September 1892.

36. *Le Figaro*, 16 September 1892.

37. *La Libre Parole* (Paris), 15 September 1892. The Huret interview was still being exploited as late as 1920, when a left-anarchist group reprinted it, adding in a footnote that the Rothschilds had made "billions" in World War I. Jules Huret, *Rothschild et la question sociale* (Paris: L'Idée Libre, 1920).

Chapter 12. Dreyfus?

1. *Le Temps*, 20, 21 December 1892; *Le Figaro*, 20 December 1892.

2. Battersea, op. cit., 76–77.

3. *La Libre Parole*, 19 December 1892.

4. *La Libre Parole*, 27 January 1893.

5. *La Libre Parole*, 26 January, 10 February 1893.

6. Goncourt and Goncourt, op. cit., 16:140.

7. Ibid., 17:40, 46.

8. *La Libre Parole*, 28, 30 December 1893.

9. Drumont, *La fin d'un monde*, iv.

10. Edouard Drumont, *La dernière bataille* (Paris: Dentu, 1890), 30–31, 40–41, 191–94; cf. Drumont, *Le testament d'un antisémite* (Paris: Dentu, 1891), 42.

11. *Le Temps*, 20 April 1890.

12. *Le Temps*, 25 January 1890.

13. Rothschild Archive, London XI-101-21 (24 January 1890).

14. Byrnes, op. cit., 1:242–43; Marrus, op. cit., 230.

15. *La Libre Parole*, 9 December 1892.

16. Archives de la Préfecture de Police Ba 1256.

17. Ibid.

18. Raphaël Viau, *Vingt ans d'antisémitisme* (Paris: Charpentier-Fasquelle, 1910), vii–ix, 26–27, 51–53, 79, 113–17, 274.

19. Pierre Sorlin, *La croix et les juifs (1880–1899)* (Paris: Grasset, 1967), 96; see plate 8 and n. 479 on p. 314.

20. For examples of Barrès's anti-Semitism, see Zeev Sternhell, *Maurice Barrès et le nationalisme français* (Paris: A. Colin, 1972), 234–35. For Barrès on Rothschild: Maurice Barrès, *Scènes et doctrines du nationalisme* (Paris: Trident, 1987), 317–19.

21. *La Libre Parole*, 3 November 1894.

22. Joseph Reinach, *Histoire de l'Affaire Dreyfus*, vol. 1 (Paris: Fasquelle, 1930), 230.

23. *La Libre Parole*, 6 November 1894.

24. Talk with Guy de Rothschild.

25. Rothschild Archive, London XI-101-25 (2 November 1894).

26. Marrus, op. cit., 244.

27. Rothschild Archive, London XI-101-25 (24 December 1894).

28. Marcel Thomas, *L'Affaire sans Dreyfus* (Geneva: Idégraf, 1978), 49–67; Reinach, op. cit., 2:93–95; Jean-Denis Bredin, *L'Affaire* (Paris: Presses Pocket, 1988), 159.

29. Bredin, op. cit., 72–73.

CHAPTER 13. FIN DE SIECLE

1. *La Presse* (Paris), 8 January 1894.

2. Archives de la Préfecture de Police Ba 142, Ba 1256; *L'Illustration* (Paris) 31 August 1895, 177.

3. Battersea, op. cit., 77.

4. By Albert Monniot, 12 March 1896.

5. Archives de la Préfecture de Police Ba 1256; *La Libre Parole illustrée*, 11 April 1896.

6. *La Libre Parole*, 11 November 1896.

7. Bredin, op. cit., 207–225.

8. *Le Matin* (Paris), 21 November 1896; Archives de la Préfecture de Police Ba 1256.

9. Rothschild Archive, London XI-101-39 (11 January 1898).

10. Bredin, op. cit., 300–6.

11. Rothschild Archive, London XI-101-39 (13 January 1898).

12. Archives de la Préfecture de Police Ba 1256, 13 January 1898 report. In February another informer reported hearing Alphonse say that he had given nothing, but that Henri de Rothschild, his distant cousin, had given 150,000 francs.

13. Quoted in Bredin, op. cit., 177.

14. Rothschild Archive, London XI-101-39 (14 January 1898).

15. Rothschild Archive, London XI-101-39 (19 January 1898).

16. Ibid., letter of 7 February 1898.

17. Ibid., letters of 9 and 12 February 1898.

18. Bredin, op. cit., 325–41. Instead of prison, Zola was to spend the year in exile in Britain. Cf. Emile Zola, *J'accuse . . . !* (Brussels: Complexe, 1988), 95–225.

19. *Le Temps*, 7, 8 June 1898.

20. Rothschild Archive, London XI-101-40 (1, 19, 23 September 1898).

21. Reinach, op. cit., 4:443.

22. *Le Matin*, 26 November 1898.

23. *Le Jour*, 1 June 1899.

Chapter 14. Edouard

1. *Le Temps*, 1, 3, 4, 13 April 1900.

2. *La Libre Parole*, 12 June 1901.

3. Archives de la Préfecture de Police Ba 1256.

4. *La Libre Parole*, 30 January 1903.

5. Archives de la Préfecture de Police Ba 1256.

6. Albert Monniot, *Que faire? . . . Réponse d'un antisémite* (Paris: Librairie Antisémite, 1904), 27–28.

7. *L'Illustration* (Paris), 2 July 1904, 2–3.

8. Marie-Jeanne Dumont, *La Fondation Rothschild et les premières habitations à bon marché de Paris (1900–1925)* (Paris: Ministère de l'Urbanisme et du Logement, 1984), 6, 14, 36, 38, 129.

9. *Gil Blas* (Paris), 24 May 1904.

10. *Le Temps*, 21 May 1905; Archives de la Préfecture de Police Ba 1256; cf. *La Libre Parole*, 20 May 1905.

11. *Le Matin*, 27 May 1905.

12. *L'Illustration*, 3 June 1905, 364.

13. *Le Matin*, 30 May 1905.

14. Archives de la Préfecture de Police Ba 1256.

15. *La Libre Parole*, 27 May 1905.

16. *Le Matin*, 30 May 1905.

17. Carlo Montagnini, *Les fiches pontificales de Monseigneur Montagnini* (Paris: E. Nourry, 1908), 184–85.

18. *Le Matin*, 30 May 1905.

19. Henri de Rothschild, *La lignée*, 18. The Frankfurt bank was closed in 1901, following the death of the last Rothschild still active in that city, Wilhelm Carl.

20. Bouvier, *Les Rothschild*, 296; cf. *Les Documents Politiques, Diplomatiques et Financiers* (Paris), February 1968, 13–14.

21. *Le Temps*, 6 July 1905.

22. *La Libre Parole*, 26, 29 March 1906.

23. *Journal Officiel, Débats Parlementaires: Sénat*, 7 April 1906: Séance du 6 Avril (transcript of 6 April session).

24. Clermont-Tonnerre, op. cit., 214.

25. *Le Monde* (Paris), 26 June 1992.

26. Rothschild Archive, London XI-101-71 (2 April 1906); talk with Guy de Rothschild.

27. Talk with Guy de Rothschild.

28. *Crapouillot* (Paris), n.s. 16 (January 1952), 17.

29. Talk with Guy de Rothschild.

30. Rothschild Archive, London XI-101-71 (4 May 1906).

CHAPTER 15. TIGHTENING CIRCLES

1. Guy de Rothschild, *Contre bonne fortune* . . . , 45–46, 49–50.

2. Paula Hyman, *From Dreyfus to Vichy: The Remaking of French Jewry (1906–1939)* (New York: Columbia University Press, 1979), 36–37.

3. Guy de Rothschild, *Contre bonne fortune* . . . , 345–46.

4. Rothschild Archive, London XI-101-71 (1 May 1906).

5. Ibid.

6. Corti, op. cit., 2:446–47.

7. Bouvier, *Les Rothschild*, 294–95; Henri de Rothschild, *La lignée*, 19–20.

8. Matrac, *Les Rothschild* (Paris: Belleville, 1909), 19.

9. Corti, op. cit., 2:446.

10. Correspondence with Prof. Eliyahu Feldman, Jerusalem.

11. Rothschild Archive, London XI-101-70 (6 and 9 January 1906).

12. Rothschild Archive, London XI-101-71 (19 June 1906).

13. Yergin, op. cit., 71–72.

14. F. C. Gerretson, *History of the Royal Dutch*, vol. 2 (Leiden: E. J. Brill, 1955), 238, 250, 275.

15. Yergin, op. cit., 121–23.

16. Ibid., 130.

17. Archives Nationales 132 AQ 262. Direction to Standard Russe, 29 December 1905.

18. Bertrand Gille, *Inventaire des papiers Rothschild* (Archives Nationales 132 AQ); Yergin, op. cit., 131–33.

19. V. I. Bovykin, "Russian Oil and the Rothschilds" (Rossiskaya neft i Rothschildi), *Vosprosy Istorii* 4 (1978), 27–41.

20. F. C. Gerretson, *History of the Royal Dutch,* vol. 4 (Leiden: E. J. Brill, 1957), 135–37, 297; Gille, *Inventaire.*

21. Schama, op. cit., 119–20, 134–39, 142–44.

Chapter 16. The Extended Family

1. *Les Documents Politiques,* February 1968, 14–16. Alphonse's widow died earlier in 1911, two days after the death of her four-year-old grandchild, Edouard's first son, Alphonse Edouard. She had worn her seventy-three years "briskly," a weekly magazine reported, printing one of the rare photographs of her, taken at Deauville some years earlier as Baron Alphonse shakes hands, bowing, with King Léopold II of Belgium. *L'Illustration,* 14 January 1911, 20. Alphonse's brother Gustave died on November 28, 1911.

2. Schama, op. cit., 196–97.

3. Talk with Elie de Rothschild.

4. *Le Temps,* 9 February 1900; *L'Illustration,* 10 February 1900, 96.

5. Clermont-Tonnerre, op. cit., 219–20; Corti, op. cit., 2:426–27.

6. Clermont-Tonnerre, op. cit., 218–19.

7. René Gimpel, *Diary of an Art Dealer* (New York: Farrar, Straus & Giroux, 1966), 200.

8. George D. Painter, *Marcel Proust,* vol. 2 (New York: Random House, 1989), 172.

9. Ray, op. cit., 26.

10. Battersea, op. cit., 79.

11. *Le Temps,* 21 February 1870.

12. Henri de Rothschild, *La lignée,* 61–63; Pascal, *Croisière,* 32–39, 41–48, 61–64, 136–37, 161–73.

13. Chernow, op. cit., 114.

14. *L'Illustration,* 5 July 1902, 10.

15. *L'Illustration,* 27 August 1904, 134–35.

16. R. Deliencourt and J. Chennebenoist, "La propriété Strassburger" (Ville de Deauville, 1981).

17. Henri de Rothschild, *La lignée,* 78–99; Pascal, *Croisière,* 13–16, 75–77, 125–73.

18. Clermont-Tonnerre, op. cit., 221–22.

19. *Le Temps,* 27 March 1898.

20. *L'Illustration,* 5 April 1913, 307.

21. Henri de Rothschild, *La lignée,* 120–24. One of Henri's books is a study of his father's collections: Henri de Rothschild, *Un bibliophile d'autrefois: le Baron James-Edouard de Rothschild (1844–1881)* (Paris: Droz, 1934).

22. *L'Illustration,* 9 May 1914, 399.

CHAPTER 17. WAR AND PEACE

1. Talk with Guy de Rothschild.

2. Dr. Eugene Kaufmann, *La banque en France,* originally published in 1910 (Paris: Girard & Brière, 1914), 166–67.

3. *Les Documents Politiques,* February 1968, 15

4. Kaufmann, op. cit., 168–71.

5. Francis Delaisi, *La démocratie et les financiers* (Paris: La Guerre Sociale, 1910), 23–27, 42.

6. Rothschild Archive, London XI-101-98 (6, 17, 23 January 1913).

7. Rothschild Archive, London XI-101-98 (6 January 1913).

8. Archives Nationales 132 AQ 34.

9. Yves-Henri Nouailhat, *France et Etats-Unis (août 1914–avril 1917)* (Paris: Publications de la Sorbonne, 1979).

10. *The Times* (London), 7 August 1914.

11. E.g., in Archives Nationales 132 AQ 35.

12. Nouailhat, op. cit., 268–69.

13. Archives Nationales 132 AQ 34. From a French translation of Morgan's remarks (1915).

14. Talk with Guy de Rothschild.

15. Roger Peyrefitte, *Les Juifs* (Paris: Flammarion, 1965), 379. A fictional character utilized to air anti-Rothschild stories in Peyrefitte's polemical novel says that when Morgan proved reluctant to renew French credits after

the disastrous battles on the Aisne and at Chemin des Dames in 1917, the New York bank obtained a Rothschild guarantee at an abusive interest rate, at which time Premier Clemenceau summoned Edouard and Edmond to tell them that if the charge wasn't canceled in twenty-four hours he'd have the Rothschilds arrested and perhaps shot.

16. Rothschild Archive, London XI-101-102 (21 December 1914).

17. Rothschild Archive, London XI-111-96 (15 March 1915).

18. Rothschild Archive, London XI-101-104 (10, 17, 27 August 1915).

19. Alain de Rothschild, *Le Juif dans la cité* (privately printed, 1982).

20. Schama, op. cit., 188–89.

21. Henri de Rothschild, *La lignée*, 127–30.

22. Quoted in "Les Gros," *Crapouillot* (Paris), January 1952, 16.

23. *Journal Officiel: Sénat*, 26 January 1917 (transcript of 25 January session), 56–66.

24. Archives Nationales 132 AQ 818.

25. Talk with Guy de Rothschild.

26. Archives Nationales 132 AQ 67. In the mid-1920s the Rothschilds contributed to the defense committees of holders of Russian bonds, part of a campaign to obtain compensation for worthless prerevolution bonds, a campaign that continues up to our own day. Ibid.

27. Talk with Guy de Rothschild; Guy de Rothschild, *Contre bonne fortune . . .* , 78.

28. Baumier, *La galaxie*, op. cit., 26–27, 31, 61.

29. Anne Sabouret, *MM. Lazard Frères et Cie.* (Paris: Orban, 1987), 10–12, 25–35, 59–62.

30. Nadine de Rothschild, *La Baronne rentre à cinq heures* (Paris: Hachette-Livre de Poche, 1985), 64–65.

31. *Journal Officiel: Annales de la Chambre des députés,* session of 1 April 1925, 1875, 1877.

32. Abbé Mugnier, *Journal* (Paris: Mercure de France, 1985), 359.

33. Jean Castex, "La Troisième République dans les Hauts-Pyrénées," *Revue de Comminges-Pyrénées Centrales* 95 (1982), 609.

34. *L'Illustration*, 29 November 1919, 432.

CHAPTER 18. SAVING THE FRANC

1. For statistics on the value of the franc from the nineteenth century to the present, the author is grateful to the Direction des Statistiques Economiques of INSEE (Institut National de la Statistique et des Etudes Economiques), and particularly to Mme. Madeleine Dangu. Cf. Bouvier, *Les Rothschild*, 297.

2. Corti, op. cit., 2:448. Cf. Jean-Jacques Becker and Serge Berstein, *Victoire et frustrations (1914–1929)* (Paris: Seuil-Points, 1990), 155–230. Later a perfidious account of this episode spoke of the Vienna Rothschilds "speculating on French currency" as if the act had been prejudicial; no mention here of its purpose: to raise the value of the franc. *Crapouillot*, n.s. 16, January 1952, 16.

3. Jean-Noël Jeanneney, *Leçon d'histoire pour une gauche au pouvoir* (Paris: Seuil, 1977), 86–89, 122–25.

4. Bouvier, *Les Rothschild*, 284.

5. Raymond Philippe, *Le drame financier de 1924–1928* (Paris: Gallimard, 1931), 95–99.

6. Emile Moreau, *Souvenirs d'un gouverneur de la Banque de France (1926–1928)* (Paris: Génin, 1954), 10–13, 42, 57, 68–70. Cf. Bouvier, *Les Rothschild*, 299.

7. Ibid.; Sabouret, op. cit., 81–84.

8. Moreau, op. cit., 108, 116–18.

9. Ibid., 157.

10. Ibid., 239–40, 295, 308–13.

11. Ibid., 572–74, 582, 590–94.

12. Ibid., 602.

13. Françoise Giroud, in *L'Express*, quoted in Jean Baumier, *Ces banquiers qui nous gouvernent* (Paris: Plon, 1983), 34.

14. Sabouret, op. cit., 68–72; Jean-Noël Jeanneney, *L'argent caché* (Paris: Fayard, 1981), 48.

15. Marcus Eli Ravage, *Five Men of Frankfurt* (New York: Lincoln MacVeagh and Dial Press, 1929), 341.

16. Archives Nationales 132 AQ 78.

17. Archives Nationales 132 AQ 329.

18. Moreau, op. cit., 345, 400–2.

19. Archives Nationales 132 AQ 67.

20. Clermont-Tonnerre, op. cit., 215.

21. Talk with Bethsabée de Rothschild, Jerusalem.

22. Hyman, op. cit., 118.

23. Talk with Jacques Getten.

24. Schama, op. cit., 230–31, 242–43.

25. Ibid., 260–62. Text of the Tel Aviv speech in Druck, op. cit., 216–22.

26. Denise Levy-Astruc, *Histoire officielle, officieuse et marginale de l'Institut de Biologie Physico-Chimique* (Paris, 1970), 1–6; *L'Illustration*, 21 February 1931, 220–21.

27. Clermont-Tonnerre, op. cit., 216–17.

28. Ibid., 217–18.

29. Castex, op. cit., 609.

30. *Journal Officiel, Annales de la Chambre des députés,* session of 1 April 1925, 1869–1882.

31. *Journal Officiel, Annales de la Chambre des députés,* session of 2 July 1926, 360–376.

32. *Dictionnaire des parlementaires français,* vol. 8 (Paris: Presses Universitaires de France, 1977), 2900–2901.

Chapter 19. Before the Depression

1. Nadine de Rothschild, op. cit., 65.

2. *L'Illustration,* 27 January 1923, 90.

3. *L'Illustration,* 28 October 1922, 418.

4. Mugnier, op. cit., 539.

5. Colette, *Lettres à Hélène Picard* (Paris: Flammarion, 1958), 119–122; Colette, *Mes Cahiers* (Paris: Aux Armes de France, 1941), 137–45; Maurice Goudeket, *Près de Colette* (Paris: Flammarion, 1956), 122–29; cf. Herbert R. Lottman, *Colette* (Paris: Fayard, 1990), 288–89.

6. *L'Illustration,* 14 February 1931, 209.

7. Henri de Rothschild, *Tour du monde* (Paris: Hachette, 1936).

8. Henri de Rothschild, *La lignée,* 145–46.

9. Herbert R. Lottman, *Colette* (New York: Little, Brown, 1991), 214–15.

10. Raymond Lestonnat, "La victoire de 'Cupidon III,'" *L'Illustration,* 16 October 1926, 424.

11. Philippe de Rothschild, *Vivre la vigne* (Paris: Presses de la Cité, 1981), frontispiece.

12. Henri de Rothschild, *La lignée,* 144.

13. Ray, op. cit., 29.

14. Colin Parnell, "The Rothschilds and Wine," *Decanter* (London), December 1991, 38–39.

15. Henri de Rothschild, *La lignée,* 142–43.

16. Archives Nationales 132 AQ 4.

17. Henri de Rothschild, *La lignée,* 35.

18. Clermont-Tonnerre, op. cit., 208–9.

19. Guy de Rothschild, *Mon ombre siamoise* (Paris: Grasset, 1993), 18.

20. Guy de Rothschild, *Contre bonne fortune* . . . , 24–34, 43, 52–60, 63–66.

CHAPTER 20. GUY'S APPRENTICESHIP

1. Guy de Rothschild, *Contre bonne fortune* . . . , 71, 78–79.

2. Corti, op. cit., 2:449.

3. Guy de Rothschild, *Contre bonne fortune* . . . , 79–82.

4. Archives Nationales 131 AQ 5; talk with Guy de Rothschild.

5. Henri Dubief, *Le déclin de la IIIe République (1929–1938)* (Paris: Seuil-Points, 1976), 11–13, 19–22.

6. Frederic Morton, *The Rothschilds* (New York: Atheneum, 1962), 249.

7. Archives Nationales 132 AQ 5.

8. Archives Nationales 132 AQ 12; talk with Guy de Rothschild; cf. Chernow, op. cit., 328.

9. Guy de Rothschild, *Contre bonne fortune* . . . , 83–84. The Paris Rothschilds advanced funds in the form of a six-year loan at 4-percent interest to December 31, 1933, 5 percent thereafter; the lenders were Edmond (70 million francs), Edouard (35), Robert (15), Henri (10), James-Henri (3), and Philippe (3). Archives Nationales 132 AQ 7.

10. Archives Nationales 132 AQ 7.

11. Talk with Guy de Rothschild.

12. Yergin, op. cit., 266.

13. Guy de Rothschild, *Contre bonne fortune* . . . , 83–90; Bouvier, *Les Rothschild*, 313–14.

14. Kenneth Mouré, *Managing the Franc Poincaré* (New York: Cambridge University Press, 1991), 1–6, 66, 74–75.

15. Talk with Guy de Rothschild. Film information from Evan A. Lottman.

16. Janet Flanner, *Paris Was Yesterday (1925–1939)* (London: Angus & Robertson, 1973), 97.

17. Guy de Rothschild, *Contre bonne fortune* . . . , 98–99, 267.

18. Ibid., 99–104.

19. See, for example, Henry Coston, *Dictionnaire des dynasties bourgeoises et du monde des affaires* (Paris: Alain Moreau, 1975), 475.

20. Widor, op. cit., 450; Schama, op. cit., 264.

21. Talk with Elie de Rothschild. On Maurice's death, his one-sixth share went to his son Edmond, Jimmy's to a charitable trust now supervised by Jacob de Rothschild.

22. Talk with Guy de Rothschild.

23. *Juvenal* (Paris), 2 July 1938.

24. Archives Nationales 132 AQ 350.

Chapter 21. The Two Hundred Families

1. Guy de Rothschild, *Contre bonne fortune* . . . , op. cit., 107–8.

2. Georges Lefranc, *Histoire du Front populaire* (Paris: Payot, 1974), 20.

3. Herbert R. Lottman, *Pétain* (Paris: Le Seuil, 1984), 204–6.

4. Hyman, op. cit., 226–27.

5. *L'Humanité* (Paris), 23, 27 July 1935.

6. David H. Weinberg, *A Community on Trial: The Jews of Paris in the 1930s* (Chicago: University of Chicago Press, 1977), 80–81; Pierre Birnbaum, *Un mythe politique: La république juive* (Paris: Fayard, 1988), 94.

7. Sedillot, op. cit., 13.

8. Milési, op. cit., 10–11; cf. Guy de Rothschild, *Contre bonne fortune . . .* , 109.

9. Sedillot, op. cit., 19.

10. Augustin Hamon et X.Y.Z., *Les maîtres de la France* (Paris: Editions Sociales Internationales, 1936), 272–73, 278–79, 287.

11. Sedillot, op. cit., 110.

12. Archives Nationales 132 AQ 721.

13. Lefranc, op. cit., 369–71. Full nationalization of the Banque de France took place in 1945. By 1993 the wheel had come full circle, with a conservative cabinet under Edouard Balladur committed to reform of the bank statutes. And a left-wing Socialist, Jean-Pierre Chevènement, in his opposition to this "denationalization of monetary power" attacked an "invisible government of money." *Le Monde*, 18 May 1993.

14. Sedillot, op. cit., 116–17.

15. *Le Temps*, 1 July 1937.

16. Kimon A. Doukas, *The French Railroads and the State* (New York: Columbia University Press, 1945), 234–43; C. Aubry, *Législation des chemins de fer* (Paris: Eyrolles, 1949), 14–19.

17. Bouvier, *Les Rothschild*, 311–13. Written *before* the nationalization of the Rothschild bank in 1981.

18. *Le Populaire* (Paris), 1 September 1937.

19. Archives Nationales 132 AQ 12; Guy de Rothschild, *Contre bonne fortune . . .* , 110.

CHAPTER 22. ROTHSCHILDS AT WAR

1. Jacques Adler, *The Jews of Paris and the Final Solution* (New York: Oxford University Press, 1987), 55.

2. Hyman, op. cit., 305–6. David H. Weinberg, in his book *Les Juifs à Paris de 1933 à 1939* (Paris: Calmann-Lévy, 1974), 101–2, says the statement as contained in Robert de Rothschild's draft was, "If they aren't happy, let them go. They are guests we receive with pleasure but they mustn't break the dishes." From Archives of the ACIP, B 132, 1935.

3. Weinberg, *Community*, 95, note 15; Maurice Rajfus, *Sois juif et tais-toi* (Paris: Etudes et Documentation Internationales, 1981), 30–31.

4. Simon Epstein, "Robert de Rothschild: Un dirigeant juif des temps difficiles (1933–1939)," unpublished ms., courtesy of Eric de Rothschild.

5. Archives Nationales 132 AQ 721.

6. Scenario, "Les enfants de la Guette" (Werner Matzdorff), with other documents, courtesy of Guy de Rothschild.

7. Flanner, op. cit., 221.

8. *L'Action Française*, 23, 24, 25, 26 January 1939.

9. Guy de Rothschild, *Contre bonne fortune* . . . , 113–14.

10. Archives Nationales 132 AQ 721.

11. Alain de Rothschild, *Le Juif dans la cité*, 285–86.

12. Ibid., 286.

13. Talk with Nicole Stéphane (née Rothschild); cf. Henri de Rothschild, *La lignée*, 132–33.

14. Philippe de Rothschild, *Vivre la vigne*, 64–65.

15. Guy de Rothschild, *Contre bonne fortune* . . . , 113–27.

16. Archives Nationales 132 AQ 719–21, 4677.

17. Talk with Guy de Rothschild.

18. "Les Rothschild," *Réalités* (Paris), March 1952, 110. The Royal Dutch shares were worth 1,534,000 Dutch guilders in 1940.

19. *New York Times*, 11 July 1940.

CHAPTER 23. VICHY

1. Lottman, *Pétain*, 182.

2. Text from *Le pillage par les Allemands des oeuvres d'art et des bibliothèques appartenant à des Juifs en France* (Paris: Editions du Centre, 1947), 259–260; cf. Joseph Billig, *Le Commissariat Général aux Questions Juives (1941–1944)*, vol. 1 (Paris: Editions du Centre, 1960), 206–7.

3. *Le Matin* (Paris), 25 July 1940.

4. *Le Matin*, 2 August 1940; cf. *New York Times*, 1 August 1940; Nadine de Rothschild, op. cit., 63.

5. *Le Matin*, 26 September 1940; *New York Times*, 26 September 1940. The *Times* account adds that Toulouse newspapers had reported the discovery in southern France of Rothschild securities and other certificates; one paper estimated their value at 350 million gold francs.

6. *Le Matin*, 10 September 1940; *New York Times*, 14 September 1940, 4.

7. Centre de Documentation Juive Contemporaine, Paris (henceforth referred to as CDJC), CLIV-54.

8. Talk with Guy de Rothschild.

9. Guy de Rothschild, *Contre bonne fortune* . . . , 133.

10. Henri de Rothschild, *La lignée*, 142–43.

11. Talk with Nicole Stéphane (née Rothschild).

12. Guy de Rothschild, *Contre bonne fortune* . . . , 134–35.

13. *New York Times*, 9 October 1940, 27; Guy de Rothschild, *Contre bonne fortune* . . . , 131.

14. Talk with Guy de Rothschild.

15. Guy de Rothschild, *Contre bonne fortune* . . . , 134; talk with Guy de Rothschild.

16. Claire Andrieu, *La banque sous l'occupation* (Paris: Presses de la Fondation Nationale des Sciences Politiques), 269–79.

17. 11 September 1940.

18. *Au Pilori* (Paris), 13 September 1940.

19. *Au Pilori*, 18 October 1940.

20. *Au Pilori*, 8 November 1940.

21. Guy de Rothschild, *Contre bonne fortune* . . . , 140–45; talk with Guy de Rothschild.

22. *New York Times*, 29 September 1940, 16.

23. Ray, op. cit., 61–63.

24. Christine Clerc, *Fondations Rothschild: 130 ans de solidarité* (Paris: Beba, 1982), 33.

25. Published in Rose Valland, *Le front de l'art: Défense des collections françaises (1939–1945)* (Paris: Plon, 1961), 237; cf. *Le pillage*, 84; Billig, op. cit., 1:206.

26. Text in *Le pillage*, 261–62.

27. CDJC LXXIX-9.

28. Talk with Elie de Rothschild.

29. *Annuaire général des finances 1942* (Paris: Berger-Levrault, 1942), 276; ibid., *1954* (Paris: Imprimerie Nationale, 1954), 687, 1000; talk with Guy de Rothschild.

Chapter 24. Goering

1. Talk with Guy de Rothschild.

2. Documents in Valland, op. cit., 235–37.

3. Ibid., 49.

4. *Le Figaro* (Clermont-Ferrand), 27 September 1940.

5. Valland, op. cit., 51–53.

6. *Le pillage*, 40–43.

7. CDJC CXLV-574.

8. *Le pillage*, 84. See chapter 23.

9. Ibid., 49–50.

10. CDJC XXI-45.

11. Photographic reproductions in *Le pillage*.

12. Valland, op. cit., 57–60.

13. *Le pillage*, 86.

14. Ibid., 85.

15. Talk with Guy de Rothschild.

16. *Le pillage,* 106–7.

17. Talk with Guy de Rothschild; cf. Guy de Rothschild, *Contre bonne fortune . . . ,* 150–51.

18. Talk with Bethsabée (Batsheva) de Rothschild.

19. *New York Times,* 21 June 1940; Georges Bernstein Gruber and Gilbert Maurin, *Bernstein le magnifique* (Paris: Lattès, 1988), 381.

20. *New York Times,* 9 July 1940, 23.

21. *New York Times,* 2 August 1940, 8.

22. Nadine de Rothschild, op. cit., 63–64.

23. Alain de Rothschild, *Le Juif dans la cité*; Ray, op. cit., 66.

24. Talk with Elie de Rothschild.

25. Talk with Nicole Stéphane (née Rothschild); Henri de Rothschild, *La lignée,* 42–43.

26. Philippe de Rothschild, *Vivre la vigne,* 61–65; ———, *Le pressoir perdu,* 41–57; Henri de Rothschild, *La lignée,* 147; *New York Times,* 12, 23 September 1940, 28 March 1941, 21 April 1941, 7 June 1941. Writing from his Lisbon exile in 1943, Henri made sure not to say where his son had gone; he has him "devoting himself to literature." If none of the French Rothschilds died in the camps, most of the family of Guy's mother (née Halphen) did. Guy de Rothschild, *Contre bonne fortune . . . ,* 134.

Chapter 25. France Without Rothschilds

1. Archives Nationales AJ 38 601.

2. *Au Pilori,* 27 March, 24 April 1941.

3. *Au Pilori,* 6 November 1941.

4. *Au Pilori,* 2 October 1941.

5. *Au Pilori,* 30 October 1941.

6. See chapter 24.

7. Henri-Robert Petit, *Rothschild: Roi d'Israël et les Américains* (Paris: Nouvelles Etudes Françaises, 1941), 46.

8. Valland, op. cit., 68–75.

9. *Le pillage*, 108–9.

10. Archives Nationales AJ 38 2448.

11. Ibid.

12. Archives Nationales AJ 38 2432.

13. Archives Nationales AJ 38 2461.

14. *Le pillage*, 196–97.

15. CDJC XIXa-35, LXXVI-7.

16. *Le pillage*, 94–98 (Note of 3 November 1941).

17. Archives Nationales AJ 38 2727.

18. CDJC CXVI-9, CXIV-79; Archives Nationales AJ 38 2727.

19. Archives Nationales AJ 38 187.

20. Guy de Rothschild, *Contre bonne fortune . . .*, 140–45; talk with Guy de Rothschild. Pucheu was the first Vichy cabinet officer to be tried for treason; he was convicted and shot in March 1944.

21. *New York Times*, 28 October 1941.

22. Guy de Rothschild, *Contre bonne fortune . . .*, 149.

23. Jean Peron, *Les Rothschild* (Paris: Editions Nouvelles, 1942), 125.

24. For example, CDJC CXVI-9.

25. CDJC CXVI-9.

26. Archives Nationales AJ 38 187, 601.

27. Alexis Carrel, *L'homme, cet inconnu* (Paris: Grasset, 1935), 359–67.

28. *Cahiers de la Fondation Française pour l'Etude des Problèmes Humaines*, vol. 1 (Paris: Presses Universitaires de France, 1943), 21.

29. On Carrel and the Germans: Dr. Robert Soupault, *Alexis Carrel* (Paris: Plon, 1951), 228–30.

30. Archives Nationales AJ 38 2764.

31. Ibid.; Levy-Astruc, op. cit., 69–87.

32. G. Arnulf, "Documents inédits sur le comportement du Dr. Alexis Carrel en France pendant la guerre 1939–1945," Communication, 27 April 1985 session, Société Française d'Histoire de la Médecine, courtesy of David Hamilton, University of Glasgow.

CHAPTER 26. LIQUIDATING THE LIQUIDATORS

1. Guy de Rothschild, *Contre bonne fortune* . . . , 151–90; ———, *Mon ombre siamoise*, 26.

2. *New York Times*, 19, 28 March, 4 April 1943.

3. Bourdrel, op. cit., 482–84.

4. *New York Times*, 10 November 1944.

5. Andrieu, op. cit., 268.

6. Guy de Rothschild, *Contre bonne fortune* . . . , 191–92.

7. *New York Times*, 11 December 1944.

8. Philippe de Rothschild, *Vivre la vigne*, 66–71; Ray, op. cit., 56.

9. Talk with Guy de Rothschild. In a final irony for the Vienna family, Austria's Soviet occupation authorities proceeded to confiscate remaining Rothschild properties as Nazi; it became necessary to prove that they had belonged to the family before Hitler's annexation of that country. (By then Louis de Rothschild was a stateless person, Eugène—deprived of French nationality by Vichy—had become an American citizen, and Alphonse had died.) Archives Nationales 132 AQ 12.

10. Valland, op. cit., 212–17; James J. Rorimer and Gilbert Rabin, *Survival: The Salvage and Protection of Art in War* (New York: Abelard, 1950), ix–xi.

11. Rorimer and Rabin, op. cit., 185–268; Valland, op. cit., 220–29; *Le Monde* (Paris), 1 November 1945.

12. Talk with Guy de Rothschild. In 1947 the French army in occupied Germany published a series of catalogs of stolen art, books, and archives not yet recovered. The volume on painting, tapestries, and sculpture alone came to 491 pages, not counting illustrations of the most important works. The Rothschilds are represented by Edouard, Maurice, Alexandrine, Henri, and Robert. Commandant en Chef Française en Allemagne, *Répertoire des biens spoliés en France durant la guerre (1939–1945)*, vol. 2 (Berlin, 1947).

13. Talk with Marie-Noëlle André.

14. Ministère de l'Education Nationale, *Les chefs-d'oeuvre des collections privées françaises retrouvés en Allemagne par la Commission de Récupération Ar-*

tistique et les services alliés (Orangerie des Tuileries, June–August 1946), courtesy of Marie-Noëlle André.

CHAPTER 27. REVIVAL

1. Talk with Nicole Stéphane (née Rothschild).

2. Talk with Marie-Noëlle André.

3. Bouvier, *Les Rothschild,* 314–15; *Les Documents Politiques,* February 1968, 19–21.

4. Guy de Rothschild, press conference (1967) in Druon, 50–52.

5. Talk with Guy de Rothschild.

6. Bouvier, *Les Rothschild,* 315.

7. Rothschild, *Contre bonne fortune* . . . , 195–97.

8. Talk with Guy de Rothschild; Bouvier, *Les Rothschild,* 315. Guy's share amounted to half the total legacy, the balance to go to his sister Jacqueline (married and resident in the United States) and Bethsabée (by then married to Donald Bloomingdale and also resident in the United States). Guy received the totality of Edouard's share of the bank partnership as part of his inheritance. *Les Documents Politiques,* February 1968, 22–23.

9. Talk with Nicole Stéphane (née Rothschild).

10. *Le Monde,* 21 December 1949.

11. *Le Monde,* 24–25 July 1949.

12. Guy de Rothschild, *Contre bonne fortune* . . . , 347–52; cf. Georges Levitte, "A Changing Community," in *Aspects of French Jewry* (London: Vallentine, Mitchell, 1969), 14–16.

13. Guy de Rothschild, *Contre bonne fortune* . . . , 105–6, 269–74.

14. "Les Gros," *Crapouillot,* January 1952, 19.

15. For example, *Le Monde,* 22 June 1951.

16. Guy de Rothschild, *Contre bonne fortune* . . . , 276–77.

17. Alain de Rothschild, *Le Juif,* 285–86; talk with Elie de Rothschild.

18. Talk with Elie de Rothschild; Ray, op. cit., 45–46.

19. Philippe de Rothschild, *Vivre la vigne,* 72.

20. Talk with Jacques Getten.

21. Guy de Rothschild, *Contre bonne fortune* . . . , 198–205.

22. Quoted in Bouvier, *Les Rothschild,* 320.

23. Ibid., 322–24.

24. Guy de Rothschild, *Contre bonne fortune* . . . , 203–7.

25. Nadine de Rothschild, op. cit., 73–74.

26. Pierre Viansson-Ponté, *Les Gaullistes* (Paris: Le Seuil, 1963), 166–70.

27. "Le Petit Pompidou illustré," *Crapouillot,* October–November 1969, n.s. 9, 42–43.

28. Guy de Rothschild, *Contre bonne fortune* . . . , 310.

29. Guy de Rothschild, *Mon ombre siamoise,* 178, 182, 184.

30. Guy de Rothschild, *Contre bonne fortune* . . . , 313.

Chapter 28. The Banks Rothschild

1. *Crapouillot,* January 1952, 8–18.

2. Henry Coston, *Les financiers qui mènent le monde* (Paris: La Librairie Française, 1955), 218.

3. Henry Coston, *La haute banque et les trusts* (Paris: La Librairie Française, 1958), 10, 12.

4. Talk with Jacques Getten.

5. Guy de Rothschild, *Contre bonne fortune* . . . , 231–32.

6. Jean-Jacques Laurendon, in Bouvier, *Les Rothschild,* 328–29.

7. Jacques Amalric in *Le Monde,* 12 November 1965, quoted in Bouvier, *Les Rothschild,* 330–31.

8. Schama, op. cit., 322.

9. Nadine de Rothschild, op. cit., 70.

10. Talk with Guy de Rothschild; Nadine de Rothschild, op. cit., 74.

11. Nadine de Rothschild, op. cit., 75, 77.

12. Jean Baumier, *Ces banquiers qui nous gouvernent* (Paris: Plon, 1983), 30–31;———, *Les grandes affaires françaises* (Paris: Julliard, 1967), 57.

13. Nadine de Rothschild, op. cit., 76.

14. Ibid., 7, 9–12, 17–32, 49–52, 55–61, 80–88, 107–18.

15. *Le Monde*, 9–10, 22 July, 27 September 1967; cf. Nadine de Rothschild, op. cit., 144–45, 187.

16. Guy de Rothschild, *Contre bonne fortune* . . . , 233.

17. Ibid., 233–34.

18. Quoted in Birnbaum, *Le Peuple*, 87–88.

19. René Andrieu in *L'Humanité*, 18 June 1969.

20. Guy de Rothschild, *Contre bonne fortune* . . . , 233–36, 245, 349.

21. Talk with Guy de Rothschild; Guy de Rothschild, *Contre bonne fortune* . . . , 251–65.

22. Talk with Guy de Rothschild.

23. Jean-Jacques Laurendon in Bouvier, *Les Rothschild*, 317–20.

24. (Paris: La Librairie Française, 1960), 163–69.

25. Peyrefitte, op. cit. The Rothschild family—Edmond joining Guy and his sister Bethsabée—went to court after publication to have the book seized; eventually the author agreed to remove passages concerning the private life of certain family members, and the complaint was withdrawn. *Le Monde*, 6, 8, 9 July, 10 September, 25 December 1965; cf. Pierre Viansson-Ponté, "Pour la plus grande joie des antisémites: 'Les Juifs' de Roger Peyrefitte," *Le Monde*, 16 July 1965.

CHAPTER 29. THE BIG CHANGE

1. *Le Monde*, 27 April 1967; extracts of press conference in Druon, 39–59; Guy de Rothschild, *Contre bonne fortune* . . . , 212.

2. Talk with Guy de Rothschild.

3. Ibid.

4. Compagnie du Nord, *Assemblées générales, Exercice 1968* (Paris, 1969).

5. Compagnie du Nord, *Assemblées générales, Exercice 1967* (Paris, 1968).

6. "La leçon de la crise de mai," interview with Guy de Rothschild by Jacques Baron, *Entreprise* (Paris), 12 October 1968, 4–15.

7. Banque Rothschild, *Assemblée générale ordinaire du 21 avril 1970, Exercice 1969* (Paris, 1970).

8. Rothschild-Expansion, *Assemblée générale ordinaire*, 27 May 1971, 23 March 1972.

9. Banque Rothschild, *Assemblée générale ordinaire*, 25 April 1972.

10. From *Lui*, quoted in Baumier, *Ces banquiers*, 27.

11. Guy de Rothschild, *Contre bonne fortune* . . . , op. cit., 258–65; Baumier, *Ces banquiers*, 28–30; talk with Guy de Rothschild.

12. Baumier, *Ces banquiers*, 28.

13. *Le Nouveau Journal* (Paris), 23 May 1973.

14. *L'Aurore* (Paris), 3 May 1974; *Les Echos* (Paris), 31 January 1975.

15. *Les Echos*, 7 February 1975, 15 March 1978.

16. *Le Journal des Finances* (Paris), 11 May 1978; *Le Vie Française* (Paris), 13 May 1978.

17. Paul Lewis, in *The New York Times*, as published in *International Herald-Tribune* (Paris), 15 November 1978.

18. Guy de Rothschild, *Contre bonne fortune* . . . , 215–16.

19. Baumier, *Ces banquiers*, 29.

20. Guy de Rothschild, *Mon ombre siamoise*, 33.

21. Alain de Rothschild, *Le Juif*, 291–93.

22. Talks with Guy de Rothschild, Mireille Munch, curator of Ferrières; Guy de Rothschild, *Contre bonne fortune* . . . , 315–16, 330–31.

23. Guy de Rothschild, *Contre bonne fortune* . . . , 314.

24. Ibid., 327–28.

25. Nadine de Rothschild, op. cit., 135–36, 140.

26. Martine Leventer, "Les vignes des seigneurs," *Le Point* (Paris), 22 December 1986, 70–71; Nadine de Rothschild, op. cit., 127–28.

27. Ray, op. cit., 107–8.

28. Promotional flyers, "Opus One," "1988 Opus One"; James Conaway, *Napa* (Boston: Houghton Mifflin, 1990), 230–35, 247–49.

Chapter 30. Mitterrand's Folly

1. *Le Monde*, 29 June 1972.

2. From *Ici et maintenant*, quoted in Sedillot, op. cit., 132.

3. Didier Linotte, "Les nationalisations de 1982," *Revue du Droit Public et de la Science Politique en France et à l'étranger* 2 (1982), 435.

4. Guy de Rothschild, *Mon ombre siamoise*, 30.

5. Guy de Rothschild, *Contre bonne fortune . . .* , 213.

6. Banque Rothschild, *Assemblée générale ordinaire du 27 mai 1981.* In addition to David as chairman of the bank's directorate, Nathaniel remained vice-chairman; Elie was chairman and Alain vice-chairman of the board of supervisors, whose members included Guy, Eric, and Evelyn of London. In addition to its branch offices in France, the bank listed representation offices in Spain, Greece, Japan, Mexico, and Venezuela, and among affiliates N. M. Rothschild of London, Rothschild Bank AG in Zurich, and New Court Securities Corporation in New York.

7. *Les Echos* (Paris), 21 July 1981.

8. *L'Humanité*, 10 July 1981.

9. *L'Humanité*, 10, 11 July 1981.

10. On the behind-the-scenes maneuvering, see Milési, op. cit., 201–2. Milési identifies Jacques Attali, special adviser to President Mitterrand, as the man who saved Lazard, at least in part because it was a "service" company and had "an international dimension." Cf. Sabouret, op. cit., 233–39. Attali had already told David de Rothschild that the government could do nothing to save his bank. Talk with Guy de Rothschild.

11. *L'Express* (Paris), 16 October 1981, 89–90; Linotte, op. cit., 443.

12. *Le Monde*, 14 October 1981.

13. *L'Humanité*, 20 October 1981.

14. *The Times* (London), 21 October 1981.

15. Linotte, op. cit., 439–40, 449–50.

16. See chapter 1.

17. Talk with Jacques Getten.

18. Guy de Rothschild, *Mon ombre siamoise*, 31–32.

19. Talk with David de Rothschild.

20. *Financial Times* (London), 18 December 1985.

21. Quoted in Milési, op. cit., 46.

22. Talk with Guy de Rothschild.

23. Talks with Guy de Rothschild and David de Rothschild; Guy de Rothschild, *Contre bonne fortune* . . . , 213. Guy de Rothschild said (in a talk with the author) that if the government had refused to remove the name Rothschild from the bank's corporate logo, the family would have taken the case to the International Court of Justice at The Hague. In 1983 the government-owned Européenne de Banque, as it was then known, entered into a working agreement with another bank nationalized in 1981, Crédit Commercial de France (CCF), leading to joint ownership of the two banks by a government-controlled holding company. Then in 1987, under a conservative government, CCF was *de*nationalized—putting the ghost of the old Rothschild bank back into the private sector. *Le Monde*, 28 April, 20 May 1987. Guy de Rothschild noted (in a talk with the author) that the sums paid out to the dispossessed Rothschilds, in addition to new investment required by Européenne de Banque, were certainly earned back by the government when CCF later sold Européenne to Barclays, Britain's largest banking group—an appropriate landlord for the historic Rue Laffitte site. Barclays paid 1.5 billion francs for the "ex-banque Rothschild" and its sixteen agencies in France, plus a sales network for the Laffitte Investment Fund. *Le Monde*, 13, 30–31 December 1990.

24. Talk with Guy de Rothschild.

25. Talk with David de Rothschild.

26. Talk with Guy de Rothschild.

27. Guy de Rothschild, *Contre bonne fortune* . . . , 215–16.

28. Talk with David de Rothschild.

29. Talk with Jacques Getten.

30. *Le Matin* (Paris), 12 April 1983.

31. Guy de Rothschild, *Mon ombre siamoise*, 20, 34; ———, *Contre bonne fortune* . . . , 369.

32. William H. Meyers, "Megadealer for the Rothschilds," *New York Times*, 4 December 1988, sec. 4.

33. Erik Ipsen, "The High Roller at Rothschild Inc.," *Institutional Investor* (New York), March 1986, 133.

34. *Paris-Match*, 4 February 1983, 34–35.

35. Milési, op. cit., 45–46; talk with David de Rothschild.

36. Talk with Eric de Rothschild; Guy de Rothschild, *Contre bonne fortune . . .*, 214.

37. *New York Times*, 14 November 1984.

38. Talk with Elie de Rothschild. Baron Elie is a resident of the United Kingdom; his Paris house now belongs to Nathaniel (whose own son Raphaël was born in 1976).

CHAPTER 31. EDMOND AND THE OTHERS

1. Jean Boissonnat, "Un Rothschild dans la France socialiste," *L'Expansion* (Paris), 4 June 1982, 91–95. On Armainvilliers: Roy and Rivaud, op. cit., 34–35.

2. Talk with Marie-Noëlle André.

3. From Michel Bauer and Bénédicte Bertin-Mourot, *Les 200: Comment devient-on un grand patron* (Paris: Le Seuil, 1987), 99.

4. Boissonnat, op. cit., 92.

5. *Magazine Hebdo* (Paris), 21 December 1984.

6. *Annuaire des sociétés et des administrateurs* 2 (Paris: Dafsa, 1989), 888–89.

7. Catalog, France Loisirs (Paris), July–September 1992, advertising Nadine de Rothschild, *Le bonheur de séduire, l'art de réussir*.

8. Nadine de Rothschild, op. cit., 218–19.

9. Talk with David de Rothschild.

10. *Paris-Match*, 4 February 1983, 34–35.

11. *Le Matin* (Paris), 12 April 1983.

12. Paul Lewis in *The New York Times*, reprinted in *International Herald-Tribune* (Paris), 6 March 1986.

13. *Le Monde*, 24–25 June 1984.

14. Milési, op. cit., 47.

15. *L'Humanité,* 23 June 1984.

16. Illustrated, for example, in *Le Quotidien de Paris,* 22 October 1986.

17. Lewis, op. cit.; cf. *Financial Times,* 18 December 1985.

18. *Le Figaro* (Paris), 10 May 1986, 126–27.

19. *Le Quotidien de Paris,* 22 October 1986; Baumier, *La galaxie,* 120–24; talk with David de Rothschild. The Rothschilds were also named as advisers on the 2.2-billion-franc privatization of the Matra industrial group. From Jean-Claude Meyer.

20. Christine Baudelaire and Yves Guihannec, "Le retour des Rothschild," *Le Point* (Paris), 22 December 1986, 68.

21. Ray, op. cit., 67.

22. Jean-Michel Gourévitch, "Sous le signe de la Torah," *Le Point,* 22 December 1986, 69–70.

23. Talk with Eric de Rothschild.

24. Talk with Eric de Rothschild.

25. Ray, op. cit., 101–3.

26. *New York Times,* 10, 22 February 1989; cf. Norman S. Roby and Charles E. Olken, *The New Connoisseurs' Handbook of California Wines* (New York: Knopf, 1991), 143.

27. Promotional literature, courtesy Baron Philippe de Rothschild, S.A., New York.

28. Talk with Guy de Rothschild.

29. *Connaissance des Arts* (Paris), September 1983, 74–79.

30. Clerc, op. cit., 39.

31. Gourévitch, op. cit., 69; Clerc, op. cit., 40; talk with David de Rothschild.

32. Clerc, op. cit., 35–38.

33. Biographical sketch, courtesy of Batsheva de Rothschild; talk with Batsheva de Rothschild, Israel.

CHAPTER 32. MODERN TIMES

1. Sabouret, op. cit., 134–35; *Le Monde,* 22 June 1993; cf. Milési, op. cit., 195–99.

2. Sabouret, op. cit., 6–7.

3. Talk with David de Rothschild.

4. Meyers, op. cit.; *New York Times*, 3, 4 November 1988.

5. Sabouret, op. cit., 134.

6. Talks with Guy, David, and Edouard de Rothschild, and Jean-Claude Meyer.

7. *La Vie Française* (Paris), 20 April 1987; *L'Evénement du Jeudi* (Paris), 19 December 1991; *Le Figaro*, 29 April 1991.

8. Talks with Jean-Claude Meyer and Edouard de Rothschild; *Le Monde*, 1 July 1994.

9. Talk with Edouard de Rothschild.

10. Rothschild & Cie. Banque, *Exercice 1991;* talk with David de Rothschild. The family holds just over 50 percent of voting rights in P.O.

11. Talk with Eric de Rothschild; Paris Orléans, *Assemblée générale mixte du 22 juin 1992;* S.H.M., *Assemblée générale ordinaire du 17 juin 1992;* Francarep, *Assemblée générale ordinaire du 15 juin 1992.*

12. *Annuaire des administrateurs, 1990* (Paris: Dafsa, 1990), 934–35.

13. *New York Times*, 23, 26 June, 17 August 1990; *Le Figaro*, 29 April 1991; Milési, op. cit., 49. The deal subsequently drew a second round of press reports when a former manager of Rothschild Bank AG in Zurich, associated with Rothschild Paris in the Suchard takeover, admitted involvement in the purchase of Suchard shares before the takeover was announced. *The Wall Street Journal*, 4 January 1991. The Swiss Rothschild bank, a joint venture between the London and Paris families, has been plagued by management difficulties. One of its senior executives, discharged by Rothschild for allegedly taking kickbacks from clients to whom he made ill-advised loans, counterattacked with charges that the Rothschilds helped Italian clients evade taxes and restrictions on exporting capital. N. M. Rothschild's Sir Evelyn branded the former manager's accusations "blackmail" and undertook a thorough housecleaning of the bank's management. "Sloppy banking isn't something normally associated with the name Rothschild,"

notes a *Wall Street Journal* reporter. *Wall Street Journal*, 2 January 1991, 3 November, 11 December 1992, 19 January 1993.

14. From Jean-Claude Meyer.

15. Rothschild & Cie. Banque, *Exercice 1991*.

16. *Wall Street Journal*, 1 December 1992.

17. *Wall Street Journal*, 22 May 1992; *Le Monde*, 7–8 August 1994.

18. Talk with David de Rothschild.

19. Matthew Schifrin, "Dr. Feelgood," *Forbes*, 4 March 1991, 78, 83.

20. *Investment Dealers Digest*, 7 September 1992, 14–18.

21. *Wall Street Journal*, 22 November 1991.

22. Pirie became co-chairman of Rothschild North America, sharing that title with David de Rothschild, while remaining CEO of Rothschild North America and chairman of Rothschild Inc. Sir Evelyn de Rothschild, until then co-chairman of Rothschild North America, became chairman of the executive committee. *New York Times*, 9 June 1992; *Wall Street Journal*, 9 June 1992.

23. Talks with David and Edouard de Rothschild.

24. Press release, Rothschild Inc., 24 May 1993.

25. Talk with Gerald Goldsmith.

26. *New York Times*, 13 January 1993.

27. *Wall Street Journal*, 9 September 1992.

28. *Wall Street Journal*, 2 February 1993.

29. *New York Times*, 7 April 1993.

CHAPTER 33. ROTHSCHILD LEGENDS

1. Stephanie Losee, "The Billionaires," *Fortune International*, 7 September 1992, 102.

2. Milési, op. cit., 324.

3. François Renard, "Le baron Edmond: un monument," *Le Monde*, 2 June 1992.

4. La Compagnie Financière Edmond de Rothschild Banque, *Rapport Annuel 1990* (Paris), 4, 14. In April 1993 Esambert left the Compagnie Financière,

soon to become president of the strategy committee of Albatros Investisse-ment, the holding company that controls the Vincent Bolloré group (Alba-tros's other owners include Kohlberg Kravis and Roberts in New York, Britain's Rothmans, and ... Edmond de Rothschild). *Le Figaro,* 10 July 1993.

5. The 3.9 million represented a sharp decline from the previous year's 41 million, attributed to difficulties encountered with certain investments in a recessionary economy and an unstable exchange market. La Compagnie Financière Edmond de Rothschild Banque, *Annual Report 1992.*

6. La Compagnie Financière Edmond de Rothschild Banque, *Rapport Annuel 1991, 1992.*

7. Talks with David, Eric, and Edouard de Rothschild.

8. Isabelle Gounin, in *La Tribune Desfossés* (Paris), 20 July 1993. On Ben-jamin: Nadine de Rothschild, op. cit., 215–16, 219.

9. Parnell, op. cit., 40–42; cf. Yves le Cannellier, "Château Clarke, ou la passion du vin," Savour Club (catalog), October 1992, September 1993.

10. *Times Literary Supplement* (London), 15 November 1991.

11. E.g., "Les bordeaux les plus chers du monde," in *Le Figaro* (Paris), 10 October 1992.

12. Ray, op. cit., 92.

13. Talk with Elie de Rothschild; Guy de Rothschild, *Mon ombre siamoise,* 40.

14. Talk with Eric de Rothschild. His responsibilities include supervision of the memorial to Jewish victims of Hitler Germany in Paris's old Jewish quarter, and the contiguous Centre de Documentation Juive Contempo-raine.

15. Talk with Christophe Salin, managing director, Domaines Barons de Roth-schild.

16. Muhlstein, op. cit., 238.

17. Suzy Menkes, "Marie-Hélène de Rothschild: Society's Star Choreographer," *International Herald-Tribune* (Paris), 16 June 1992.

18. *Le Figaro,* 10 October 1992.

19. Hélène de Turckheim, "Guy de Rothschild," *Madame Figaro* (Paris), 15 May 1993.

20. *Le Pays d'Auge* (Lisieux), 25, 28 August 1992.

21. Talk with David de Rothschild.

22. Talk with Eric de Rothschild.

23. Talk with Edouard de Rothschild.

24. *Le Figaro*, 10 August 1992.

25. *Le Figaro*, 10 August, 12 September 1992.

CHAPTER 34. KING DAVID

1. Guy de Rothschild, *Mon ombre siamoise*, 161–62.

2. Talk with David de Rothschild.

3. Talk with Jacques Getten.

4. Talk with David de Rothschild.

5. *Financial Times*, 30 July 1993.

6. *Rothschilds*, published by N. M. Rothschild (1992?).

7. Talk with David de Rothschild.

8. From David de Rothschild and Jean-Claude Meyer.

9. Talk with Jean-Claude Meyer.

10. Gilles le Gendre, "De Paris à Londres," *L'Expansion*, 2 April 1992, 46–49.

11. Ibid.

12. Marc Roche, in *Le Monde*, 2 June 1992.

13. Nicholas Bray, "Britain's Rothschild Seeks to Rebuild Banking Links with French Family," *Wall Street Journal*, 10 August 1992.

14. Talks with David and Eric de Rothschild.

15. Roche, *Le Monde*, 2 June 1992. The journalist describes the rivalry existing between Sir Evelyn and his cousin Jacob, the present Lord Rothschild, who runs his own highly successful financial services group. In 1980 Evelyn moved into Jacob's preordained position as chairman of NMR—doing it with the help of Jacob's own father, Victor (Lord Rothschild), a man who preferred scientific research to banking. Amschel is Victor's second son and Jacob's half-brother.

16. François Renard in *Le Monde*, 2 June 1992.

17. Bray, op. cit.

18. Roche, op. cit.

19. Jeanne Villeneuve, "Les nouvelles 200 familles," *L'Evénement du Jeudi* (Paris), 19 December 1991, 66.

20. Milési, op. cit., 23. Nearly one-third of the two hundred leading French companies were still in family hands in 1988. Ibid., 57.

21. *Le Monde*, 25 August 1992; talk with Guy de Rothschild.

22. Quentin Hardy, "Financial Markets Turmoil in Japan Leads to 'Jewish Conspiracy' Article," *Wall Street Journal*, 3 July 1992.

23. *Manhattan Jewish Sentinel* (New York), 11 August 1993.

24. *New York Times*, 1 March 1994.

25. Told by Dominique le Guilledoux, in *Le Monde*, 29–30 August 1993.

INDEX

Abetz, Otto, 229
Academy of Fine Arts, 119, 134, 163, 333
Academy of Science, 249
Action Française, 200, 236
Action Française, L', 164, 212
Aldobrandini, Prince, 307
Aleichem, Shalom, 341
Alexander II, Czar, 81
Alexander III, Czar, 92, 99–101
ʿAli, Muhammad, 27, 28
Allégret, Marc, 180
Allenby, Gen. Edmund, 161
American Friends Service Committee, 212
Amsterdam Overseas Corporation, 285
André, Marie-Noëlle, 259
André, Pierre, 259
Angoulême, Duc d', 18
anti-Semitism, 72, 84–92, 104–14, 119–20, 128–29, 135–36, 140, 176–77, 195, 200, 209–11, 252, 281–82, 340
    in German-occupied Paris, 239–42
    from left, 31, 87
    Popular Front and, 203
    post–World War II, 273–74
    in Russia, 81–82, 92, 97–101, 141
    during World War I, 161
    See also Dreyfus affair
Anti-sémitique, L', 87

Apponyi, Rudolf, 26, 51
Arago, François, 37
Argent, L' (Zola), 87, 122–23
Arliss, George, 195
art collections, 79, 91, 94–95, 119, 147, 148, 163, 277, 292, 305
    donated to museums, 312
    Nazi plundering of, 228–34, 241–43
    recovery of, 256–60
Asiatic Petroleum Company, 142
Aspects de la France, 280
Association Consistoriale des Israélites de Paris (ACIP). *See* Jews, Consistory of
Astronomer (Vermeer), 233, 259, 292, 312
Aumont, Jean-Pierre, 180
Au Pilori, 223, 239–41
Aurore, 123

Babinet, Georges, 335
Bagatelles pour un massacre (Céline), 203
Balladur, Edouard, 309, 332
Balzac, Honoré de, 21, 26, 30, 34–37, 39–40, 48
Banca Privata, 306
Banca Solari e Blum, 327
Banca Tiburtina de Credito e Servizi, 306
Bank of California, 327

Bank of England, 12, 27, 60, 76, 155
Bank of Japan, 340
Banque de France, 2–4, 20, 38, 60,
    63, 104, 118, 136, 155, 156, 159,
    162, 166–68, 170, 184, 190,
    203–5, 219, 231, 241
Banque de l'Eurafrique, 327
Banque de Paris et des Pays-Bas (Pari-
    bas), 72–73, 144, 162–63, 168,
    201, 231, 241, 269, 284, 287,
    297, 309, 322, 337
Banque Lazard, 301
Banque Nationale de Paris, 287
Banque Ottomane, 268
Banque Privée Edmond de Rothschild,
    327
Banque Rothschild, 284, 285, 289,
    295–98, 300, 303, 334
Banque Stern, 289, 339
Banque Worms, 339
Barber of Seville, The (Rossini), 24
Barrès, Maurice, 87, 113–14
Bat-Dor dance studio and troupe, 314
Batsheva Crafts Corporation, 314
Batsheva Dance Company, 314
Batsheva de Rothschild Foundation for
    Art and Science, 313
Batsheva de Rothschild Foundation for
    Art and Learning, 314
Battersea, Constance, 25, 37, 57, 120
Baum, Vicki, 180
Baumier, Jean, 290
Beaumont, Count Etienne de, 212
Bel-Ami (Maupassant), 87
Belin, Edouard, 147
Belmont, August, 22, 27, 40–41, 56,
    161
Belmont, August, Jr., 162
Ben-Gurion, David, 92, 264, 277
Bérégovy, Pierre, 318
Bernstein, Henry, 235
Berry, Duc de, 312
Bibliothèque Nationale, 153, 264
Bismarck, Otto von, 61, 65–70, 76,
    225
Bleichröder, Gerson von, 61, 66,
    67, 70
Blum, Léon, 164, 175, 202, 204, 205
Blum, Robert, 236
Bnito, 100, 142–44
Bodenkreditanstalt, 191
Boissieu, Michel de, 298
Bolloré, Vincent, 337

Bolsheviks, 162, 202
Bonheur, Rosa, 259
Bonnard, Pierre, 233
Bontoux, Eugène, 84–86, 92, 122
Bormann, Martin, 233
Boucher, François, 95, 148, 228
Bourbons, 15, 20, 147
Bourse, 309
Bouvier, Jean, 74, 86, 275–76
British Airways, 321
British Automobile Association, 216
British Petroleum, 336
British Telecommunications, 336
Brynner, Yul, 292
Buderus, Carl Frederick, 8
Byrnes, Robert, 31

Caesarea Development Corporation, 306
Canal Plus, 319
Canard Enchaîné, Le, 279
Caprivi, Count Leo von, 100
Carême, Marie-Antoine, 24
Carlisle, Lady, 19
Carrefour, 319
Carrel, Alexis, 247–49, 313
Castro, Fidel, 276
Catholics, 31, 55, 78, 84–85, 132–34,
    152, 156, 164, 335
    anti-Semitic, 90, 113, 125, 130, 176
    marriages of Rothschilds to, 306,
        310
Caussidière, Marc, 37–38
Cavour, Count Camillo di, 45–46, 61
Céline, Louis-Ferdinand, 203, 240
Center of Documentation and Vigilance
    (CDV), 210
Chalone wine group, 331
Changarnier, Gen. Nicolas, 42–43
Channel Tunnel Company, 83
Chapelle Darblay paper mills, 321
Chaplin, Charlie, 179
Charles X, King, 20
Chase Manhattan Bank, 327
Chautemps, Camille, 205
Chicago Tribune, 56
Child with Buddha (Fragonard), 233
Chirac, Jacques, 309
Cinzano, 321
Civil War, U.S., 56
Clarke vineyards, 292–93, 329
Clemenceau, Georges, 125, 164
Clermont-Tonnerre, Elisabeth de (née
    de Gramont), 147

Cloisters museum, 256
Club Méditerranée, 277, 306, 320
Cluzel, Louis, 175–77
Cohn, Albert, 92
Colette, 179, 180
Collège Bourbon, 55
Columbia University, 235
Comédie Française, 181
Commissariat for Jewish Questions, 222, 226, 231, 239, 240, 242–49
Committee of Assistance to Refugees (CAR), 210
Committee of Jewish Social Action, 310–11
Common Platform, 295, 298
Communists, 1, 4, 167, 176, 201–4, 210, 213, 280, 295–99, 308
Compagnie AEP, 327
Compagnie Agricole de Lukus, 198
Compagnie Auxiliaire du Nord, 285
Compagnie des Chemins de Fer de l'Est, 73
Compagnie Européenne de Banque, 289, 296, 299
Compagnie Financière, 277, 288, 304, 306
Compagnie Financière Benjamin et Edmond de Rothschild, 304, 327
Compagnie Financière Edmond de Rothschild, 308, 309, 320, 328
Compagnie Financière Martin Maurel, 320
Compagnie Financière de Suez, 303, 337
Compagnie Française de Pétroles, 268
Compagnie Luxembourgeoise de Télé-diffusion, 306
Compagnie du Nord, 30, 39, 55, 82, 133, 134, 152, 159, 160, 171, 184, 195, 205–6, 266–69, 275, 283–86, 288–90, 299–300, 302, 309
Compagnie de Suez, 269, 297
Compagnie de Trésorie Benjamin de Rothschild, 327
Comptoir d'Escompte de Paris, 102
Conseil Représentatif des Institutions Juives de France (CRIF), 291, 307
Constitutionnel, Le, 28
Copperweld, 288
Corti, Count Egon Cesar, 9, 10, 12, 56, 73, 141, 188, 194

Coston, Henry, 274, 281
Cranach, Lucas, 231
Credit-Amstel, 191–92
Creditanstalt, 46
Crédit Foncier, 99
Crédit Lyonnais, 72–75, 99, 144, 281, 287, 337
Crédit Mobilier, 43, 46–48, 57, 61–62
Crédito Mobiliario Español, 45
Crémieu-Foa, Capt. Ernest, 116, 117
Crémieux, Adolphe, 28, 252
Crémieux decree, 252–53
Croix, La, 90, 113
Croix de Feu, 201–2
Crown Zellerbach, 317
Curie, Eve, 235

Daladier, Edouard, 201–3
Dalberg, Carl von, 10–12
Damascus affair, 28–29
Darlan, Adm. François, 222, 244–46
Daudet, Alphonse, 90, 110
Daudet, Léon, 111, 164
David-Weill, Michel, 315–16
David-Weill, Pierre, 317
David-Weill family, 257, 315
De Beers Consolidated Mines Ltd., 75, 121, 263, 268, 277
Decazes, Elie, Duke of, 16
de Gaulle, Charles, 194, 224, 237, 250, 251, 253, 254, 270, 271, 275–76, 278–81, 294, 297–98
Del Val, Merry, 132–33
Delahaye, Dominique, 134
Democratic party, 22, 27
Denfert-Rochereau, Eugène, 102
Dernière bataille, La (Drumont), 111
De Rothschild Frères, 133, 140, 142, 144, 146, 148, 154–55, 163, 189, 194, 195, 197, 261–63, 267, 271
    becomes Banque Rothschild, 284
    during World War I, 157
    during World War II, 219, 244, 245
Deterding, Henri, 142
Devisenschutz-kommando, 226
Dietrich, Marlene, 196
Discount Bank of France, 289, 290, 296, 297
Disraeli, Benjamin, 75–77
Domaines Barons de Rothschild, 311, 335
Doumer, Paul, 183
Drexel Burnham Lambert, 323

Dreyfus affair, 72, 86, 87, 90, 114–18, 120–28, 132, 135, 152, 273
Drinker, The (Hoogh), 312
Drumont, Edouard, 72, 85, 88–90, 101, 104, 105, 107–14, 127–30, 132, 134, 135, 204, 274
 and Dreyfus affair, 116, 119, 120, 122, 124
Du Camp, Maxime, 54, 79

E. F. Hutton, 323
Ecole des cadavres, L' (Céline), 203
Ecole Nationale d'Administration, 318
Edey, Russell, 319
Edward VII, King of England, 76, 139
Eiffel Tower, 111
1848 revolution, 36–40, 67, 192
Einsatzstab Rosenberg, 230–33, 257, 260
Elizabeth, Empress of Austro-Hungary, 147
Emmanuelli, Henri, 305
Ems dispatch, 66
English Channel tunnel, 82–83
Ephrussi, Michel, 127
Européenne de Banque, 308
Esambert, Bernard, 306, 327
Esterhazy, Maj. Ferdinand, 116–17, 121–24, 126
Euris investment company, 319, 321
European Coal and Steel Authority, 194
European Community, 194, 338, 340
Expansion, 305, 332

Faure, Félix, 101
Favre, Jules, 68, 69
Fédération Continental insurance, 321
Feldpolizei, 226
Ferdinand VII, King of Spain, 29
Ferruzzi Agricola Finanzaria, 306
Feydeau, Ernest, 37, 44, 48, 49, 68
Fifth Republic, 275–76, 279, 280
Fillon, René, 186, 252, 270, 271
Figaro, Le, 63, 90, 105, 107
Finaly, Horace, 201, 202
Financière Boréale, 327
Finlay, Horace, 162
Fin d'un monde, La (Drumont), 111
First Boston, 337
Fitzroy, Henry, 25
Flanner, Janet, 196, 212
Flaubert, Gustave, 151
Fleck, Peter, 234

Flight to Egypt, The (Memling), 312
Fondation Alphonse de Rothschild, 247
Fondation Edmond de Rothschild pour le Développement de la Recherche Scientifique, 173
Fondation Marie-Hélène and Guy de Rothschild, 291
Fondation Ophtalmologique Adolphe de Rothschild, 312
Fondation de Rothschild, 312, 313
Fondation Salomon de Rothschild, 182–83
Fonds Social Juif Unifié (FSJU), 264, 272, 307
Forte hotel-restaurant group, 321
Fortune magazine, 325, 326
Fouché, Joseph, 4, 51
Fould, Achille, 43, 58, 60
Foundation for French Judaism, 307
Fourier, Charles, 21, 23, 31, 87
Fourth Republic, 262
Fragonard, Jean-Honoré, 95, 233
Francarep, 269, 206, 320, 335
France, La, 63
France juive, La (Drumont), 88–91, 111
Francis Ferdinand, Archduke, 157
Franco, Francisco, 213, 280
Franco-Prussian War, 65–73, 252
Frankfurt Allgemeine Zeitung, 193
Frederick II, Prince of Hesse, 7–8
Free French, 224, 235, 237, 250–55, 275
Freemasons, 88, 223, 244
French Committee of National Liberation, 253
French Forces of the Interior (FFI), 255
French Foundation for the Study of Human Problems, 248
French Revolution, 9, 12, 14
French Tunnel Society, 82
French Workers Party, 91
Freycinet, Charles, 80–81
Fry, Christopher, 180

Gabriel, Jacques-Ange, 25
Gainsborough, Thomas, 231
Gambetta, Léon, 80
Gaudin de Villaine, Sylvain, 161
Gaullists, 2, 227, 251–52, 254
Générale Alimentaire, La, 288
Génévale Occidentale, 289

Geneva, University of, 276
Gestapo, 226, 240, 254
Getten, Eric, 335
Getten, Jacques, 5, 267, 274, 300, 318, 335
Gide, André, 180
Gil Blas, 130
Gille, Bertrand, 15, 20, 34, 38, 41, 64
Gimpel, René, 148
Giraud, Gen. Henri, 250, 252–53
Giscard d'Estaing, Valéry, 295, 300
Gladstone, William, 66
Goering, Hermann, 225, 232–34, 241, 242, 258, 260
Goldman Sachs, 318, 337
Goldsmith, Gerald, 323
Goldsmith, James, 288, 289, 301, 315–17, 325
Goncourt, Edmond de, 47, 52, 56, 59, 88–90, 94–97, 110–11
Goncourt, Jules de, 47, 52, 56
Goudchaux, Michel, 37
Goya, Francisco, 231, 312
Graham, Martha, 313, 314
Gramont, Agénor, Duc de, 103
Gramont, Elisabeth de, 103–4, 148, 152, 171–73, 183
Grand Metropolitan, 321
Granville, Lady, 19
Great Exhibition of 1851, 51
Great War. See World War I
Guardian, 3
Guesde, Jules, 91
Günzberg, Horace de, 81, 82

Hachette, 306
Halévy, Ludovic, 80
Hals, Frans, 231, 312
Hanska, Anna, 26, 30, 34–37, 39
Hanson Trust, 317
Harcourt Brace Jovanovich, 316–17
Harrison & Abramowitz, 283–84
Harvard University, 318
  Business School, 303
Havas press agency, 99–100
Hayard, Léon, 104–5, 131
Hebrew University, 172–73, 216
Heine, Heinrich, 19, 24, 28–30, 33, 48
Henry, Col. Joseph, 124, 125, 126
Hepburn, Audrey, 292
Hermès, 320
Herriot, Edouard, 166, 168
Herzl, Theodore, 93, 96, 144–45, 173

Hitler, Adolf, 193, 206, 207–9, 213, 215, 216, 220, 223, 224, 226–34, 241–43, 249, 255, 258, 260, 264, 334
Hohenzollern-Sigmaringen, Leopold von, 66
Hoogh, Pieter de, 312
horse breeding and racing, 102–3, 124, 196, 265, 320
Hortense, Queen, 189
Hottinguer bank, 141, 339
Houdon, Jean-Antoine, 148
Hugo, Victor, 47, 83
Humanité, L', 201–4, 280, 296
Huret, Jules, 105–7

"I Accuse" (Zola), 123
IBM, 267
Illustration, L', 129, 164, 179
Imétal, 288, 290, 296, 299, 320
Ingres, Jean-Auguste-Dominique, 19, 24, 260, 292
Inno-France, 277
Inpravbank, 171
Institut de Biologie Physico-Chimique, 173, 248–49, 313
Institut d'Etudes Politiques, 302
Institut Pasteur, 104, 249
Interborough Rapid Transit (IRT), 171
Isabelle II of Spain, 29
Ismail Pasha, Khedive, 75–77, 80
Israel Center for Dance Medicine, 314
Israel European Company, 306
Israel General Bank, 277, 306, 326
Istel, Yves-André, 324

Jacobs Suchard, 321
Janico, Maurice, 226–27, 244, 245, 247
Janson de Sailly, 302
Jaujard, Jacques, 257
Je Suis Partout, 235
Jeu de Paume museum, 230–33, 241, 257–59
Jewish Colonization Association, 144
Jewish State, The (Herzl), 96
Jews, 19, 22, 33, 49–50, 59, 63, 156, 278–79, 305–7, 339–41
  in Britain, 12
  charitable activities for, 25, 53–54, 79, 313
  Consistory of, 78, 112, 138–39, 172, 201, 202, 208–10, 234, 252–53, 264, 272, 278, 291, 307, 310

Jews (cont.)
  in Damascus affair, 27–28
  Fourier and, 21, 22
  Free French movement and, 252–55
  Metternich and, 15–16
  Napoleon and, 11, 12
  Nazi persecution of, 208–13,
    223–34, 240–44
  North African, 310
  Palestine settlement of, 91–93,
    95–96, 144–46, 161, 172–73,
    210–12, 278
  of Papal States, 54–55
  Pompidou and, 280
  in pre-Revolutionary Europe, 6–7
  and privileges of wealth, 53
  Prussian attitude toward, 69, 70
  in Saint-Simonian movement, 31
  sense of patriarchy of, 183
  Sephardic, 95
  in United States, 27
  veterans of World War I, 201
  Vichy regime and, 220, 222–24,
    236, 242–49
  See also anti-Semitism
Jews: Kings of Our Time (Toussenel),
    31, 273
Jockey Club, 53, 111, 307
Joint Distribution Committee, 255,
    264
Journal des Débats, 63, 65
Journal de Mickey, Le, 247
Journal de Paris, 63
Jouvet, Louis, 180
Jovanovich, William, 316

Kahn, Zadoc, 111–12, 132
Kaiser, Henry, 287
Kaiser Aluminum, 287
Kaplan, Jacob, 202
Karen Hayesod, 307
Karloff, Boris, 195
Kaufmann, Eugene, 154
Keitel, Field Marshal Wilhelm, 226,
    230
Kennedy, Edward, 292
Knox Partners, 327
Koenig, Gen. Pierre, 252, 255
Kohl, Helmut, 340
Kristallnacht (Night of Broken Glass),
    210, 211
Kuhn Loeb, 288
Kymmene Oy, 321

Labori, Fernand, 126
Labriffe, Christian de, 319
Ladies' Lake (Baum), 180
La Fayette, Marquis de, 20
Laffitte, Jacques, 16
Lafite vineyard, 62, 181, 225, 227,
    231, 255–56, 266, 292, 293, 310,
    311, 330, 331
Lamartine, Alphonse de, 27
Langlois Bridge in Arles (Van Gogh),
    233
La Rocque, Col. François, 201–2
Lattre de Tassigny, Gen. Jean de, 259
Laval, Pierre, 222, 246
Lazard, Abraham, 136
Lazard Frères, 163, 168, 170, 257,
    297, 315–19, 321, 337, 339
Lead Industries Group, 288
Left Cartel, 166, 167, 174, 175
Legion of Honor, 77, 118–19
Lenin, V. I., 171
Leonino, Baron Emmanuel, 104
Leonino, Baroness Juliette, 104, 131
Le Pen, Jean-Marie, 340
Lesage, Charles, 75
Lesseps, Ferdinand de, 75
Librairie Antisémite, 129
Libre Parole, La, 107, 110, 112, 114,
    116, 119–21, 125, 128, 130–32,
    134, 161
Lichine, Alexis, 330
Ligue de la Patrie Française, 127
Lindbergh, Charles, 186, 248
Lohse, Bruno, 258
Loubet, Emile, 126
Louis XIV, King, 26
Louis XV, King, 25
Louis XVI, King, 90
Louis XVIII, King, 13, 16
Louis-Dreyfus, Louis, 168
Louis-Napoleon. See Napoleon III
Louis-Philippe, King, 16, 20, 28,
    35–37
Louis Vuitton, 321
Louvre museum, 95, 229, 257, 312
Lubersac, Count de, 127
Ludwig II, King of Bavaria, 242
Luftwaffe, 228, 232, 257
Lycée Carnot, 302

Macmillan Inc., 317
Man the Unknown (Carrel), 248
Marchais, Georges, 295

Marie-Christine, Spanish regent, 29
Marlowe, Christopher, 180
Marone-Cinzano family, 321
Mathilde, Princess, 59, 88, 94–97
Maupassant, Guy de, 87, 88
Maurel, Martin, 308, 320
Mauroy, Pierre, 297, 307
Maurras, Charles, 212–13
Maxwell, Robert, 301, 316–17, 324
Mayer, Capt. Armand, 112, 116
Mayer, René, 194–95, 270, 276
Mazout marketing company, 143
Meling, Hans, 312
Mendès-France, Pierre, 237–38
Mercier, Ernest, 201
Mesa Inc., 324
Metropolitan Museum of Art, 256
Metternich, Prince Clemens von,
    15–17, 19–21, 26–29, 39, 61, 67
Metternich, Victor, 17
Meulemans, Jules, 118
Meyer, Jean-Claude, 319, 321
Michelangelo, 95
Michelet, Jules, 19
mining interests, 74–75, 102, 121,
    161, 268, 276, 280–81, 285,
    287–88
Mirbeau, Octave, 88
Mirecourt, Eugène de, 49–50
Mirès, Jules, 46
Mitterrand, François, 1, 3, 5, 295, 300,
    304, 305, 309
Modigliani, Amedeo, 147
Mohilewer, Shmuel, 92–93
Mollien, Nicolas, 12
Moltke, Helmuth von, 68
Mondavi, Robert, 293
Monniot, Albert, 134
Montagnini, Monseigneur Carlo,
    132–33
Montefiore, Moses, 28
Montesquiou, Comte Robert de,
    148–49
Montijo, Eugénie de, 47
Moreau, Emile, 168, 170
Morès, Marquis Antonio de, 110, 112,
    113, 116
Morgan bank, 49, 157–58, 166, 171
Morgan Stanley, 337
Morton, Frederic, 191
Mouton vineyards, 34, 62, 149, 181,
    225, 231, 255–56, 264, 266, 293,
    311–12, 329–30

Mövenpick hotel and restaurant chain,
    321
Mugnier, Abbot Arthur, 164
Muhlstein, Anka, 17, 23, 34, 331
Münster, Georg von, 100
Musée de l'Homme, 265
Muslims, 95, 252, 275

N. M. Rothschild & Sons, 281, 301,
    308, 318, 319, 321, 328, 335–39
Naouri, Jean-Charles, 318–19, 321
Napoleon, Emperor, 4, 9–14, 32, 41,
    42, 51, 89, 195, 203, 334
Napoleon III, Emperor (Louis-
    Napoleon), 40, 42, 46–48, 57, 58,
    61, 65–67, 70, 189, 252
Nathaniel Rothschild Holdings, 303
National Bloc, 164, 167
National Gypsum Company, 324
nationalization, 294–300, 308–9, 311,
    322, 334
NATO, 276
Nattier, Jean-Marc, 148
Nazis, 208–13, 236, 238, 252, 253,
    265, 273, 294, 332, 334
    annexation of Austria by, 206–7
    occupation of Czechoslovakia by, 220
    occupation of Paris by, 25, 113,
        221–24
    plundering of Jewish assets by,
        225–34, 256–58
    rise to power of, 192, 193
Nesselrode, Countess von, 26
Nesselrode, Karl von, 26
New Court Securities, 288, 301
New Deal, 195
New Economic Policy (NEP), 171
New York Central railroad, 161
New Yorker, The, 196, 212
New York Times, The, 217, 235, 254,
    289, 301, 309, 317
New York University, Graduate School
    of Business Administration, 320
Nicholas I, Czar, 26
Nicholas II, Czar, 141
Nickel, Le, 75, 161, 268, 276, 280–81,
    285, 287–88, 296, 302
Nicolay, Count François de, 272
Nicolay, Philippe de, 272
Nobel, Alfred, 100
Nord Financier, 296
Nuremberg war crimes trials, 220
Nureyev, Rudolf, 331

Olympia & York, 324
Oesterreichische Credit-Anstalt für
    Handel und Gewerbe, 191
Office of Strategic Services (OSS), 258
oil interests. See petroleum
Ordman, Jeannette, 314
Oréal, L', 319
Orléans, Philippe d', 87
Ottoman Turks, 21, 27

P.O. Banque, 308–9, 320
P.O. Gestion, 300, 307
Païva, La, 55–56
Panama Canal Company, 102, 104
Paribas. See Banque de Paris et de
    Pays-Bas
Paris, University of, 173, 249, 291
Paris Commune, 71–72
Paris-Match, 307
Paris-Orléans investment house, 4–5,
    300
Paris-Soir, 222–23
Paris Tribunal de Commerce, 13
Pascal, André. See Rothschild,
    Henri de
Pascal, Philippine. See Rothschild,
    Philippine de
Pasteur, Louis, 130
Paxton, Joseph, 51, 270
Peck, Gregory, 292
Pèlerin, Le, 113
Peñarroya, 268, 280–81, 285
Pereire brothers, 23, 43, 44, 57, 58,
    61–62, 84
Peron, Jean, 246
Perrin, Jean, 173
Persigny, Duke Fialin de, 46, 56–57
Pétain, Philippe, 1, 3, 219–22, 226,
    229, 234, 240, 244–46, 248, 249,
    254, 304
petroleum, 75, 100, 142–44, 162, 194,
    287
Peyrefitte, Roger, 282
Philip Morris, 321
Piatigorsky, Gregor, 234
Picasso, Pablo, 147
Pickens, T. Boone, 324
Picquart, Maj. Georges, 116, 121
Pinault group, 321
Pirie, Robert, 301, 316, 317, 322–23
Pius X, Pope, 133
Pius XII, Pope, 188
PLM, 296

pogroms, 92, 141
Poincaré, Raymond, 134, 156, 158,
    166, 168–70, 186–87, 195
Point, Le, 310
Poliakov, Léon, 86–87
Pompidou, Georges, 194, 270–71,
    274–77, 279–82
Populaire, Le, 206
Popular Front, 2, 136, 202–5, 213,
    236, 266, 294, 299
Presses de la Cité, 316
Prévost-Paradol, Lucien, 63
Protestants, 6, 31, 88, 141, 156, 203,
    339
Proudhon, Pierre, 31, 87
Proust, Marcel, 35, 94, 148
Publications Filipacchi, 306
Pucheu, Pierre, 246

Quakers, 212
Quinta do Carmo, 331

Racine, Jean, 212
railroads, 23, 29–35, 39, 45, 55, 60,
    73, 75, 82, 84, 182, 205–6, 266
Rasche, Karl, 220
Ravensbruck concentration camp, 238
Ray, Cyril, 310, 311, 330
Reglesperger, Yves, 239, 245
Régnier, Marthe, 179, 237
Reinach, Joseph, 125
Rembrandt van Rijn, 95, 231, 312
Renault automobile works, 294, 322
Réunion Financière, 44
Reynolds, Joshua, 231
Ribbentrop, Joachim von, 229, 233
Ribbentrop-Molotov treaty, 213
Ribot, Alexandre, 158
Ríotinto mines, 121, 280
Robert, Hubert, 148
Rockefeller, John D., 100
Rockefellers, 326
Romain, Jules, 148, 180
Roosevelt, Eleanor, 245
Rorimer, James J., 256–58
Rosenberg, Alfred, 230–34, 241–44,
    257, 258
Ross, Wilbur, Jr., 301–2, 323, 324
Rossini, Gioacchino, 24, 58
Rothschild, Le, 87
Rothschild, Adele Hannah de, 56, 182
Rothschild, Adelheid de, 92, 95
Rothschild, Adolph de, 147, 148

Rothschild, Alain de, 183, 214, 216, 235–36, 242, 261, 263, 266, 268, 274, 278, 284, 286, 290–91, 293, 302, 306, 311, 313

Rothschild, Alexandre de, 306, 307, 332

Rothschild, Alix de, 196–97, 213, 216, 221, 246, 250, 264–65, 271, 291

Rothschild, Alphonse de, 2, 25, 45, 49, 56–61, 74–82, 118–19, 127, 140, 149, 165, 180, 233, 292, 333
accession of, 64–65
anti-Semitic attacks on, 87–89, 91, 104–5, 107–14, 119–20, 128–29
birth of, 34
death of, 130–35, 138, 141, 146
and Dreyfus affair, 115–17, 123–25
education of, 34–35, 55
during 1848 revolution, 37, 39, 40
during Franco-Prussian War, 66–71
health problems of, 127–28
home life of, 103–4
Huret's interview with, 105–7
as man about town, 55–56
marriage of, 53
and Palestine settlement, 93, 96
and Paris Commune, 71–72
petroleum interests of, 142
Russian Jews and, 81–82, 92, 97–101
stable of, 102–3, 124
and Suez Canal, 75–77
and Union Générale crisis, 86, 87
in United States, 40–41

Rothschild, Alphonse de (son of Edouard), 183

Rothschild, Arielle de, 332

Rothschild, Arthur de, 150, 152

Rothschild, Amschel de (British cousin of David), 338

Rothschild, Amschel (son of Mayer Amschel), 8, 12, 16

Rothschild, Benjamin de, 278, 313, 328, 330, 339

Rothschild, Bethsabée (Batsheva) de, 185, 214, 217, 234–35, 237, 312–14

Rothschild, Bettina de (daughter of Alphonse), 67

Rothschild, Bettina de (wife of James), 18–19, 24, 25, 34–35, 37–39, 43, 50, 53, 58, 72, 79, 92

Rothschild, Carl, 8, 11, 12, 16, 24

Rothschild, Charlotte de, 24, 34, 58–59, 62, 97, 149

Rothschild, Charlotte Béatrix de, 67, 104, 135, 259, 333

Rothschild, Claude de, 237

Rothschild, Cécile de, 183, 213, 214

Rothschild, David de, 4, 5, 250, 289, 291, 296–303, 305, 306–12, 315–16, 318–22, 328, 330, 332, 334

Rothschild, Diane de, 183, 214

Rothschild, Edmond de (son of James), 64, 74, 91–97, 117, 129, 133, 135, 140, 146–48, 174, 225, 269, 276, 277, 305, 325, 332–33
art collection of, 94–95, 163
birth of, 34, 35
death of, 197, 198
Goncourt and, 79, 94–97
Institut de Biologie Physico-Chimique endowed by, 173, 248
and James's death, 55, 91
in Jockey Club, 307
in old age, 172, 188, 192, 209
and Palestine settlement, 91–93, 95–96, 144–45, 161, 172–73
and Russians, 141, 143–44
during World War I, 159–61

Rothschild, Edmond de (son of Maurice), 178, 235, 242, 269, 276–79, 284, 288, 291–93, 304–6, 309, 312, 313, 325–30, 335, 339

Rothschild, Edouard de, 2, 25, 67, 111, 112, 127, 138–40, 144, 147, 155, 156, 165, 183, 184, 194, 259, 261, 266
accession of, 133, 135–37
and Alphonse's death, 131–33
and Edmond's death, 197–99
American investments of, 170–71
ancestral home of, 182
country house of, 185
death of, 263, 265, 267
family life of, 171–72
and Guy's apprenticeship, 188, 190, 195
liquidation of estate of, 312
marriage of, 138
and Nazi rise to power, 208, 209, 211
and Popular Front, 204–5
and stable, 196, 320
and value of franc, 165–70, 176, 186

Rothschild, Edouard de (*cont.*)
and Vienna crisis, 192–93
during World War I, 159–60, 162
during World War II, 212–214,
216–18, 220, 226, 228, 229, 231,
232, 234, 239–41, 244, 245, 247,
250, 252–53
Rothschild, Edouard Etienne Alphonse
de, 272, 303, 319–20, 330, 332,
339
Rothschild, Elie de, 183, 214, 217,
235, 236, 242, 261, 263, 266,
268, 274, 284, 286, 287, 289,
290, 293, 300, 303, 310, 313,
330, 332
Rothschild, Eric de, 236, 293, 302–3,
305, 306–12, 320, 321, 328, 331,
339, 340
Rothschild, Eugene von, 231
Rothschild, Evelyn de, 301, 303,
337–39
Rothschild, Gabrielle de, 214
Rothschild, Germaine de, 138, 172,
183, 184, 186, 211–12, 214,
217–18, 234, 250, 259, 292, 312,
313
Rothschild, Gustave de, 34, 39, 40, 55,
56, 64, 69, 74, 93, 101, 102, 124,
127, 129, 133, 140, 146, 154,
159, 172
Rothschild, Gutele Schnapper, 8, 19
Rothschild, Guy de, 2–4, 138, 139,
183–90, 200, 277, 283–92,
298–306, 310, 313, 318, 319,
331, 332, 334
apprenticeship of, 188–90, 194–95
birth of, 183
charitable donations of, 312
childhood of, 183–84
divorce and remarriage of, 271–72
education of, 184–87
marriage of, 196–97
nationalization and, 295, 296,
298–300
Pompidou and, 270–71, 274, 275,
279–81
during postwar years, 261–68
stable of, 196, 265, 320
during World War II, 213–17, 221,
224, 227, 236, 237, 239, 244–46,
250–52, 254–55
Rothschild, Hannah de, 25
Rothschild, Hélène de, 182

Rothschild, Henri de, 34, 113, 150–53,
161, 163, 178–82, 199, 214, 220,
221, 231, 236, 241, 254, 264
Rothschild, Jacob, 303, 320, 328, 330,
338, 339, 340
Rothschild, Jacqueline de, 185, 234,
312
Rothschild, James de, 2, 4, 15–55, 68,
88, 91, 92, 94, 97, 103, 149, 162,
165, 172, 174, 189, 198, 259,
266, 286, 293, 305, 307, 315,
325, 331, 339
ascension of, 15–18, 20–21
birth of, 8
Bismarck and, 61
charitable activities of, 53–54, 79
country estate of, 51–52, 69, 291
death of, 62–65, 129
during 1848 revolution, 36–40, 67,
192
home life of, 34–35
marriage of, 18–19
Metternich and, 16, 28–29
Napoleon III and, 42–43, 57, 58
during Napoleonic wars, 10–13
in old age, 59–60
Pereire brothers' rivalry with, 43–48,
57, 61
railroads and, 23, 29–35, 45, 285
United States interests of, 40, 41
Rothschild, James Armand de (Jimmy),
133, 141, 144, 146, 159–61, 172,
173, 197, 225, 235, 276, 330
Rothschild, James Edouard de, 149–50
Rothschild, James-Henri de, 182, 221,
236–37, 264
Rothschild, Julie de, 147–48, 173,
277
Rothschild, Laura Thérèse von, 150,
152
Rothschild, Lavinia de, 307
Rothschild, Leonora de, 53, 57, 59, 67,
78, 104, 128, 130, 184
Rothschild, Leopold de, 58, 59
Rothschild, Lili de, 214, 238, 240–41
Rothschild, Lionel de, 24, 46, 53, 59,
75–76
Rothschild, Louis von, 190–93, 206–7,
231
Rothschild, Margaretha Alexandrine
von, 103
Rothschild, Marie-Béatrice, 310, 311,
331

Rothschild, Marie-Hélène de, 271–72, 279, 291–92, 319, 331, 332
Rothschild, Mary de, 235–36
Rothschild, Mathilde de, 150, 161
Rothschild, Maurice de, 147–49, 159, 163–64, 173–78, 197–99, 205, 212, 213, 220, 229, 231, 235, 242–43, 269–70, 276, 277, 304, 312
Rothschild, Mayer Amschel, 6–9, 11, 12, 16, 19, 51, 128, 195, 325, 340
Rothschild, Mayer Carl von, 56, 65, 103, 182
Rothschild, Miriam de, 173, 197, 243, 277, 333
Rothschild, Monique de, 237
Rothschild, Nadine de, 276–78, 292, 304, 306, 326
Rothschild, Nathan de, 8, 10–13, 15, 16, 19, 23, 24, 26, 34, 46, 51, 60, 62, 149, 195
Rothschild, Nathaniel de (son of Elie), 5, 289, 300, 303, 332
Rothschild, Nathaniel de (son of Nathan), 25, 34, 46, 58, 62, 97, 113, 149, 180, 331
Rothschild, Nelly de, 160, 332
Rothschild, Nicole de, 214, 221, 236–37
Rothschild, Noëmi de, 163, 178, 235
Rothschild, Olimpia de, 307, 310
Rothschild, Philippe de, 34, 179–82, 214–15, 220, 231, 237–38, 241, 255–56, 264, 266, 293, 311–12, 329–30
Rothschild, Philippine de, 181, 214, 255, 312, 329–30
Rothschild, Robert de, 133, 146, 147, 172, 197–98, 261–62, 266, 290, 313
  death of, 262
  in duel, 127
  and Gustave's death, 154
  and Guy's apprenticeship, 188, 195
  and Nazi rise to power, 208–11
  and Popular Front, 202, 204
  during World War I, 159, 160
  during World War II, 213, 214, 220, 228, 231, 235, 244, 245, 247
Rothschild, Salomon de, 8, 11, 16, 18–21, 23, 37, 56–57

Rothschild, Salomon James de, 34, 54, 56, 64, 182, 272
Rothschild, Stéphanie de, 307
Rothschild Asset Management, 335–36
Rothschild & Associés Banque, 309, 328
Rothschild Bank AG, 336
Rothschild & Cie. Banque, 319, 320, 328, 336, 338
Rothschild et Compagnie Banque, 328
Rothschild Continuation Holding, 320
Rothschild España, 328
Rothschild Europe, 338
Rothschild Foundation for Social Hygiene, 129
Rothschild Inc., 281, 301, 303, 316, 317, 322–24
Rothschild North America, 337
Rothschild Zurich AG, 308
Rothstein, Adolphe, 98
Rouvier, Maurice, 99, 141
Royal Dutch Oil, 142–44, 162, 194, 217, 263, 268
Royal Seed Establishment, 216
Rubens, Peter Paul, 231, 326
Russian Revolution of 1905, 142
Russian Revolution of 1917, 162, 165, 171, 294
Russo-Japanese War, 142

S. M. Rothschild und Söhne, 166, 191, 206
S.H.M./Francarep, 320
Saga shipping company, 267, 271, 274, 296, 302–3
Saint-Honoré Finance et Conseil, 327
Saint-Honoré-Matignon, 309, 320
Saint-Simon, Claude-Henri de Rouvroy, 23, 106
Saint-Simonians, 30, 31, 32
Samuel, Marcus, 142
Saragossa railroad, 75
Savour Club, 329
Say, Léon, 55, 65, 72, 75, 80, 82, 103
Schama, Simon, 92, 95, 144, 172–73
Schwab, Charles, 151
SCM, 317
Second Empire, 43, 47, 58, 65, 70, 82
  fall of, 67
  foreign policy of, 45
Sem (caricaturist), 151, 152
Shell Oil, 142–44

Simone, Simon, 180
Six Day War, 278–80
Smith New Court PLC, 337, 338
Socété Générale, 144
Socialiste, Le, 91
Socialists, 1, 3, 4, 174, 175, 206, 308
    nationalization by, 294–300
    nineteenth-century 31, 87, 91,
        105–6
    Radical, 164, 166, 167, 201, 202,
        204, 205
Société des Agriculteurs de France,
    110, 120
Société Commerciale et Industrielle de
    Napthe Caspienne et de la Mer
    Noire, 100
Société Continentale de Banque, 289
Société Financière de Banque, 306
Société Française des Hôtels de Mon-
    tagne, 304–5
Société Française de Pénicilline,
    268
Société Générale, 319
Société Nationale des Chemins de Fer
    (SNCF), 205–6
Société Transocéan, 271, 277
Soncantar, 285
Sorbonne, 187, 314
Soros, George, 324
Spanish Civil War, 213
Spiegel, Der, 3
Stalin, Joseph, 142, 213, 294
Standard Oil, 100, 142
Standard Russe, 142, 143
State Department, U.S., 253
Statut des Juifs, 222, 244
Stavisky scandal, 200
Stendhal, 1
Stéphane, Nicole, 3
Straus, Emile, 88
Straus, Madame Emile, 94
Südbahn railroad, 75, 84
Suez Canal, 75–77, 85
Supreme Headquarters Allied Expedi-
    tionary Forces (SHAEF), 252
Swanson, Gloria, 292

Taj Mahal casino, 323
Talleyrand, Prince de, 24, 25
TAT, 321
Temps, Le, 67, 107, 152
Théâtre Pigalle, 180
Thiers, Adolphe, 28, 70–72, 80

Third Republic, 65, 70, 78, 219–20,
    224
    Catholics and, 132–33
Time magazine, 265
Times (London), 58, 63, 83, 298
Time Warner, 322
Tolstoi, Dimitri, 81
Tour de Monde (Henri de Rothschild),
    179
Toussenel, Alphonse, 31, 204, 273
Très belles heures de Notre-Dame (illu-
    minated manuscript), 312
Trump, Donald, 323
Twentieth Century–Fox, 195

U.S. Steel, 151
Union Club, 111
Union Générale, 84–87, 92, 122
United Jewish Appeal, 307

Valland, Rose, 232, 256–59
Van Gogh, Vincent, 233
Velasquez, Diego Rodríguez de Silva,
    231, 233
Vermeer, Jan, 231, 233, 259, 292,
    312
Verne, Jules, 179
Veuve Clicquot Ponsardin, 321
Viau, Raphaël, 113, 120–21
Vichy regime, 1–3, 219–27, 229–38,
    240, 242–50, 253, 254, 263, 313,
    332
Victoria, Queen of England, 75, 77
Vienna, Congress of, 15
Villèle, Count Joseph de, 18
vineyards, 34, 62, 149, 181, 225,
    292–93, 311–12, 329–31
Vishnegradski, I. A., 97–98
Voltaire, 292

Wagons-Lits restaurant chain, 321
Wall Street crash (1929), 169, 170,
    190, 191
Warburg Brinckmann Wirtz, 321
Warburg, Eric, 236
Waterloo, Battle of, 13, 89
Watteau, Antoine, 95, 259
Wehrmacht, 230
Weill family, 163
Weizmann, Chaim, 210
Welles, Sumner, 253
Wellington, Duke of, 16
Wendel, François de, 170

Wertheim investment bank, 320
Wildenstein, Nathan, 148
Wilhelm IX, Prince of Hesse, 7–12
Wilhelm, Kaiser, 66, 68, 225
William Tell (Rossini), 24
Wilson, Woodrow, 161
Witte, Sergei, 100
Women's International Zionist Organi-
    zation (WIZO), 278
Work Table (Bonnard), 233
World War I, 129, 140, 152, 153,
    157–63, 165, 182, 183, 201, 215,
    222

World War II, 2, 25, 182, 199,
    213–56, 287, 294
  recovery of Nazi plunder from,
    256–60

Yergin, Daniel, 142
Youth Aliyah, 265

Zanuck, Darryl, 195
Zionism, 92–93, 96, 145, 210, 264,
    278
Zola, Emile, 87, 115, 122–25, 140
Zurich Polytechnical School, 302